CHARLES BUKOWSKI

Also by the same author and published by Virgin:

ALLEN GINSBERG: A BIOGRAPHY
JACK KEROUAC: KING OF THE BEATS
WILLIAM BURROUGHS: EL HOMBRE INVISIBLE

CHARLES BUKOWSKI

Barry Miles

First published in Great Britain in 2005 by
Virgin Books Ltd
Thames Wharf Studios
Rainville Road
London
W6 9HA

A catalogue record for this book is available
from the British Library.

ISBN 1 85227 271 6

Typeset by TW Typesetting, Plymouth, Devon
Printed and bound in Great Britain by CPD Wales

CONTENTS

Introduction   1
1. House of Torture   4
2. High School Nazi   34
3. On the Road   53
4. Drinking With Jane   82
5. Writing Again   105
6. Outsider of the Year   123
7. Chinaski Rides Out   149
8. Years of Fame   175
9. Boogie in the Mud   200
10. San Pedro   219
11. The Old Man and His Cats   240
Index of Sources   266
Bibliography   300
Index   307

INTRODUCTION

In the early 60s there were scores, if not hundreds, of small literary magazines with names like *Wormwood Review*, *Dust*, *Ole* and *Nadada* being published in America, often from small towns I had never heard of. They were occasionally hand printed, like the *Outsider*, often mimeographed, and almost always produced as a labour of love, usually by someone with a factory job, or sometimes by a sympathetic academic in a midwestern college. They were available from a dozen or so bookstores worldwide, but were mostly sold by mail order; many of them ran lists of other magazines that carried similar material, often with brief reviews of the latest issue. The same names of contributors occurred time and again, but none so frequently as Charles Bukowski.

From 1965 until 1970 I had a bookshop of my own and carried everything of Bukowski's that I could lay my hands on: books, magazines, and even a record. First we stocked the little mimeograph chapbooks, then the beautiful, signed limited editions from Black Sparrow. And in 1967 the underground newspapers began, together with a flood of small broadsides and pamphlets.

In 1968 I was made the label manager for Zapple, an experimental division of Apple, the Beatles' record company. John Lennon and Paul McCartney asked me to record a series of poetry albums for them and so I prepared a list which included Lawrence

Ferlinghetti, Richard Brautigan, Michael McClure, Allen Ginsberg, Kenneth Patchen and half a dozen others. High on the list was Charles Bukowski. All four Beatles gave the project their blessing so, in January 1969, I travelled to Los Angeles to make a spoken word album with him.

I arrived at 5125 1/2 DeLongpre Avenue in a slummy part of East Hollywood near the 20th Century Fox Studios on Sunset in a rented green Mustang that looked gleamingly conspicuous in the shabby street. The single storey wooden-frame house had peeling paint and there were holes in the screen doors. Hank's house had a struggling hedge to one side, and his '57 Plymouth was parked on the patchy remains of his front lawn. The overflowing garbage cans had paper sacks filled with bottles and beer cans were stacked around them, awaiting collection.

The screen door opened straight into his living room. The shades were drawn. Rickety bookshelves were overloaded with books, magazines, old newspapers and racing forms. The settee had a hole where the stuffing was bursting out. There was a pile of car tyres in the corner and many empty beer cans. In another corner was Hank's desk with his huge, battered, sit-up-and-beg, black cast-iron Remington, dusty but for the carriage and keys, surrounded by cigar butts and ash, crumpled paper. Hank went straight down to the corner store and returned with a six-pack of Miller Light in glass bottles.

He was still working at the post office and wondering if it would ever be possible for him to make it as a professional poet. Essex House had just published *Notes of a Dirty Old Man*, a collection of his underground press columns, as a mass market paperback and he had been encouraged by this latest development.

We talked about the record. He was casual, relaxed and said that he had made a lot of home recordings before but he had not yet done a public reading. He hated the idea of performing in public. He said it was show business, an ego trip, but actually he was also shy, and concerned that he would make a fool of himself. I was unable to persuade him to come to a recording studio, unknown territory with ample opportunities for him to embarrass himself. He wanted to make the record at home, alone: 'Sure, just show me how the machine works and come back in a few days. I'll just curl up on the rug with some packs of beer, my books, turn on the machine and . . .' I wired up an Ampex 3000, arranged a microphone stand and microphone, headphones and twelve reels of blank tape. He refused to allow me, or anyone else, to be present to supervise the recording, saying he was too shy.

When I returned a week later, Hank was looking a bit hungover. There was a middle-aged woman with him, in black fishnet stockings and a black slip. She disappeared into the bedroom without speaking, emerging some time later ready to leave, looking tired and worn-out. Hank crushed some notes into her hand. 'Car fare', he said, as much to me as to her. Nothing in the room had changed. The Ampex was where I had left it and, for a moment, I was worried that he had not recorded anything. But it was done. He had filled every reel with the poems and stories that we had selected: six hours of his favourite pieces. In fact he had attempted to record 'on the other side', not realising that professional tape recorders do not work like that, and he had, therefore, inadvertently wiped his first recordings. He said to be sure to listen to the story called 'The Fire Station' as he liked that best of all.

I thought the results were wonderful, a mix of poems and stories – perfect for the series I had planned. We called it *At Terror Street and Agony Way*. Unfortunately, before I even had time to edit the tapes, the Zapple label was closed by the Beatles' new business manager Allen Klein and the poetry recordings were left unedited and unreleased. Over the years I managed to get most of the tapes out on other labels, but it was not until 1993 that *At Terror Street and Agony Way* finally reached the stores as a double CD on the King Mob label. Sadly, even that is now unavailable.

In rereading Hank's books for this biography I found that his work was still fresh, it has not dated, it goes straight to the point. He gave a voice to the disenfranchised, the marginalised, the mad and dysfunctional, the factory hand, the working people, the drunk and disorderly. He made a point of always trying to write clearly so that people knew exactly what he was saying. He did not use a dictionary. He avoided long words and tried to use the easiest, simplest words possible. He told Jean-Francois Duval: 'I like it raw, easy and simple. That way, I don't lie to myself.' In other words, he told the truth.

AUTHOR'S NOTE

Henry Charles Bukowski Junior was called Henry by his parents. His friends called him Hank, or sometimes Buke. He disliked being called Buck, as in fuck, 'I'm *Buke*, like in puke.' Both words, of course, would have appealed to him as a way of shocking the conformist neighbours. I shall call him Hank, throughout, in order to distinguish between father and son.

1. HOUSE OF TORTURE

It was the summer of 1939; Charles Bukowski had just graduated from Los Angeles High School. As usual, the Senior Prom was held in the girls' gym, which had been decorated with white crepe paper and had balloons in a net over the dance floor ready to be released on the dancers. A live combo played numbers like 'Deep Purple' and all the teenagers dressed in formal wear: tuxedos for the boys and long satin ball gowns for the girls. Hank did not have anyone to take but something drew him to the dance. He walked the two and a half miles from his parents' house and stood outside in the starless darkness, peering in through a wire-mesh covered window. He was amazed at the sight of his friends and classmates transformed from schoolchildren into adults so that he almost didn't recognise them as they danced, the boys very upright and straight, holding their dates in their arms, faces pressed into the girls' freshly permed hair. The girls had become women, very grown-up, stately, lovely. They looked wonderful. The boys were also transformed: they were handsome, confident, behaving with exaggerated politeness. Then Hank caught a glimpse of his reflection in the glass, staring in at them: the boils and scars on his face, his ragged shirt. He felt like some jungle animal drawn to the light and looking in. He wondered why he had come. He felt nauseous but kept watching. The dance ended and there was a pause while everyone left the floor. The couples chatted easily to each other. It all seemed natural and civilised. Hank could not understand where they had learned to converse like that and to dance. He couldn't converse or dance. Everybody was possessed of this secret knowledge but him. In any case, he knew that he would be too terrified even to look at one of those girls, let alone be close to her and talk. To look into her eyes or dance with her would have been beyond him.

The music began again and the mirror globe revolved overhead washing the couples in moving points of red, blue, green and gold light. In *Ham On Rye* Bukowski remembers: 'And yet I knew that what I saw wasn't as simple and good as it appeared. There was a price to be paid for it all, a general falsity, that could be easily believed, and could be the first step down a dead-end street.' But it became too much for him to take, waves of loneliness swept over him, and he began to hate them, he hated their beauty, their sureness and confidence, their untroubled youth and their happiness. He repeated to himself: 'Someday I will be as happy as any of you, you will see.' Suddenly Hank's soliloquy was interrupted by the night-watchman, who appeared with a flashlight and demanded to know what he was doing. Gesturing, he told Hank to get lost before he called the cops. Hank protested that he was a senior and this was the Senior Prom and he had every right to be there. 'Bullshit,' said the man, shining his torch on Hank's scarred face. 'You're at least 22 years old.' The man followed him down the path, his flashlight edging him on, step by step off the campus, the music fading behind him. There are parallels between this archetypal scene and Charlie Chaplin's *The Gold Rush* where Chaplin's 'Little Man' watches a New Year party in full swing through a window. It is Hank as the outsider, the loner, the Frozen Man. Hank's life and that of the 'Little Man' have much in common: the series of menial jobs, the slapstick humour, the buffoonery, even a boxer theme; the park benches and dead end jobs, the destitution, the poverty. And, in the best Hollywood tradition, Hank's story even has a happy ending.

The German–Americans constitute one of the largest ethnic groups in the United States; there are more of them than English–Americans or Irish–Americans. By the beginning of the twentieth century, 10 per cent of the population was of German extraction.

Hank's grandfather Leonard emigrated to the United States in the 1880s after fighting in the war of 1870 when Bismarck defeated Napoleon III. In Cleveland he met eighteen-year-old Emilie Krause, whose family had emigrated to the United States from Danzig (now Gdansk), which was then in Germany. They married, settling in Pasadena. In 1904, after many years as a carpenter, Leonard started his own construction company. Pasadena and Los Angeles were both booming; at the top end of the scale this was the period of the Greene Brothers and the Craftsmen movement in California, and at the bottom end it was a time when thousands of sub-standard Spanish stucco boxes were thrown up. Anyone who knew how to build was inundated with work. Leonard did very well for himself and built a large two-storey home for his family. He and Emilie had four sons and two daughters, beginning with John who was born in 1881. Next came Charles followed by Hank's father Henry, then Emma, Eleanor and the youngest, Ben.

The origin of the Bukowski family name is not known: they may well come from Bukowsko, a village in the L'vov district in Galicia near the present Polish border. Bukowsko is probably a derivation of Bukowski, the family name of a minor squire named Buk, from the Ukrainian 'buk' or beech. He was ennobled as a reward for his service as armour-bearer to his knight fighting the Turks in Vienna, a famous victory that stopped Islam in its tracks. Thus Buk became Bukowski. (Another version has the village simply named after some beech trees.) The Bukowskis are therefore either descendants of minor Polish nobility or, more likely, descendants of the many Jews who settled there in the eighteenth century, attracted by the town's annual trade fair and later by the establishment of a powerful Hasidic court.

Hank's parents met when Henry Bukowski was a sergeant in the American army of occupation after the defeat of Germany in 1918. He was stationed in Andernach, a small town on the left bank of the Rhine, ten miles northwest of Koblenz in the Rhineland-Palatinate. Andernach is one of the oldest towns in Germany; it is the old Antunnacum, the Roman Castellum ante Nacum, a frontier garrison town founded by Drusus in 12 BC when the Romans began their wars against the Germanic tribes on the right bank of the river. They enlarged the river harbour and built the town walls, the foundations of which are still standing. In 1253 Andernach joined the confederation of the Rhine cities and was the southernmost member of the Hanseatic League. In 1794 Andernach passed to France, but was ceded to Prussia in 1815 together with the left bank of the Rhine. Its long history has left a treasure house of monuments and old buildings including the thirteenth-century Romanesque basilica, the Pfarrkirche Maria Himmelfahrt, whose four towers dominate the town.

Sergeant Henry Bukowski had an office job; Hank referred to him as a typist, but he had an advantage over most of the other American troops in that he spoke fluent German. He got to know Heinrich Fett, who managed the canteen for American troops, and they became friends. Heinrich lived at home with his parents, Nanatte and Wilhelm, a seamstress and a musician. Apparently music ran in the Fett family as we know that Wilhelm's father was a violin player who went from bar to bar, passing his hat until he had collected enough to buy a few drinks. He was often thrown out for being drunk and disorderly and simply moved on to the next bar and repeated the scenario. This was one family story that Hank enjoyed.

The war had caused many shortages and Henry was sometimes able to give the Fett family meat and other scarce foodstuffs. He had already glimpsed Heinrich's sister Katherine, but it was not until he was invited to dinner that they were able to talk; she had previously resisted his advances and not replied when he shouted up to her from the street. Now they began an affair which quickly resulted in her becoming pregnant. Though Bukowski often claimed that he was born out of wedlock this was not so; Henry and Katherine were married on 15 July 1920 when she was eight months pregnant. The reason for the delay was so that Henry could first get demobilised. A month later, on 16 August, Heinrich Karl Bukowski was born at home in their apartment on the corner of Aktienstrasse near the railway station. Katherine's parents were Catholics, as were the Bukowskis, and so Henry was baptised into the faith in the magnificent medieval font in the Mariendom.

There has been some speculation about Katherine Fett's background as her mother's maiden name, Nanatte Israel, suggests that she might have been Jewish. This would have made Hank Jewish as the transmission is through the maternal line. As Bukowski is also likely to be a Jewish name, Hank's flirtation with Hitler and Nazism in the 40s was particularly unfortunate.

Out of the army, Henry first worked for the Rents, Requisitions and Claims Service before setting himself up as a self-employed building contractor; a boom industry following the destruction wreaked by the conflict. Two years after little Hank's birth, his father moved the family to Pfaffendorf, on the outskirts of nearby Koblenz. This was a much larger city and even had an American consulate. It was a beautiful city with a medieval centre and, as the centre of the local wine industry, a thriving economy. The river Mosel joins the Rhine here. It seems likely that Henry would have settled there, but postwar inflation, largely caused by the stiff reparations imposed on Germany by the French at Versailles, brought the economy to the point of collapse. Unable to make a living, Henry decided, like his father before him, to take his family to the USA and, on 18 April 1923, they sailed from Bremerhaven to Baltimore on the SS *President Fillmore*.

They spent some months in Baltimore, but Henry was unable to find suitable employment so they moved on, back to Pasadena to join his parents.

There is not one building that you could show in a backdrop that people would instantly recognise as a Los Angeles setting, as you could with New York, London or Paris. The city is not that well known, it is formless, lacking in definition. The Hollywood sign on Mount Lee is the most recognisable structure in Los Angeles and that was originally an advertisement for the Hollywoodland subdivision. It is now given historic building protection: appropriate in a city where billboards are the main architectural feature. In Los Angeles there is no sense of place, the street landscape is so similar from one block to the next that the residents have to devise recognition tricks in order to cope with the long commutes, and an unfamiliar destination can often result in getting lost in the seemingly endless sprawl.

When three-year-old Hank arrived there were already 53 movie studios in Los Angeles, and the oil industry was rapidly expanding across the southern part of the city. During the 20s the landscape of Los Angeles was transformed by wooden oil derricks in what was to become the most intensive oil field development in American history, producing 20 per cent of the world's output for that decade. In 1920 Los Angeles counted 576,673 residents but a decade later the census showed a population of 1,238,000. Hank arrived at a time of unprecedented growth. In the 20s Sunset Strip was still a dirt track; wheel ruts through citrus and avocado fields, subject to mudslides and flooding from the Hollywood Hills in the rainy season. Then came Prohibition, and because the Strip was outside the City Limits where the county sheriffs were easily bribed, it quickly became home to brothels and speakeasies and, by the mid-1930s, accommodated some of the fanciest nightspots in the world, including the Trocadero, El Mocambo and Ciro's. Sunset

Strip was ideally located between the Hollywood studios and Beverly Hills where the stars had just begun to build their homes. Developers tried to open up the Hollywood Hills and, in 1923, construction began on Mullholland Drive (then called Mullholland Highway) but the lack of water, frequent fires and mudslides deterred the population and it wasn't for another generation, not until after World War II, that property above the foothills was developed for anything except stables and riding schools.

Meanwhile the city spread south, following the Los Angeles River, and along the foothills, both east and west. Orange and citrus groves became freight yards and factories. There was a brutal open-shop, anti-union economy with wages generally about one third lower than other cities in the country, but the people still swarmed in, gulled by the boosterism of the Los Angeles Chamber of Commerce.

There was a tremendous beauty in the mountain landscape. In *The Day of the Locust* Nathanael West captured the setting: 'Hills rose directly behind his garage. They were covered with lupins, Canterbury bells, poppies, and several varieties of large yellow daisy. There were also some scrub pines, Joshua and Eucalyptus trees.' The intense colours and the sunshine affects every writer who comes to Los Angeles. Even the normally hard-core John Rechy in *City of Night* felt moved to describe the flowers: 'Blue and purple lupins, joshua trees with flowers held high,' but added 'You can rot here without feeling it.' There were also the ubiquitous palm trees, including the indigenous California palm. In the 20s it was easy to reach the countryside, every third lot was vacant and you were never very far from the orange groves that surrounded the city. Oranges were everywhere, they not only gave their name to Orange County, due south of Los Angeles County, and to more than 140 streets, but entered everyday consciousness. When Raymond Chandler needed a simile in *Farewell My Lovely* he wrote: 'A yellow window hung here and there, all by itself, like the last orange. Cars passed spraying the pavement with cold white light, then growled off into the darkness again.' Everyone in southern California would have known what he meant.

The air was still clean and the sky was blue; the motor age only began in the 20s and there were very few cars. No freeways were built until after World War II with the exception of the Arroyo Seco Parkway, built in 1938, but that was only six miles long.

Pasadena was still best known as a winter retreat for eastern millionaires. This was where passenger trains terminated. The

Union Station in downtown LA was only built in 1939, the last of the great train stations before air travel destroyed the railroads.

By the time Henry, Katherine and Hank arrived in Pasadena, Emilie and Leonard were estranged; a situation caused largely by Leonard's fondness for whiskey. Though not divorced they lived separately, not seeing each other, and his name was never mentioned in her presence. Financially she was well cared for, having taken charge of most of Leonard's money from his construction business. After the children had grown, Emilie had moved to a smaller house, one of several that Leonard owned, built under a grove of overhanging pepper trees. She had canaries, each one in a different cage and every evening she would cover each cage with a white cloth so that the birds could sleep. She had a piano and on one visit, while the adults talked, little Hank played random notes on the keyboard. When his father told him to stop, his grandmother encouraged him, saying 'Let the boy play.'

Emilie was religious and always attended the sunrise Easter service. Movies she thought were sinful and would not see them but she always watched the Rose Bowl parade; she and Leonard had originally lived on South Pasadena Avenue, just down from the Rose Bowl in Brookside Park. She enjoyed the southern California lifestyle and liked to visit the beach where she sat primly on a bench, looking out to sea. Her austere German ways – no show of emotion, no kissing or touching her grandchildren – seemed completely out of place in the warm sunlight surrounded by brilliantly coloured flowers and shrubs, birds with bright plumage in the flowering bushes and waving palm trees. This frigid carapace did not mean she had no feelings; such restraint was common across the whole of Europe in the days of large families and very high child mortality; to get too close and then have the child die could be devastating. Many parents continued to maintain a heartbreaking distance between them and their children which only the 1960s generation really broke down. Jazz musician Art Pepper, born in 1925, had a parallel experience to Bukowski, brought up by a German grandmother in Los Angeles. In *Straight Life* he wrote: 'She was a solid German lady ... but she was cold, very cold and unfeeling ... I saw that there was no warmth, no affection. I was terrified and completely alone. And at that time I realised that no one wanted me. There was no love and I wished I could die.' At least Hank had better than this.

Most of our information about Bukowski's childhood comes from his *bildensroman Ham on Rye*, but the same incidents are described again and again in scores of poems and interviews, each one adding a little more to the story: a new angle, an extra detail. Bukowski opens *Ham on Rye* with a description of hiding under the table in 1922 Germany, but as this memory includes his grandmother Emilie, it must have occurred in Pasadena. Most children remember nothing of their first three years of life but food was very important in the Bukowski family and one of the first things Bukowski tells us in *Ham on Rye* is what they ate: knockwurst and sauerkraut, chicken, green peas, carrots, spinach, string beans, meatballs and spaghetti, sometimes mixed in with ravioli. For breakfast they had waffles or hotcakes with scrambled eggs and bacon or French toast and sausages. On Sunday, when Emilie Bukowski came to visit, it was usually roast beef, mashed potatoes and gravy, followed by strawberry shortcake or apple pie with vanilla ice cream. German food remains the basis of American coffee shop cooking today and hamburgers and frankfurters have become symbolic of America itself.

Emilie was big and heavy and wore full-length skirts and dresses, her collar trimmed with antique lace and set off with a large glass brooch. According to Hank, she had a serious gas problem and would fart in loud bursts, four or five times, about a minute apart, just as the food was being served. Then she would say: 'I will bury you all.' Hank wrote: 'Every Sunday it was death and gas.' She enjoyed her food, and ate enormous helpings. After apple pie and ice cream there would usually be a big argument with her son over nothing and Emilie would run out of the door and take the red car back to Pasadena. After she left, Henry would stride around the room, fanning the air with a newspaper to get rid of the smell, saying: 'It's all that damned sauerkraut she eats.'

Bukowski wrote about his grandmother a lot, always misspelling her name as Emily, using the American form. Emilie enjoyed visiting Henry and Katherine because Katherine, like her, had been born in Germany and had old-fashioned German manners which in Emilie's eyes made her superior to all the other wives and husbands of her children. Emilie Bukowski was self-sufficient and very independent. She regarded hospitals with disdain and never used them or called a doctor. One evening, when she was 87, she keeled over and died while feeding her canaries.

Katherine and Emilie spoke German together; Katherine knew very little English when she arrived and always retained a thick German accent. German was also Hank's first language, but he soon forgot it. He struggled hard to lose his accent, too, because the neighbourhood children teased him mercilessly about it. When they arrived in Baltimore, Henry had quickly anglicised his family: Katherine became Kate or Katey, and little Heinrich became Henry. When they were together Hank's parents spoke German. Hank could hear them in the other room after he had gone to bed, and they also 'turned on the Deutsche' whenever they wanted to discuss something without him understanding.

In 1924, after a few months in Pasadena with Emilie, the family moved to Trinity Street, just south of downtown Los Angeles, near the old industrial district and the newly created Central Manufacturing District which extended along the already polluted Los Angeles River. The countryside was not far away, but things were changing rapidly; that same year three hundred acres of cauliflower fields near the river were dug up and replaced with the Union Pacific and Southern Pacific freight yards. They had a small house in a poor neighbourhood but little Hank was not allowed to play with the other children because they were poor. Their families were no more deprived than Hank's own parents but the Bukowskis aspired to be rich and they didn't want their son mingling with 'bad' children. The children would have only teased him anyway as Hank was dressed in clean formal clothes at all times in the German tradition and must have looked like a freak to them. The first time he played with children of his own age was when he went to kindergarten. He did not know how to relate to the other children. Because his father had not allowed him to join them in the street, he did not know how to catch a ball or swing a baseball bat. He was put in a game, someone threw a ball at him and he didn't know what to do. He dropped it. 'They seemed very strange, they laughed and talked and seemed happy. I didn't like them.'

Nonetheless he enjoyed kindergarten; they planted radish seeds and two weeks later they had grown and the children were able to eat them with salt, they painted in watercolours and did all the usual group activities. In the manner of the day, Hank was very strictly toilet trained and had been taught that everything to do with going to the bathroom was 'dirty'. This created big problems for him at kindergarten because he was ashamed to tell the teacher or to let the others know that he needed to go, so he held it. 'It was really terrible to hold it. And the air was white, I felt like vomiting.' When the other, less-repressed children, came back from using the toilets, Hank would look at them and think they were dirty, that they did something dirty in there. He always wanted to go to the bathroom. For Hank: 'Kindergarten was mostly white air.'

Henry took a job delivering milk for the Los Angeles Creamery Company, making his rounds with a horse and cart. The horses provide one of the few tender moments with his father that Hank ever wrote about. One morning, when Hank was almost five, his father woke him. 'Come on, I want to show you something.' It was still dark and Hank walked outside with his father in the moonlight, still in his pyjamas and slippers. The horse was standing very still, harnessed to the wagon. 'Watch,' said his father and he put a sugar cube in his hand and offered it to the horse. The horse ate it from his palm. 'Now you try it . . .' said Henry, putting a sugar cube in Hank's hand. Hank was afraid the horse would bite him, but Henry pushed him closer, telling him to hold out his hand. 'The head came down. I saw the nostrils; the lips pulled back, I saw the tongue and the teeth, and then the sugar cube was gone.' His father gave him another lump to feed the horse. It was a magical experience for the four-year-old child. The horse was so big, towering over him and he was aware of its great strength and was scared it would stand on his feet, but it was the most exciting thing that had ever happened to him. In 'Ice for the Eagles' he wrote: 'The horses were more real than/my father/more real than God.' The horse shook its head in pleasure. 'Now,' said Henry, 'I'll take you back inside before the horse shits on you.'

In another tender moment from *Ham on Rye* Hank describes his father playing games with the packaging of Camel cigarettes, having Hank count how many pyramids there were on the packet. His father could always find more. There were tricks to do with the camel's humps and the words on the package. It was a constant source of wonder to the little boy. Though we come to know his father as an argumentative, bombastic brute who dominated his cowed wife, Hank didn't actively dislike him until he started beating him, something which appears to have begun after Hank had started school, though it was very common in those unenlightened days for parents to beat their children.

If grandmother didn't visit, the family would drive out to the nearby orange groves on a Sunday. They had a metal chest that held dry ice in which they kept frozen cans of fruit. In the picnic basket went the weenies and liverwurst, the salami sandwiches and bananas and potato chips; good German fare. The fizzy drinks were continually switched from the icebox to the basket so that they would not freeze solid.

One memory that Hank revisited several times was a picnic trip during which his father climbed a fence and filled a picnic basket with oranges, only to be confronted by the orange grove's irate owner who ordered them off his property at gunpoint and without their stolen fruit. For all his lectures about the glories of the American way of life, Henry was not above breaking the property laws himself when he thought he might get away with it.

We only have a series of vignettes from Hank's early life. Hank was six years old the first time he met his grandfather. Leonard was a big, solidly built man, six foot three inches, and wore a long white beard and moustache. He had pure white hair and brilliant, sparkling blue eyes. Hank thought he was the most beautiful man he had ever seen. They drove over to see him in his father's Model T Ford. Hank's grandfather had been an army officer and stood up tall and straight in front of his little house. Hank's parents did not get out of the car so Hank walked alone over to the porch to meet him. He said, 'Hello Henry. You and I, we know each other.' There was the smell of whiskey on his breath, though Hank could not have known what that was at the time. Leonard clearly had a bootleg supply as this was in the middle of Prohibition. He took Hank into the house and invited him to sit down. Leonard went into another room and returned with a small tin box which he gave to Hank. Hank's small fingers could not open it so his grandfather did it for him. Inside were his medals from the war of 1870 including a Maltese cross on a ribbon. He gave them to Hank. They met only one more time (though in *Ham on Rye* the two meetings are conflated into one). This time he gave Henry his gold pocket watch on a long gold chain. Henry wound it up too tight and broke it, something he always felt bad about.

In 1927 the family moved to a small Spanish-style bungalow at 4511 South 28th Street in Jefferson Park. Hank was sent to Virginia Road Grammar School, two blocks away between 29th and 30th. He felt like an outsider, the other children knew what to do; they used elaborate rituals to choose sides, they played complicated ball games that he did not know the rules for, they made circles and sang songs. He stood watching them, asking himself, What are they doing, why are they doing that, why run in a circle like that? Even at that age a part of him thought, This is stupid. He told Fernanda Pivano: 'I used to look at them and say, "What's wrong with you?" And they'd look at me and say, "Hey, there's something wrong with you." The crowd was always here, and I was always there, from the very beginning. And there's just an impasse.' He told Steve Richmond: 'I've never felt good with the crowd and it started in grammar school, I sensed that they touched each other, but that I did not belong.' It was something that stayed with him: 'The worst part is that I do not even belong with the *best* ones, the living ones, I seem sliced off forever by some god damn trick, either my imagining or some type of insanity, but even the good ones leave me dangling and I feel like a fool, and I know that I am a fool for I feel what I know.' It was the schoolyard he really disliked; the embarrassment of always being chosen next to last on the baseball team.

But it wasn't all alienation at school: his teachers praised his painting, calling him a genius, and he relaxed enough to begin using the bathroom, but only to piss. Hank was often constipated, sometimes so much so that his mother would take him to the doctor. Hank's bowels were of great interest to him and the subject of numerous poems and asides in his books. In the poem 'Poop' he described his problems in digesting his food while facing his father across the table. Henry would wipe up the gravy on his plate with a piece of bread and chew his food with greasy lips, spittle flying as he engaged in idiotic conversation. He noisily slurped his coffee then wiped his face with a huge white napkin and then leaned back to relax with a Camel, lighting it with a kitchen match that he would put, still burning, into the ashtray. Hank tried to swallow his food but 'it all turned to glue inside'.

It was at Virginia Road Grammar School that Hank had his first problem with teachers. It appears he had some form of dyslexia; in the poem 'Education' he says he had trouble differentiating between the words 'sing' and 'sign', he couldn't get the order of the letters right. There was something there he couldn't overcome. The teacher, Mrs Sims, asked Hank's mother to come and see her and told her he was not learning anything and not trying. Dyslexia was unknown then, so it seemed that he was either dumb or slacking. Mrs Bukowski began to cry, upsetting the teacher so much that she said she would give Hank another chance. His mother said: 'Oh Henry, your father is so disappointed in you, I don't know what we are going to do.' She shared the teacher's view that he was just being lazy, but her reaction also showed her own fear of her husband. The event was burned into Hank's memory and more than forty years later he could still remember Mrs Sims's fierce pointed face thick with white powder.

Hank was, in one incident, picked on by a school bully and provoked into a fight. When the teacher broke it up, Hank was blamed and he found himself in the headmaster's office. Regarding him as a troublemaker, the headmaster taunted him, 'Think you're a tough guy, eh?' and shook his hand, squeezing it harder and harder until he screamed in pain. He gave Hank a note in a sealed envelope to take to his parents. In Germany, teachers had the same status as a judge or a doctor and Hank's mother was beside herself with anxiety at the shame and disgrace of it all. It was either for this, or for the sloppy work caused by dyslexia – reports vary – that Hank was beaten when his father got home. It was the first time that Henry used his razor strop.

The first blow shocked him more than anything else, but each following blow increased the pain. At first he saw the confining walls, and the toilet and bath, but after a while he couldn't see anything. With each stroke Henry upbraided him, but Hank couldn't understand the words. Suddenly Hank began to sob, swallowing and choking on the tears and mucus in his throat and Henry stopped. Hank's mother was standing outside in the hall. 'Why didn't you help me?' he asked.

'The father is always right,' she said.

To her the father and husband was the unquestioned head of the household. To Hank it simply meant that she had no love for him and the incident permanently alienated him from his parents. He did not love them, or care anything for them, and had all the usual children's fantasies that they were not his real parents but that they must have adopted him. Somewhere, he felt, there were some real parents, capable of love not just the blind obedience to authoritarian dogma. He did not feel rejected, he just felt as if he were in the wrong place, with the wrong parents. Like many children he would lie in bed in the dark and think: 'Those aren't my parents in the other room, that's somebody else.'

This was at a time when corporal punishment was commonplace, both at home and in most schools, particularly Catholic ones. 'Spare the rod and spoil the child' and 'children should be seen and not heard' were typical of the reactionary clichés that guided the lives of many unthinking people and, though most survived it relatively unscathed, there were some particularly sensitive children whose lives were destroyed or warped by such casual brutality. No one doubts the pain and trauma inflicted on Hank, or that there was an obvious element of sadism in his father's behaviour, at least when Hank was older. We can also see a mindless vacuity in his mother's blind acceptance of her husband's authority; however, Bukowski managed to parlay his whippings into something possibly a great deal more sinister than they actually were. At least in these early days the Bukowskis sound like a typical working-class, authoritarian family, determined to 'beat sense' into their recalcitrant child in the days before knowledge of Freud, Dr Spock and popular psychology was widespread or even existed. Later, during the Depression years when the family was under considerable strain, and Hank was an adolescent questioning his father's authority, there is no doubt that Hank's beatings were part of an Oedipal power struggle.

Fighting was part of everyday life, something Hank grew up with and was even enamoured of. As a teenager he fought a lot; as an adult he enjoyed and sought out bar fights. Later he followed boxing and attended matches, even toying with the idea of entering the ring himself. When he was little, however, he avoided violence if he possibly could. It was hard to be a German kid in Los Angeles in the 20s. The Great War was not long over and anti-German feeling still ran high. Hank used to be chased by the neighbourhood kids yelling: 'Heinie! Heinie! Heinie!' but they never caught him. He knew all the back alleys and dead ends, the backyards and chicken coops, the empty lots filled with brush, the garage roofs and crawl spaces. It was a game. They didn't really want to catch him either in case he turned into a real German and bayoneted them.

Hank's mother no doubt suffered, also, from anti-German feeling. She desperately missed her family and was lonely for German friends. Sometimes Henry would take her to the Deutsche Haus, at 634 15th Street, a German social centre not far from their house where they could eat, listen to a German band and buy German magazines and newspapers. Sometimes there were movies and documentaries about Germany. They usually went after church on Sundays, but it was a boring event for Hank because he didn't speak the language.

Each afternoon, when school ended, there would be a fight between two of the older boys out by the back fence. They were never fair fights; there was always a smaller boy whose face would be pounded bloody. 'The smaller boys took their beatings wordlessly, never begging, never asking for mercy.' It was the survival of the fittest and Hank quickly became adept at the ways of the jungle. He seems to have avoided fights at Grammar School but on the street it was different.

One day he got into a fight with three kids he had never seen before. He saw off two of them but the biggest one carried on fighting, and Hank was losing. There was a little girl who lived next door, who from the age of six or seven had made a habit of showing him her panties. The girl, called Lisa in the poem 'Panties', came up behind his aggressor and cracked him over the head with a large bottle. That ended the fight and the boy ran off screaming, holding his head. For some inexplicable reason, the girl never showed Hank her panties again.

Henry Bukowski's true character begins to emerge in a series of stories illustrating his irascibility and short temper. In 'The Monkey' we see him at his most unpleasant. A fat organ grinder wearing a red fez, badly faded by the sun, came down the street with his monkey; the monkey was dressed in a little hat, waistcoat and pants and danced and did somersaults to the music. When the music ended the organ grinder passed his cup around. Other parents gave nickels and dimes, the children gave pennies, but Hank's father came storming out of the house, yelling 'What's all the goddamed noise' and immediately got into an argument with the man, frightening the monkey so that it bit the organ grinder's hand, making it bleed. Henry ordered the man off the block, spoiling the entertainment for everyone.

Hank's descriptions of his childhood do not include any toys or games, but focus very much on his parents: hatred of them when they were at home or pleasure at their absence. The most time he spent with them was at dinner and Hank gives many descriptions of the aspiring German bourgeoisie at table: his father loved pancakes for breakfast, with syrup, butter and bacon, and he liked his coffee so hot that it burned his throat. Sometimes it was so hot that he spat it out across the table, though this probably only occurred once, as described in *Ham on Rye*. He liked pork chops, mashed potatoes and gravy, chilli and beans, which made him fart for hours afterwards and he grinned with each fart. He liked to end a meal with strawberry shortcake and vanilla ice cream.

While demolishing his food, Henry liked to talk. His favourite topics included food, his job, at which he excelled and everyone else was a dolt, his retirement – he never made it – or he mouthed his favourite aphorisms: 'If you can't succeed, suck eggs', 'My country right or wrong', 'The early bird gets the worm', 'Early to bed and early to rise makes a man healthy wealthy and wise', 'Don't do as I do, but do as I say!' while his wife looked on admiringly. Astonished by her husband's wit and wisdom she would turn to Hank and admonish him: 'Henry, you *listen* to your father.' Henry also liked the racist rhyme: 'Eenie, meanie, miney, mo./Catch a nigger by the toe./If he hollers make him pay./Fifty dollars every day.' Intriguingly he sometimes included a snatch of Edgar Allan Poe in the performance.

Henry's mother was caught in an impossible situation. She was living in a foreign country, with the victors in the war against

Germany. She had been brought up to believe that the husband was to be obeyed, that the father was always right and that her role was to keep the house and bring up the child. Her English was not good, she had a strong German accent, and she had a limited understanding of American cultural values despite her attentive reading of the *Saturday Evening Post*. She had no friends and relied on Henry for almost everything. Hank seemed to recognise this, despite his many criticisms of her:

> She never had much of a chance, she believed everything she had been told, or taught, and she never stumbled upon any counter-sources to pull her out of that. Of course, maybe she didn't have the will, or spirit to escape the obvious. She might have been simple minded. I remember hearing throughout my childhood: 'Smile, Henry, be happy.' I mean, she actually thought that if I smiled I'd be happy.

Hank interpreted her seeming coldness as a lack of love, though she wrote to relatives in Germany saying that she doted on the child. Hank had a hard time of it, and it was only to get worse: 'Between the imbecile savagery of my father, the disinterestedness of my mother, and the sweet hatred of my playmates: "Heinie! Heinie! Heinie!" things were pretty hot all round.'

Every Saturday morning his houseproud parents took up all the rugs in the house and waxed the hardwood floors before covering them again. They cleaned the house assiduously, paying particular attention to the bathroom. 'Silverfish!' Hank's father would yell and his wife would come running with the spray can to kill them. In the afternoon they would go out together. These were Hank's happiest times, left alone in the house, late in the afternoon when it was shady and quiet. They had a stand-up Victrola in the living room housed in a mahogany cabinet with a handle on the right-hand side to wind it up between each playing. If you did not wind it, it played slower and slower, so by the third record it slowed and stopped. Hank liked to let it do that. The sound was amplified by a wooden sound box and the volume controlled by shutters on the front. The steel needle had to be changed with each play, but most people played at least three records before changing it so the record grooves had a white sheen of worn steel. The records were old even then, as the Victrola had belonged to Hank's grandfather and the records were originally his. Hank would take all the phonograph records and spread them around the room on the floor and look at the coloured labels; he liked the dark purple label and only played those. He didn't really enjoy the music, he enjoyed the game of holding his thumb against the edge of the green baize turntable to slow it down. The wobbling, slowed-down voices brought images to his eyes: he recalled his father pulling on his leather slippers in the morning; or saw a waterfall or a tiger in the jungle attacking its prey. Brief glimpses of things before they vanished: 'Nothing I could think of/in my life then/seemed better than listening/to that/victrola/when my parents weren't/home.'

Another game, played alone in the house, was to time himself holding his breath. He would wait until the second hand of the clock reached twelve then take a deep breath. He would hold it so long that he had to clench his fists and roll on the rug to stop himself taking a breath while flashes of red, blue and purple light exploded in his head. Finally he would breath in and look at the clock, hoping to have knocked a few seconds off his record. Then he would go to the kitchen and drink a glass of water.

When he was old enough, Hank went to the Saturday matinee for children at the local picture palace, waiting in line for an hour before the theatre even opened, then being shown to his seat by an usherette with a torchlight. There was an adult movie – often Fred Astaire and Ginger Rogers – then came Popeye or another cartoon followed by a Buck Rogers space movie. Hank and his friends sat there with 'jawbreakers' gobstoppers. Hank and the other kids loved movies about World War I aviators such as Paramount's *Wings* (1928), the story of the aviation battles. The dog fights between the German Fokkers and the Allies in their Spads were always protracted, and the Germans always lost. The remaining Spads would then limp home and that night the pilots would all gather in the bar and drink whiskey, their arms round slinky blondes. Hank's hero was Baron Manfred Von Richthofen, the German air ace who shot down eighty planes. Even though Germany had lost the war, Hank was permitted to admire this German, who was universally recognised as a great flyer. To advertise the film, the movie house had the wing of an actual Spad and a propeller and attracted attention with a searchlight, lighting up the Hollywood sky. Hank and his friends studied *Flying Aces* magazine and knew about all the heroes.

Hank had a friend called Frank Sullivan, whose father had been a pilot in the Great War. Frank introduced Hank to air shows. There were air races, parachute jumps and stunt flyers in brightly coloured bi-planes painted in stripes and checks; a handkerchief was hung near the ground and a stunt flyer in an old German Fokker would fly in low and pick it off with a hook on one of his wings, then do a barrel roll right near the ground. There were lots of crashes. Hank and his friends built models of Spads and Fokkers from balsa wood kits which cost 25 cents each, a lot of money then but each kid had his own plane.

In 'Buddies' Hank says that when he was nine or ten years old his first real friends were Moses and Red. Moses was a quiet Jewish boy who one day did something to a five-year-old girl in the large yellow and white garage down the block and the police took him away. That left Red. Red's right arm was deformed, ending in rudimentary fingers and he wore a half-arm of pure white enamel with a hand covered in a brown leather glove. As is to be expected the other children picked on him, but they soon found that to be hit on the head with an artificial arm was a very salutary experience and as long as there were only four or five boys against Red and Hank they soon defeated them. Red and Hank went swimming in the public pool but there were always more new kids who didn't realise the situation and began taunting them until these children too were sent running, tears streaming down their cheeks.

Hank's parents bought him an Indian suit, complete with feathers, headband and tomahawk. It was the worst thing they could have done. Bukowski: 'Here I was, with my German accent, dressed up like a goddam Indian while all the other little boys had cowboy outfits. That put me in a tough spot, believe me. But I got very good with that tomahawk. It did a lot more damage than their toy guns.'

In the childhood jungle you either bullied or you were bullied. Hank described how he and his friends bullied one of the local boys, called Harold in 'Fun Times: 1930'. They would pretend to hang him, two or three times a week, cornering him on the back porch of a neighbour's house where there was a thick beam over the porch. They would put a rope around his neck and tell him that this time it really was it. He would cry, tears running down his freckled face. They would give him a choice, if he didn't want to die he either had to drink piss or eat shit. He always chose piss and they would pee all over him, laughing as they wetted his shoes and pants and he sobbed. Then he moved away. The children passed on the sickness from one generation to the next: sensitivity was ruthlessly crushed and stamped on; emotions were to be repressed; boys don't cry; you have to be tough to survive. And as the Great Depression began to bite, this was ever more so.

Hank frequently wrote about the lonely, the shy or sensitive boys at school and how they were persecuted, first by their schoolmates and then by the parents. He would take peanut butter sandwiches to school for lunch in a brown paper bag, but one of the boys brought a lunch pail which had different compartments containing a thermos of chocolate milk, apples, bananas, ham sandwiches, beef sandwiches, a pickle and a bag of potato chips. Even though the other boys derided him for it and the boy was the school sissy, Hank always sat beside him at lunchtime. The boy, called Richardson in 'Those Marvellous Lunches', and 'David' in *Ham on Rye*, would give him potato chips. His friendship with the boy meant that no one else would speak to him – clearly an exaggeration – but Hank was hungry and the potato chips meant more to him than friendship. He claimed the boy was his only friend, they walked home together after school and the other boys would gang up against them and push the boy around and knock him down, but they didn't dare attack Hank. He and Hank rarely actually spoke to each other.

David would arrive home dishevelled, his clothes grass-stained and torn. His mother demanded to know how he got this way each day but he maintained the code of silence and so, after being beaten up by the schoolboys, he was then beaten by his mother. Hank would stand outside his house, listening to his friend sobbing. Then David had to practise on his violin. 'The afternoon light hurt my eyes. I felt like vomiting.'

In 'Me Against the World' Hank describes running away from four boys who were about to beat him up and, on reaching his home, finding his father beating his mother. She was screaming and on the floor were broken objects from the fight. Hank threw himself at his father and began swinging but his father was too tall and all Hank could hit were his legs. He saw a flash of red and purple and green and found himself on the floor. 'You little prick!' his father yelled, 'you stay out of this!'

'Don't you hit my boy!' his mother screamed. Hank felt good because his father was no longer hitting his mother and was concentrating on him instead. Just to make sure, Hank charged him again and got beaten to the floor once more. When he got up his father was sitting on one chair and his mother sitting on another and they were both looking at him. This traumatic event was reworked a number of times in his later poems.

Things were evidently going badly wrong between Hank's parents, a situation which came to a head when Henry Bukowski fell in love with one of the women on his milk round, something Hank also wrote about a number of times. Henry took a room on West Adams Boulevard, a block from home. He did not live there, just used it to meet with his mistress. Hank wrote that he arrived home from school to find his mother in tears and a strange woman sitting in the living room while his father was forced to choose between them. Hank's reaction was to threaten to kill his father, which resulted in him once again being knocked to the floor. After a fierce argument the other woman left, taking off in the family car. Hank was locked in his bedroom while his father vented his anger on his wife. As she screamed and Henry kept beating her Hank climbed out of his bedroom window but found the front door locked. He tried the back door and the windows but everything was locked. All he could do was stand in the backyard and listen to the screaming and the beating.

Despite his own infidelities, Henry Bukowski was very censorial towards his brothers. The Bukowskis did not get along with each other. His brother Ben would drive up in his Model-A and come in with a new lady; they would sit on the couch in the living room and chat. Then Ben would follow Henry into another room and ask him for money, 'Come on Henry, let me have a couple of bucks.' Henry would always react the same way, 'You're nothing but a bum, get yourself a job!' Ben always lied, saying he'd tried a number of places that morning, but Henry was obdurate: 'You're lying, you just want money for that whore.' Ben would protest but Henry was convinced, 'Get her out of my house! We don't allow those kinds of women in here.'

'Just two bucks?' he would wheedle.

'Get her out of here before I throw her out.'

They would leave and Hank's parents would run about the house opening doors and windows, 'She stinks, that cheap perfume!' his mother would shriek.

'We're going to have to fumigate the place,' his father screamed.

Then a week later, the Model-A would pull up and Ben would saunter in with a different woman.

'Come on Henry, just two bucks.'

As far as Hank could see, Ben never did get two bucks from his brother but he never gave up trying. Hank's parents would mutter to each other. 'Those women are so ugly,' his mother would say. Then a great gloom would descend on his parents, they would stop talking and just sit in the living room, thinking how terrible it was that Ben was imposing his women on them, daring to intrude on their lives. For his part, Hank wondered where Ben got the petrol for his car.

Ben borrowed a lot of money from his mother but contracted TB and was hospitalised in a sanatorium, high in the Hollywood Hills, paid for by Emilie. Hank describes a visit made by the family to take him some flowers. Hank's father hectored Ben about the cigarettes that he continued to smoke, against the sanatorium regulations, and about his 'prostitutes' as Henry called them, but Ben wasn't going to be drawn by Henry's ill-will. He told him that he'd had a good life and enjoyed it. He was prepared to die, even though he was only 24.

Henry's oldest brother John chewed tobacco and rode a motor-cycle. He was also impecunious and, in *Ham on Rye*, Hank describes a visit to the small court where he lived, occasioned by the fact that the police had come to Henry's house looking for John who was wanted for rape. His beaten down wife and two daughters, Katherine and Betsy, were half starving and Hank's mother had brought several boxes of canned food for them. Though the visit no doubt took place, the family have angrily denied the rape charge as a fantasy of Hank's alcoholic brain. John died in 1933 aged 52.

In October 1929 the Stock Market crashed, heralding the Great Depression. By 1933 almost 27 per cent of the wage-earning population was unemployed. Grim-faced, bewildered men in their fedoras gathered on street corners and in bars, overwhelmed by events beyond their control. Money became very scarce. Bukowski could remember the rag and bone man coming down his street, hearing his shout of 'Rags! Bottles! Sacks!' long before the old wooden wagon pulled by a decrepit sway-back horse came into view. Hank remembered the saliva dripping in white streams from the horse's mouth, ribs showing, the swarms of flies round its eyes. The rag and bone man was very dirty, unshaven and sat on top of a large pile of canvas sacks, whip in hand. In 'Rags, Bottles, Sacks', Bukowski wrote that he was the first, and only, man he ever wanted to kill; his cruelty to his horse upset him so much.

People searched vacant lots for edible weeds and kept scrawny chickens in their backyards. The children used to gather to watch when the neighbours killed gophers by attaching a hose to the car exhaust and sticking it down their holes. The gophers would come out and the cats would attack them, then the dogs would attack the cats and everyone had a good time watching. Wings cigarettes were 10 cents a pack but many of the men rolled Bull Durham; it was regarded as particularly accomplished to be able to roll a cigarette with one hand. 'If somebody looked at you wrong you cracked him one right in the mouth. It was a glorious non-bullshit time, especially after we got rid of Herbert Hoover.'

In 1931 the Bukowski family moved a few blocks north to 2122 Longwood Avenue, a subdivision south of Washington Boulevard: 'the house of agony'. It was here that Henry imposed strict discipline on Hank, and beat him for the slightest infraction. Bukowski: 'I could not understand why he beat me. He would search very hard for a reason.' Katherine acquiesced, though it is hard to see how she could have done otherwise since Henry beat her as well.

In 1985 filmmaker Barbet Schroeder returned with Bukowski to the house on Longwood Avenue and filmed him in the bathroom. Bukowski:

This is the torture chamber. This is where I learned something. The old man had a razor strop he used to hang here. He'd just pick it off. Drop your pants and your shorts. I would stand about here and he would begin. And I don't know how many lashes he'd give me. They'd be hard. Eight – ten – twelve – fourteen. And of course you can't help screaming, especially when you're six years old, seven years old ... So this place holds some memories all right. Its just a terrible place to stand and talk about.

You're a small creature and you have a large creature beating on you. And the mother says OK ... And at that time it's very difficult because there's no place to go, there's nothing you can do.

Though Hank's father undoubtedly did beat him before they moved to Longwood Avenue, it was not until Hank was eleven that the regular corporal punishment began, using the lawn as an excuse.

On Saturdays, from the age of eleven, while the other children in the neighbourhood were playing football, little Hank had to mow the front lawn, first one way and then the other. After that he had to use the edger, not missing anything growing underneath the overhanging hedge. Then he was to take the shears and clip any tall blades that the mower had missed. If there was a single blade of grass standing above the others when he was finished, Hank was beaten. His father would get down on his hands and knees and put his eye to ground level, searching for rogue blades. Naturally he always found some and would fly into a rage: 'There, I SEE IT! YOU MISSED ONE! YOU MISSED ONE! Then he would call to Hank's mother, who always watched the proceedings from the bathroom window: 'HE MISSED ONE! I SEE IT! I SEE IT!' And Hank's mother would go along with the farce: 'Ah, he MISSED one. Ah, shame, SHAME!' Then it was her turn to crouch down and look and add her opprobrium. Hank thought they were both insane, as they were. 'INTO THE BATHROOM! Henry would scream. 'INTO THE BATHROOM!' Then they would all troop into the house. Hank would go into the bathroom and pull down his pants and shorts and his father would take down the razor strop and the beating would begin. Each stroke increased Hank's loathing and hatred for his psychopathic father and his stupid, cowed mother. After the beating Hank had to water the lawn. Then he was given a pillow to sit on.

The lawn does appear to have become something of an obsession for Henry. In 'I Was Born to Hustle Roses Down the Avenues of the Dead' Bukowski describes how his father got so angry one time because Hank was not sweating as he mowed the lawn that he threw a two by four piece of wood at him, hitting him on the back of his left.leg and leaving a broken blood vessel that jutted out for the rest of Hank's life. In revenge Hank threw the wood into Henry's beautiful rose border before limping back to finish the lawn, still not sweating.

Bukowski always maintained later that his father's brutality was good training for the world: 'I'd say one thing they taught me was not to weep too much when something goes wrong. In other words, they hardened me to what I was going to go through: the bum, the road, all the bad jobs and the adversity. Since my early life hadn't been soft, the rest didn't come as such a shock.'

Elizabeth Barrett Browning caught the situation when she wrote: 'But the child's sob in the silence curses deeper than the strong man in his wrath.' Hank managed to contain his rage and fury, tending it in a boiling pit of resentment, refining it, until he was ready to express it in a novel, a series of stories, and innumerable poems.

One of the main reasons Bukowski is an important writer is because he managed to preserve some of his sensitivity despite the conditioning regime which was designed to break and bury it. Part of him was always an outsider from an early age and he was able to take a disinterested view of his parents and their madness – the madness of everyday life:

I guess that's where it all started – the disgusted realisation that it takes something extraordinary, like drinking or writing or classical music, to move beyond such people. That's why I took to Dostoevsky so quickly because you remember what he says in *The Brothers Karamazov* – 'who doesn't want to kill the father?' Who exactly? . . . The disgust he made me feel for life never left. But disgust is better than anger. When you're angry you just wanna get even, when you're disgusted you just wanna get away; and with disgust you can laugh.

The hardest part was the crying. He didn't want to cry and so one day he just decided not to: 'All that could be heard was the slashing of the leather strap against my naked ass. It had a curious and meaty and gruesome sound in the silence and I stared at the bathroom tiles.' The tears flowed down his cheeks but he made no sound. Henry was puzzled and stopped beating. He usually gave Hank fifteen or twenty lashes but he stopped at a mere seven or eight. He ran out of the bathroom, 'Mama, Mama, I think our boy is CRAZY, he don't cry when I whip him!'

'You think he's crazy, Henry?'

'Yes, Mama.'

'Ah, too bad!'

It was the first recognisable appearance of what Hank was to call the Frozen Boy. He knew there was something wrong with him but he also knew he was not insane. He just could not understand how other people could become so enraged. But this distance came at a terrible price. He wrote: 'I was BORN into the Frozen Man Stance . . . When I got into a fist fight with one of my friends I could never get angry. I only fought as a matter of course. No other out. I was Frozen. I could not understand the anger and fury of my opponent . . . every now and then I would land a good one to see if I could do it, then I would fall back into lethargy.'

Fighting was a major part of his childhood experience, and it stayed with him into the barfights of his youth. He had two buddies, called Eugene and Frank in the poem 'Practice', and he had wild fist fights with each of them once or twice a week. The fights lasted for three or four hours at a time. They crashed through people's hedges and rolled through strange backyards and vacant lots as people screamed at them and dogs barked. They fought up and down the road and the pavement and on people's front lawns. They never quit until their parents' called them for supper, which they couldn't afford to miss. Afterwards they had bruised knuckles, fat lips, black eyes and swollen noses, sprained wrists and purple welts on their bodies. Sometimes there would be blood. Their parents said nothing, just let them fight, sitting on their porches, glancing at them from time to time then turning back to their newspapers. Only if they tore or ruined their clothes did their parents become angry during the fight, but, if Hank lost, his father would complain bitterly that he let some boy beat him and his mother would say, 'Shame!' Hank described one epic fight, lasting from ten in the morning of a Saturday until six in the evening when the sun went down; afterwards their arms were so tired they couldn't lift them. The next day Hank's entire body was purple from bruising and he had a couple of loose teeth as well as swollen lips. He often exaggerated these fights, claiming that an all-day fight was a regular occurrence, but in *Ham on Rye*, it only happens once.

Eugene, who was a year older and a bit bigger than Hank, featured in several poems; in 'The Bee' Bukowski describes how he and Eugene leaped off a garage roof together to prove their guts. Eugene managed it but Hank twisted his ankle and was bedridden when it swelled up. His parents raged about the cost of medical attention.

When Hank was eleven or twelve, he used to hitchhike twenty miles to the beach at Santa Monica, which was much cleaner in those days. Or they sometimes took the tram which cost seven cents, which also got you two transfers. Hank went with his friend, called Frank in 'Streetcars', who was very bold, going up to people and asking them if they were going to use their transfers. They loved to sit in the open section as the W line tram tore along the tracks, shooting sparks from the wheels, the conductor banging the bell with his foot pedal. It was particularly thrilling at night because large sections of the city were still vacant lots and so they were riding through velvet blackness.

Hank moved to Mount Vernon Junior High and when President Hoover came to Los Angeles for the opening of the 1932 Los Angeles Olympic Games, Hank's English class was given a project to write about the visit. In his paper Hank described the Saturday crowds at the LA Coliseum, the secret service men, the excitement of the crowd. But Saturday was the day he had to mow the lawn. So on Sunday he simply let his imagination flow and created the scene in his own head: 'I just made the whole thing up. I wasn't even there. I wrote how his car entered the Coliseum and he had garlands on and was followed by other cars and the people stood up to see the President's face . . . it was total bullshit.' The teacher read his piece aloud to the class and praised him highly but afterwards she kept him behind when the class was dismissed. She asked if he had been there and he admitted that he was not. 'That makes it all the more remarkable,' she told him. Bukowski: 'So that was the first recognition. When the teacher stood up, I said "Oh-oh" I thought, *"something's happening here"*.' But he did not build on this encouragement; it was not yet time.

His parents gave him a bicycle, and by the age of fourteen in the summer Hank would ride his bicycle all the way to Venice beach and back. He had powerful legs and it was not difficult for him. He attempted to shorten the journey time of each ride and beat his own record. He really moved and one day got into an altercation with an old man in a late-model red sports car – typical of Bukowski's almost photographic attention to detail that he should remember the colour and year. The man challenged him and Hank took him up on it, yelling 'Park it!' The man parked but when Hank got alongside the car, the man started up and roared away. There was a young woman with long blonde hair sitting next to him and Hank knew that as they drove away, it was him that she was thinking of. He ends the poem, 'I had become a man.'

In seventh grade at Mount Vernon Junior High he became friendly with William 'Baldy' Mullinax. In 'Those Girls We Followed Home' he writes how he and Baldy followed sisters Irene and Louise home from Junior High. Described by Bukowski as 'astonishingly beautiful', so much so that boys stayed away from them, they wore high heels, silk stockings, blouses and skirts. Hank and Baldy walked ten or twelve feet behind them, saying nothing, and when they went into their house, Hank and Baldy stood outside smoking cigarettes and talking, acting like hard men, but the girls never invited them in.

Unfortunately, becoming a man caused Hank even more distress. Acne is not uncommon in adolescents, but in Hank's case it took the form of a severe case of acne vulgaris. At the age of thirteen the pimples and boils covered his face and neck, his back and he even had some on his chest. He was just getting a reputation as a tough guy and a leader but now he had to withdraw, he was too vulnerable. At the same time Hank's home life grew steadily worse. In 'On and Off' he wrote that his first thought of suicide came at the age of thirteen and it stayed with him ever since. He botched some attempts and some were not really serious, he was just playing at it as if he was rehearsing. But there were other times when he tried hard, though it must be said, he couldn't have tried *that* hard as he always survived.

Henry continued to beat his wife and son but, as Hank wrote, bullies do sometimes get their comeuppance. One day, when Hank was thirteen, he came home from school and his mother told him, 'Your father was in a terrible fight.' Hank found him sitting on the toilet with the bathroom door open, his face bruised and puffed up, the eyes colouring prior to turning black. One arm was broken and in a cast. Hank stood and looked at him for some time until his father screamed: 'What the hell you staring at? What's your problem?'

Hank had long ago concluded that his father was insane, it was the only way to account for the way he got into violent arguments in stores, in the street and in car parks over the most trivial incidents; to account for the way he drove his car, honking and cursing at everyone; and for the way he beat his only child upon the slightest provocation.

Katherine escaped into her own world; she and Henry attended Catholic Mass each Sunday at Saint Agatha's on West Adams Boulevard, walking distance from home, taking Hank with them against his will. She had become very straight-laced and disapproved of her husband's use of four-letter words. In the amusing yet sad poem, 'Snails', Hank remembers his mother standing at the window looking at her husband in the backyard flower garden, bent over, intently viewing something. She went to see what he was doing, creeping up behind him. Then she screamed and came running into the house, 'My God, my God, my God!' Hank asked what was wrong. Sobbing she explained, 'He's watching two snails doing it to each other!' Then she screamed a long and horrible scream, tears rolling down her cheeks. Visibly angry, Hank's father came back into the house and snapped at his wife to shut up. Hank retired to his room, the screaming continued, eventually accompanied by breaking glass. After his father had left, slamming the door, Hank ventured out. His mother was sitting on the couch, the tears still pouring down her face. 'Why did he do that?' she asked. Hank didn't know.

As with when they wouldn't let Hank play with the 'poor' kids, though they were poor, his parents pretended they were wealthy. As they sat down to beans and wieners, his father would say, 'Not everybody can eat like this.' At the height of the Depression he still included 'Anyone who wants can make it in America', and 'God helps those who help themselves!' among his aphorisms at dinner. Because of his pretensions he always voted Republican: for Hoover against Roosevelt, then Landon against Roosevelt. Hank thought that his father made him want to become a bum, if someone like him wanted to be rich, then he wanted to be poor. Then he found that most bums wanted to be rich too. Hank was an outsider, as usual.

Henry's views about America changed somewhat when he found himself unemployed. He was so ashamed at not having a job that each morning he got in his car and drove off, as if he was still working at the dairy and he returned the same time each day. Katherine managed to find a badly paid house cleaning job but this didn't last long. With both parents unemployed, the family qualified for free food from the market but they were too proud to let their neighbours see them collecting their tins of bologna, corned beef hash and potatoes so they walked two miles along Washington Boulevard past Crenshaw to a distant market. They didn't use the car because Henry had to save petrol for his make-believe job. Katherine learned how to make potato pancakes.

The Great Depression continued and people got desperate. When Hank was thirteen, one of their neighbours tried to rob their house. He had been stealing cans of beans, radios, waffle irons and garden equipment from all the people in the nearby streets. It was noon and Henry caught him climbing in through the window and pinned him down on the floor; Henry was a strong man. As the neighbour pleaded with him, 'Henry! Henry let me go!' Henry cursed him while his wife phoned the police; there was no sympathy or understanding there. Hank noticed how the handcuffs glittered in the sun as the police, handguns drawn, slipped them around his wrists. Another neighbour set his house on fire to attempt to collect the insurance but he was found out and jailed instead. They were surrounded by human misery. There was nowhere for Hank and his friends to go and nothing to do in the hot summers in the mid-30s in Los Angeles, and in the hot sleepless night they could hear 'the terrified talk of our parents'.

During the day Hank was supposed to play in the streets if he was not at school; he was locked out of the house. However, he knew how to get in. He would unlock the screen door using a piece of cardboard to push back the lock. The back door was locked but the key was in the door. He slid a sheet of newspaper under the door, jiggled the key until it fell out and then dragged it under. He left by the front door which locked behind him. Once inside he hid behind the red curtains at the window and spied on the woman directly across from the Bukowski house who liked to sit on the steps of her front porch directly across from the Bukowski house.

Using his father's binoculars, Hank was able to examine her legs as he masturbated. He did the same to the woman who lived next door, peering through their side window into their living room. These were all subjects for poems such as 'My Secret Life'. He was still the loner, the outsider, but things were changing.

His interest in sex was stimulated by 'Mrs Gredis' who sat on top of the front desk in English class and crossed her legs high and told them all about Hawthorne and Poe and Melville while the fourteen-year-old boys stared at her black high-heeled shoes and her silk stockings as she crossed and recrossed her legs, the image burning into their brains.

At the age of fifteen Hank and his friends Frank Sullivan and Bill 'Baldy' Mullinax lied about their age and managed to get into the Burbank and the Follies burlesque theatres on Main Street. The girls had quite an impact on the adolescents and, fifty years later, Hank could still remember some of their names: Darlene, Candy, Jeanette and Rosalie. Rosalie was the best stripper: she made them squirm in their seats as the lights changed colour, and the music was loud as she shook and stripped. The front row was dubbed 'Bald-headed row', a sad line of old men, some of whom jerked off. There was a comedian dressed in floppy clothes, big shoes and suspenders with a flat felt hat turned up in the front and back. The most beautiful stripper always came on last and once in a while she showed them everything if she was sure that no vice squad men were in the audience. The place was raided periodically but Hank was never there at the time.

The boils on Hank's face, neck and shoulders got worse and eventually the teachers suggested that Hank be withdrawn from school. He had huge boils all across his back and face, even on the eyelids. He spent his days in bed, his face covered in a white ointment that set hard like plaster. One day his grandmother came to visit. Hank's mother was not at her cleaning job that day and was obviously expecting her. The two women came into his bedroom and his mother told him to lie on his front. His grandmother began praying and waving a crucifix over his body, yelling 'Purge the devil from his body, Lord!' She got very excited and lunged at his back, puncturing several boils, making the blood spurt out. Hank leapt up yelling: 'What the fuck are you doing?' His grandmother explained that she was making a hole for the devil to be pushed out by God. Hank threw them both out of his room. Emilie prayed for Hank constantly, telling him, 'Poor boy, the devil is inside of you.' It was shortly afterwards that Katherine lost her job and Hank was eligible for free treatment at LA County General. The doctors and nurses discussed his case as if he was not there: 'Worst case I've ever seen', 'Look at his face!' They drilled the boils with an electric needle, then a nurse had the unpleasant task of draining all his pustules. She was the only person in the hospital who was nice to him, and chatted as she squeezed each boil until it bled. In *Ham on Rye* he described her as 'the kindest person I had met in eight years'.

Each day he took the number seven tram to and from the Charity Ward at the LA General. Children would stare at him and ask their mothers: 'What's wrong with that man's face?' and, embarrassed, the mothers would try to shut them up. He would sit for hours on a wooden bench in the old brick building waiting to be drilled, staring out of the window, watching the Sierra Madre mountains change colour as the sun went down. The needle was threaded like a wood drill and he could smell the lubricating oil burning as it would bring up blood and pus while the doctors brought students to see him. He felt acutely self-conscious, a freak. He was fourteen then.

Bukowski: 'You toughen up to physical pain. When I was in General Hospital they were drilling away, and a guy walked in, and he said, "I never saw anyone go under the needle that cool." That's not bravery – if you get enough physical pain, you relent – it's a process, an adjustment.' The tears and pain remained frozen inside. Bukowski believed, 'It was my hatred of my father coming out through my skin – an emotional thing.' The boils were like bubbles of hatred rising to the surface of his frozen musculature. The deep freeze itself would take a lifetime to thaw, though in old age he found relief. For most of his life it took massive amounts of alcohol or a good fist fight to break through the armour.

The hospital had little luck with draining the boils because new ones grew in their place so they tried ultraviolet treatment followed by a full facial bandage. He emerged looking like the invisible man, except that everyone was looking at him. This new approach actually worked, the boils diminished in size and flattened out, though his face was left badly scarred: 'I felt as if no woman would want to be with me.'

Around this time his father got a job as a security guard at the LA County museum so Hank was no longer eligible for free treatment, and his father had no intention of paying for a doctor. It was 1936. Hank was fifteen; he had been out of school from February until September.

2. HIGH SCHOOL NAZI

Number 2122 Longwood Avenue was in the catchment area of Los Angeles High School on Olympic Boulevard. Determined to blame all his trials on his father, Hank claimed that Henry insisted that he attend LA High because it was an 'elite' school, hoping that some of the attitude and wealth of the other kids would rub off on him. In fact this was the same school attended by all his friends from Virginia Road Grammar – Bill 'Baldy' Mullinax, Jim Haddox, Bob Stoner, Bill Cobun, Ray Shuwarge and Hal Ortner – his father didn't force him to go. It was in fact far from elite although some wealthy kids did go there. It was a huge school with kids from all walks of life and is remembered by most of them as being an enjoyable experience. The father of crime fiction writer James Ellroy, who came from the same part of Los Angeles, pulled strings to make sure his son went to Fairfax High instead of LA High. In his autobiography Ellroy wrote: 'LA High was full of tough Negro kids. The old man figured they'd kill me the first time I opened my mouth.' This was because Ellroy held the same pro-Nazi views that Bukowski had done 25 years before. Maybe the neighbourhood had changed.

There was another writer at LA High at the same time as Hank; Ray Bradbury was in the year above, graduating in 1938, but their experiences could not have been more different. Bradbury joined the Drama Club and the Poetry Club and was encouraged in his work by two of his English teachers, Snow Longley Housh, who taught him about poetry, and Jeannet Johnson, who taught him to write short stories. There was also an informal writing club that Bradbury joined, but Hank did not. Hank never looked for help with his writing: 'I hadn't heard crap all about poetry then, and never had any desire to.' Academically there was no reason why Hank should not have done well: he had good marks in languages and maths and was obviously smart. His father wanted him to be an engineer and he took draughting and Spanish but he ended up in a vocational programme because he couldn't pass Spanish and didn't like draughting. His father gave up in disgust so Hank took the easiest courses.

Hank had a choice between sports or officer training (ROTC). ROTC was for rich kids whose parents were very patriotic or for misfits who hated sport. Hank did not want to have to wear a tracksuit or shower with the other boys because his back was still covered with enormous boils. At least an army uniform would cover them but shouldering the rifle caused the boils to bleed, soaking his uniform so his mother sewed in cloth patches to protect his skin from the rough khaki. Hank was in Company A commanded by Captain Harcourt Hervey Jr. They were taught how to tie tourniquets and extract the venom from a snake bite, to dig a field latrine and bayonet the enemy. There was rifle practice on the firing range and field manoeuvres and Hank got his marksmanship medals. They did field exercises in the nearby hills, Reds versus the Blues, with coloured ribbons on their rifles. They had rifles but no ammunition. The officers had wooden sabres. The exercises usually degenerated into fights between the opposing sides, resulting in bloody noses, fractured skulls, a broken arm, all of which Hank enjoyed immensely.

There was a manual of arms competition and the winner in each squad was entered in the final competition. Each time someone made a mistake they dropped out. First there were 50, then 25. Hank was good and eventually they all dropped out, leaving just him and the son of a famous criminal lawyer. Hank claimed he won by just acting mechanically, not trying to win, not caring in the slightest. A few days later a colonel, all covered in Great War medals pinned a medal on him. Afterwards Hank took the medal off and walked along the street, holding it in his hand: 'Then without rancour, fear, joy, without anger or direct reason, I threw the medal down a sewer drain outside a drugstore.' Bukowski claims it meant nothing to him, that ROTC meant nothing, and yet he finished up with the rank of Cadet Sergeant which, together with his medal, suggests that like most of his scholarly achievements, he later played down those that contradicted his outsider image and instead played up the misery and suffering.

Hank was friendly with the group of boys from Virginia Road Grammar who had transferred with him. In *Ham on Rye* he wrote: 'Meanwhile the poor and the lost and the idiots continued to flock around me . . . I didn't care much for any of them: Baldy, Jimmy Hatcher [Haddox], and a thin gangling Jewish kid, Abe Mortenson . . .' In fact Hank was only on the fringe of their group, it was Bill Mullinax who was the popular one and the centre of attention. Hank never fully belonged to their group because they enjoyed going to dances, belonged to the ROTC Officers' Club, were members of Buildings and Grounds and, crucially, they all had girlfriends. Hank was convinced that he was ugly and that no girl would ever go out with him, a self-fulfilling prophecy. He never went on a date the whole time he was at High School and college. He developed a big chip on his shoulder from largely imaginary slights and humiliations. While his friends were joining sports teams or the many school clubs, he turned instead to the German–American Bund.

As Hitler consolidated his hold on Germany in the 1930s, murdering and exiling his opponents, the Deutsche Haus became a centre for Nazi propaganda. At the Aryan Bookshop upstairs, Hank was able to buy all the poisonous anti-Semitic, superiority-of-the-master-race tracts that he liked. It was filled with English language books and magazines about Germany, including *Mein Kampf*. In *Ham on Rye* he said, somewhat ambiguously, 'I had never read *Mein Kampf* and had no desire to do so,' but if not then, he read it not long afterwards. Hank absorbed German music, German films, German food and German politics. In 1936, the year that the Olympic Games were held in Berlin, his parents took him to celebrate Hitler's birthday at a torchlight parade in Hindenburg Park in La Crescenta. The German–American Bund attended in full Nazi uniform. From then on Hank looked to the Fatherland for inspiration.

Increasingly he saw himself as German. Having been born there he had a natural loyalty and did not like the way that the media depicted the German people and derided their culture as trash. He claimed that movie newsreels speeded up footage of Hitler and Mussolini to make them look like madmen. But much of it was a part of his adolescent fight with his father: his father was pro-America so he was against it; the teachers were anti-German, he was for it. His mother was pro-Hitler and his father was against him. Hank began to read William Randolph Hearst's pro-Nazi *Los Angeles Examiner*, which published columns by both Hitler and Mussolini and, until Germany declared war on the USA, was the main voice of fascism in California. Hank had built himself a tough protective shell to conceal his feelings of hurt and alienation and by associating with the Nazis, whom he saw as victims of pro-British and French factions in the USA, he felt part of a community.

Bukowski mythologised his childhood to make every slight, every rejection, every embarrassment, into a fight for survival. According to him, it was an unrelievedly miserable period and he undoubtedly saw it so. On the surface, however, he appears to have had a comfortable American suburban upbringing. He had few household chores compared with some kids: he had to take out the garbage, run to the grocery store and mow the lawn every Saturday morning. He had the rest of the weekend free. We have to take his word for it that the lawn really was the focus of his father's sadism though no one can doubt the trauma involved in his beatings, he wrote about them so often. He was living in a quiet suburb where only two-thirds of the lots were built on so there was plenty of open space where the kids could play, but, in Hank's writer's eyes, it was like growing up in Hell's Kitchen:

> On the slum streets of LA it was balls-up in those days, and only the tough survived. I was a big, rawboned, tough kid. I made it. Trouble was, I liked it. Liked the impact of knuckles against teeth, of feeling the terrific lightning that breaks in your brain when somebody lands a clean one and you have to try and shake loose and come back and nail him before he finished you off.

There were slums in LA, in the Mexican section to the east, but not where he was, his neighbourhood was not even fully built yet. 'It's not nice to be followed home by eight or ten people threatening to beat you up. And for your own survival you must do something about this or you keep taking the beating. So I started beating people up. And I found it wasn't bad. Better to beat than to be beaten. It feels better.' This was the tough-guy image that he was to foster later in his career.

At the age of seventeen he finally tried to lose his virginity by going with two school friends to a whorehouse in Tijuana. They were drunk and the place was filled with American servicemen, hollering and beating on the doors. There were lines in front of the doors, some of them long. One friend threw up and went back to the car, one plucked up courage and got it over with. Hank went into the room, was intimidated by the pimp there, gave the whore the money and left without doing anything. One the way back to LA they all boasted of their conquests to each other.

His image of himself vacillated between looking in the mirror and seeing a monster, to pride in certain, albeit rather unlikely, attributes. For instance he was very proud of the size of his testicles and mentioned them on many occasions. He first became aware of their formidable aspect when he was seventeen. In gym class the students would strip off and comment on each other's body, comparing cock size and so on. They pointed at Hank and said, 'God, look at the balls on that guy.' He proudly told the Italian literary critic Fernanda Pivano: 'I had the biggest balls of any guy in the gym.' He was also pleased with his legs and the massive size of his thighs which enabled him to walk with a giant stride. In a poem called 'The Stride' he described walking with a friend through the night-time streets and his friend commenting: 'Jesus Christ, I bet nobody walks with giant strides like we do!'

It was during his eight months off school that Hank discovered the little La Cienega Public Library next to an old church between Washington Boulevard and West Adams Boulevard near his house. The librarian was a stereotype with rimless glasses and white hair pulled into a tight bun behind her neck. His first discovery there was Upton Sinclair, then came Sinclair Lewis's *Main Street*, each book read in a single evening. He was attracted to the title of Josephine Lawrence's *Bow Down to Wood and Stone* but he was turned off as soon as he opened the pages. As he replaced the book, his hand grazed a volume by DH Lawrence who he later described as: 'Lawrence of the tight and bloody line'. He read everything by Lawrence that the library had. Lawrence was always there for Bukowski; even in the later years when Hank became bored by him, he remained in Hank's consciousness, not the lusty sexuality but the 'washing of feet and skin, the thin pin-point structured line'. Hank moved on to Hilda Doolittle (HD) and the Imagists followed by Aldous Huxley, whom he had not expected to enjoy. John Dos Passos's *USA* trilogy took Hank almost a week to read. And he became a lifelong fan of Sherwood Anderson. He approved of his pictorial style 'like blood or paint' on the paper. He liked writing that created strong pictures in the reader's head and told Neeli

Cherkovski that he would like to do with words what Picasso did with paint. Theodore Dreiser's ponderous Great American Novels were not to Hank's taste but then he finally discovered Ernest Hemingway, who, along with John Fante, he claimed as having the biggest impact of all.

Many critics have remarked on the influence of Hemingway on Bukowski but there are more differences than similarities. Hank shared Hemingway's insistence on honesty: 'Write the truest sentence that you know', and there are parallels in the romantic attitude towards drinking which we get with Hemingway from the very beginning – in *The Sun Also Rises* the characters spend much of their time drinking, each drink lovingly described. A story such as 'The Light of the World', consisting entirely of a dialogue between drinkers in a bar, may have provided the model for Bukowski's many stories set in bars. Certainly the spare style is an influence, though Hemingway employed much more description than Bukowski, who is closer to the hard-boiled detective writers in his prose. The biggest difference is that Hemingway wrote fiction whereas all of Bukowski's important work involves the author himself as the central character, being thinly veiled autobiography. Hemingway had also travelled widely and been in both the Spanish Civil War and World War II and so had a far greater fund of material to draw upon (he was once in two plane crashes within 48 hours); Bukowski's close focus on bars, whores, the racetrack and drinking becomes monotonous after a time because he was not selective in what he released. In this he could have learned a lesson from Hemingway, whose emphasis was always on economy and the paring down of any redundancy. Hemingway tightened his prose to the point where he could challenge a colleague to find even one word that could be removed from a paragraph as redundant. Bukowski's lack of revision meant that his work often sprawled and was excessively wordy.

Bukowski often spoke about Hemingway: 'He wrote a very serious melodrama with a lot of humour, and it often had a lot of soul. But it was taut, and it was interesting, and it was readable, simple, and I think it was moving in my direction. What I'm trying to do is move in that direction and still have the content of humour, blood, sparkle. Hemingway's was too much wood.' He told Fernanda Pivano: 'He said things with these easy lines, which influenced me, I'm sure. Subconsciously, I try to do the same thing, say it as simple as possible and still say what is needed to be said ... Keep it simple, and make it simpler yet. And then make it simpler yet. Hemingway – the line is what I pick up on.' Bukowski's competitive feelings towards Hemingway, and the equally threatening Thomas Wolfe, are revealed in the hilarious story 'Class' in which he challenges Hemingway to put the gloves on and join him in the ring. 'I'm here to kick your ass.' Naturally he knocks him out and afterwards has sex with Thomas Wolfe's glamorous girlfriend.

Hemingway's poetry was probably of greater influence than his prose, the way he pinpointed some trivial event or action and gave it universal significance. Bukowski: 'These poems are encouraging to any young (or old) writer to show that something almost can come out of almost nothing.' He compared it to buttoning a button correctly or knowing how to open a door; it was so easy to write that 'almost nobody can do it'. Then came the Russians: Turgenev and Gorky and Tolstoy. Dostoevsky came a little later.

The Bukowski household went to bed very early, a legacy from Henry Bukowski's days as a milkman. Hank's father rose at 5 a.m. and insisted that everyone got to bed at 8 p.m. 'Lights out!' he would yell and turn off all the lights, which gave Hank very little time to read. But Hank, in the grand childhood tradition, would take his bed light under the covers to read. Sometimes it got so hot that the lamp began to smoke and he had to hold it outside to cool down. He felt that without those books he would have surely murdered his father. He wrote: 'a good book/can make an almost/impossible/existence,/liveable.' These books saved his life, they moulded his writing style, his appreciation of literature, his approach to writing. These years of study were crucial in his development and he wrote extensively about his influences, of which virtually all (except Céline) come from this period.

By this time Hank had developed an attitude, and the teachers did not like it. He never really knew what the teachers meant when they said this, he just felt blank, uninterested, but he was continually being sent to stand in the hall because they detected a sneer on his face. He was taciturn, withdrawn, guarded and very cynical. His only weapons against authority were irony, sarcasm and silence. Mr Sanderson was principal of Los Angeles High School. The teachers would send Hank down to see him with a sealed envelope. Sanderson would open it and he would always say the same thing: 'Well, here we are again. We just can't behave ourselves, can we?' The punishment was to go into the phone booth and close the door and not come out until told to do so. It was a glassed-in booth with a little seat and a pile of old Ladies Home Journals. It was stuffy and there was nothing to do except think, something Hank didn't want to do, as Mr Sanderson well knew. Hank was usually there for about two hours, knees racked up against the wall, his head lolling back pretending to sleep. He read later that Sanderson had been prosecuted and jailed for embezzlement of school funds, which gave him some satisfaction.

He had always had good grades in English, and passed all the tests; in fact he was known for his Great War pilot stories, but on the next to last day before report cards were issued, right in the middle of the lesson, his English teacher suddenly leaped up from her seat behind the desk and pointed at him, sobbing with rage, tears on her cheeks and yelled: 'Henry, I am going to FLUNK you!' Hank complained to his mother, who went to the school and cried for hours until the teacher relented and passed him. Hank never found out what caused that outburst; it was something about his attitude. Bukowski's curious explanation was that the teacher must have been in love with him and wanted him to stay in the class next year. He told Ben Pleasants that this was not the only time he was saved by his mother, and other school friends have described him as something of a mother's boy.

At about the same time as his discovery of literature and Nazism, Hank's friend Baldy introduced him to drinking. Baldy's father had been a successful surgeon but had lost his licence because he was an alcoholic. Though he had stopped drinking, he still had a number of barrels of wine in his basement. Baldy invited Hank down to try some. He showed him how to stick his head under the spigot and turn it on. At first Hank didn't want to, then he tried some but hated the smell. Baldy had some, then Hank asked to try some more, and took a big swallow. 'I grew, I expanded, I was twelve feet tall, I was a giant of a man. And my heart felt wonderful. And life was good. And I was powerful. And I said, "Baldy, this is good stuff." And that was it. I've been hooked ever since.'

When he was about seventeen he began drinking with a group of older boys; a 'fast crowd' who robbed petrol stations and liquor stores, though one of them had a part-time job as a messenger boy at Western Union. Hank would wait until his parents were asleep, then at about nine o'clock he would sneak out of his bedroom window to join his friends. He did not have a latchkey. The biggest problem was getting back in again, climbing up over a berry bush and in through the narrow window drunk. His new friends were impressed by his icy demeanour which they thought was a lack of fear, and shared his disgust with the world. He was popular precisely because he didn't care whether he was or not, and because no matter how much whiskey, wine or beer they gave him, he never seemed to get really drunk. Nothing could shake him out of his frozen state, nothing could animate him.

He found that his ability to hold his liquor could be used to make money and by the time he was eighteen he was winning between $15 or $20 a week at drinking contests. One of the gang, a guy called Stinky, always gave him a run for his money. Sometimes Hank would break his confidence by ostentatiously downing an extra drink in between bouts but one night Hank thought Stinky had him beat. He blearily looked up from his drink and Stinky wasn't there. Hank went to the bathroom to throw up and admit defeat but there in the bathtub was Stinky, passed out cold. Hank didn't vomit. He walked out and picked up the money.

They drank and sometimes slept in rooming houses, somehow getting the keys to vacant rooms. They would begin by pulling down the shades and drinking quietly so as not to be detected, then a fistfight would erupt and they would wake the whole building breaking mirrors, chairs and tablelamps before running quickly down the stairs to make their escape just before the police arrived. Three of his friends from this gang were later killed in World War II.

Hank's parents very much disapproved of his drinking but he was unable to disguise his morning hangovers, which added to the tension at home. Hank was only seventeen and still at school, so they could hardly throw him out. One night he arrived at home and knocked on the door – he still did not have a key – and his mother opened the little window in the door and screamed: 'He's drunk! He's drunk again!' From the living room Hank heard his father repeat her words, 'He's drunk AGAIN?'

His father's face replaced hers at the little window. He told Hank he was a disgrace to his mother and to his country and he was not going to let him in. Hank was drunk, it was cold, he had walked all the way from his friends' house and intended to sleep in his own bed. He ordered his father to open the door or he would break it down. His father began his speech all over again. Meanwhile Hank had walked to the back of the porch. He lowered his shoulder and charged. He was not angry, he was just doing what had to be done. The door splintered when he hit it, a large crack appeared down the centre and the lock was half broken. Hank walked back down the porch for another try at it. His father, not wanting the door smashed completely off its hinges, let him in.

Hank walked unsteadily into the living room but the exertion of smashing the door was too much for his overloaded stomach and he threw up all over their living room rug, one with the Tree of Life woven on it. Even in a situation like this, he remembered the tiny details. 'I vomited, plenty,' he said.

'You know what we do with a dog who shits on the rug?' his father yelled.

'No,' he said.

'We stick his NOSE in IT! So he won't do it NO MORE!' his father shrieked and put his large hand behind Hank's neck. 'You are a dog,' he said as he pressed Hank's head down towards the pool of vomit on the Tree of Life rug.

'Stop,' said Hank; he wasn't feeling at all well. 'I'm asking you one last time to stop!' But Henry continued the pressure, pushing Hank's head down lower to the vomit. Hank twisted and swung from his heels, catching his father very accurately with a hard uppercut full on the chin.

Henry toppled over backwards and fell heavily, spreadeagled on the sofa, his eyes wide with surprise. Hank walked to the couch and stood in front of him, ready to continue but his father either would not, or could not, get up. He just stared in astonishment at Hank.

Hank's mother, who had been standing watching in her white nightgown, threw herself upon Hank, clawing at his face, screaming over and over again, 'You hit your FATHER! You hit your FATHER! You hit your FATHER!'

Bukowski: 'I turned my face full toward her and let her rip and scream, slashing with her fingernails, tearing the flesh from my face, the fucking blood dripping and jerking and sliding down my neck and my shirt, spotting the fucking Tree of Life with flecks and splashes and chunks of meat. I waited, no longer interested. "YOU HIT YOUR FATHER!" and then the slashes came slower. I waited then they stopped. Then started again, one or two, "you . . . hit . . . your . . . father . . . your . . . father . . ."

' "Have you finished?" I asked. I think the first words I had spoken to her outside of "yes" and "no" in ten years.'

It was clearly nonsense to say that they had not had a meaningful conversation in that time. The point was that, by defying his father, Hank was threatening her entire system of values; if the father was not always right, then what was she doing in this terrible city, away from her family and her country, subject to Henry's authority?

Hank, however, saw her viewpoint as a withdrawal of her love. His reaction was to claim there never was any love, that there was little or no contact between mother and son when he knew she was always intervening on his behalf at school, demonstrating her concern for him by such things as sewing the patches on his ROTC uniform, shielding him from his father as best she could given that she, too, suffered from abuse. As with Henry's mother, Emilie, Katherine was not demonstrative in her love and comes across as cold and distant, but she no doubt loved Hank in her way. But Hank would have none of it. In his writing, both parents were his enemies and his tribulations were all their fault.

'I have often let shackjobs and whores slash my face as my mother did, and this is a most bad habit; being frozen does not mean let the jackals take control and, besides, children and old women, and some strong men, now wince, as they see my face.' By the time the doctors had finished drilling him and his mother had clawed his face, he had developed a carapace of scar tissue, heavily lidded eyes half-closed like a Chinese mask or a watching reptile; he had made himself an armoured helmet, what Freudian psychoanalyst Wilhelm Reich called 'character armouring'. Similarly the frozen pain and anger in his shoulders came to resemble a hunchback, in fact the title of one biography calls him *The Hunchback of East Hollywood*.

From now on it was Hank's turn to terrorise the household. Every morning he would get the black looks, their fierce disapproval. One morning he challenged them: 'Christ, so I got drunk . . . You people treat me like a murderer . . .'

'That's it! That's it!' they said. 'What you have done is worse than murder!' His parents meant it. To them there might be an excuse for murder, but to socially disgrace them in front of their neighbours by drinking, never.

Hank graduated from Los Angeles High in the summer of 1939. He and Jimmy Haddox sat in their mortarboards and gowns, waiting their turn on stage to receive their diplomas. As usual, Bukowski told conflicting stories about the occasion. In one he made sure his parents did not attend, and afterwards he walked home alone with 11 cents in his pocket; in another they were in the audience, but he argued with his father afterwards and they drove home in silence broken only by his mother sobbing. On the strength of his writing Hank was accepted on a scholarship to study journalism at Los Angeles City College.

He took a summer job as a stock boy at Sears Roebuck on Olympic Boulevard but that soon fell through – according to *Ham on Rye* it was because he got into an argument with some of the kids he had been with at high school and took them to the roof for a fight. He spent the rest of the summer hanging out on Pershing Square, the only architectural element in Los Angeles with full metropolitan dimensions and proper city feel. The periphery of the square was used as a public forum, with many orators speaking at once. There, among the statues of soldiers, the cannon and the statue of Beethoven with a cane, the palm trees and the two rushing fountains, he listened to the Black preachers delivering their fiery messages, quotations from the Bible written in chalk on the pathway. Hank heard out the proponents of obscure religious sects and political agitators. He relaxed on the cool grass or the benches, listening to the drummers and guitarists; some benches had RESERVED FOR LADIES stencilled on them, an injunction that was scrupulously obeyed. He watched the cops and the drunks, the runaways and the junkies, the beggars and the pushers, the unemployed and the transvestites, and the homosexual hustlers, sitting with their shoulders hunched on the railings facing 5th Street. There was a bar beneath one of the big hotels and Hank let the gays buy him drinks until things got difficult, then he'd beat a swift departure. But they soon caught on and the free drinks no longer came his way. He was already hooked: 'I love this town. Well, I don't love it, but it's the only place I ever want to live. I couldn't write anywhere else. I hope I die here.'

At City College, Hank's English class began each morning at 7 a.m. It was taught by Mr Richardson and it was here that he learned Gilbert and Sullivan; songs that stayed with him throughout his life as they were particularly suited to drunken singalongs. Richardson liked his writing but Hank just could not get to class on time. He always arrived late at 7.30 with a hangover. Finally Richardson told him: 'Mr Bukowski, there isn't any use in you showing up anymore. You'll get your grade.' Richardson had to give him a 'D' because his attendance was so poor but Hank understood it was not personal.

Hank had one teacher for three units who gave them an assignment to hand in a story a week, or more if they wanted. At midterm she read out the class roll and how many papers each student had handed in. Most had submitted three or four, Hank appears to have handed in more than thirty, and, as the teacher told the astonished class, 'they are all good!' The class gasped and turned to stare at him. It was then he thought he must have something going for him, some talent yet to be realised. 'It's just like you plant a seed of corn in the ground, here comes the tree.' This was a story that he told many times and the number of essays written by him varies, according to the interview or poem, between 38 and 72.

Hank enrolled in the creative writing class but it did not work out: 'The teacher turned me off immediately. The guy was a goddamned Dork. Tea and cookies and students at his feet on a soft rug. If that's poetry I'm a striped ass baboon . . . Anyway, that did it for me. My first and last class in writing.'

When an arsonist set fire to the Los Angeles library in April 1986, a large part of Bukowski's youth went with it. (Twenty per cent of the two million volume collection was completely destroyed, many more were fire- or water-damaged.) He had read his way through most of the classic literature, philosophy and religion, then branched out, reading texts on geology and medicine. 'I even made a study of the operation of the mesacolon. That operation was damned interesting. You know, the type of knives, what you do: shut this off, cut this vein. I said, "This isn't bad. Much more interesting than Chekhov." When you get into other areas, out of pure literature, you sometimes really get picked up. It's not the same old shit.'

He read almost at random, grabbing a book from the shelves, reading a few lines and thrusting it back. If he liked a writer he would voraciously read everything of theirs that he could lay hands on. He was an autodidact, very knowledgeable but unsure of his standing and with some surprising gaps in his reading. He was defensive. As an adult he mispronounced words that he'd read but never heard spoken, something which further embarrassed him and made him shy away from any literary discussion and for a long time prevented him from reading his work in public. Complex proper names like Dostoevsky or anything in French was a big problem for him.

Bukowski's other major influence, almost as significant as Hemingway, was William Saroyan, the author of 'The Daring Young Man On the Flying Trapeze'. Hank really liked his easy flowing line and his uncluttered style, and picked up on it right away. Years later, in a poem to Saroyan called 'The Still Trapeze', Hank critiqued his work, saying that the tremendous brave optimism that buoyed everybody up so well during the Depression turned to sugar water when better times came along. But, at the time, he was a giant.

Then, on 8 November 1939, a book was published that would change the way he looked at writing. John Fante's *Ask the Dust* did not receive very good reviews when it first appeared; Fante was recognised as a good writer, but his subject matter was deemed to be 'cut wholly out of Saroyan's cloth', and the book was compared unfavourably with his previous novel, *Wait Until Spring, Bandini*, which Bukowski seems to have missed when it came out. Copies of *Ask the Dust* no doubt appeared on the open shelves by Christmas of that year. Bukowski: 'He had a great influence on me. I liked his writing style. It was open and easy, and it was clear and it was emotional, and it was just damned good writing.'

John Fante became a very important role model for Bukowski. Fante had struggled hard to be a writer, taking employment wherever he could get it: digging trenches, delivering ice, heavy-lifting on the docks, at warehouse jobs, as a night clerk at a hotel, a bus boy, and working in a fish cannery on Terminal Island – the view from Bukowski's window when he moved to San Pedro late in life. Fante never kept a job for very long, he worked hard but very reluctantly. He knew the harsh reality of the unregulated labour market and the reciprocal harshness that this produced in its victims: the hard case, the domestic violence, the bar-room brawling, the wisecracks and cold-fish unemotional attitudes of the period as expressed in the hard-boiled fiction that the era produced.

Fante was raised a Catholic and became an alcoholic; throughout the early 30s he lived and wrote in cheap rooming-houses in Bunker Hill. It would not be long before Hank emulated him in that. In fact, Hank mirrored his life in every respect but one: unlike Fante he did not sell out to Hollywood. Fante squandered his talent for the high wages he was paid to write screenplays, most of which were never filmed. By the time *Ask the Dust* was published, he was just starting to get big Hollywood money. As a successful screenwriter, Fante ate regularly in the famous back room of Musso Frank's Grill along with William Saroyan, Dashiell Hammett, Erskine Caldwell, Nathanael West and other heavyweights. Later, when he was a successful writer, Bukowski aped his heroes by also becoming a regular at Musso Frank's, to the extent that they stocked the dreadful sweet German Riesburgs and Liebfraumilch that he liked. (They cancelled the order when he died as he was the only person who ever drank it.)

When the Nazis rolled into Poland on 1 September 1939, Hank continued his support for Hitler. He was still a teenager, insecure in his identity, he had rarely even spoken to a girl and certainly never dated one; he was perfect material for fascist recruitment. At City College he ran into a White Russian named Veloff who sided with the Nazis because he saw them as anti-Communists who were going to destroy the Bolsheviks who had killed one of his relatives.

Veloff had a revolver and used to play Russian roulette with it. Hank sensibly refused to play. Hank, Baldy and Veloff attended a meeting of the New Vanguard Party, a right-wing outfit set up to combat the Communist Menace, held in the basement of a very large mansion in Glendale. Hermann Max Schwinn, the leader of the Los Angeles Bund was the speaker. He sat behind a desk on a low stage with a large American flag behind him and the meeting began with the audience standing to pledge allegiance to the flag, something which alienated Hank straight off. This was what his father would do. Hank was pro-German, not pro-American. Then Schwinn started talking about the Communist Menace and how they had to fight force with force. From his accounts of the meeting Hank was not as enthusiastic as his fellow fascists.

Afterwards they went to Veloff's house and they all got drunk on buttered rum. According to *Ham on Rye* they played Russian Roulette but Veloff cheated and Baldy refused to do it. Veloff drove them to MacArthur Park and they rowed out on the boating lake to catch a duck for dinner and to finish off the rum. After a lot of rowdy talk, no duck, and with the bottle empty, Veloff shot holes in the bottom of the boat, which began to sink. They waded waist deep to shore, cursing and laughing. Hank arrived home drunk and soaking wet and had to climb in his bedroom window over the berry bush having had a very enjoyable evening. It sounds more like a student prank than a serious involvement with the Nazi Party and appears to have been the only meeting Hank ever attended outside those at the Deutsche Haus.

At High School, Hank had watched as the earnest, caring American anti-fascists joined the Abraham Lincoln Brigade and went off to fight for the Republicans in Spain and were mowed down by Franco's trained troops. He was unmoved, even when Hitler's Condor Division bombed Spanish civilians. He says he would leap up in class and spout the Nazi slogans he got from the pamphlets: 'Breed a plough horse to a race horse and you get an offspring that is neither swift nor strong. A new Master Race will evolve from purposeful breeding.' In *Ham on Rye* he wrote: 'I don't know where I got my stuff,' but he knew full well where he got it from: the Aryan Bookshop at the German–American Bund and from Nazi party meetings he attended there. Now, with Europe actually at war, a surprising number of his fellow students listened and agreed with him and he was asked if he intended running for student body president. Some students spoke out and said that the US should enter the war and destroy Nazism before it took hold everywhere but it was four years before Germany declared war on the United States, forcing it to become involved.

Bukowski always played down his involvement with fascism, with the most puerile of excuses: 'I avoided any direct reference to Jews or Blacks, who had never given me any trouble. All my troubles had come from white gentiles. Thus I wasn't a Nazi by temperament or choice; the teachers more or less forced it on me by being so much alike and thinking so much alike and with their anti-German prejudice.'

It is hard to imagine that anyone could be so ignorant when every day the newsreels showed tens of thousands of innocent civilians dying from German bombs as Europe's cities were subjected to Blitzkrieg, but Hank was only concerned with the affront to his pride and ego when his teachers criticised the country of his birth. He went to the Deutsche Haus to see the Nazi propaganda film *Blitzkrieg in the West*, which showed how the German army had crushed Holland, France, Belgium and Denmark. The cinema was filled with cheering Nazi sympathisers, including Bukowski. As he said in *Ham on Rye*: 'The war was going well, for Hitler.' Hank's father's refusal to see the film is probably the main reason the young Bukowski was such a Nazi supporter.

Anti-Semitism was common and largely tolerated in the USA at this time. Its most vocal proponent was a young Roman Catholic priest, Charles E Coughlin, whose Sunday broadcasts from the pulpit of his church in Royal Oak, Michigan, were listened to by Catholics across the nation. He received more letters than the President – an average of 80,000 letters a week – and, in 1933, a national poll voted him the 'most useful citizen of the United States'. He is now regarded as the father of 'hate radio'. His message was that Jewish bankers ('international bankers') were to blame for the Depression and the rise of Communism and that Jewish interests were leading America into the war. Bukowski probably heard much the same thing from the pulpit at his own Catholic church. Coughlin was not taken off the air until 1940, and his right-wing journal, *Social Justice*, continued publishing until 1942 when the Federal Government threatened to charge him with sedition.

It would be a mistake to place too much significance on Bukowski's flirtation with fascism as it appears to have been mostly an attention-drawing device. He wrote letters supporting Hitler to the *Los Angeles Examiner* and, according to him, most of them were published, though they are not listed in Dorbin, Bukowski's most complete bibliography. In 'What will the neighbours think?'

he says that the letters brought 'interesting results', that is to say hate mail and death threats. The letters also put him in contact with right-wing fanatics who wanted to get him involved with their cause. He calls them 'people who believed that I meant what I had written in those letters', because Bukowski later tried to distance himself from his Nazi past by claiming that it was just teenage rebellion and he hadn't believed in any of it. 'What will the neighbours think?' describes secret meetings in cellars and attics, guns, pacts, plans and speeches; probably a reference to the one meeting in Glendale and to Veloff's revolver. In the same poem he reveals that his father was disgusted by his support for Hitler and told him 'I don't believe that you are a son of mine!' A lot of it probably *was* teenage rebellion, but he didn't know it at the time.

He says that he gathered a small band of followers who believed in his ideas more than he did. According to one version, they were attracted to him because he got into a fight with a heavyweight fullback from the football team and scrapped with him for half an hour on the campus lawn before unexpectedly winning the bout.

They would sit in the malt shop listening to Glenn Miller on the jukebox, watching the girls dancing with the football players and the more popular boys. Hank didn't dance. He sat with a couple of what he terms his 'disciples': 'We were supposed to be outlaws/the explorers of Truth.'

One day a communist speaker set up a platform on a vacant lot south of the City College campus and Hank and his followers went to listen. Hank stood and listened but Veloff – who was in all probability his *only* follower – produced a bag of rotten tomatoes he had brought along. 'When you give the word, we'll begin throwing them,' he told Hank.

'Put the tomatoes away,' Hank told him.

'Piss, I wish they were hand grenades,' said Hank's now ex-follower. Hank walked away as Veloff and his friends began throwing rotten tomatoes.

A key ingredient to the Bukowski myth is that he was a real tough guy at school, that he was feared, or at least disliked by many of his teachers. He slouched in his seat 'hungover and dangerous'. He was insolent to the teachers, answering back, and never read the books he was assigned. 'I was the meanest son-of-a-bitch in the/world. /I would leap up and make incoherent/speeches challenging whatever the professor had just/said.' It was mostly wild exaggeration though he did keep a bottle in his locker. When Ben Pleasants did some preliminary research for a Bukowski biography, it turned out that it was Baldy Mullinax who was the leader, the centre of the gang, if it could be called a gang, and many of Hank's schoolmates had no memory of him even being in their class. This is in part because he was not a joiner. Baldy went to the introductory dance – the Howdy Hop – but Hank didn't. The school magazine, *The Collegian*, advertised a Journalism Club, 'Our purpose is to better acquaint new journalism students', but Hank didn't join. Despite his interest in aviation he ignored the Aero Corps who were looking for new members, nor was he attracted by the German Club, Deutscher Verrien, perhaps because it was headed by a girl. Since he was studying journalism it would have made sense to become involved in *The Collegian* and get hands-on experience, but he told Ben Pleasants: 'I walked in and looked around. There were these guys with little paper hats on. Tremendous egos. I couldn't stand it. So I walked right out . . . I got into the Nazi trip instead.' It was as if he saw the two as interchangeable student activities.

Despite his image as a loner, Hank actually knew quite a few people at City College. One of the people he met there was Robert Stanton Baume, who was paying for his journalism classes by working as a bicycle messenger for Western Union. He lived by himself in a place on West 11th Street having left his family in Minneapolis where his father was a journalist. They compared their work; Hank liked Baume's short stories though he found them derivative of Thomas Wolfe. Through Baume he met Robert Knox, who also became a friend, and visited Hank at Longwood Avenue where, for some reason, Katherine was introduced as being French. Bukowski, Baume and Knox hung out in coffee shops together and it might be Knox and Baume that he described as 'disciples'. Knox, however, told Neeli Cherkovski that he remembered Hank as being very shy and withdrawn in those days – hardly the rabble-rouser, goading the teachers and leading a neo-fascist gang that Hank liked to claim.

Inspired by Hemingway, Lawrence and the other authors he had discovered, Bukowski began writing short stories of his own in addition to the work assignment at college. Though it is not known what the stories were about, they were clearly not of the sort his mother read in the *Saturday Evening Post* and they caused yet another major confrontation at home. Hank had hidden the pages under the lining paper in his sock drawer where his father, snooping through Hank's things, found them. Hank was on his way home from school when he encountered his mother waiting anxiously for him a few blocks from home. Hank's father had flown into a rage and thrown all of Hank's things out on the lawn: the typewriter they had given him when he went to journalism school, his coats, shirts, shorts and socks as well as his stories – 'No son of mine is going to write stories *like that* and live in *my house!*'

Katherine was frantic and thrust ten dollars into his hand, telling him to take the money and go and get a room until his father calmed down. Hank took the money but still continued to walk home. She ran on ahead and, as she entered the house, Hank yelled to her for Henry to hear: 'Tell him to come out here, I'll knock his god-damned head off!' There on the lawn were his typewriter, his clothes and the pages of his short stories, blowing about in the breeze, trapped in the gutter and around bushes. First he collected his manuscripts, trying to find every page. He put each one in his suitcase, holding them down with a shoe. Then he put his typewriter back in its case; it had sprung free when Henry threw it out. His parents watched from behind a curtain. When he had collected everything – he left his dirty laundry knowing that his mother would wash it for him – he walked north up Longwood towards 21st Street and Westview Hill. There he took the W tram to downtown where he got a room.

There is some confusion whether this was the occasion of his leaving home for good or whether it was just for a few nights. He reported the substance of his conversation with his parents about his writing many times:

Henry: 'Nobody wants to read stuff like this!'

Katherine: 'Yes, people like to read things that will make them happy.'

That conversation must have occurred at home, but the giveaway is the report of a subsequent event. Despite the ruckus, Hank's father continued to rifle through his son's belongings. One evening, his father approached him, carrying pages he had found in Hank's room and told him: 'This is a great short story.'

'OK,' said Hank, taking it from him to read. It was about a rich man who had a fight with his wife and stormed out into the night to get a cup of coffee. In the café he had carefully observed the waitress and coffee cups, the spoons and forks, the salt and pepper holders and the neon sign in the window. Then he had gone back to his stable to visit his favourite horse. He petted it and the horse kicked him in the head, killing him. The story obviously touched a chord in his father, who perhaps also sat in cafés musing over life. Hank told him he could keep it. His father took the pages and walked out of the door. Hank wrote: 'I guess that's/as close/as we ever got.'

3. ON THE ROAD

H ank continued to take courses at City College until June 1941; he didn't graduate, just had a good time and only took the courses he liked, which in his final semester had consisted of one gym class and four art classes. Whatever the exact sequence of events, Hank did move out of his parents' home before finishing at City College, renting a small second floor room on Temple Street in the Filipino district for $1.50 a week. There was a Filipino bar on the ground floor where he could drink. He loved it; he felt that he was finally living the bohemian writer's life, starving in his artist's garret like his hero John Fante.

His college friend Robert Baume lived a little further uptown from Hank; he left City College a semester before Hank and had taken a job as a Western Union messenger. They both wanted to be writers and would meet in the public library on 5th Street and sit on the stone benches and discuss Steinbeck and Thomas Wolfe. Hank said that Baume's short stories were good and he was the better writer. They would take their only meal of the day together, usually at Clifton's Cafeteria, where you could eat for less than a dollar in 1941. They sent their stories to *Atlantic Monthly*, the *New Yorker* and *Harper's*, and hung out with a gang of young men who did not care about literature but liked to drink and gamble and fight. They all had a good time together.

At night Hank drank and ran a gambling saloon in his room: he told John William Corrington that his place got to be known and every night it was packed out with aircraft workers and pimps; however, in *Ham on Rye* he says it was just his schoolfriends Jimmy Hatcher and Becker who came by, which sounds more likely. In both places he describes one evening when he made substantial winnings, between $200 and $450 depending on which story we read, but that a fight developed during which the mirror and a couple of chairs got broken. This is covered in the first story in *Notes of a Dirty Old Man*, in which he describes how he woke up in the morning lying under the bed to find everything smashed, the ashtrays, the dresser, lamps, even the bed itself. He had a large cut under his chin and scraped knuckles, but he could stand up and the money was still there in the closet where he had thrown it each time he went for a piss before the fight started.

Bukowski reinvented the myth so often that it is now impossible to sort out truth from fantasy. The version told to Neeli Cherkovski is the most plausible: one day his friend Robert Baume showed up wearing a marine corps uniform. 'I want to prove something to myself,' he told Hank. It was not long before an argument about literature and patriotic duty turned into a fist fight. Hank hit Baume with a couple of good punches, knocking him across the room. Baume told him that he'd won and they had a couple more glasses of wine. When they finished those Hank asked, 'No hard feelings?'

'Hell no, Buddy,' replied Baume, punching Hank hard in the stomach. After a brief scuffle, Baume knocked his buddy out and left. Hank came to surrounded by broken furniture and his landlady calling his name through the door. He yelled for her to go away and surveyed the situation. Rather than pay for all the damage he decided to make a run for it. Once again, his mythomania steps in.

To Corrington he claimed that he knew the aircraft workers and pimps would be back for the money he had won from them so, early in the morning he caught a bus for New Orleans. In *Tales* he described how he packed his steel portable typewriter, borrowed from the wife of a friend and never returned, put the money in his wallet and packed his few remaining belongings in a cardboard suitcase. But one of the landlady's Filipino workers was watching his room from the hallway, pretending to lay carpet. Bukowski described rushing from his room, smacking the Filipino hard on the side of the head with the metal typewriter and charging downstairs. There was a cab outside. He took it straight to the bus station where he waited for an hour for a bus to New Orleans, wondering if he had killed the man.

It suited Hank's sense of drama to make a scene more desperate than it was. If he was there at all, the Filipino was probably just laying carpet tacks and Hank accidentally banged him with the metal carrying case as he passed, saw that he had hurt the man and ran in embarrassment. Bukowski the novelist intensified the incident to a potential murder. This is the problem with deciphering Bukowski's stories. He claimed they were 95 per cent accurate, with embellishments here and there. The percentage is probably closer to 50 per cent fact, 50 per cent fantasy. We do know that his next move was not to New Orleans, but to Bunker Hill, a few blocks away, where he took a $2.50 a week plywood hut behind a rooming house on Figueroa Street. It was number three of four wooden shacks in the backyard and had everything he needed: a cot, a blanket, a hotplate, a single electric light bulb and a small dresser. The backyard led to an alley and there was a long wooden stairway that led down the yellow clay cliff to the street below. At the bottom was a liquor store. This was the neighbourhood where Fante wrote his early work and to a certain extent Hank was living out a fantasy version of the same life.

He often walked past Fante's old rooming house at the foot of Bunker Hill, at Third Street and Hill, next to the Angel's Flight railroad, and fantasised that he *was* the young John Fante struggling to become a writer. He took the nickel ride on the little funicular railroad up and down the hill: the two fourteen-seater cable cars, purpose-built in 1901 for that precise incline and named after the two Biblical mountains Olivet and Sinai. The area was more or less unchanged since Fante's day. It was only in the early 60s that Los Angeles finished the destruction of its only historic neighbourhood. In the 50s the Santa Ana, the Santa Monica and Harbor Freeways were cut through downtown, demolishing scores of blocks for cloverleafs and on and off ramps, then came the Dorothy Chandler Pavilion, The Mark Taper Theater and the Ahmanson Theater, which opened in 1964. Even though The Angel's Flight railroad was a profitable operation it was closed down in 1969 and the cable cars stored away as part of the 'urban renewal' project that bulldozed away every trace of history and landscape to replace the neighbourhood with a row of soulless anonymous high-tech high-rises and luxury apartments that could be anywhere in the world.

Before all this change, Hank rejoiced in the seedy bars and alleys, particularly the small Mexican bars around the Plaza. In 'Training For Kid Aztec' the protagonist starts the evening at a large, well-frequented bar, but finds it too mellow and full of decent working men. He finds a dark alley and follows it, his switchblade in his pocket, until he comes upon a little Mexican bar at the alley's end. He orders a bottle of beer, gets off his stool and sneers: 'Anybody here want to spar a little, huh?' No one responds. 'I had only bored them with/my dangerousness.' It sounds a true story.

Hank moved to Ma Norman's rooming house. It was just south of downtown LA, a little east of Broadway, in a neighbourhood now long ago replaced by warehouses and parking lots. Hank would come down in the morning and Mama and 'Old Jeff' would be sitting in the kitchen. Hank would get some grain from the sack and go out into the backyard to feed the chickens, then Ma would pour him half a glass of whiskey. He enjoyed having two older people, landlords, who treated him as an equal. There was a large whore in the room to the south of his who would knock on his door 'naked and round and white and terrible' and tell him what happened to her the night before, and about her sons, one of whom she said looked just like him. They would sit and drink the port wine he kept in his room.

Hank's mother would come to visit and poke about in the dresser drawers: 'Henry, you don't have any clean stockings? Do you change your underwear?' She worried that Hank might be seeing the woman down the hall: 'Henry, you can get a terrible disease!' There was no danger of that; the woman visited only to drink. Naturally Katherine talked to his landlady, who complained that Hank read a lot of books in bed because when he went to sleep the books fell on the floor, and woke the other lodgers. They could hear it all over the house, heavy books falling, one at midnight, another at 1 a.m., another at 2 a.m. another at 4.

When Hank ran out of money, his mother came to his aid, as usual, and through a friend of hers she got him a job working in the Southern Pacific Railroad yards, down by the Los Angeles River. His job was to scrub the sides of the freight cars with Oakite and use a steam gun to wash away the grime on the railroad carriages. He learned quickly that the workplace was just as much a jungle as the schoolyard had been. On his first day on the job three of his co-workers blocked his way, one of them holding his crotch. 'What the hell's that supposed to mean?' Hank asked them, then, without hesitation, informed them he would take on any one of them and challenged them to give it a try. Later, as he was scrubbing the dirt off a boxcar the leader sidled up and told him they were going to get him. 'Maybe,' he said. 'But it won't be easy.' Six weeks later they still hadn't made their move; they were scared.

On 7 December 1941 Hank was walking past a penny arcade when he saw Robert Baume playing one of the machines. They laughed about their fight and went to a bar where they resumed their discussion of their plans for literary success. They moved on to a second bar when suddenly the music on the radio was interrupted with a news flash. Japan had attacked the American fleet at Pearl Harbor. Baume turned white. 'That's it,' he said. Hank agreed, but what Baume meant was that it was time for Hank to sign up. 'You're needed.'

Hank walked with his friend to the Greyhound Station where Baume bought a ticket to return to his base. He asked Hank to join him, but Hank had already made his position clear: 'I'm not getting on the bus with damn fools.' Baume, pale and clearly anxious about the future, asked Hank if he had any advice. Hank had nothing to say.

He never saw Baume again; he was killed in the Pacific only three months after completing basic training. Baume used to tell him: 'Bukowski, about half of what you say is bullshit.' Hank always meant to dedicate a novel to him, but never did.

Hank saved enough money from Southern Pacific to quit his job and take a Trailways bus to New Orleans, taking with him a fifth of whiskey for the trip. 'I went on the road not like Kerouac, as a fulfilling [experience]. I went on the road because there was no place to go. I just moved on because everything was ugly. All I wanted to do was find a small room somewhere, find a bottle of wine, and start drinking.'

There were a lot of troops on the bus, on their way to camp, and Hank and one other were the only two young men not in uniform. Soldiers came on board and demanded to know where everyone of draft age was from and where they were going. Hank answered them civilly but, instead of saying that he was born in Germany, he lied and said Pasadena. They let him alone. The other young man objected to being interrogated about his patriotism and the soldiers roughly hustled him off the bus and commanded the driver to go on his way, which he did, taking the young man's luggage with him.

Hank read Hemingway on the bus but couldn't understand it and threw it out of the window. A red-haired girl he got talking to made a sketch of his face and wrote her phone number in Fort Worth on the back. They got on so well that the bus driver and several of the other passengers expressed their surprise that he had not left the bus with her. He carried on to Dallas, showered and shaved at the Y then took a bus back to Fort Worth. The redhead lived with her mother, so Hank had to find accommodation. He took a room in a whorehouse by mistake and spent the night listening to doors slamming, people screaming and toilets flushing. It was a large, clean room for $5 a week. The maid offered him sex for $5 but he says he told her he was too tired. This incident prompted the story: 'Life in a Texas Whorehouse'. It was one of the man-of-the-world pieces that made his reputation about listening to a pimp beat up his whore, which ends, 'If I had known that was going to happen I would have let her have a little.' Hank had never been on a date, let alone had a woman.

He met up with the redhead and she was friendly and nice. They sat in the living room and talked while her mother hovered discreetly in the bedroom. Then the girl began talking about Jesus, the power of prayer and her boyfriend, and Hank realised that he had been gulled. As usual there are numerous versions of this story, including one where Hank didn't know how to contact her and a local newspaper advertised for the girl as a human interest story, claiming that they met on a plane, and she telephoned the newspaper. The outcome of the reunion, however, was the same. He continued his journey to New Orleans.

Hank arrived in New Orleans in a downpour at 5 o'clock in the morning. At first he sat in the bus station, but the atmosphere was so depressing that he started out in the rain, looking for the poor part of town where he might find a cheap rooming house. His suitcase was made of cardboard with a black coating which had peeled off in places. He had tried to make it look presentable by rubbing black boot polish on the exposed cardboard. As he walked along in the rain, switching the heavy suitcase from one hand to another, he inadvertently rubbed the black polish all over his pants.

He took a small dark room on the second floor of a rooming house just west of Canal Street. It smelled of piss and decay. Across the street, in the saddest bar he had ever seen, the drinkers were silent; it was very brightly lit, the bartender moved with glacial speed and Hank's wine had dust on top of it when it finally arrived. He remembered that he had something to drink in his room, and left. He could see into the bar from his window. Nothing had changed. The glaring overhead lights showed the drinkers, each at their separate tables like an Edward Hopper painting.

He was 21 years old, all alone, 2,000 miles from home. There were two lively girls living at the end of the corridor who kept knocking at his door, trying to get him to come out with them. The more he told them to go away, the more they persisted, pushing notes under his door and taping flowers to his doorknob. But he was scared of them and wanted to be alone to drink green beer and cheap wine in his mouse-infested room. He liked to watch women, but he was too shy, too unsure of himself, too frozen to contemplate having an affair, or even being friendly towards them. This was why he drank; to loosen up the frozen man, to feel more human. As Dr Johnson said: 'Wine gives a man nothing. It neither gives him knowledge nor wit; it only animates a man, and enables him to bring out what a dread of the company has repressed. It only puts in motion what has been *locked up in frost.*'

Instead Hank befriended the old man with swollen ankles in the next room. During the day Hank went for long, slow walks, drifting aimlessly all over town. He sat on public benches and watched the pigeons. He ate one meal a day in a cheap café where he got a huge breakfast of grits, sausages and hotcakes for very little money that lasted him all day. In the evenings he wrote short stories. This was exactly the life he wanted. He walked into a bar drunk, covered in mud after falling down on a rainy night and watched a knife fight. As one man stabbed his opponent, Hank strolled over and put a nickel in the juke box. He loved it there, it was exciting and manly. New Orleans became one of his favourite towns.

He drank his money up and took a job with a magazine distributor, checking that the piles of magazines and comic books matched the orders on the invoices. He lasted a week. The other workers couldn't stand his superior attitude. Next he worked in the composing room of one of the local newspapers, finding the pre-set type or zinc plates for ads for regular advertisers. And there were other jobs, including one at an auto parts warehouse; they all meld into one and it is impossible to establish a chronology. He went to Miami Beach, Atlanta, New York, St Louis, Philadelphia, San Francisco, Los Angeles again, New Orleans again, Philadelphia again, San Francisco again, Los Angeles again. Around and around. A couple of nights in East Kansas City, Chicago. After the initial few they become a blur, impossible to track.

He thought that he would be working an eight-hour-a-day job for the rest of his life, and the only way he could remain sane, the only way to save a little of himself, was to change jobs all the time, no matter how bad the jobs were, to work as little as possible, and to travel from city to city. That way he got some variety.

This image, of the wanderer, the alienated loner, is an old theme central to the work of Norwegian novelist, dramatist and poet Knut Hamsun, who won the Nobel Prize for Literature in 1920: the starving writer in *Sult* (*The Hunger*) (1890), and the itinerant labourer in the two *Wanderer* novels. Between 1882 and 1884 Hamsun roamed around the United States before returning to Oslo. From 1886 to 1888 he again travelled around America, working as a tram attendant in Chicago and as a farmhand in North Dakota. In Minneapolis he gave lectures; his books were based very much on his own experiences and Hank read them avidly.

In *Hunger* Hamsun wrote:

If one only had something to eat, just a little, on such a clear day! The mood of the gay morning overwhelmed me, I became unusually serene, and started to hum for pure joy and for no particular reason. In front of a butcher's shop there was a woman with a basket on her arm, debating about some sausage for dinner; as I went past, she looked up at me. She had only a single tooth in the lower jaw. In the nervous and excitable state I was in, her face made an instant and revolting impression on me – the long yellow tooth looked like a finger sticking out of her jaw, and as she turned toward me, her eyes were full of sausage. I lost my appetite instantly, and felt nauseated.

It is easy to see how Hank related to this writing. One night in Miami Beach, Hank had not eaten in sixty hours and took his last remaining money to a corner grocery and bought a loaf of bread, planning to savour each slice, chewing it slowly, imagining it was a steak or slice of turkey. Back in his room he opened the wrapper, and the slices of bread were all green with mould. He threw the bread on the floor and went to bed. The next morning, all that remained was the green mould – the mice had eaten the rest. He may have also liked Hamsun because of the controversy surrounding the Nobel laureate, who was a strong supporter of Hitler and the Nazis, even after the German occupation of Norway in 1940, something which destroyed his reputation. (In 1943 Hamsun met Adolf Hitler and Josef Goebbels, and gave Goebbels his Nobel Prize medal as a token of his esteem. After the war he was ostracised as a traitor and his work was ignored.)

The loner image is an American archetype: Chaplin's Little Man, the indomitable vagabond; the alienated individual of Sam Fuller's movies; the maverick; the gunslinger; the lone riverboat gambler; the disenfranchised; the dysfunctional; the lone man living in a rooming house. Bukowski:

> At the worst of times, in the worst of cities, if I could have a small room, if I could close the door of that small room and be alone in it with the old dresser, the bed, the torn window shade, I would begin to fill with something good; the unmolested tone of the singular self. I had no problems with myself, it was those places out there, those faces out there, the wasted, ruined lives – people settling for the cheapest and easiest way out. Between church and state, the family structure; between our educational and entertainment systems, between the eight hour job and the credit system, they were burned alive. Closing the door to a small room or sitting in a bar night and day was my way of saying no to all that.

This was one of Bukowski's major themes and he returned to it time and time again. One good example is 'Blue Collar Solitude', a meditation on alienation: about picking up a couple of six-packs after work, not bothering to eat dinner, just going home to his apartment, stripping down to his underwear, throwing his clothes on the floor and climbing straight into bed with no shower or bath; sitting propped up against the pillow, lighting a cigarette and cracking open the first can of beer, yesterday's dishes in the sink, nothing to do, nobody to talk to, no television, drinking, looking at the wallpaper and the knobs on the dresser as the light fades and the room becomes dark. This could also have been the protagonist of Hamsun's *Hunger*.

San Francisco was one of Hank's early destinations. It was there his 80-year-old landlady introduced him to classical music when she gave him an old green wind-up Victrola gramophone and an album of Beethoven's Fifth Symphony – it needed a number of the fragile 12-inch 78 rpm discs to play the whole symphony, which is why they came in hardback albums. She helped him drag the Victrola up the stairs. In his room he had a large bucket filled with beer and bottles of wine. He put on the symphony and played it until his neighbours beat on the wall. In a San Francisco bar he once drunkenly set his pants on fire with the ashes from his corncob pipe and deliberately smashed a glass, but was not thrown out. San Francisco was famous for its tolerance and quickly became another of Hank's favourite cities.

In Philadelphia Hank took an attic room for $2 a week: Just what I need, Hank thought. I can live here forever and be creative! But the pigeons woke up at 5 a.m., scores of them, and they marched about on the roof cooing. He moved around the corner. One day in July 1942 he was listening to the second movement of Brahms' First Symphony on a small record player when there was a knock at the door. Two large men stood there. One of them flipped his FBI badge. They told him to come with them and to bring a coat as he might be some time. One of them shut off the record player. Heads peered from the windows. 'And the eternal woman's voice; oh, there goes that horrible man, they've got him.'

Hank couldn't imagine what he had done wrong that would merit the FBI; had he killed someone while drunk? 'Keep one hand on each knee and don't move your hands!' There were two men in the front and two in the back of the car. Hank's air of indifference was interpreted as sang-froid and irritated the men: 'Hey, this guy's pretty cool!' one of them said. Not wanting to be beaten up Hank quickly piped up: 'Now wait! I'm scared,' which seemed to please them. To Hank they were like creatures from outer space, there was no common ground, he could not relate to them at all. At the office he was shown rows of framed photographs displayed on all four walls. 'See those photographs?' he was asked. Hank looked, but he didn't recognise any of the faces. He was told they were men who had been killed in the service of the FBI. He didn't know what to say so he said nothing. In another room a man screamed at him, 'Where's your Uncle John?' Again he didn't know what they were saying, what was his uncle John, some kind of weapon? He was nervous.

'John Bukowski!'

'Oh, he's dead.'

'Shit, no wonder we can't find him!'

Hank was put in an orange-yellow holding cell. It was a Saturday afternoon and from his cell window he could see people walking around. Across the street was a record shop with a speaker directed at the street, so he could hear the music. 'I stood there trying to figure what I had done. I felt like crying but nothing came out. It was just a sort of sad sickness, sick sad, when you can't feel any worse.'

He was wanted because he had not registered his address with the draft board the last time he moved. He had only moved eighty yards away, and had given the post office his forwarding address, assuming that was enough. He had drawn a very high draft number and was not expecting ever to be called up. The FBI sent him to Moyamensing Prison, a mock gothic castle with crenellations and turrets dating from the 1830s (demolished in the 60s.) As the two large wooden gates swung open to let them in Hank thought there should have been a drawbridge. His cellmate was a fat man called Courtney Taylor, who described himself as Public Enemy No. 1. They bet on how many bedbugs they could catch, Hank caught thirteen, Taylor had eighteen and won a dime. Hank later found out that Taylor had broken his in half and stretched them 'He had been a swindler, a real pro.'

At first Hank let his beard grow in prison because he was a long way down the line for the razorblade, but then his luck changed. While the other inmates played football in the prison exercise yard with a torn-up shirt tied into a ball, Hank ran a crap game and claimed that he made $15 or $20 a day. It was enough to live a life of luxury behind bars with shaving cream, new razorblades and the latest issue of the *New Yorker*. After lights out the cook arrived with plates of the same food the wardens ate: steaks, pie, ice cream, followed by good coffee and cigars. Taylor told Hank not to give the cook more than fifteen cents, that was tops, and warned him that the cook was there for murdering two men. Each day the cook whispered his thanks and asked if he should come back the next night. 'By all means,' Hank told him.

It took the FBI seventeen days to decide that Hank was innocent of deliberate draft dodging and sent him to the nearest induction centre. He passed the physical and went to the psychiatrist. They had raided his room and seized his papers. The psychiatrist had been reading through his short stories, which he described as 'these mad garbled writings'. Fortunately there were no Nazi pamphlets there as Hank had dumped all his Nazi propaganda, including his copy of *Mein Kampf*, down a storm drain as soon as Germany declared war on America. They asked if he believed in the war. 'No,' he told them.

'Are you willing to go to war?'

'Yes,' Hank said.

The doctor said that they were having a party the next Wednesday for doctors and artists and writers and Hank was invited. Would he like to come?

'No,' he said.

'All right,' the doctor said, 'you don't have to go.'

'Go where?'

'To the war.'

Hank looked at him in astonishment.

'You didn't think we'd understand, did you?' asked the doctor.

'No,' Hank told him. He was given a piece of paper to take to the next desk. It was folded and attached by a paper clip but Hank peeked and was able to read a fragment: '. . . hides an extreme sensitivity under a poker face . . .' He now had an 'unfit for service' draft card and was free to go.

Philadelphia was memorable for him in another way; it was here that he had sex for the first time. He was 23 years old and his partner was a '300 lb whore' who he picked up at a bar. He went at it with such vigour, all those years of frustration, that they reduced the bed to splinters and she declined payment on the grounds that she had not had that much fun in years. The landlady and her housemaid sniggered behind their hands the next day as they installed a new metal bed frame, as if defying him to break *that* one.

Throughout this time he had been writing three or four short stories each week and most of his money was going on stamps and envelopes as he mailed them out to *Atlantic Monthly* and *Story*. They all came back. It wasn't until he was in St Louis, working as a packer in the mail room of a dress shop, that *Story* magazine finally accepted a piece. The familiar envelope obviously contained a returned manuscript but, when he read the letter, the editor said they couldn't use the enclosed, but they would be running 'Aftermath of a Rejection Slip' in their issue for March–April 1944. Hank was amazed, it was his dream come true: Saroyan published in *Story*, all the greats. 'That was the magazine of the day then. It was *the* thing. Once you hit *Story* you were supposed to be "ready" . . .'

His peripatetic wanderings took him next to New York City. He usually did well in ports: San Francisco, New Orleans, Philadelphia, Los Angeles. He arrived at the Port Authority bus terminal and walked down 42nd Street to Times Square just as people were getting out of work. It was already dark and they shoved their way into the subway stations, shouldering him to one side, spinning him around on the pavement as he stood there like some country bumpkin, staring up at the tall buildings. The people were more brutal than he'd seen anywhere else. He had seven dollars in his pocket, nowhere to stay and no job. He told interviewer Robert Wennersten: 'Of course, I deliberately went to New York broke. I went to *every* town broke in order to learn that town from the bottom . . .' This was when he still thought that the only 'real men' – people whose company he could put up with for more than ten minutes – were at the bottom of society and not at the top. He later realised that such people are not at the top, middle or bottom, they are just very scarce and you don't meet many of them.

In *Notes of a Dirty Old Man* he described his arrival in New York: how he asked the way to Greenwich Village, how he took a room there and was surprised to find that it was furnished with an easel. He sat behind the easel, drinking his wine and looking out of the dirty window. When he went to buy more wine, he passed a young man talking on the hall phone, dressed in a beret and sandals, with a 'half-diseased beard'. The young man was evidently gay and talked excitedly on the phone. Hank hated the Village: 'They sat in the cafés, very comfortable, in berets, in the get-up, pretending to be Artists.' As this was fifteen years before the Beatniks with their berets and beards, one wonders quite who Bukowski encountered or if he was mixing it up with a later visit, or simply making it up; the Village in the 40s was a poor, run-down area mostly filled with working people and the scattering of artists and writers who did live there were attracted by the cheap rents, not because it was fashionable. Hank was disgusted by what he says he saw in the old Italian coffee shops in 1944: 'No men burning in agony, dreaming knives, just con-babies. Berets, goats, sipping tea by the window, or whatever they were sipping, I never went in. They looked too comfortable, they looked too money, too phoney.' Perhaps he visited again in 1958. He did, however, like the art movies that were playing there such as Luis Buñuel's *Un Chien Andalou* (1928): 'I was a sucker for Art movies.' He also liked films about the lives of the great composers and saw many of them, including a life of Schubert.

He finished out the rent, then took a room outside the Village. He walked across town until he reached Third Avenue and found a rooming house with a vacancy sign. He wondered why the room was so cheap but soon found out. He was right next to an 'El' stop. The Third Avenue Elevated ran right past his window. When the train stopped, the entire room was lit up and he would look out at a carriageful of faces: 'Horrible faces: whores, orangutans, bastards, madmen, killers.' Then, with a terrible screeching of metal, the train would pull rapidly away from the stop, plunging the room into darkness again.

His building was owned by a Jewish couple who also ran a tailor and cleaning shop across the street. They quickly conned him into buying a suit, an incident that he used in a comic tour de force worthy of Wodehouse or Tom Sharp: 'As I got into the pants the entire crotch split up the back. Well, I was game. It was a little cool, but I figured the coat would cover. When I got into the coat the left arm ripped out at the shoulder spilling out a sickening, gummy padding. Taken again.' It was such a good story he told it again in *Factotum*.

He knew that writers needed first-hand experience to draw on, and this restless, seemingly random, movement from city to city served no other purpose than to place him in situations where things might happen; from his point of view, the incident of the suit was a triumph even though more than twenty years would pass before he wrote about it. He was consciously accumulating material: stories, images, pictures of cities and people. He found another place, this time in a basement below the stoop of an old brownstone. One night he lost his key and, as he only wore a thin white California shirt, he had to ride a bus back and forth to keep from freezing. Eventually he finished up at the end of the line and found himself standing outside Yankee Stadium in the Bronx, home of his childhood hero Lou Gerhrig. After warming up with coffee and a doughnut at Father Divine's Mission he began the long walk back to lower Manhattan. No one answered the bell at his apartment house so he stretched out on top of the garbage cans and went to sleep hoping that the rats would not find him there. More grist.

One day Hank went to Pete's Tavern on Irving Place where O'Henry wrote *The Gift of the Maji*. He went down the steps, past the red-check tablecloths and up to the bar. The bartender said, 'Sorry Sir, I can't serve you.' Hank was sober but very hung over. He didn't argue but 'it made me feel filth as if he smelled some inner stink in me and I had been feeling mad, thinking suicide, maybe I looked too ugly, too vile.'

The next day he took a job replacing the cardboard advertisements in the subway cars. The carriages were parked on a stretch of elevated rail about ninety feet above the street and to get from one to another he had to skip along the railroad ties, carrying his heavy load of cardboard. The ties were three feet apart and he was terrified of falling between them to his death or brushing against the third (electrified) rail. When he reached the second car he told his colleagues he was quitting and demanded to know how to get out of there. He had to cross two or three third rails to reach the stairway. 'Each time I reached a third rail I stepped high and fancy. They had a soft and calm look to them in the moonlight.' Luckily there was a bar at the bottom of the stairway.

He lived on loaves of bread, sometimes with bologna sausage or peanut butter. He hadn't eaten for three or four days so one night he finally decided to treat himself to a big bag of popcorn. The popcorn was hot and greasy and salty and he hadn't tasted food for so long, it tasted so good that he walked along in a beautiful trance:

Each kernel, you know, each one was like a steak! I chewed and it would just drop into my poor stomach. My stomach would say: 'Thank-you, thank-you, thank-you!' I was in heaven, just walking along. And two guys happened by, and one said to the other, 'Jesus Christ!' The other one said, 'What was it?' 'Did you see that guy eating popcorn? God it was awful!' And so I couldn't enjoy the rest of the popcorn. I thought, what do you mean, 'it was awful.' I'm in heaven here. I guess I was kinda dirty. They can always tell a fucked-up guy.'

He hated New York: the harsh weather, the lack of food and lack of success as a writer had all conspired to bring about a terrible depression. He was walking down a street one day, broke, thinking about suicide, not 'because of artistic failure but more the failure of myself stuck down inside of life with all that happens and doesn't happen', when he passed by a corner drugstore and there on the rack was the April issue of *Story* Magazine. He snatched it up: 'It was a very odd feeling indeed.' They had used the story on the endpapers, beginning on page two, continuing on pages four and five, and finishing on the last three pages of the magazine. With the exception of letters to the *Examiner* and the college magazine it was his first time in print: 'A hell of a feeling, believe me, when you're 24 and half mad. A hell of a feeling anytime, I'd imagine.' Even though he felt that the piece had been taken by *Story* for its entertainment value, considering where they had run it in the magazine, he was elated and mightily encouraged.

This was his chance at the big time. *Story* magazine paid him $25 for his piece and he was approached by a literary agent, offering to represent his future work, inviting him to meet for drinks or a meal. But he turned her down, telling her: 'I'm not ready yet. I just happened to hit on one story – and it was a bad story.' He was right, at 24 he was probably too young to enter the New York literary rat race; he was too naïve, callow and would never have been able to play their games. In addition, he had never experienced a city as tough as New York and he knew that one false step there and he would be in real trouble: 'In New York you've got to have all the luck. I knew I didn't have that kind.' He left town almost immediately after *Story* came out, heading to East Kansas City.

He writes about this period with the worldly wise tone of an old trooper, but he was 24 years old, he'd had sex just once, he'd been published just once, he had no job, no skills – at least none he was prepared to use to make money – and was broke. But he was doing the right thing and a sense of calm and tranquillity comes through even in his macho description of yet another pimp beating up his whore: 'Maybe the next day when I wasn't so tired from the bus trip I'd let her have a little. She had a nice ass. At least he wasn't beating on that. And I was out of New York, almost alive.'

Encouraged by *Story* magazine Hank continued to write: '20 Tanks From Kasseldown' appeared alongside Henry Miller, Lorca and Sartre in the third issue of Caresse Crosby's luxurious fine art production *Portfolio: An International Review* in spring 1946. It was issued as a series of loose leaves each printed in a different typeface on coloured papers with drawings housed in a folder. Caresse Crosby and her husband Harry ran the legendary Black Sun Press. She wrote to Hank saying that his contribution was: 'a most unusual and wonderful story. Who ARE you?' He wrote back, 'Dear Mrs Crosby: I don't know who I am. Sincerely yours, Charles Bukowski.'

That same year he made a number of appearances in *Matrix* a local Philadelphia magazine: summer 1946 had a story called 'The Reason Behind Reason' and a poem called 'Hello', his first poetry in print; the winter 1946 issue contained the story 'Love, Love, Love', a poem called 'Voice In a New York Subway' and another called 'Object Lesson'; and he had another story, 'Cacoethes Scribendi', in the fall–winter 1947 issue. The spring–summer 1948 issue published a story called 'Hard Without Music' which suggests he did not completely give up writing in 1945 as he has claimed. There was even something by him in a 1951 issue of *Matrix*.

He continued his self-appointed round of cities. He claimed that he used to decide where to go by letting his finger fall randomly on an open map in the library, then head off to the bus station. He never rode freight trains; the picture of him hanging on the ladder of a boxcar was posed for a photographer. He would get a cheap room in the poorer section of town and write eight or ten short stories each week, hand printing them in neat letters whenever his typewriter was in the pawnshop, which was often. He never descended to Skid Row and always kept himself neat and clean, shaving, washing his shirts and shorts in the bathtub each day so that he always had a clean, though probably crumpled, outfit.

He rapidly became streetwise. He learned to carry his wallet in his front pocket, a switchblade in his pocket and most of his bills in his shoe. He had no girlfriends but after picking up a few prostitutes and waking in the morning to find his wallet gone it became so ingrained that even when he returned to his room alone, he automatically hid his wallet and his money. In the mornings he would often spend hours searching his room, trying to find the ingenious hiding place, which was often in a book; the last place a prostitute would think of looking. Once, returning some books to the library he stopped the librarian just as she was taking the books away because he saw a line of green protruding from between the pages. She returned it to him and he opened the book and pulled out three twenties and a ten.

Another morning, waking up in a Texas rooming house after a night of ferocious drinking, he found his wallet but no money. The rent was due that day and he explained to his landlady that he had somehow lost it. He went for a walk to clear his head, and returned full of self-pity to his room. The landlady met him. She was holding a handful of dollars. She told him that she was vacuuming his room and the vacuum kept hitting a bump in the rug. When she pulled it back, there was Hank's money.

Much of his money went on stationery, envelopes and stamps as he sent his stories out to *Harper's*, and the *Atlantic Monthly*. Strangely he never submitted anything else to *Story*. The manuscripts would come back but he pressed on, drinking too much cheap wine, taking low-paid service jobs to buy himself more time to pay the rent and buy alcohol, half starving in small rooms lying on the bed, staring blankly at the window shade or the knobs on the dresser before one day suddenly taking the bus to the next town. He felt that he needed the time to get something done and that the only way he could buy time was with poverty. 'I worked not so much with craft but more with getting down what was edging me toward madness – and I had flashes of luck.'

This theme is also explored in 'You Don't Know', a superb, effortlessly crafted poem in which he explains how good it is to return to your room from work in a strange city where no one knows you, you don't know the street names or the name of the mayor. Instead of eating dinner you take off your shoes, climb into bed with the lights out, to listen to the crackle of the cockroaches behind the peeling wallpaper and the scampering feet of the mice across the floor. To sit there in bed in the moonlight or the light from street lamps or neon signs through the window, and feel the wine enter your body, to see the flare of a match illuminate the room for a brief moment. He relishes being there without a woman, without a telephone, with no car or TV, listening to the voices of the other boarders as they make dinner, flush toilets, argue and laugh. Then to finally undress, take the last drink, pull the warm covers up around you. 'You don't know/how good it can be/until you've been/there.'

When Hank ran out of money he usually tried for an easy stopgap job that didn't involve too much hard work, such as a stock boy pulling orders or a packer, a shipping clerk or cleaner. Once he worked as a doorman in a Texas whorehouse. Sometimes he got so spaced out from excessive drinking that no one would hire him for this type of work. This meant getting a manual job such as working in the meat packing plant or a factory, exhausting, back-breaking work for more or less the same money. At a rubber factory, he was one of three men whose job was to lift a mass of rubber and place it in the machines that heated it and chopped it into the various things the factory made: hot-water bottles, bathing caps, bicycle pedals. It was a delicate job because the machine could easily shear your arm off, it had happened to two men in the last three years, so Hank was particularly careful when he had a hangover. After an eight-hour shift there was compulsory overtime.

He worked in a dog biscuit factory putting metal screens filled with stamped-out dough into the oven. The flames in the oven leaped fifteen feet high and Hank's job was the one nobody wanted because the screens were heavy and the oven burned your hands. He came in for work at 4.30 p.m. and stayed until 1 a.m. He arrived drunk every day and quit after two weeks.

At each of these jobs he entered into someone else's world; the workers had often been there for some time, and most saw themselves as staying there for the rest of their working life. Hank observed the menial jobs, the petty world of bickering, of officious managers and mean foremen, of jealousies and feuds, of meticulously observed precedent and job descriptions. He saw it all and remembered it. He could never have faced the foremen 'with their little rodent eyes', were it not for drink. He despaired of his fellow workers with their group insurance and holiday plans: 'the actual/human slavery/of men who didn't/know/that they were/slaves'. He dreamed all day about getting home, stretching out on the bed, unscrewing the cap of the bottle and taking his first long swig.

* * *

It was in Philadelphia that Bukowski claims he evolved a master plan. Depending on which interview you read, Bukowski either gave up writing and forgot all about it because he became an alcoholic, or it was all part of a master plan to gather material. In his poem 'Master Plan' he claims 'of course, I never really considered quitting the/writing game. I just wanted to give it a/ten year rest.' It is a well-constructed, very funny poem, and it may be partly true. He gave a completely contrary account to Robert Wennersten, however:

> It started around 1945. I simply gave up. It wasn't because I thought I was a bad writer. I just thought there was no way of crashing through. I put writing down with a sense of disgust. Drinking and shacking with women became my art form. I didn't crash through there with any feeling of glory but I got a lot of experience which later I could use – especially in short stories. But I wasn't gathering that experience to write it, because I had put the typewriter down. I don't know, you start drinking; you meet a woman; she wants another bottle; you get into the drinking thing. Everything else vanishes.'

The fact is that neither account is strictly accurate because he continued to publish, and therefore presumably submit, throughout his 'ten year drunk', albeit on a much reduced scale.

It was about one in the afternoon when Hank walked into a run-down bar in the poor neighbourhood at 16th and Fairmount in the Spring Garden district of Philadelphia to have a beer. He took a seat at the bar. To his surprise the place was packed; everyone was drinking beer and they were all drunk. All of a sudden a bottle came flying through the air. The man seated next to him stood up and yelled at his assailant: 'You ever do that again, man, I'll kill you!' Another bottle came flying through the air. The bartender just poured another drink, not bothering to even say anything. Hank thought: 'This is a place I want to be! Something's finally happening ... Decent, open violence!' Then two guys got into a fight and began slugging it out. Hank went to take a piss and had to pass between them. 'OK, pardon me, gentlemen,' and they paused to let him through. On his way back they were still at it but stopped once more to let him pass. He thought: 'This is my heaven. I'm going to drink in this bar. I'm going to fight like this and I'm going to live like this.' But the strange thing was, it never happened again. 'It was like they all planned it for me. The same people were there, and I waited and waited. I waited two and a half years.' That first afternoon was it. 'I was trapped into a dream that I wanted.'

There was an early barkeeper called Jim who started work at 5 a.m., mopping down the floor, washing glasses, bringing up supplies. Hank would arrive at about 5.30 and tap on the door and Jim would let him in for the company. They talked quiet and easy. Hank listened to the wet slosh of the string mop and heard the traffic outside as the people went to work. Every so often Jim would pour him a whiskey, and one for himself. Drinks were on the house. Then at 7 a.m., official opening time, he'd say, 'Well Hank, I've got to charge you now, I'm opening the door,' and Hank would thank him. Then the regulars would come swinging in: alcoholic office workers in need of a drink before they got to their desk, the early shift whores, drinkers of all types, but none of them stayed. Hank was the only one who was not caught up in the rat race. He told Doug Blazek, a fellow poet and the editor of the hard-hitting poetry magazine *Ole*: 'I was the only one who stayed and it worked into my mind that if I could just get onto that stool each 5 a.m. somewhere somehow there, I wouldn't be too much touched by the asshole war of the world, and it was a strange and necessary time: many hours of not talking, staring at the bar wood, watching the sun come up and go down.' He became a fixture on the end bar stool. He would sit there and just hope that someone would buy him a drink. Sometimes, if the morning whiskeys had not done the trick, he would beg for one, play the buffoon, or shake the pin-ball machine for change. He became a neighbourhood character, the bar clown, someone with quite a way of telling stories, and drinks often came his way.

But even in 'The City of Brotherly Love' you cannot live for free and Hank had to work to pay the rent and buy his food and cigars. When he filled in his employment record for the post office in order to show continuous employment he claimed that he worked at Fairmount Motors, at 16th and Fairmount Street, between January 1942 and August 1945 so, although he was in New York in March 1944, and St Louis before that, and we have to assume that he did, at some point, spend some time sitting at the bar all day, he must have worked at Fairmount Motors at least some of the time – unless he made it up: it has the same address as the bar.

He ran errands for sandwiches, picked up a dime here, a dollar there, but it wasn't a nine-to-five job, it was a five-to-two a.m. job. 'I guess there were good moments, but I was pretty much out of it. It was kind of a dream state.' One classic bar moment came when the other barflies refused to believe that he was a published writer. With a bet of three drinks hinging on it, he went to his room and returned with one of his copies of *Portfolio* III, Caresse Crosby's $10 magazine. The patrons were amazed, the bargirls marvelled at the long words, the thick handmade paper and the beautiful printing. He won his bet, he was a hero. Somehow they all finished up outside; there was a very strong wind which sent the pages flying down the street, people running after them. Hank stood and watched, drunk, as his literary career was literally washed down the gutter. A big window washer who always ate six eggs for breakfast put his massive foot in the centre of one of the pages, yelling triumphantly: 'Here! Hey! I got one!'

'Fuck it, let it go, let all the pages go!' Hank told them, and they all trooped back inside.

But such excitement was not usual. It was normally pretty quiet. Bukowski: 'The bar was so run down, old, smelled of urine and death, that when a whore came in to make a catch we felt particularly honoured.' He liked to say he stopped in for a quick one and stayed five years; it was probably just a few months.

At about 11 a.m. each morning, when the alcohol kicked in, Jim the bartender would say that he'd had enough and tell him to go take a walk. One story Hank told many times, always in the plural as if it happened a lot, was that he would go around to the back of the bar and lie down in the alley because delivery trucks ran up and down there delivering to the warehouses 'and I felt that anytime might be mine'. This sounds an exaggeration and more probably something he did once, though it does show his often mentioned suicidal recklessness. Of course, in the middle of the day, the truck drivers would most likely have seen him. There were some shacks in the alley where black people lived and he claimed that every day little black children would throw rocks at him or poke sticks in his back until he'd hear their mother's voice saying: 'All right now, leave that man alone!' After a while he would sober up enough to be allowed back in the bar and continue drinking. The whitewash in the alley was a problem. 'Somebody always brushed the lime off of me and made too much of it.'

Hank was not at the bar all the time, however. He still fired off stories to the *Atlantic Monthly* 'because I felt pretty bad and didn't know what else to do.' He was evicted from room after room for being drunk or not paying the rent or causing a disturbance. Within a four-block area he lived in nine different rooms, the longest being at 603 North 17th Street.

One winter in Philadelphia he almost died in a snowstorm. He was sitting in a tiny bar, giving his line to two women, when the bartender began quoting Shakespeare. For some reason this irritated Hank who responded with a diatribe about Hitler and Mussolini and the next thing he knew he was out of there in the snow. He stopped to piss against the side of a church and took a shortcut through the churchyard. It was a clear, cold night with a full moon but as he stumbled drunk towards his room, he tripped over a wire surrounding a patch of grass, buried ankle deep in the snow, and fell. He lay there, too drunk to get up and yet knowing that if he stayed there he would freeze to death. After a long time the coldness of the snow on his face sobered him enough to stagger to his feet and he made it home. The next morning he resolved to stay out of the snow country in winter.

As there were no bar fights to join in with, he had to provoke some of his own, often with the night-time bar tender Tommy McGillan. McGillan won most of them as he was well fed and not drunk, he may also have been the stronger man. Hank was never vicious or worked up: 'My violence was against the obvious trap. I was screaming and they didn't understand. And even in the most violent fights I would look at my opponent and think, why is he angry? He wants to kill me. Then I'd have to throw punches to get the beast off me. People have no sense of humour, they are so fucking serious about themselves.'

One time, fighting Tommy McGillan in the alley behind the bar for the benefit of the patrons, and getting beaten as usual (all the bar girls were rooting for Tommy who was a handsome, muscular Irishman), something clicked in Hank's brain that said, 'It's time to do something else.' He gave Tommy a good hard crack on the side of the head that shook him up. He stared at Hank, as if to say, 'This isn't in the script.' Then Hank gave him another, and he could see the fear rising in him. Hank closed in and finished him off quickly. Hank didn't really know what had happened except that he had stayed out of the bar that day and drank muscatel and ate boiled potatoes and rye bread to build up his strength. They dragged Tommy inside and the girls all sat there holding his head and wiping him with their hankies while Hank sat at the bar and hollered: 'Hey, what the fuck is this? I want a drink!' But the relief bartender leaned close and told him: 'I'm sorry, sir, we can't serve you.' Hank walked to another bar a block away, sat down and ordered a beer. Three days later he was allowed back in.

His love of brawling sometimes got him into trouble. In 'Garbage' he describes one fight where he took a tremendous beating, where, even after Bukowski was unconscious, his opponent continued to kick his head, again and again, and then emptied several garbage cans over him. He awoke, lying in the alley, at 6 a.m., his face a mess, eyes almost swollen shut, and somehow staggered back to his room. Often his opponents were well-fed, burly truck drivers, and even though Hank had studied fighting, and even once contemplated a career in the ring when he was in high school, he was no match for them. In 'Looking Back', written in old age, he wrote that he couldn't understand the man he was then: continually choosing the biggest meanest bastard in the bar to come and fight in the alley, and getting himself slammed by blows he didn't see coming, his brain jolted, flashes of coloured light exploding in his head, feeling his mouth fill with blood. Hank loved fighting. He told his friend AD Winans that he 'liked the impact of knuckles against teeth, the rush to the brain when a blow landed to a man's body, the feeling of having to shake loose and nail the other person before he finished you'. It was never personal, even when he became violent in bars and the fight spilled out into the street. Fights were Hank's way of making human contact, a necessity of life:

I think violence is often misinterpreted. Certain violence is needed. There is, in all of us, an energy that demands an outlet. I think that if the energy is constrained, we go mad. The ultimate peacefulness we all desire is not a desirable area. Somehow in our construction, it is not meant to be. This is why I like to see boxing matches, and why, in my younger days, I'd like to duke it in back alleys ... The best feeling is when you whip a guy you're not supposed to whip. I got into it with a guy one time, he was giving me a lot of lip. I said, 'OK. Let's go.' He was no problem at all – I whipped him easy. He was laying there on the ground. He's got a bloody nose, the whole works. He says, 'Jesus, you move slow man. I thought you'd be easy – the goddam fight started – I couldn't see your hands anymore, you were so fucking fast. What happened?' I said, 'I don't know, man. That's just the way it goes.' You save it, you save it for the moment.

The desire to pick a fight was always a problem for Hank until he became too old to challenge people. His one-time friend Harold Norse wrote to William Childress: 'He's a truly great poet. But he is always wanting to fight. To stay around him too long is to invite disaster.'

His face was never completely healed, he always had a black eye, a swollen nose, a fat lip. He developed bone spurs on his knees from falling on them so hard and so frequently. It was the Frozen Man trying to shake loose some feeling, as if violence would shake him out of his torpor, make him feel something. His father's beatings suggest that, to Bukowski, violence was a medium of communication: if you can't love me, at least recognise that I exist. Beating was that recognition.

What was Hank doing, sitting there on his stool in the bar, watching the flash of light when the door opened change from dark to daylight and back again, and the customers come and go? The same as he did later at the racetrack. He may not have known the word but Bukowski was the epitome of the French *flâneur*: the solitary observer, invariably male, originally strolling about Paris, though by definition he could occupy any urban space. *Encylopédie Larousse* defines him as a fritterer away of time, a loiterer. The idea of the *flâneur* has been written about most extensively by philosopher Walter Benjamin, who described the lone individual in the crowd, his leisurely strolling, his aimless wandering, most notably his alienation or detachment. Baudelaire famously wrote: 'The crowd is his domain, just as the air is the bird's, and water that of the fish. His passion and his profession is to merge with the crowd. For the perfect idler, for the passionate observer, it becomes an immense source of enjoyment to establish his dwelling in the throng, in the ebb and flow, the bustle, the fleeting and infinite.'

The *flâneur* is the solitary walker as a detective, a philosophical stroller, an urban reporter. In '59 Cents a Pound' Bukowski wrote: 'I like to prowl ordinary places/and taste the people –/from a distance,/I don't want them too near.' If they got too close, that was when attrition started. He liked to view them in supermarkets, laundromats and cafés, on street corners, at bus stops, hot dog stands and drug stores. Then he could look at their bodies and faces and their clothing and observe the way they held themselves or walked or completed an action. He compared himself to an X-ray machine. He liked to see them on view like that. He felt sorry for them all, including himself, and glad for them all 'caught alive together', awkwardly living their lives.

And so, just when the myth suggests that Bukowski had exchanged writing for drinking, we actually find him at his most active as a poet, for, as Baudelaire wrote: 'The poet is possibly at his busiest when he seems to be at his laziest.'

Hank's withdrawal, his dislike of his fellow humans, his three-day-four-night bed marathons parallel the bedroom patrol of the greatest of indoor *flâneurs*, Marcel Proust. Part of the definition of *flânerie* is that it produces little but the *flâneur* accumulates a great deal. Hank's ten-year drunk accumulated the raw material for his subsequent career as a writer. Though not working from a cork-lined room, his position on the end barstool enabled him to join in or not, to observe or take centre stage as a raconteur or bar brawler; he was in control, he was a barfly and yet he was far removed from that community of regular drinkers who were to supply so much of the material for his work. Baudelaire wrote, 'he makes it his business to . . . distil the eternal from the transitory.' That was the great genius of Charles Bukowski.

One day he did not show up at the bar; he gave several reasons for this, including the flippant (and therefore most plausible) one that they installed a television in the bar and so the conversation stopped. 'I was waiting for something to happen. Somebody to say something . . . I was waiting for some magic to occur in this bar . . . It never did.'

Hank made several trips to Atlanta, Georgia, and during the war he worked at the Coca-Cola bottling plant there for $60 a month because of the government wartime freeze on wages. In Atlanta he nearly died of starvation and experienced something of an epiphany. His many accounts of this appear to conflate several visits to the city but, considering the weight loss he was experiencing, it was probably just after his spell at the bar in Philadelphia, and just before he took his long break from being a writer. Arriving in Atlanta, as usual, he knew no one, had no job and was broke. He headed for the cheaper part of town. It was already dark and he was cold, still wearing only a thin, white, California shirt. He saw a Room For Rent sign, but the landlord looked him up and down and said, 'I see you don't dig me. So I don't want to be bothered,' and told Hank, rather forcefully, to leave. By now he was shivering. He tried to find shelter in a church, but the door was locked. Eventually he found another Room to Rent sign, and an old woman answered the door. There was a tarpaper shack in the front yard. The door was hanging from one hinge. It was a dollar and a half for the week: 'Ain't no lock but nobody's gonna bother ya in there,' she told him.

It had a dirt floor with old newspapers laid on it like a rug, a bed but no sheets, just one thin blanket. No electricity, just a kerosene lamp. He lit the lamp, but pretty soon the oil was used up and the flame shuddered out. The outdoor toilet had no seat and seemed to go miles into the earth. It stank and there was a spider web spun across the mouth of the bowl with a big black spider sitting in the middle of it. 'Suddenly all desire to shit left me.' His weight had dropped from 198 to 133 pounds. He was on the edge of starvation.

Hank had always been in love with the photographs of two people: Kay Boyle and Caresse Crosby. In one account he says he wrote to them both, telling them he was starving and if they would just send him $10 – and hurry! – he would pay them back double, triple, only he needed it now! He wrote many letters, telling the few people he knew who might be sympathetic that he had made a mistake, that he was starving and trapped in a small freezing shack in a strange city. He wrote a long letter to his father, saying he was starving and asked him for the bus fare back to LA. He mailed the letters and waited the long days and nights, hoping for a kindly response. Hank had reached some kind of nadir. As he put it: 'slowly then health and courage began to leak away,/and the night arrived when everything fell apart – and fear, doubt, humiliation entered.'

He had a loaf of sliced bread and he ate one slice a day followed by a nibble at a Payday candy bar. 'No steak more glorious than a small nibble at that.' He had reached bottom. This experience was returned to time and time again in stories, poems and interviews. It is central to the Bukowski myth. There was an electric wire dangling overhead which at some point had fed a lightbulb but the light and its fitting were long gone. Toying with his suicidal impulses he reached for the wire, not knowing whether it was alive or dead, waving his hand closer and closer to it. Then he saw the newspapers on the floor, used as a floor covering. He had used all his writing paper but saw that there were wide margins around the printed text. He pulled his hand away from the wire. Though it is very unlikely that the wire was live, the suicidal impulse was there but the desire to write overwhelmed it. 'It's no good quitting, there is always the smallest bit of light in the darkest of hells.' He had pawned his typewriter but he still had a pencil stub, so he began writing around the edges. He could not afford oil for the lamp so he sat in the open doorway, shivering in the moonlight so that he could see what he was doing. He filled margin after margin.

One cold night, Hank stepped outside his shack and stood looking at the warm lights of his landlady's house. Through the window he could see the fireplace blazing. For a moment Hank really wanted that life, to be that sort of normal person. He was a writer but nobody was reading his work, even when he managed to get it out to the New York magazines. They were publishing well-written formula pieces, written by people who knew the game. He wasn't playing the game. All this spun through his mind as he stood in the yard, freezing and starving. He had dedicated himself to the word and there he was up against the wall. He was an idiot. All he really had was a conviction that there was a better way to write than what the professionals were doing. He had no girlfriends, no friends, no money, and he stood watching the flames rise into his landlord's chimney. It was a tempting life, but Hank didn't quit.

He says that only two people responded to his letters, and both arrived on the same day. He quickly opened the pages and shook them out for money. There was none. One was from Caresse Crosby saying she was no longer publishing her literary magazine and had found God and was living in a castle in Italy and helping the poor, though he later wrote that this letter followed him around from address to address until it reached him in New Orleans. (He also later said that he didn't write to Kay Boyle because he had run out of stamps.)

The other letter was from his father, ten pages of bile, telling him that he deserved everything he got, that he should have become an engineer as Henry suggested. For page after page Henry pointed out Hank's failures and his refusal to face reality, telling him to make something of himself. Twenty years later Hank wrote to Doug Blazek: 'Ten fucking vindictive pages about AMERICA and MAKING GOOD, and it was worse than silence because he was rubbing it in.' The hurt was still there.

Bukowski gives various accounts of his next move, one of which says he escaped Atlanta by signing on to the track crew that took him back to California. In *Factotum* this trip originated in Louisiana so he may have gone there first, receiving Caresse Crosby's letter when he was there. We cannot be sure. He signed on to a railroad track crew to work out of Sacramento but first he had to get there.

The railroad transported the men and issued them with tickets good for a night in the local hotel at each overnight stop as well as meal tickets for a local café. On board the windows wouldn't open and they were given cans of food but no openers. They busted the cans against the side of the seats and ate raw hash and uncooked lima beans. The water tasted foul. Hank didn't mix with the other men. He stretched out on the wooden seat and dozed. The seat was old with many cracks in the wood. He felt a breeze blow dust up through the cracks into his face, then realised it was a man crouching behind the seat who was blowing the dust through, on to him. He sat up and the man scrambled to his feet and ran to the front of the coach to join his friends, asking them to protect him from Hank. They switched trains at El Paso. He heard them plotting to beat him up and decided it would be more prudent to sleep on a park bench than join them at the company hotel.

He picked the wrong night for sleeping in the park. That night there was a sandstorm and he awoke covered from head to foot in dust. He brushed himself off as best he could and made his way to the local library. The librarian frowned at his appearance but he was otherwise respectable as he browsed the shelves. It was here that he found another book in the pantheon of influences upon his writing: Dostoevsky's *Notes from Underground*. 'This guy has got it!' he thought. He spoke less over the years about the Russian's work than of some of his other influences, but this might be because he didn't know how to pronounce his name – something which often prevented him from engaging in literary discussion for fear of embarrassment. Hank was reading Dostoevsky at the same time that members of the Beat Generation were first discovering him – they referred to him familiarly as 'Dusty' – and he was a considerable influence on them all.

In Los Angeles there was a two- or three-day stop-over and they were again issued with hotel and meal tickets. Hank gave his hotel tickets to the first bum he met and headed for the café where he could use his meal tickets. He ran into two of the rail crew who, instead of being hostile, were now friendly. The café also sold beer and Hank soon used up all his tickets. That left him just enough change to take a street car home to his parents. His mother was delighted to see him: 'Son, you've come home!', but when his father got home his first words were to tell him that he was going to charge him room and board, plus laundry, payable as soon as he got a job. Hank didn't stay long; that would have seemed like defeat. He continued north to San Francisco, where he managed to live for several weeks by selling blood. But it was hopeless, he was too rundown. Tired and exhausted, he returned to his parents and stayed almost two years. He took a steady job at the Merry Company at 634 South San Pedro Street. It was only in October 1947 that he felt strong enough to once more leave home and take up the challenge again.

As far as his parents were concerned, Hank regarded himself as ever the victim. Years later he wrote to rare book dealer Jim Roman: 'They hated my guts. Charged me room and board, atrocious prices.' But what was a 26-year-old man doing living at home? Perhaps a month of home cooking to bring his weight up but why stay there if he loathed them so much? If he didn't like the price of room and board he could have taken a room of his own. This is a period that Hank diplomatically kept very quiet about; running back to mom and dad hardly squared with the hard-man image. He appears to have been defeated by life on the road, by starvation and, most importantly, by rejection by the magazines. He stopped writing and, apart from a few appearances in the Philadelphia magazine *Matrix*, where he presumably knew the people, he entered a ten-year silence. To compound the ignominy, Hank's father now stole his identity as a writer and passed himself off as the author of the piece in *Portfolio III* in order to get a better job at the LA County Museum. They had the same name and, though it must have puzzled his bosses, Henry was promoted from security guard to floor assistant helping to hang pictures.

There is a photograph of Hank in his parents' garden taken in July 1947. He wears a light-coloured double-breasted summer suit, a neatly tied necktie, his hair is carefully groomed and his brown shoes highly polished; he looks like a car salesman.

4. DRINKING WITH JANE

Then began the legendary, mythical life of Charles Bukowski: the whores, the drinking, the fights and carousing, the rooming houses and the tawdry glamour of Hollywood lowlife. If for no other reason, Bukowski's place in literary history is secure for his celebration of Los Angeles. He captured many wonderful images of downtown, before all the energy was drained out of it. He is the poet of sprawl: no other poet has written so many poems about freeways, palm trees and lawns, as well as the racetrack, going to the bank, the minutiae of everyday life in Los Angeles. In September 1947, when he moved out of Longwood Avenue and once more found a room of his own, downtown was still the centre of Los Angeles and only a few scattered miles of freeway existed.

This was the area he knew from living on Bunker Hill. Hank preferred the cheap residential neighbourhood of West Lake around MacArthur Park and Alvarado Street, a mixture of grimy brick apartment buildings and rooming houses converted from Victorian mansions, interspersed with strip joints, pawnshops, liquor stores, cigar stores and cheap bars. The buildings were low-rise, with scruffy palm trees in the yards and storm fences snagged with trash. The population was not much different than over at Main: cheap whores, alcoholics, the ever-present pensioners, lonely men eating at the counters of cheap cafeterias or soda fountains, and a few tanned derelicts, dodging the cops. Hank had an abundant choice of decaying rooming houses with torn shades, screens smooth with decades of grime and a sheen of cooking fat grease on the crumbling plaster walls. Most of the small rooming houses had no receptionist, which suited Hank as he didn't want anyone monitoring his movements. The rooms had a sink but the toilet was down the hall and shared with other tenants.

If he felt like a night out he would head over to the medieval carnival of Main Street with its frenzied night-time action: three-feature movie houses ablaze with neon; burlesque joints with photographs of impossibly well-endowed women; porno magazine shops filled with cellophane-wrapped photographs of women in underwear; shoeshine stands where the bootblack could direct you to anything in the world you could want, legal or not; jukeboxes blaring from bars filled with young male hustlers, predators and the preyed upon, cowboys, queens, and the vice squad wagon cruising the streets around 6th and Main, where the transvestites gathered, and outside Hoopers all-night coffee-shop. Gangs of servicemen on leave, just waiting to get fleeced but determined to have a good time. The long, narrow bars jammed with humanity, broken neon flickering outside reflected in the smeared mirrors, the peeling plaster yellow from nicotine, the booths slashed and patched, the air thick with cigarette smoke, the smell of stale beer, piss and disinfectant; pawnshops filled with suits and rings; army and navy surplus stores; coffee shops smelling of stale coffee and onions, the walls dripping from the steam tables; liquor stores selling the cheapest rot-gut; and, above it all, the black, starless, Los Angeles night.

Hank rarely strayed further east than this; one block over was Los Angeles Street and beyond that was Skid Row. Mostly he stuck to West Lake, and it was at the Glenview bar on Alvarado Street that he first encountered Jane Cooney Baker. In *Factotum* he described how the bar was crowded and yet there was a seat remaining to the left of an attractive woman, which surprised him. He queried the bartender, who told him that she was crazy; she had a bad habit of suddenly smashing her glass into the face of any man talking to her. She rarely spoke, just sat and stared at her drink, now and then raising her head to pronounce 'Shit!' Naturally, Hank was intrigued and took the seat. There is only one photograph of Jane, from her high school yearbook. When asked, Hank always called her 'a looker', and said she wore high heels and had lovely long legs. She was a rather dark blonde in her late 30s who had gained a bit of weight; her neck and cheeks now fleshy, but her face still had a lingering beauty. There was a large wart on her left hand and she dropped her cigarette ash everywhere. Her beer belly grew larger through the years he knew her. She was obviously an alcoholic and many of her friends were hookers. In many poems he described her as 'an Alvarado Street whore' yet he was immediately attracted to her. 'She had a kind of mad sensibility that knew something, which was this: that most human beings just aren't worth a shit. And I felt that and she felt it, so we had a working ground.'

If Hank knew nothing else, the years in Philadelphia had taught him good bar etiquette. He bought her a drink and another. After four drinks he told her that was it, he was now out of money. She told him to come with her and they went to the nearest liquor store. She asked the man to charge two-fifths of Old Grandad, a six-pack, cigarettes and some snacks. He phoned someone who okayed her purchase. They went back to Hank's room. All of this was used in the movie *Barfly*.

Jane was ten years older than Hank. She was born on 7 July 1910 in Carlsbad, New Mexico, but she grew up in St Louis, where her father Daniel C Cooney was a successful doctor. Unfortunately when she was nine, he contracted pneumonia and moved his family to Glencoe, New Mexico, but he died not long afterwards. Jane's mother, Mary, took her family – Jane had at least one older sister – to nearby Roswell, another desert community, later famous as the site of a supposed UFO crash. Daniel and Mary were devout Catholics and, though Jane never lost her faith – she always slept with a rosary under her pillow when she was with Hank – she became known as a party girl at high school, always wanting to drink and dance. In 1927, shortly after she graduated from Roswell High School, one of her boyfriends, Craig Baker from nearby Artesia, made her pregnant. She married him on 25 January 1928 and the next morning they left for El Paso where she gave birth to her son Joe. Three years later she and Craig had a daughter they named Mary.

Hank maintained that Craig Baker was from a wealthy Connecticut family but this was not so. Almost everything that we know about Jane comes from Howard Sounes's research for his biography *Locked in the Arms of a Crazy Life*; virtually everything that Hank told his first biographer, Neeli Cherkovski, about Jane proved to be false, although Hank probably thought he was giving him accurate information. Jane and Craig lived with her mother because they couldn't afford to do otherwise; Craig's business, whatever it was, did badly, and he was a borderline alcoholic. Things began to go badly wrong. She and Craig divorced even though she apparently still loved him. Shortly afterwards, in 1947, Jane's mother, Mary Cooney died, and not long after that Craig Baker was killed when he crashed his car while drunk, something that Jane blamed herself for. With her husband and both parents gone, Jane's life fell apart and she began drinking heavily. She moved to Southern California to make a new start. Her children, now almost grown up, were living with Craig's family. She eventually lost touch with them, which was one of the many demons that troubled her. She told Hank: 'Losing my kids, that was the most painful thing.' She talked lovingly about her children every night before sleeping.

Hank was in love. He was 27 and he said that Jane was only the second woman to have sex with him; the first being his one night stand that broke the bed in Philadelphia. If that is true then many of the early stories of waking to find his money gone are fabrication and the early Bukowski myth begins to look even more spurious (though he made up for it later). He loved Jane because she 'was the first person who paid attention to me in my life'. It is likely that Jane fabricated her past almost as much as Hank did because she told him that she was an ex-showgirl, and offered to show him clippings and photographs to prove it. She claimed to have almost won a Miss America competition. Jane had clearly been in Los Angeles for some time when Hank met her. The career as a showgirl, if it happened, is more likely to have occurred there than in New Mexico and she had already found a sugardaddy to pay for her drinking habit – possibly the man to whom her charges at the liquor store were made. Hank found her physically very attractive: 'Some class, but just a hint and little more.' She was at a stage when, as he put it: 'a woman is still nicely put together, just dangling on the edge of falling apart, which is when they look sexiest to me'.

They moved in together, first at 521 South Union Drive, a short, curving street five blocks east of MacArthur Park where they posed as a respectable newly married couple. The landlady was pleased to have them as tenants and even gave them a new rug, but her hopes were quickly dashed and she was forced to evict them. Jane drank even more than Hank, and they soon smashed the place up in a drunken argument. They moved constantly, always in the West Lake area, taking rooms in hotels and rooming houses, sometimes lasting only two or three days. They were evicted from so many places for being drunk and disorderly, fighting and keeping the neighbours awake that they couldn't remember them all. On one occasion, they were looking for a new hotel room and knocked on a rooming house door, to be confronted by a landlady who had only thrown them out days before. She turned white with rage, screamed at them and slammed the door.

They truly were the neighbours from hell. In 'Piss' Hank tells how Jane came in drunk one evening and told him she had been unable to hold it and had pissed in the elevator. He went out to investigate, wearing only his shorts, and another couple came to the elevator as he was looking in; they naturally thought he was responsible. In another poem, 'Sloppy Love', he described how the receptionist called to say that Jane was lying in the elevator and refusing to move until he came to get her. She was using abusive language and had urinated over herself but they had not wanted to call the police. Hank went to get her. He would drag her into the room and pull off her wet clothing, put a drink on the coffee table and wait. Suddenly she would sit up straight and look around the room, wondering where she was, calling his name. She would see the drink and gulp it down.

Some of the rooms they shared were so cheap that they didn't have a hot plate so Hank and Jane had to run hot water in the sink and put cans of beans in to heat them up. They drank so much that they had a bottle problem. In order not to alert the hotel managers to the extent of their drinking they would hide them in neighbourhood trash cans, but even then the empties began to build up in their room. When they had dozens of carrier bags and paper sacks filled they would sneak out late at night and fill the car with them, then drive very slowly, clinking and clanking, south to the Baldwin Hills. They were terrified that the police might stop them as they naturally had a couple of open bottles with them as well. Hank would cut the headlights and they would drive through the forest of silent oil wells until they found a likely spot among the rocks and scrub, then they would rapidly throw the bottles out in a great cacophony of noise. To save on petrol, Hank would disengage the gears and they would glide silently back down the hill to the waiting city below.

Hank wrote many poems about Jane later, some reflective, such as 'My First Affair With That Older Woman', in which he looks back on the abuse he took from her and feels shame for being so innocent and allowing it to happen; it was the first time he had lived with someone. He realised that her life had been ruined somewhere along the way and she saw him as no more than a temporary companion, more of a drinking buddy than lover. Considering how much they drank, and how inexperienced Hank was, it is unlikely that he was a very good sex partner. He later wrote that he must have been a terrible lover because it was not until many years later that he learned – from Linda King – anything about foreplay and pleasing a woman. Before then his descriptions make it sound more like a container shipping operation: roll on – roll off.

Hank was a slow starter and, by the time he got good at something, everyone else had moved on. He began as the worst baseball player and became the best, but, by then, everyone else was getting ready to go to college. He was timid when young but became a tremendous brawler just when no one else wanted to fight. He secretly honed his skills, but always arrived late when these achievements no longer counted. He listed his useless skills as football, high-speed driving, drinking, gambling, clowning, debating, bullshitting, going to jail, going crazy, lifting weights and shadow boxing with fate. Those of his contemporaries who had survived the war all had jobs, mortgages, wives and children, life insurance, pet dogs, lawns – all the things that terrified him. He saw himself as a retarded child, still looking for playmates but they had all grown up. Though she was already a mature woman, Jane became his missing childhood playmate.

In pieces like 'Fire Station' he gives her a Betty Boop voice and portrays her as being like the dizzy blonde character Marilyn Monroe played so often. Bukowski's portraits of women are rarely three-dimensional so, despite the depths of his feelings towards her from his love poems, Jane herself remains strangely outside the myth. They used to drink together every night until two or three in the morning. She introduced him to a world of raucous adventure. She appears to have been a casual prostitute, thinking nothing of turning a trick to get enough money to buy more alcohol. Bukowski often referred to his girlfriends as 'whores' even if they were not, a habit picked up from his years with Jane. Many of her girlfriends seem to live the same life. There is a hilarious story about a yacht belonging to someone called Willie or Wilbur (Bukowski uses both) which occurred soon after Hank first met Jane, before he felt possessive enough of her to be jealous. He might even be the same person who enabled Jane to charge alcohol and supplies to his account at the liquor store.

Willie (or Wilbur) had three or four girls who hung out at his house for food and drink in return for sex. Jane brought Hank along to meet him because Willie was writing an opera called *The Emperor of San Francisco* and needed someone to help him with the libretto. The floor of the living room was covered with coins. He used to throw handfuls at the girls, saying that that was all they were worth. Hank began gathering them up but Jane advised him to leave some because they belonged to the girls.

In *Factotum* Hank reconstructed some of Willie's conversation. He was sitting on a stool at the wet bar in the living room and told Hank: 'The girls were up here the other night, and then somebody hollered RAID! You should have seen them running, some of them naked, some of them in panties and bras, they all ran out and hid in the garage. It was funny as hell. I sat up here and they came drifting back, one by one, from the garage. It was sure funny!'

'Who hollered 'RAID?' Hank asked.

'I did,' Willie said.

When Willie didn't have a hangover they would sometimes pile into his car and drive down to San Pedro where he kept his yacht. The car was so old it had a rumble seat. On one trip, Willie got annoyed by the girls and took off for three days, leaving Hank and four girls stranded on the yacht with plenty of booze and food. According to Hank, the only way to keep warm at night was for the girls to creep, one by one, into his sleeping bag and for him to fuck them in turn to heat them up. The story is repeated several times, which usually suggests there is some truth in it. Clearly he was beginning to make up for lost time.

Hank made three or four trips to the yacht but then Willie died and the girls were out on the street again.

Jane and Hank never knew where the rent was coming from and they were both too sick from drinking to look for work. 'Every time we worried, all we could do about our worries was fuck, that made us forget for a while. We fucked a lot.' And yet money always appeared from somewhere. One time Hank found a pile of 50-cent pieces on a seat in the row in front of him on the bus. He moved up a row and put them in his pocket. When his pockets were full he pulled the cord and got off at the next stop. No one tried to stop him or said anything. Another time he received a delayed income tax refund, then an uncle died and left him $300 in his will. Each day they would go to MacArthur Park and sit on a bench and watch the ducks on the lake. Once in a while one of the hotel people would catch a duck at night, kill it and take it to their room to cook. Hank and Jane thought about copying that but never did it, largely because the ducks were very hard to catch. Most of the time they ate small pancakes made out of flour and water. One of the neighbours had clumps of corn in his garden and they would sneak out at night and steal an armful of cobs.

One morning Hank awoke with one of the worst hangovers he had ever had: 'like a steel band around my head'. Jane was already in the bathroom throwing up and Hank was sitting at the open window, trying to get some air. Suddenly a man fell past the window, standing upright, fully dressed with his necktie neatly knotted. 'He seemed to be going in slow motion. A body doesn't fall very fast.' He called to Jane to come and see but she thought he was making a joke. When Hank insisted that he wasn't trying to be funny, she put her head out of the window and looked down.

'Oh God almighty!' Jane gasped and just made it back to the bathroom in time before she threw up again. Bukowski: 'He plopped right apart like an old tomato! We are just made of guts and shit and slimy stuff!' Hank went to the refrigerator and got a beer. His headache felt better.

During this time, Hank was storing up raw material in buckets for the future. He told Fernanda Pivano: 'I was doing much more drinking then. And I knew I wasn't quite ready to be a writer then; I hadn't lived enough.' One day, while he was having coffee at a counter, a man three or four stools down asked him if he was the guy who was hanging from his heels from the fourth floor window of the hotel the other night. Yes, Hank said, it was him. Years later he got a poem 'Coffee' out of it.

On Monday mornings, after a weekend of revels, Hank usually found that he was unable to make it into work even though the rent was often due and they frequently had no money for food. At about 11.30 he would struggle into his clothes and go out into the street and look through trash cans until he found the Sunday papers, unless he had gathered some in on Sunday night. He would bring them back to the room and they would sit in bed, reading the funnies, the world news, the entertainment section, the travel section. Talking, laughing, drinking, coughing and spitting: they reinforced each other, he was soon as cynical as she was. Then they would hit the streets; while everyone else worked they would visit friends. They always knew someone who would have a drink, they would tell stories and laugh and laugh. 'We were very close to freedom.'

Somehow they always found money for cheap wine and rent. They barricaded themselves against the other roomers and on one occasion the police. The other residents hated them for their noise and fighting and late night screams and the receptionist was scared of Bukowski's threatening looks and stature. 'and it went on/and/on/and it was one of the/most wonderful times/of my/life.'

This period is the source of many of Bukowski's finest lowlife images: of throwing his shoe and smashing the window at 3 a.m. and sticking his head through the jagged shards of glass and screaming with laughter as the phone rings; the landlady demanding that he be quiet. The whiskey roaring through his blood made him invincible.

He was quick to identify iconic details and store them for later use. He recognised the alienation of the Los Angeles landscape; the brilliantly lit empty residential streets at night fanning out before you at each compass point. It was where Hank felt most at home: 'Los Angeles, the only city in the world . . . It was my town . . . I almost loved it.' One of their rooms was downtown, near Union Station, with a good view of a red Mobil sign; a winged horse that flew in red neon on the side of a building to the east of Hank and Jane's building. All night it flew, flapping its red neon wings. They would count the flaps; when it reached seven it would stop and the horse froze. Their whole apartment was lit in the red glow of the sign. In the brief moment before the horse began another sequence, their apartment was lit by a white flash from an advertisement beneath the red horse. Then the horse would start flapping its wings all over again. It was an image that Hank later used in the *Barfly* movie.

The police visited them in this same room. It was 3 a.m. and Hank was pacing up and down the room barefoot, as usual, picking up bits of broken glass in his feet, filled with artificial confidence, proclaiming to Jane 'I'm a genius and nobody knows it but me!!' while Jane slumped in her chair told him 'Shit! You're a fucking asshole!' and the receptionist called to say there were complaints from the other guests. Jane grabbed the phone and told the receptionist: 'I'm a fucking genius too and I'm the only whore who knows it!' Then Hank and Jane put the chain on the door, and together pushed the settee in front of the door, turned out the lights and sat on the bed and waited for the police to arrive. They each had a chair, either side of the bed, and on each chair was an ashtray, cigarettes and wine. The police pounded on the door with their night-sticks and yelled so that anyone who had not been disturbed by Hank and Jane was now fully awake, but as the landlord didn't want his door reduced to matchwood he forbade the cops from breaking the door down. Hank and Jane sat in silence, watching the red Mobil sign.

There is a story which Bukowski told several times, including in *Factotum*, of looking for Jane after an argument and finding her in a bar on Sixth Street near Alvarado. She was sitting between two men, flirting with them. He hadn't objected before when she turned tricks to provide the money for booze but this time he was angry. He marched along the bar:

> I walked up behind her, standing near her stool. 'I tried to make a woman out of you but you'll never be anything but a god damned whore!' I back-handed her and knocked her off her stool. She fell flat on the floor and screamed. I picked up her drink and finished it. Then I slowly walked toward the exit. When I got there I turned. 'Now, if there's anybody here . . . who doesn't *like* what I just did . . . just say so.' There was no response.

Even allowing for the macho prose, inspired largely by novelist Mickey Spillane rather than his usual high-minded literary influences, this suggests that the cause of their frequent arguments, and ultimately of his physical violence, was sexual jealousy. Hank's jealousy played a major role in every relationship he ever had and we know that with most of his later women friends the infidelities were almost always imaginary. With Jane, however, his paranoia seems rooted in fact; she was casually promiscuous, and he found it very difficult to handle. She caused him a great deal of pain.

There is little other evidence of physical abuse. Hank specialised in verbal putdowns, but there are a few stories of violence against women that seem grounded in reality. This is the theme of 'Chickens': first he lifts the foldaway Murphy bed back up into the wall with his woman in it, then he slaps her across the mouth and breaks her false teeth. Hank often took his stories from the experiences of his friends and acquaintances so there is no indication that he was responsible for this piece of abuse. He remained unreconstructed all his life, however, violence against women was something he very much disapproved of and he told several different interviewers that there were only one or two incidences of it in his life. If so, this was remarkable given his lifestyle and propensity to drunken rages.

The key seems to be that he did not know how to deal with his feelings of jealousy because he had always been unable to express his love; the power of his feelings towards women scared him. He looked for ways to negate them, sometimes resorting to extreme measures, at least in fantasy. Perhaps the answer is embodied in his castration complex poems. In 'Freedom' the events leading up to the fantasy appear to be very factually based though the castration itself is obviously not. Here he describes how Jane was out again when he came home from work, how he drank wine all night, the night of the 28th – the poem is that specific, though he does not give the month or year – and describes his torment, of how he kept thinking of her, of how he knew the colour of each of her dresses and her shoes, of how he knew the wear and curve of each heel and every detail of her legs – he was especially fond of Jane's legs and mentioned them often – of the way she walked and talked and made love and the way she told him such convincing lies. He waits, the hours drag by, until she returns at 3 a.m. in the morning 'with the special stink again', wearing her yellow dress, his favourite.

In the poem he takes out a butcher's knife and she screams and backs up against the rooming-house wall: 'still pretty somehow/in spite of love's reek', and he finishes his glass of wine before cutting off his balls which he proceeds to flush down the toilet.

Castration was the theme in at least two stories: 'No Way to Paradise' where Anna castrates George so that no other woman can have him, and another where a man castrates himself so that his wife will not have power over him sexually. It is also the subject of the poem 'True story' in *Burning in Water*, about a man found walking down the freeway having severed his penis and put it in his pocket. Bukowski:

> I've been wondering about this castration complex of mine. I've written a couple of poems about it too. I just thought of it the other day. I said, 'What am I about here? What does this mean?' I really don't know, unless … I think it's more symbolic than actual. In other words it's … at times we all try to figure ways to escape the female and the power she has over us. I would never take that route; it's probably a symbolic gesture though. It's the only thing I could think of at those moments, you see, of frustration and panic and dominance and loss. It just happens to my characters. I can't figure it; I can't figure the meaning of it.

There is a well-documented example of domestic violence against him that he used in *Barfly*. After an argument, Jane stalked out of the door, which he held open wide for her like a doorman. She turned and stood facing him. He started to close the door as she raised her purse over her head. 'You rotten son of a bitch!' she screamed. He saw the trajectory of the purse, but he stood with a calm smile on his face. He had been in some tough fights so a handbag was not something to cause him worry. Jane's purse was full, and in the front corner, the part that hit him, was a white cold-cream jar. It was like being hit with a rock. His legs folded, and as he sank to the ground she had more leverage for the top of the head. She was furious and pounded him, faster and faster as if she was trying to crack his skull. It was his third knockout but his first by a woman. He woke up to find the door closed. He was alone, lying in a deep puddle of his own blood. He found some whiskey and poured it over the wound. They were on the fourth floor and as he sipped the whiskey he began to throw Jane's clothes down into the vacant lot next door. The next morning he went out to gather them up but they were gone; a neighbour had collected them for the Salvation Army but fortunately they had not yet collected the carton.

Clearly it was impossible to live in Los Angeles for very long without working, and so Hank took a series of dead-end jobs, which he then used as the basis for stories and poems. There was Milliron's Dept Store at 5th and Broadway, then there was the Sunbeam Lighting Co. at 777 East 14th Place, between San Pedro and Central. Hank told the post office that he worked here for more than two years, starting in January 1949, but it is doubtful he survived that long with his absentee record. At Sunbeam Hank was one of only two white men among a staff of 150. His job was to wrap and tape up the fluorescent lighting fixtures as they came off the line. They quickly cut his thick gloves to pieces with their sharp edges and after that they sliced into his hands. The other workers watched him, waiting for him to give up. One day something snapped and he suddenly screamed aloud the name of the firm they were all slaving for: 'Sunbeam!!' The girls on the assembly line cracked up. Then he yelled it again, and they laughed again. Then one of the girls yelled it, and they all laughed. It was a great release. Someone on the line yelled and there was more laughter. Then the foreman came in and broke it all up. But it stayed in Hank's head for forty years, until he wrote it down in the poem 'Sunbeam'.

Hank worked for a Christmas decoration company as a warehouseman, loading and unloading trucks, but it was a temporary job as there was no business after Thanksgiving. He worked in hotels and was fired from one for drunkenness and for holding the assistant manager captive in the men's room for half an hour, something he had no memory of doing and no explanation for. When they were really desperate he went to the Farm Labor Market at Fifth and San Pedro where you reported at 5 a.m. for back-breaking jobs picking fruit or vegetables. Despite the diatribes about being a misanthrope, about hating humanity, Bukowski had a tremendous empathy for the plight of working people. He sympathised with and cherished them, using terms which in Europe would be regarded as left wing: 'there are men out there now/ picking tomatoes, lettuce, even cotton,/there are men and women dying under the sun,/there are men and women dying in factories,/ for nothing, a pittance . . ./I can hear the sound of human lives being ripped to/pieces . . .'

Early in his relationship with Jane, they lived at the Beacon Street Hotel, next to a housing development where they had a ground-floor room and were plagued by the local children. He was hampered in his ability to get a job by his alarm clock, on which the spring was broken. He shortened it and reattached it; this made the clock run at three times normal speed, so they never knew what the time was. It was possible to calculate the time by knowing when it was last set accurately, just the thing for a pair of drunks to ponder over and laugh about. One morning he set the alarm for 5.30 a.m. to go to the Farm Labor Market. Cotton-pickers were wanted in Bakersfield, with food and lodging provided. A number of labourers got on the back of a truck and Hank stood politely aside to let the ladies on before him. When his turn came, the Mexican foreman slammed the tailgate up and drove off, leaving him behind. It took him an hour to walk back to the hotel.

In one version of the story, when he got home Jane had been joined by two of her girlfriends and a drinks party was in progress. As the day and evening progressed Hank managed to have sex with all three without the others knowing because they had passed out from alcohol. As with many of Hank's stories, it sounds like pure fantasy until small references to the same incident in several poems and letters suggest a basis in reality.

Hank had certainly found his long-sought playmate. Jane had no intention of settling down; she lived to drink and party. One time in 1953 Jane had been gone for two or three days. Then the door of the rooming house opened and there she was. 'Just leave before I throw you through the wall,' yelled Hank. 'Now don't get nasty,' she said, and explained that one of her friends, a hooker, had just found the ultimate john. He set her up in a room, gave her a fifty dollar bill and a fifth of scotch. 'Let's go,' said Hank. Jane's friend had the radio tuned to a country station and was flipping through a copy of *Life*. She had an enormous smile on her face, she had never been paid fifty dollars for a trick before and was very proud of herself. She produced paper cups and began pouring the scotch. The man had sent his chauffeur over to pick her up and take her to his mansion. All she had to do was suck off his wife while the chauffeur took photographs. His wife was fat. 'This is great whiskey,' Jane said.

Like many drunks, Hank and Jane enjoyed a singsong while inebriated. In *Factotum* and elsewhere he lists the songs that he and his various girlfriends sang, to the distress of their neighbours who apparently rarely complained about their fights, but did about their singing: 'If I'd Known You Were Coming I'd a Baked a Cake'; 'How the Hell You Gonna Keep Them Down on the Farm'; 'I Want a Gal Just Like the Gal Who Married Dear Old Dad'; 'Poor Little Lambs Gone Astray'; 'I Married an Angel'; 'A Tiskit a Tasket'; 'When the Deep Purple Falls'; 'Who's Afraid of the Big Bad Wolf'; 'No More Money in the Bank'; 'Keep Your Sunny Side Up'; 'I Get the Blues When It Rains'; 'Bonaparte's Retreat'; 'Tumbling Along with the Tumbling Tumbleweeds'; 'Buttons and Bows'; 'Old Man River'; 'I Got Plenty of Nothing'; and, a sure hit with the neighbours: renditions of 'God Bless America' and 'Deutschland über Alles'.

In 1950 Hank took a temporary job at the post office for the two-week Christmas season. Eighteen months later, in March 1952, he took a job as a postman delivering letters for $1.61 an hour. At first he was a substitute postal carrier, which meant that, after closing the bars at 2 a.m. with Jane, he had to be sitting with the other subs on the little ledge outside the magazine cases at 5.30 a.m. When he did get a round his tiredness and hangover made him dizzy and sick as he dragged the sack around, the sweat running down his face and beneath his armpits. In *Post Office* he wrote about the old ladies who stood in the street asking if he had anything for them, as if he should know who they were; the attack dogs and dangerous neighbourhoods, the punishing schedules presided over by vindictive and sadistic supervisors, the pointless bureaucracy of the US Post Office which was structured as any other government department.

In April 1951 Hank and Jane took an apartment at 268 South Coronado on the 2nd floor. The woman downstairs worked in her garden wearing a bathing suit, something guaranteed to get Hank's attention. It was here that Hank used to get drunk and throw the radio through the closed window. The window would shatter and the radio would land on the roof below, still playing. Hank would tell Jane: 'What a marvellous radio!' Next day he would take the window off its hinges and take it to the glass repair shop. Other versions of the story suggest it is a bottle that goes through the window on a weekly basis. At any rate, the window really did need fixing regularly. Each week he would take the fitting down to the hardware store at the corner and get a pane of glass put in. The man who worked there looked at him very strangely but he always took Hank's money.

Jane got a job as a typist so, when Hank got up around 10.30 a.m., he had the house to himself. He played with the new dog that Jane had bought, entertained the striptease artist who lived in front and flirted with the wife of the mechanic who lived in the back. The arguments with Jane got fiercer and clearly more traumatic. He probably felt more for her than she did for him; she had already had numerous boyfriends, been married and had children and, though she stayed with Hank for many years, it sounds as if it was more of a convenient arrangement with a friend and fellow-drinker than a deep love affair for her. Considering how much he was drinking, their sex life must have been virtually non-existent; the fun came from getting roaring drunk together. They remained in Westlake for years, close to the lake and palms of MacArthur Park, moving from apartment to apartment: 521 South Union Drive; 503 South Union Drive; 334 South Westlake; 268 4/6 South Coronado St; 2325 Ocean View Ave; 323 1/2 North Westmoreland. In 1954 they were evicted from the Aragon apartment building at 334 South West Lake Avenue where their notice to quit was for: 'excessive drinking, fighting and foul language, disturbing other tenants', so they were clearly still going strong. Bukowski's mood was fluctuating from drunken glee to suicidal depression and he does seem to have made one or two half-hearted attempts on his own life during this period.

Hank lived with Jane for seven years. His parents hated her and he hated them, as he always had, but nonetheless they socialised, which again suggests that his professed antipathy to his parents was not as extreme as he claimed. One day they went on a picnic together in the Hollywood Hills where they sat and played cards and drank beer with potato salad and weenies. He was surprised because his parents talked to Jane as if she were a real person instead of the usual dismissive joking and laughing. Later Hank told Jane that he was glad they were finally treating her with some respect. Jane called him a damned fool: 'Don't you see? They keep looking at my beer belly. They think I'm pregnant.'

Jane seems to have regarded Hank almost as a son, she wanted to put him through college but she was restless, always wanting to move on. She left often but always came back. She needed a place to hang her clothes, and she said that Hank was funny and made her laugh, though he was not being intentionally funny. He first knew heartache with Jane, returning from his two-mile walk home from work, turning the corner into the alley and looking up at the window to find it dark.

Hank's health was beginning to break down, he was now 35 years old and had abused his body terribly. There had been warnings of something wrong, terrible stabbing pains in his stomach, but he had ignored them. His image of himself was of a tough guy, a bit of pain was just bad luck, something to ignore and get over: 'I just poured whiskey on top of the pain and went about my business. My business was getting drunk.'

One morning in the spring of 1955, he jolted awake to find blood streaming from his mouth and ass: 'Black turds. Blood, blood, waterfalls of blood. Blood stinks worse than shit.' Jane called a doctor and an ambulance. The ambulance attendants told him he was too big for them to carry down the stairs and asked him to walk down. He staggered down with their help and, once outside, they popped open the stretcher and he climbed on. The neighbours had their heads out of the windows and were standing gawping on their steps as he went by. He let go a mouthful of blood over the side of the stretcher and they all gasped. The ambulance stacked patients in tiers and Hank was on the top, bleeding onto the people below. Hank had no medical insurance and so he was taken to the charity ward of Los Angeles General, where he had spent so much time as a child having his boils lanced.

On an examination table they began asking questions: his religion, place of birth, were his parents alive, was he married and, most important, did he owe the county any money from previous treatment? He was taken to a dark basement along with four or five other people and given something in a glass of water. One of the men was drunk and seemed insane to Hank, who grabbed a water pitcher, ready to hit him, but the man never came near him. Hank was kept in the basement room all night and until noon the next day when he was transferred to an upstairs ward.

The second night he tried to get to the bathroom but didn't make it. He threw up blood all over the floor, he fell down and was too weak from loss of blood to get up. He called for a nurse, but the doors were covered with a thick layer of soundproof tin and they didn't hear. They checked the wards every two hours to see if anybody had died. When he regained consciousness he was surrounded by lights and two nurses were trying to get him upright. 'I couldn't talk. Drums were in my head. I felt hollowed out. It seemed as if I could hear everything, but I couldn't see, only flares of light, it seemed. But no panic, fear; only a sense of waiting.' They eventually managed to get him into a chair and slid him along the floor. Suddenly he was surrounded by people. An angry doctor in a green operating gown was yelling at the head nurse: 'Why hasn't this man had a transfusion?' It seemed that Hank didn't have any blood credits. In America health care was and is only available to the wealthy.

'I want some blood up here and I want it now!' yelled the doctor. They began feeding him blood: nine pints of blood and eight of glucose in all. After his first bottle of blood they took him to the X-ray room and asked him to stand for them to take the pictures but he was so weak that he kept falling over and ruining their film. After two failed attempts they angrily sent him back to the ward for more blood. A nurse appeared with a meal of roast beef, potatoes, peas and carrots. He told her it would kill him if he ate that. 'Eat it,' she demanded. 'It's on your list.' He left it. Five minutes later she came running back into the ward screaming, 'Don't eat that! There's been a mistake!' She gave him the glass of milk he'd been asking for all along. Being in the charity ward was apparently almost as dangerous as being on the streets.

He was moved to the terminally ill ward, a special place for the poor and dying with doors that were thicker and windows that were smaller than the normal wards. In addition to the nurses, there was a priest there to administer last rites. The priest was around all the time but they seldom saw a doctor. The priest kept pestering him because he had listed his religion as Catholic on the admission form. 'That was just to be social,' Bukowski claimed.

'My son, once a Catholic, always a Catholic,' the priest told him.

'That's not true,' Hank said. 'Father, no offence, but please, I'd like to die without any rites, without any words.' The priest was so shocked that he swayed and rocked on his feet in disbelief.

Patients in the ward who died in the night were rolled in their beds straight to the morgue elevator. Hank described the elevator as being very busy and that in the course of a night three or four corpses were taken into it. The most he witnessed was eight in one night as he lay there, trying to sleep.

Then suddenly he was transferred back to the wards. The black homosexual orderly who pushed his gurney through the corridors asked him: 'You know the odds of coming out of that ward? Fifty to one,' the man told him. Hank asked him if he had a cigarette. He said he'd get him some.

The worst thing that happened in the main ward was the Salvation Army Band right there in the ward that woke everyone up at 5.30 a.m. on Easter morning by playing religious music badly and loudly. Hank joked that of the forty or so in the ward, the Salvation Army killed ten or fifteen of them before 6 a.m. and said that he felt as close to death that morning as he had ever felt, thanks to them.

The best thing about the ward, however, was the two Mexican nurses who giggled and joked and flirted with the patients as they changed the sheets. One of them pointed at him and said: 'I'll take this one and you take that one and we'll make them well and then we'll all shack-up together!' He began feeling better right away. The Mexican nurse clearly had a profound impact on his mood because he wrote about her two or three times.

One day Henry showed up with Jane who was completely drunk; her face red and puffy, she reeled against the bed a few times but was so out of it she could not speak. Hank's paranoia naturally made him assume that his father had deliberately given her money so that he could bring her before him drunk to make him unhappy. 'Why did you bring her like that?' he asked. 'Why didn't you wait until another day?'

'I told you she was no good! I always told you she was no good!' yelled Henry

'You son of a bitch, one more word out of you and I'm going to take this needle out of my arm and get up and whip the shit out of you!' Henry took Jane's arm and managed to steer her out of the ward.

When Hank was discharged, he took the bus home. They were living at 334 South West Lake Avenue; a long block from the park. He climbed the steps to the walkway leading to his doorway on the upper court and stood in front of his door for a while, feeling the sun on his arms. He told Robert Wennersten: 'When I walked out of that place, I felt very strange. I felt much calmer than before. I felt – to use a trite term – easygoing. I walked along the sidewalk, and I looked at the sunshine and said, "Hey, something has happened." You know, I'd lost a lot of blood. Maybe there was some brain damage. That was my thought, because I had a really different feeling. I had this calm feeling. I talk so slowly now. I wasn't always this way. I was kind of hectic before; I was more going, doing, shooting my mouth off. When I came out of that hospital, I was strangely relaxed.'

He found his key, opened the door and climbed the stairs to his room. In 'Reunion' he has Jane (here called Madge) sitting on the couch, wearing an old green silk dress, drinking a glass of port with ice. He asks if there's anyone in the bedroom, which she dismisses with 'Don't be silly', and asks him if he wants a drink. Hank tells her that the doctors have told him not to, and that he has to eat only items on his list, things like boiled chicken and soft-boiled eggs. He asks how much money is left. Fifteen dollars she tells him. 'You spent it fast.' He asks how much time is left on the rent. Two weeks.

Then he asks where his car is. She loaned it to someone who crashed the front and it was in the corner garage but it still ran. Hank said that as long as the radiator worked and the lights then it was OK to drive. He emptied her purse. In addition to the $15 she told him about there was a $5 bill and a single dollar bill that she was keeping back. The garage was just round the corner. They had a new grille installed and the bill was $75. Hank explained that the whole car wasn't worth that, that he was just out of hospital, and the only way they might get their money was if they gave him the car so that he could look for a job. He gave them $5. In the story he then buys two six-packs of Millers in bottles, a pack of Pall Malls and two Dutch Masters on the way back. He goes in, drains a beer, then drains her wine glass before dragging her into bed. He ends the story with an account of his finances: he has $13.75 plus two six-packs, two cigars and a pack of cigarettes; he owes the LA County General Hospital $225, the Japanese guy at the garage $70 and a few utility bills. He had two weeks on the rent and no job. The financial details are probably true.

This story is a powerful part of the Bukowski myth. He told journalist Silvia Bizio: 'I got out of the hospital – they had told me never to have a drink again or I was going to die – and the first place I went was to a bar and had a beer. No, two beers.' It is a story he told again and again; and it was just that: a story, a romantic exaggeration. He himself contradicted it in several of the many versions, the most reliable dating back to 1962, before he was consciously creating a public persona. He told publisher Jon Webb that six days after leaving hospital he returned to his job at the post office, driving the mail truck, lifting 50-pound packages and mail sacks and wondering if the blood would come again. And it was a couple of days after that he had his first drink. He mixed a little wine into a glass of milk, then tried it again with very little milk, but it was a tentative experiment, he did not want the bleeding to begin again. In *South of No North* he says that the first drink was a week after he began driving the mail truck.

A huge part of Hank's life had revolved around alcohol but while he was still on the wagon, before he experimented with wine and milk, he he asked Jane: 'What the hell am I going to do now?'

'We'll play the horses,' she told him.

'Horses?'

'Yeah, they run and you bet on them.'

She had found some money on the boulevard, as he put it, and so she took him to the track. He had three winners, and one of them paid over fifty dollars. It seemed very easy money to Hank. They went a second time and he won again. He was hooked. It was that night he decided that if he mixed some wine with milk that it might not hurt him. There were no races on Sundays in those days so Hank would nurse the old car down to Agua Caliente and back. He was always treated kindly by Mexican bartenders and never had any problems even though he was sometimes the only gringo in the bar.

The 50s were the good old days for the racetrack, jam-packed with people, sweating, shouting, screaming as the horses thundered past, pushing and jostling towards the overcrowded bars. There were crap games in the parking lots, fist fights, between 50,000 and 60,000 people at weekends, all determined to have a day out, to have a good time. Hank remembered it in *The Captain*: 'Bravado and glory. Electricity. Hell, life was good, life was funny. All us guys were men, we'd take no shit from anybody. And, frankly, it felt good.'

Horse racing has always belonged to that fringe category in American life where upper and lower classes mix to the exclusion of middle-class moralists. This is 'the sporting life', a wide category, based around hedonistic enjoyment that includes not only race-tracks, bookies and gambling outfits, but after-hours drinking and gambling joints, private stag shows and orgies, strip shows, floating poker and crap games, bars where prostitutes operate and illegal drinking places. When Bukowski was first on the scene, the list would have also included poolrooms and whorehouses, burlesque shows and possibly even opium dens. They were all places of heavy drinking, gambling and whoring, three main themes in Bukowski's work. These are closed areas; you need specialised knowledge to operate there. At the racetrack there was usually one race a day that was fixed – 'One for the boys' – but that still left eight that were more or less legitimate; the trick was to either have inside knowledge on the fixed race, or at least know which one it was in order not to bet on it, as the results were apt to be unexpected. Bukowski was a sporting man: 'Horse racing does something to you. It's like drinking: it joggles you out of the ordinary concept of things. Like Hemingway used the bullring, I use the racetrack. Of course, when you go to the track every day, that's no damned joggle: it's a definite bring-down.'

Hemingway did not just write about the bullring, he also wrote many short stories about the racetrack when he was in Paris with his wife Hadley in the 20s, but all of them, with the exception of 'Out of Season', were lost when Hadley's suitcase containing both the manuscripts and carbon copies was stolen in the Gare de Lyon. Had Hemingway's stories survived, then maybe Bukowski would not have written about the track. Had Hemingway not gone to the track, then Bukowski might not have gone either, it seems to have been just a way of filling in time. Bukowski: 'I didn't give a fuck about the horses; they looked nice and shit a straw flat sort of shit, that's all I knew. I went to the tracks to try and get out of the factories, out of the US Post Office. I went to the tracks as a chance of life.' The majority of his many poems about the track are not about horses, or even gambling, so much as about the people observed there.

Bukowski's near escape from death was a transcendent experience for him. Without it he would probably never have written again, but he emerged, reborn, blinking into the sunlight, knowing himself to be a changed person. His memory which was once good was now bad, probably caused by brain damage; he had lain there for two days in desperate need of blood, hammers pounding against his brain. He now spoke in the painfully slow Californian drawl that is familiar to fans from his many recordings. He felt old, somehow different.

A week or so after getting out of the hospital he bought himself a used typewriter and began writing again: 'I found my fingers making the poem. Or rather the bar-talk. The non-lyrical, non-singing thing . . .' This description was actually a paraphrase of a critical remark by one of Hank's friends who told him: 'You do not understand the true meaning of poetry. You are not lyrical. You do not *sing*! You write bar talk. The type of thing you write you can hear in any bar on any day.' He was writing from experience, most of which had been in bars. With his grounding in 20s High Modernism, in William Carlos Williams' notion: 'No ideas but in things' he did believe, to quote Williams, that 'Art can be made of anything,' and, as Williams constantly demanded, that American poetry should be the voice of the American streets, with the raw cadences, the phrasing and delivery of the working people, not the aristocratic voice of English intellectuals. 'The American idiom' Williams called it. Williams himself never delivered this, but Bukowski did.

It is a style fraught with danger; as Raymond Chandler, one of its greatest practitioners put it: 'American is an ill-at-ease language, without manner or self control. It has too great a fondness for the faux naïf, by which I mean the use of a style such as might be spoken by a very limited sort of mind. In the hands of a genius like Hemingway this may be effective . . . When not used by a genius it is as flat as a Rotarian speech.'

In his ten years of study, Bukowski had internalised the shape and rhythm of American language, and now it came pouring out of him, almost effortlessly. 'Once I sit there, there's no planning, there's no effort, there's no labour. It's almost like the typer does it by itself. You get in a kind of trancelike state . . . [the words] come out sometimes like blood, sometimes like wine.' It is a familiar condition, once described by Allen Ginsberg as a case where 'The typewriter imagination tells the writer what to write.'

Artists and writers are all familiar with the semi-trance state, half-sleeping, half-conscious, where the mind is not quite under control and memories and fantasies can reach consciousness. It is a warm comfortable place, free from self-censorship and good behaviour. It is a door to the unconscious mind and fertile ground for artistic production. As Leon Trotsky, in his role as a political philosopher, said: 'The creative union of the conscious with the unconscious is what one usually calls "inspiration".' It is a well-documented phenomenon: a state that artists often retreat to while painting, or the drowsy half-consciousness that John Lennon and Paul McCartney put themselves in to write a song. Here all the experiences of previous years were gathered, waiting to be used.

Hank is the protagonist in virtually all of his writing, he shapes his experiences into a text, his thought and actions modified for clarity so that the chaos becomes order. Though he was mostly writing poetry, he was working in the field of autobiographical fiction where thinly disguised private life is presented as public life. It was the modernism of Ernest Hemingway, John Fante, F Scott Fitzgerald, Marcel Proust, e.e. cummings, L-F Céline and Henry Miller that he now raided and made his own. Bukowski: 'So I was writing again and had all these poems on my hands. I started mailing them out. I was luckier this time, and I think my work had improved.'

Hank was upset that Jane had damaged the car when he was in hospital. It was his first. He had bought it for $35; it had no suspension or reverse gear and in order to get the headlights to work he had to hit a hard bump in the road. He had to park it on the hill in order to get a rolling start. It ran for two years without him ever changing the oil and when it finally died he just left it and walked away. He learned little tricks to keep it alive: taping up loose wires, cleaning the spark plugs, keeping the radiator topped up. Some of the time he was with Jane he ran two cars, both of them wrecks, so that if one didn't go, he had a fall back.

The drinking and the fights continued, sometimes getting out of hand. When it came, the break-up with Jane seems to have been an almost casual affair. She told him she'd had enough; he packed up and left. He took the first room with a For Rent sign. They seem to have tried getting together again. One time at a hotel on 6th Street, he sat waiting for her, drinking wine with the lights turned off. Jane called to say she would be along in a little while and to wait for her. When the bottle was empty he took the lift downstairs and went to the store to buy another. When he came back he asked the receptionist if there were any messages. He looked at him as if he were crazy. He was halfway through the second bottle when she called again. 'I'll be there real soon,' she told him. He sat in the dark and finished the bottle. Then he took the lift down and walked half a block, took a left and walked to the bar. Through the blinds he could see her sitting at the bar, smoking and drinking, talking to an old man in a grey wrinkled suit. He went to his car and drove away. He ran into her a couple of weeks later. 'Gee, Hank, what happened? I went to that room and there was nobody there.' She knew it was over.

In 1965 Bukowski told fellow poet William Wantling: 'I only loved one woman and, unlike all the others, she was the only one who never demanded or asked for the spoken word of it. And even over her grave I said nothing, not even in my head, but the sunlight knew and my shoelaces and [illegible].'

5. WRITING AGAIN

In May 1955, Hank took a job with Supreme Lighting Co. at 600 East Turner Street between Alameda Street off Santa Fe Avenue, processing orders for light fixtures. In his poem 'Sparks' he describes it as being the best job he ever had. He worked a ten-hour day, four hours on Saturday, at union rates, which was good for unskilled labour. There were not many whites on the job; they weren't strong enough to flip the heavy fixtures and didn't last long. Most of the workers were blacks or Mexicans. They wore white T-shirts and jeans, smoked cigarettes out of the side of their mouths and sneaked beers while the management looked the other way. Hank liked the camaraderie, the sound of drills and cutting blades and the sparks flying.

One day the old wooden racks that held the light tubes pulled away from the filthy peeling wall and came tumbling down on the concrete floor in a tremendous crash of broken glass. Hank and the other workers lashed them together again in an even more precarious manner. In the poem 'Yankee Doodle' he describes how an Irish worker who had been there for years, whistled the same tune all day: 'Yankee Doodle Dandy'. Hank began whistling it right along with him, hoping to provoke him; the Irishman counting out screws and Hank packing eight-foot-long fluorescent lamps into long shipping boxes. They piled the boxes into stacks six high, then the loaders would come and clear his table and he and the Irishman would start on the next six. It was only after the man became sick and retired that Hank realised that he had not hated him for his whistling along with him; it was Hank who had done all the hating.

Meanwhile, poems poured out of him. With Jane not there to talk to, he sat at the typewriter every night, writing poems and stories, smoking cheap cigars, drinking a little more each week but still afraid that it might provoke another haemorrhage, feeling very pale and weak, but not lonely. He always valued solitude. He quickly found himself with a pile of fifty or so poems and wondered what to do with them. It was just like the old days. He looked in *Trace* magazine for addresses of literary magazines. A magazine called *The Naked Ear* took one, *Quixote* took two. There was a magazine called *Harlequin* down in Wheeler, Texas, edited by Barbara Frye that was asking for poems and he decided to send her some. As he told it: 'I might as well send them and *insult* somebody. . . This is probably an old woman – she doesn't like dirty words or this type of poetry, you know. She probably likes rhymes and lives in a little rosy hut with canaries – I think I'll wake her up and see what happens.' He dropped a big packet of poems in the mail and received a letter back telling him he was a genius. 'And they published forty of them . . . We corresponded back and forth. We finally met, got married, and *then* I found out when we went to her home town that, uh, she *owned* the place.' It was a classic Bukowski story, and, as with many, mostly pure fiction. Barbara Frye was from a quite wealthy family but was hardly a millionaire. Also, it appears that *Harlequin* didn't publish anything by Bukowski until long after they married. Dorbin's usually authoritative bibliography only lists one issue of *Harlequin*: volume two, number one, printed eight poems and three short stories by Hank but that was dated 1957 and by then he was co-editing the magazine with his wife.

Barbara Frye, called Joyce in *Post Office*, was only 23 – born 6 January 1932 – eleven years younger than Hank, and was brought up by her grandparents after her parents divorced when she was two years old. She was born with two vertebrae missing from her neck and a slight spinal curvature which meant she was unable to turn her head, which appeared to sit directly upon her shoulders. In the course of her correspondence with Hank, she complained that her deformity meant that no man would ever marry her. As they continued to exchange letters, a certain intimacy developed so that one night, while drunk, he responded to one of her letters about being left on the shelf by telling her to relax, he would marry her. He mailed the letter and forgot about it, but Barbara didn't and she took him at his word. They exchanged photographs. She sent some of herself that made her look attractive, but after Hank told her he would marry her, she sent him some which showed the extent of her physical problem; it was noticeable but that was about all. According to Hank he studied the photographs and got really drunk. He was terrified, wondering what he had done. He had given his word so it was a matter of honour to go through with it, but he got on his knees in the centre of the rug and said, 'I hereby sacrifice myself. If a man can make just one person happy in a lifetime, then his life has been justified.' He would look at one of the photographs and his 'whole soul would shake and scream' and he would throw up a whole can of beer.

Their literary romance seems to have been like the internet romances of the present day. She was lonely for a man and Hank was on the rebound from his relationship with Jane and looking for a companion. She gave up her job in the county clerk's office and took the bus to Los Angeles. Hank met her at the bus depot. He sat there, half-drunk, waiting for a woman he had not even spoken to on the phone but whom he had promised to marry. What had he got himself into now? He felt he must be insane, a madman that should not be allowed out on the streets. Her bus was called and he watched the people get off: 'Here comes this cute sexy blonde on high heels, all ass and bounce and young. Young, 23, and the neck wasn't bad at all. Could that be the one?'

She wouldn't go to bed with him until they were married so they got some sleep and the next day, 29 October 1955, drove all the way to Las Vegas and back without sleep. Bukowski's biographer Howard Sounes reports that the first time they had sex, Hank struggled and struggled and concluded that she was too big for him, but the next morning, when he spoke about it, she told him he hadn't even penetrated her. She had assumed it was a new way of doing it. He knew so little about sex, and was so inexperienced – Barbara was possibly only the third woman he had taken to bed – that he hadn't realised that he was not in her. (This further contradicts the stories of whores and wild orgies with Jane's friends.) By Hank's own accounts, however, their sex life was dynamic to the point of exhaustion. Barbara had told him she was a nymphomaniac and, after the third or fourth round, he believed her. This is a recurring point in his writing and interviews, and in his *Open City* column he complained that he had to have sex with her 'seven or eight or nine or eleven times' a week.

Shortly after their marriage, Hank gave up his job at Supreme Lighting and they made a trip to her hometown, though, strangely, she picked a time when her grandparents, whom she referred to as 'Mom and Dad', were away. This suggests that there was considerable family opposition to her marriage. They arrived in Wheeler, a small town of about 1,000 people 80 miles east of Amarillo, towards Oklahoma City. Hank, in his regular two-piece suit, looked to the Texans like a city slicker and he was forced to borrow the cowboy gear that the locals wore, something that made him look ridiculous. There was more bad news when Hank found that Wheeler County was dry.

He did, however, have some memorable experiences while in Texas that he was able to use in his later writing. It was in Wheeler that he watched a crow blast: 100 farmers armed with 100 shotguns 'jerking off the sky with a giant penis of hate' and watching the crows fall from the sky, half dead, half living, to be clubbed to death by the farmers in order to save their ammunition. They ran out of shells before they ran out of crows: 'and the crows came back and walked around the pellets and/stuck out their tongues/and mourned their dead and elected new leaders/and then all at once flew home to fuck and fill the gap.'

Hank claims that he enjoyed lounging about in Wheeler, but it would have driven him mad if he had stayed there for any length of time. As it was, Barbara had never lived in a big city and was desperate to move to Los Angeles, so after a couple of weeks they boarded the Greyhound and set off back across country. Barbara was artistic and, because of her unusual looks, she had channelled much of her energy into culture, she was well read and had a large vocabulary, she published a poetry magazine from a small Texas town, she wrote poems that Bukowski thought were 'pretty good' and she painted – 'badly' in Hank's opinion. She enjoyed the company of artists and artistic types and liked to attend art classes. She had what Hank called 'a superior air', which he attributed to always having had money. Her family owned property and some of her relatives ran successful companies, but Barbara herself had a secretarial job and expected to work when they got to Los Angeles.

Barbara didn't like living in a rooming house so they rented a small house at 2254 1/2 Branden Street in Echo Park, a hilly neighbourhood between West Lake and Elysian Park and one of the first housing developments to the west of the original downtown. It was a mixture of cottages, courts and small single-storey houses, a bit rundown; it was a cheap working-class neighbourhood lived in mostly by Mexicans, Japanese, Filipinos and blacks. It was a pleasant place to be, with the rise of Bunker Hill to the south and Echo Park with its palm trees and pleasure boats on the lake. Their house was one of two at the top of a rise and it had long grass filled with flies in the backyard. Every day Hank would go out with a big can of spray and kill hundreds of them, but the next day there were just as many buzzing around.

His neighbours in the front building had previously lived in Hank and Barbara's house and had installed shelves on the walls all around the bed which held pots of geraniums, big pots, little pots, all of them filled with flowers. When Hank and Barbara had sex, the bed would shake the walls, and the walls would shake the shelves, and Hank would hear the ominous sound of the shelves giving way and stop. 'Don't stop!' Barbara would yell, 'Don't stop!' and he would pick up the beat again, and down would come the shelves, striking him on his head and arms and legs and bare ass, and Barbara would laugh and scream with delight. Afterwards, battered and bruised, Hank would swear he was going to rip the rest of the shelves off the wall but Barbara begged and pleaded for him not to and was so persuasive that he relented and hammered them back up again, cleaned up the mess, put the geraniums back in the pots and the pots back on the shelves and waited for the next time. Hank was pleased with the story, which he told to great effect in both *Notes of a Dirty Old Man* and in *Post Office*.

Barbara bought a little dog and a new car, a 1957 Plymouth which Bukowski drove for many years after they broke up. She took an exam and went to work for the Sheriff's department, LA county. Hank had been fired from his job as a shipping clerk and used to wash the car every day then drive down to pick her up after work. She joined an art class and spent all her free time painting. He went three or four times, and the rest of the class found it very funny because he just sat there watching her. Eventually the instructor told him he had to paint something, not sit there looking at the paper. Hank said he had forgotten to buy brushes. The instructor lent him one, saying to make sure he returned it at the end of the class. He was told to paint a bowl with flowers sticking out of it. He worked fast, finished, then went for a coffee and cigarette while everyone else was still painting. When he returned, everyone was crowded around his picture. A blonde with big breasts 'turned to me and put those breasts up against me and said, "Ah, you've painted before, haven't you?" "No, this is my first thing." She wiggled the breasts and drilled them into me, "Ah, you're kidding!" "Ummmmmm" was all I could say.'

The instructor took Hank's painting and displayed it in front of the class, saying: 'Now here is a man who is not afraid of colour.' He told the class: 'This is what I want. See the feeling, the flow, the naturalness!' Barbara was unhappy. She took her work into another studio where they normally made collages. She threw paint around, tore up her work and destroyed someone else's collage hanging on the wall. The teacher asked Hank if Barbara was his wife. On Hank's admission that she was, he warned him: 'We don't tolerate prima donnas around here', but said that they would like to use his work in the art show. Everything Hank did, the instructor wanted for the art show. Barbara quit the art class in disgust and Hank dropped out too, leaving all his work behind. Could this have been the course in commercial art that Bukowski mentioned in a letter to *Harlequin* contributor CE Harper, where he says he is going to night school four nights a week taking a two-year course in commercial art? Hank continued to paint at home, but the paint got on his hands and on his cigars as he drank and listened to music so he got paint in his mouth from the cigars, which made him sick in the morning. He switched to drawing.

By now Hank was working a 44-hour week at the Graphic Arts Center, at 1534 West 7th Street. The art supply store was one of his best situations and he used it as the source of numerous stories in *Factotum* and in his poems. He always had a keen eye for the absurd, for the detail. As he pasted FRAGILE labels on the packages he noted the management swindles, such as pasting different labels on tins of paint if they had run out of the type ordered, the staff's petty theft loading stolen stock in their cars in the back alley – and the sexual tension between the workers. He observed the office hierarchy and how secretaries gave him their jobs to do.

One thing Hank and Barbara had in common was their interest in literature. Hank became very involved with *Harlequin* and became virtually co-editor with her, finally publishing a selection of his own poems and short stories in the first issue of 1957. He took revenge on little magazine editors who had rejected his work by firing off rejections when they submitted to *Harlequin*, but he already had the clear no-bullshit vision of writing that characterised his life work. He was writing a lot himself and in November 1956 started his first novel, *A Place to Sleep the Night*.

The problem was that he didn't love Barbara. They got along, but never really hit it off. Bukowski: 'I had a wife once who divorced me because more in essence than reality I would never say I loved her. How could I say this without dragging in Hollywood and my next door neighbour and patriotism and the barber's cough and the cat's ass?' Hank, preoccupied with his writing and his drinking, offered Barbara very little in terms of marriage. She wanted children, Hank didn't, but, as they did not use contraception, she inevitably became pregnant. She miscarried and blamed Hank, thinking that he had damaged his sperm by years of alcohol abuse. He agreed with her and felt guilty. He was not what she had expected him to be. She had been impressed by the poet who had published alongside Lorca and Sartre in *Portfolio*, and could not understand why he made no contact with whatever intellectual society Los Angeles offered. By his own definition he was an alcoholic, he did not attend church, he was surly and difficult with her relatives whom he disliked, he cursed and used bad language when drunk, he was antisocial, he was coarse, he shaved carelessly and sometimes stayed in bed for two or three days running. Not surprisingly, she began to look around.

In December 1956 Hank found out that his mother was in hospital. Hank and Barbara went to visit. Katherine was in a small, airless room with no windows at the top of a stairway. The room reeked of sickness and Hank, who had a terrible hangover, thought he was going to throw up. She had been operated on two days before for cancer of the womb. She was in pain and was unable to straighten her legs. She told him, 'You know, you were right, your father is a terrible man.' The smell overcame him and he had to rapidly excuse himself and run down the stairs, leaning over the rail, gulping for air as he tried not to vomit. Eventually he recovered and returned to her room.

Katherine told him how Henry had had her committed to a mental hospital. Hank told her he knew, and that he had told the doctors that they had the wrong parent in there. Henry had become more and more abusive and Katherine had made the one supreme effort of her life to escape his tyranny and moved out. She had apparently enjoyed her time living alone, but her financial circumstances had forced her back to her husband.

Hank told her he would be back the next day. When he got outside he threw up in the rose garden. He returned as promised, carrying the most beautiful rosary he could buy on Christmas Eve, and a bouquet of flowers. When he reached her room it was locked and there was a wreath on the door. As he stood there, twisting the doorknob, a nurse walked up and said, 'She just died.' As he approached his car he saw two little girls, about six or seven years old, and gave them the flowers.

It was a quiet Catholic funeral with a closed coffin. Afterwards Hank went straight to the racetrack where he had a lucky day. In *Notes of a Dirty Old Man* he claimed that he met a 'light yellow girl' there and they went to her apartment where she cooked steaks and they had sex, but, as this was originally written for one of the sex magazines where he always had to introduce some action, it is pure fantasy.

At work in the sheriff's office Barbara met a Turkish gentleman who wore a purple stickpin and who kissed her lightly on her forehead and told her she was beautiful. He told her that he owned a drive-in movie theatre which he operated at night as well as working for the county by day.

The pivotal moment which ended their marriage came when Hank was shopping at the market. He saw a gourmet shelf: 'I bought the whole rack: tiny octopi, snails, snakes, lizards, slugs, bugs, grasshoppers.' First he cooked the snails in butter. He served them to her and asked her how Purple Stickpin was. Barbara hated the snails and claimed she could see their assholes. 'Everything you eat has an asshole,' he told her. 'You have an asshole, I have an asshole . . .' she ran to the bathroom and began throwing up. Hank laughed and ate them, washing them down with beer.

Early one morning a few days later, someone knocked at their door. Hank got out of bed and answered it. The man served him with divorce papers. Hank went back to bed and showed Barbara the papers. 'Baby, what's this?' he asked. 'Don't you love me, baby?'

Barbara began to cry. She cried for a long time, while Hank tried to console her, saying maybe Stickpin would be the right man for her. She stopped crying, then they brought the flowerpots down for one last time and afterwards he could hear her humming and singing in the bathroom as she got ready for work. She left around 8 o'clock, looking the same as ever, possibly even better than usual, Hank thought. He didn't even bother to shave; he called in sick and went straight down to the corner bar.

That night Hank helped her to find a new place. She didn't want to stay in the house; she thought it would break her heart. He helped her pack and move out. Their divorce was finalised on 18 March 1958. He saw her a few more times and she told him that she only had sex with Purple Stickpin once. She later moved to Aniak, Alaska, where she married a Japanese fisherman called Hayakawa and had several children. In 1991 Hank heard that she had died in India where she was part of some religious sect but that nobody in her family wanted the body. One of her daughters committed suicide not long after. Bukowski: 'She divorced me and she should have. I wasn't kind enough or big enough to save her.'

Hank also moved. He had no need of a house and garden; he returned to his old habitat, the single bachelor room. He took a shabby cold-water room on the fourth floor of an old apartment building in East Hollywood at 1623 North Mariposa Avenue between Hollywood Boulevard and Sunset. Room 303 was off a long institutional style corridor and had a Murphy-bed that pulled down from the wall and a tiny kitchenette. The bathroom was down the hall and shared with the other residents. The Hollywood Bureau of Public Assistance was on one side and the Kaiser Foundation Hospital on the other. The Hollywood Hills rose steeply at the north end of the street giving way to the greenery of Griffith Park. Hank could see the Griffith Observatory from his window looking north. He was to live in room 303 from mid-1958 until 1 May 1964.

In June 1958 Hank had already published enough poems in small literary magazines for the editor of *Hearse* magazine, EV Griffith, to agree to publish a chapbook of his work to be called *Flower, Fist and Bestial Wail*. (Hank originally thought to call it *Fire, Fist and Bestial Wail*.) He was initially delighted to be published, and told Griffith he was honoured to be singled out by him from his other contributors, but as the months passed, and the chapbook had still not appeared, he grew exasperated. It took eighteen months, until October 1960. Then, responding to a card left in his mailbox, he went down to the post office to collect a package. He opened the carton right there in the street, between the post office and a new car agency, spilling the little books all over the sidewalk. He got down on his knees among them, picked up one and kissed it. 'Never a baby born in more pain, but finally brought through by the good doctor Griffith – a beautiful baby, beautiful!' He was immediately contrite and begged forgiveness for all the irritable letters he had sent Griffith complaining about the delay. He was forty years old, and had returned to writing late, so the publication of his first book was a very emotional event after so many years of rejection and starvation for his art.

On 4 December 1958, at 7 a.m., Henry Bukowski died. He had just got up and was standing at the sink, drinking a glass of water, when he was felled by a heart attack. He was found by his fiancée, Shirley.

Hank felt no sorrow, just a sense of relief that his tormentor was no longer alive. At the funeral in Alhambra everyone commented on the tremendous family resemblance between Hank and his father, 'You could have been twins', people said. The $1,500 mahogany coffin was left open and Shirley, moaning and crying, reached into the coffin and cradled Henry's dead head and kissed it. The attendants pulled her off. Hank approached the coffin for a last look. His father lay there surrounded by folds of purple velvet. To Hank 'his face looked like ice/painted yellow'. A boy soprano, hired for $15, sang behind a purple velvet curtain.

Hank turned and walked down the steps but there he was grabbed by his father's distraught girlfriend, whom he had never met. She threw her arms around him and began kissing his face, saying: 'Oh, you look just like your father!' To his embarrassment this caused Hank to get an erection and when he shoved her away he was very concerned that the other mourners might see it. After they closed the coffin lid, Hank and his Uncle Jack went out for hamburgers and fries. Jack told him that his father was a good man. 'Good for what?' Hank asked. He drove straight from the funeral to the racetrack, but the good luck he had after the death of his mother did not recur and this time he lost money.

The funeral was fictionalised in 'The Death of the Father I' where, instead of attending the burial after the service, he takes Shirley back to his father's house, gets drunk and spends the night with her. Shirley wasn't much older than him. In 'Father, Who Art in Heaven' he says he dated his father's girlfriend twice but got nowhere with her so he gave it up, which is probably what happened.

Henry left no will and no money to speak of, but Hank inherited the house on Doreen Avenue in Temple City, near the Santa Anita racetrack, as well as its contents and his father's four-year-old Plymouth. In 'The Twins' Hank described moving through the house after his death, looking at his father's shoes, noticing how his feet had curled and shaped the leather. He looked at the last cigarette Henry had smoked and the rumpled sheets from his final sleep before he had risen to make his last breakfast. There were his father's bulbs, set out by the screen ready for planting. He walked around the garden and peeled himself an orange while neighbours peeked from behind curtains. He watered the lawn and the flowers. Back inside the house he tried on a light blue suit. It was much better quality than anything Hank owned, but his father was much taller than him and the sleeves hung down over his hands. 'It's no good:/I can't keep him alive/no matter how much we hated each other.' Worst of all was the family resemblance; he hated the fact that people commented upon his strong likeness to his father. In 'With Vengeance Like a Tiger Crawls' he cries: 'Oh, let me lose my father's face!'

He began to sort through Henry's personal effects and some nights he stayed over at the house. He got to know the neighbours, particularly the man in the house to the north, the manager of a laundry, who had $5,000 worth of cage birds in his backyard, some of which talked, squawking 'Got a match?' or 'Go to hell!' over and over again. The neighbour and his wife came over some nights and they all drank. Hank used this for one of his more amusing sex stories where all the birds get released and Hank and the neighbours have an orgy.

Shortly before his father died, Hank had run into Jane again and now she told him: 'This is going to be your one chance to get a house because you don't have sense enough or ability enough, you don't know how to make money. You better hold on to that house.' But Hank didn't like the neighbourhood and told her: 'I can't live next to these people! I'd rather live anywhere. They go out and they mow their lawns on Saturdays . . . To hell with it!' After about a month he sold the house for $16,000, sold his father's car and his furniture and put his dog in the pound. In 'The Death of the Father II' he allows the neighbours to strip the house of its contents in a way that is all too familiar: the gardening tools, the cooking pots, the dishes and his clothes. He let them take all his parents' paintings except one, and gave them his mother's bottled fruit. The details are too accurate to have been imagined so something like this must have happened before he put the house on the market.

Naturally Henry's death was the subject of many many poems and stories over the years, and the details vary. In 'Father Who Art in Heaven' he says: 'I gambled and drank away the money', purposely squandering it at the racetrack and on drink as a rebellion against everything his father stood for. This is unlikely and several of his friends say that he was always very worried by poverty and put most of his inheritance in the bank. Though a generous host, he was naturally parsimonious and, as he approached middle age, he saved as much of his money as he could. He had no trade and had been used to getting a labouring job or working in a factory when impecunious, but these jobs were drying up. The factories were closing and being replaced by service jobs, fast food, McDonald's, jobs that did not hire the downtown floating population but took unqualified school leavers at minimum wage. Hank realised that he needed a more secure form of employment so he rejoined the post office and trained as a mail sorter. He stayed for twelve years, mostly working the night shift so that he could spend the day at the racetrack.

The racetrack became his beat, his personal space. It was here he really became a *flâneur*, the observer, the man *of* the crowd as opposed to the man *in* the crowd: 'the secret spectator of the spectacle of the spaces and places of the city'. As Keith Tester wrote in *The Flâneur*: 'Flânerie can, after Baudelaire, be understood as the activity of the sovereign spectator going about the city in order to find the things which will occupy his gaze and thus complete his otherwise dissatisfied existence; replace the sense of bereavement with a sense of life.' The *flâneur* needs the city and its crowds, yet he remains aloof from both. Hank was dissatisfied unless he visited the track regularly, he felt incomplete, he needed to watch the world go by. He told Jon Webb: 'Nothing is quite real to me. Streetcars. Bombs. Bugs. Women. Lightglobes. Areas of grass. All unreal. I *am* outside.' He investigates traces of human activity, like a detective story. He is like Christopher Isherwood: 'I am a camera, quite passive, recording, not thinking.' Bukowski:

> I'm not so much a thinker as I am a photographer . . . I have nothing to prove or solve. I find that just photographing is very interesting. Especially if it's people you see and then you write it down; it can get a little bit holy here, but there's a message or sense of direction after you've written it down. It says something which you didn't even quite know. So that works better for me.

This is the surprise revelation identified by William Burroughs: 'You can only write what you know, even if you don't know that you know it.'

Hank had developed a friendship with a young man in San Bernardino called Jory Sherman who had a great interest in literature. Hank wrote to him about his drinking and feelings of alienation, telling him that these days he drank mostly alone and discouraged company. He found most people's conversation irrel-evant or they were too eager or too vicious or too obvious. In August 1960 he told Sherman he was still drinking heavily and that his girlfriend – presumably at that time Jane – complained that he was more drunk than she had ever seen him. He used vile language then yanked the mattress off her bed before lecturing her for two hours on the arts.

Hank had to moderate his drinking while he had a regular job. However, in June 1961, he found himself once more up before the judge after a night in the drunk tank. He was concerned that another court appearance might cost him his job. He already had more than a dozen arrests to his name and he knew that the post office had access to his records.

Drink was a subject that interested him enormously and he discussed it at length in many articles and interviews. He believed that if he hadn't been a drunkard he would probably have committed suicide. He used it to escape:

You work a goddam lousy job, you come home at night, you're tired, what are you going to do? Go to a movie? Turn on your radio in a $3 a week room? Or are you going to rest up and wait for the job the next day for $1.75 an hour? Hell no! You're going to get a bottle of whiskey and drink it and go down to a bar and maybe get into a fist fight and meet some bitch – something going on! Then you go to work the next day and do your simple little things, right? I'm all for alcohol, I'll tell you. It's the thing!'

Bukowski thought that alcohol had prevented many people from committing suicide and that for them: 'Drink is not a slow form of suicide but a deterrent to it. Drink is the only music and dance they are allowed. The last cheap and available miracle. When I came in from the slaughterhouse or the parts factory, that bottle of wine was my god in the sky.'

Nonetheless he does seem to have once again contemplated suicide during this period. One time at the Mariposa Avenue apartment he closed all the windows, turned on the oven and the gas jets and stretched out on the bed. The escaping gas had a very soothing hiss and he nodded off to sleep. He might have succeeded had the gas not given him such a terrible headache that it woke him up. He got up off the bed laughing and saying: 'You damned fool, you don't want to die!' and turned off the taps and opened up the windows. He kept laughing because it seemed very very funny to him. Then, in true Bukowski style, he went out and bought himself a good bottle of whiskey and some very expensive cigars.

Hank still saw Jane from time to time. Just before his father died he had encountered her on the street and they had gone for a beer. She had grown old fast; she was heavier, the flesh hung at her throat and her face was lined. Hank felt sad but recognised that he had also aged. She was out of a job; the café where she worked as a waitress was torn down to make room for an office building. The dog had been run over and now she was living in a small room in the Phillips Hotel on Vermont Avenue in Hollywood, a seedy residential hotel where she had a part-time job changing the sheets and cleaning the bathrooms. She went back to her room, put on her high heels and changed into her best dress. They bought a fifth of whiskey and some beer and went to Hank's room to drink. In *Post Office*, where she is called Betty, he described calling in sick and the post office sending round a nurse to make sure he wasn't malingering, standard practice at the time. Jane hid under the covers while he signed the form at the door. There is a terrible poignancy about his description of them getting back together, which, even if fictionalised, sounds very much based on real life observation:

We drank a little longer and then we went to bed, but it wasn't the same, it never is – there was space between us, things had happened. I watched her walk to the bathroom, saw the wrinkles and folds under the cheeks of her ass. Poor thing. Poor poor thing. Joyce had been firm and hard – you grabbed a handful and it felt good. Betty didn't feel so good. It was sad, it was sad, it was sad. When Betty came back we didn't sing or laugh, or even argue. We sat drinking in the dark, smoking cigarettes, and when we went to sleep, I didn't put my feet on her body or she on mine like we used to. We slept without touching. We had both been robbed.

Jane had grown old and her beer belly was now enormous; Hank felt repulsed.

They began to see each other again, though mostly for companionship. Unfortunately, being with Jane only encouraged Hank's drinking and there was one time when he reported for work at 5.30 a.m. at the post office that the man sitting next to him at the casing racks thought he smelled petrol. Hank told him not to light a match as he might explode: 'I thought the stuff tasted worse than usual.'

Hank had Jane over for Christmas in 1961. He got in a large quantity of alcohol and she baked a turkey. Jane had always liked large Christmas trees so they bought a huge one, seven feet tall and half as wide, which filled the corner of the room. They decorated it with tinsel and coloured lights. They drank a couple of fifths of whiskey, had sex, ate the turkey, and drank some more. Jane passed out on the bed and Hank sat on the floor in his shorts, drinking and periodically straightening the tree, which had a loose nail in the stand and was leaning ominously. He eventually lay back and closed his eyes. Something made him open them just in time to see the tree, covered in hot coloured bulbs, falling straight towards him, the star on top like a dagger. It landed right on top of him, the hot lights burning his bare skin as he wriggled and hollered. He finally got out from under it, his body covered in red burns from the lights. Cursing, he pulled out the plug. 'Oh, my poor tree,' wailed Jane.

A few days after Christmas Hank stopped by to see Jane at her hotel. It was 8.45 a.m. and she was sitting in her room on the top floor, watching the morning traffic, already drunk. Everyone in the building had given her liquor as a Christmas box and the room was littered with bottles of the cheapest brands. 'If you drink all this stuff it will kill you,' Hank told her. In *Post Office* he wrote: 'Betty just looked at me. I saw it all in that look.' He understood. Her two children never visited, her looks were gone, the well-dressed, elegant woman was reduced to being a scrubwoman in a cheap hotel. Hank tried to take the bottles with him, promising to dole them out to her in small quantities but she told him to leave them.

A couple of weeks later he went over to visit. There was no reply to his knock. He opened the door. The room was empty, the bottles were gone and there was a bloodstain on the sheet. The French woman who owned the hotel stood in the doorway. She told him that Jane was at County General Hospital. She had been very sick the night before and the French woman had called for an ambulance. Hank drove to the hospital. There were just three or four beds in a small ward. He pulled the curtains around Jane's bed for privacy and sat next to her on a stool. He called her name quietly, and touched her arm

Her eyes opened. 'I knew it would be you,' she said. Then she closed her eyes. Spittle had caked around the side of her mouth and he tried to wipe it away with a damp cloth. He wiped her face, and her hands and throat, tidied her hair and tried to get her to sip some water but she did not respond. Jane died on 22 January 1962.

That evening, consumed by grief, Hank tried to distract himself by writing letters but found that it was impossible. He wrote to John William Corrington: 'I am unable to write. The woman I have known for so long has been critically ill since Saturday and died 2 hours ago. This is going to be the longest night of them all.'

Hank bought a cheap black suit for the occasion, fitted in a rush; it was his first in years. Jane had had the address of her son Joe's father-in-law written on a slip of paper and Hank had managed to locate Joe by making two long-distance calls to Texas. But by the time he got to Los Angeles his mother was already dead. No one knew where his sister was. The son drove Hank to the funeral at the San Fernando Mission in a new Mercedes Benz. There were just three of them: Hank, Joe and the mentally retarded sister of the woman who owned the hotel where Jane had worked and lived. Her son had an argument with the priest over whether Jane was a true Catholic or not; the priest was a stickler for technicalities and wasn't convinced. They finally settled for a compromise: the service could not be in church but he would say it over the grave. The funeral was held on 24 January 1962. It was hot despite the time of year; Hank's flower wreath had been left out in the sun and the roses had all wilted. The three of them stood there by the grave and as the priest waved his arms about and droned through the ritual, Hank thought she should have been buried in Mexico; Jane had always liked Mexico. He remembered how she talked about Arizona and New Mexico, hot places, and how she liked tacos, but not the flies.

Afterwards the mourners had coffee. Joe dropped Hank off at his building and told him that he would write to him about a headstone, but they both knew that, if anyone was going to buy a stone, it would be Hank.

Bukowski wrote to fellow writer John William Corrington: 'I went back to my whore who had once been such a cruel and beautiful woman, and who was no longer beautiful (as such) but who had, magically, become a warm and real person, but she could not stop drinking, she drank more than I, and she died.' Hank felt guilty for allowing Jane to live alone in the state she was in, but knew that their relationship had been an impossible one and could not have continued: she treated him badly, deserting him for days on end, sleeping with other men, engaging in casual prostitution to get money for wine. She lied, she stole from him and from others. In a sad, reflective poem called 'My First Affair with That Older Woman' he concluded: 'She brought me immense pain.'

He cleaned out her room and took some of her things, including her goldfish, to his place. He hung her dresses in his closet. Only with Jane dead was he able to express his love for her; as a living breathing woman he had been too scared, too afraid of rejection. Jane was sarcastic, caustic, and, even if she knew his feelings, she did not want to hear them expressed. Love was not a word Hank used lightly: 'Love, which I hardly know and am very afraid of.' He mourned her deeply and in his grief he wrote some of his most moving poems: 'for Jane: with all the love I had, which was not enough:– I pick up the skirt,/I pick up the sparkling beads/in black,/this thing that moved once/around flesh, and I call God a liar.'

A painting by the German artist Erich Heckel hung on his wall (one of the few things he kept from his parents' house when he sold it) and now Hank tucked photographs of Jane between the frame and the glass. They had taped some of their drunken conversations and some evenings he would open a bottle and sit and listen to her voice, talking and laughing: 'I had love/and love died; a photo and a piece of tape/is not much, I have learned late.' He had not had such strong feelings before but this grief broke through his frozen carapace and shook him to his centre. He told his friend AD Winans that he felt he would never again be the same, that his feelings were too powerful to put down in prose. He tried but they didn't come out right. She became his muse. Almost thirty years later he was still writing about her: 'I remember your bones/in flesh/and best/in that dark green dress/and those high-heeled bright/black shoes,/you always cursed when you/drank,/your hair coming down you/wanted to explode out of/what was holding you: rotten memories of a/rotten past, and/you finally got/out/by dying, leaving me with the/rotten/present; you've been dead/28 years/yet I remember you/better than any of/the rest.

He drowned himself in alcohol, barely managing to hold down his job. But beer and drinking were, of course, an essential component of his self-image: half the self-pity of the alcoholic, half bravado. He loved to boast about his drinking. In the series of letters to fellow-poet Ann Bauman written a few months after Jane's death, he mentions beer or drinking in every one: 'Sitting here having a beer' (10 May 1962); 'God, I am running out of beer! This is madness . . .' (19 May 1962); 'Getting this off while drinking a beer and listening to a little Sibelius. . .' (21 May 1962); 'It is 26 minutes before 9 a.m. and I am out of beer . . .' (20 June 1962); and, to John William Corrington: 'Just off a four day drunk. Bloody ass. Glass on floor. Broke . . .' In September he described his mood as 'German gloom' to Ann Bauman (4 September 1962). One morning he awoke from a wild rampage to find that he was missing $455 and that Jane's remaining goldfish was lying stiff on the rug (one had already died from overeating). Hank put it back in its bowl in a vain attempt to revive it but then flushed it down the toilet and put the empty bowl in the corner. He felt suicidal. He sat on the couch and attempted to read, trying hard not to think that Jane had now been dead for six months, and that the world was going on without her.

Jane's demons were caused in part by a rejection – perhaps unconscious – of the traditional role of women. In her day women brought up the children and respected the husband as the head of the household. She dressed in the stockings and slips and suspender belts and all the paraphernalia that Hank – also from the same generation – loved so much. She never lived to see the changes brought by the 60s but she was a precursor of women's freedom in her personal rejection of the straight middle-class life; her cynicism could only find an outlet in casual whoring and alcoholism. In just a few years there would be other ways, but she was trapped in an era when women were 'broads' and 'dolls' and 'dames'.

The 60s, as the decade of the counterculture, passed Bukowski by. He was never sympathetic to the hippies, but he was a fellow traveller; the hippies discovered him and loved his stuff because they could relate to his extreme honesty; he wrote what he saw, even if he changed it a bit. He described real human feelings and, like the hippies, he rejected the consumer society. The smile in his work was real, not a Hollywood grimace. By the end of the decade he was famous.

In 1960, Hank's first book of poems, *Flower, Fist and Bestial Wail*, was published and the next year Jon Webb's *Outsider* magazine introduced his work to the Beat Generation readership. He began writing a column for the underground paper *Open City*, which brought his work to the attention of a wide group of Hollywood movers and shakers as well as the countercultural underground. By the end of the decade he had met his mentor and saviour, John Martin, publisher of the Black Sparrow press, who put him on a retainer for the rest of his life and gave him the financial security he needed to write.

6. OUTSIDER OF THE YEAR

Hank had a friend called Jory Sherman who was well informed about literary magazines and small presses. It was Sherman who put Hank in touch with Jon Edgar Webb, then about to start a literary magazine in New Orleans. Webb and his wife had bought an antique 8 by 12 Chandler & Price letterpress, intending to set the whole thing by hand. Webb called it the LouJon press, named after himself and his wife Louise. Their magazine, the *Outsider*, was designed to be noticed: a lavish production, hand-printed with tissue interleaves on different coloured papers and illustrated with photographs and drawings.

Jon Webb was twenty years older than Bukowski. He came from Cleveland where he'd been a police reporter on the *Cleveland Plain Dealer*. He did a three-year stretch in Mansfield Reformatory in the 30s for armed robbery and, while there, he edited the prison newspaper, *The New Day*. The *Outsider* was dedicated to the new poetry and writing spearheaded by the Beats and such writers as Henry Miller, who had always been one of Webb's heroes. Webb had written some tough, hard-bitten stories about his own experiences and responded immediately to Bukowski's work.

It was a portfolio of Hank's work published in the first issue of *Outsider* in the autumn of 1961 that first brought his work to the attention of the Beat Generation writers. He appeared in the company of postwar American heavyweights: Henry Miller, Allen Ginsberg, William Burroughs, Gregory Corso, LeRoi Jones, Gary Snyder, Michael McClure, Diane di Prima, Lawrence Ferlinghetti, Charles Olson, Ed Dorn and others.

The second issue of the *Outsider* appeared in the summer of 1962 and, once again, Hank was in august company: Henry Miller, Kenneth Patchen, Jean Genet, William Burroughs, Jack Kerouac, Gregory Corso, Jack Micheline, Philip Lamantia and many others. Hank felt ambivalent about being placed alongside the Beats. He thought there was something too 'chummy' about them in the way they appeared to do everything as a group, though this was actually a press myth: for instance, William Burroughs never went west of the Rockies until 1974 and did not meet most of the San Francisco poets until then, long after the 'San Francisco Renaissance'.

The Webbs quickly became Hank's main sponsor and in 1963 devoted a special section of the third issue of *Outsider* to his work. This was a time when Bukowski was sending his poems to virtually every little magazine that he heard of, mailing them off in batches of eight or ten, but for some self-destructive reason not keeping carbon copies of them or any record of which poems were submitted to which magazine. As a consequence he complained to Webb about editors not sending his poems back and calculated that he had lost between two and three hundred this way since 1955. He railed against editors who didn't respond to his queries, loading them with invective, but it seems very foolhardy on his part not to have kept carbon copies and to trust the post office to get the poems there and back in the first place. He also knew that most of the magazines were small mimeograph efforts, brought out in the editors' spare time, where manuscripts were quite likely to get lost.

That year, in addition to *Outsider*, he had poems published in: *Mica, Brand X, Simbolica, Quicksilver, Satis, Sun, Signet, Black Cat Review, Targets, Choice, Midwest, Renaissance, South and West, El Corno Emplumado, Outcry, Northwest Review, Rongwrong, Mummy, In/Sert* and the *Wormwood Review*, often more than one poem in each issue and often in more than one issue during the year. The *Wormwood Review* was to become one of his major outlets, and publication in *Renaissance* began a tumultuous relationship with editor Jon Bryan.

By this time Bukowski had established a writing routine that did not change much for the rest of his life. He wrote directly on to the typewriter, rarely keeping a notebook or diary. He tuned his radio to a classical music station while he worked, eventually narrowing his choice to two stations, KUSC-FM and FFAC-FM, and drank while he wrote. In the early days he rarely corrected his work though sometimes a poem would be discarded. The racetrack continued to be important to him and he felt that he wrote best after losing at the track. These were all magical ingredients; they enabled him to reach that semi-trance state where the poems came into being.

Going to the track was the first thing: 'I go out there and the people, the action, the drabness of it, everything . . . it's a loosener. I'm able to write that very night, especially if I lose a lot of money. If I lose a lot of money I'll get drunk and really write some poetry. I guess it's fear.' He would get home and approach the typewriter. Sometimes he would circle the room before sitting down at his typing table. Then he would open a beer. The look of the electric light on the sheet of paper was important for him. He told Michael Perkins: 'It is the sound of the keys and the electric light. Then the fingers hit the keys . . . the words arrive by themselves, without thought, without pressure. I don't know how it works.' Sometimes there would be a pause and he would think the poem was finished, but then it would begin again. When the magic happened it resulted not just in one poem, but four or six. They would often all be on different subjects. The way he saw it, he let the material build up within him, then it would take something to trigger them – such as losing a hundred dollars at the track – and then they would all come out.

Being at the track helped to focus the line. As he spent so much of his time there he had very little time to write. He had no time to play at being a writer, he had to be serious: 'When I write it is the line I must write. After losing a week's pay in four hours it is very difficult to come to your room and face the typewriter and fabricate a lot of lacy bullshit.' It was a tough methodology.

He began his writing career with stories, though he did have a few poems published in the 40s. By the 1960s he wrote nothing but poetry, but as he came to them from a short story background, they retained a strong narrative style, making them very accessible. At the end of 1962 Hank told editor Raymond Federman that he had written only two short stories in years, and one of those, called 'The Murder', was more of a prose-poem. His early poetry he described as 'personal – action things – things that had happened to me personally. Rather subjective and maybe a little bit bitter.' He took everyday events, no matter how trivial, and gave them a certain universality.

Though he often presented himself as an unacademic, callow practitioner, Bukowski was actually very aware of what he was doing. He was well read on poetic theory but didn't like to discuss it. Clarity of vision and simplicity were matters of great importance to him: 'I thought, let's open up and clear up the line – be able to hang out a clothesline, a simple line, and be able to hang emotion on it – humour, happiness – without it being cluttered. The simple, easy line, and yet having the simple easy line to hang all these things – the laughter, the tragedy, the bus running through a red light. Everything.'

Ezra Pound made quite an impression on him but he was not intimidated; in fact he read him with an amused, critical eye. He could see that Pound did not obey his own strictures, and knew that he came closer himself to what Pound was trying to do than any other poet. In 'Horse on Fire' he commented that Pound demanded that poets write so that a man on the West Coast of Africa could understand it, then wrote his own Cantos filled with quotes in dead languages and newspaper clippings.

Bukowski's early poetry shows the powerful impact that the Big Sur poet Robinson Jeffers had on him: 'He influenced me a great deal with his simple lines – his simple long lines. Using the precise language, you know, not "pretty language" – just saying it. And that's what I've been trying to do, keep it simple . . . keeping it clear.' Jeffers influence was defined more simply when Bukowski told Jory Sherman: 'Jeffers is my god.' This was a view he expressed in many other interviews, though he usually specified that it was Jeffers' long narrative poems that he preferred because in the shorter works he tended to 'preach'. Jeffers' long narrative poems, such as 'Tamar' or 'Roan Styallion' sometimes run to almost a hundred pages. They are more conversational than lyrical in form and consequently would have appealed to Bukowski, who was in the process of moving away from lyricism himself. There was also their subject matter: murder, rape, incest and a primitive view of human sexuality that was as misogynist as Bukowski's own.

Jeffers used the term 'inhumanism' to describe his approach to the world, he disliked most people and said so – what Alfred Kazin described as Jeffers' 'disgust with the human species *in toto*'. Louis Untermeyer summed up the central message in Jeffers' work simply as 'Life is horrible.' It is easy then to see why Bukowski felt empathy with him.

Bukowski himself never attempted a long narrative poem of his own, with the exception of 'Horsemeat', an episodic poem in twenty sections, some poetry, some prose, some in between. It was the centre of *War All the Time, Poems 1981–1984* and featured characters observed and met at the racetrack, his everyday activities there, his thoughts and, at 27 pages, it was almost a chapbook in itself.

Jeffers took an extreme isolationist position on World War II which made him very unpopular when America joined the war. His epic 'The Double Axe' was certainly a powerful antiwar statement, even if he did hold the view that Europe was corrupt and needed to be smashed and cleansed. Also clear in his work was his misanthropy: 'Guard yourself from perceiving the inherent nastiness of man and woman . . ./(Expose your mind to it: you might learn something.)'

Bukowski liked Jeffers because he was a real loner. He liked him where the style was almost prose, but where the images were hard as stone, as Bukowski put it: 'where everything is up against the knife and very real'. This was also the reason he liked Antonin Artaud, the creator of the Theatre of Cruelty: 'Artaud wrote the *iron* line, like reaming fire through cement . . . Artaud is one of the few writers I look up to.' He was another loner, whose line was pared down to the wire and alive.

Some critics have made much of the fact that Bukowski was attracted to right-wing or fascist writers such as Knut Hamsun, Jeffers and Pound, but he also wrote favourably of Steven Spender, WH Auden and, at times, Allen Ginsberg. On Spender, for instance, he told Robert Wennersten:

Once I was lying in bed, and I opened this book up. You know what happens when a poem hits you? I was thinking of that one with the touch of corn about the poets who have 'left the air signed with their honour'. That was pretty good. Spender got them off . . . I know that he set me off three four five six times. The more modern poets don't seem to do this to me.

On Auden he commented: 'I liked a lot of Auden. I was in a liking mood. I liked that whole gang: Auden, [Archibald] MacLeish, [TS] Eliot.' He read them in the 30s and 40s but when he returned to their work they didn't strike him the same way. They were not loose enough, they didn't take risks, they didn't gamble. 'They say good things and they write it well; but they're too careful for me now.' However, late in life, he revised his position and concluded that Auden was probably the best of them all. Throughout his career he often wrote poems that were little more than a Whitmanesque catalogue of the poets and writers he read in his youth, usually bemoaning the fact there were no present equivalents (one such was 'Nowhere' in *Septuagenarian Stew*). He bemoans Auden, Jeffers, Eliot, Pound, Spender, cummings, Carl Sandburg, Dylan Thomas: 'let's admit it, the giants have gone and there have not come up any giants to replace them.'

He often mentioned the New Jersey poet William Carlos Williams to the extent of referencing his 'red wheelbarrow' in a number of poems including 'John Dillinger and le chasseur maudit' where he also mentions that he is sitting reading Robert Herrick, Edmund Spencer, Andrew Marvell, Gerard Manley Hopkins and Emily Brontë, while listening to Dvorak's 'Midday Witch' and Cèsar Franck's 'Le Chasseur Maudit', which gives an idea of the wide range of his reading. One thing he may have taken from Williams is the idea of dropping in to his work notes and letters. Just as Williams reproduced whole a long letter from the young Allen Ginsberg, then still living with his father in Paterson, New Jersey, so Bukowski appropriated a note left by one of his girlfriends when he was delayed at the post office and couldn't get home in time: 'sun of a bitch:/I wated until 5 after ate/you don't love me/you sun of a bitch/somebody will love me/I been wateing all day' (though the use of the colon suggests that Hank may have made it up, or at least modified it).

Bukowski's pride and competitiveness kept him from ever entering into a reasoned discussion of his many influences, even though there are many. The New York School of poets would have to figure high on the list, Frank O'Hara in particular. Bukowski would certainly have studied Donald Allen's enormously influential anthology *The New American Poetry 1945–1960*, which included O'Hara's 'The Day Lady Died'. Written in 1959 it is a perfect example of O'Hara's 'I did this and then I did that' style of poem. It was also probably not as a throwaway gesture that Hank named Larry Eigner when asked who was the greatest living poet, by interviewer Arnold Kaye in 1963.

Bukowski was very critical of the poetry establishment, in particular the old Black Mountain school of poets led by Robert Creeley and Charles Olson whom he saw as 'the biggest snob outfit ever invented'. He regarded their work as an elaborate confidence trick, played on the universities and reading public. He saw Creeley as feared and revered more than any other poet but felt that his poetry was dull, 'very dull, so dull that the dullness is taken for hidden meaning – the meaning is hidden all right, so well hidden that there isn't any meaning'. As Hank saw it, if you didn't enthuse over this type of work then you were seen as lacking in soul and sensitivity. If you were not moved by it then you had better try harder and, failing that, at least keep your mouth shut. Naturally Hank could not keep quiet and spouted forth his opinions on Creeley at every possible moment. Creeley became a bête noir.

In fact Bukowski and Creeley had much in common, for instance many of Creeley's poems were written straight off, with no changes, just like Hank's. Creeley was also a drinker and someone who, in his younger days, frequently got into bar fights. Creeley lost an eye at the age of two, his father died when he was four, and he was advised to leave Harvard for excessive drinking. He spent a year in India and Burma with the American Field Service during World War II, spent the years 1951–1955 living in France and Mallorca, before working as a tutor in Guatemala on a coffee finca.

Creeley was 36 before his work received any acclaim which was when *For Love, Poems 1950–1960* was published in 1962. This secured Creeley's reputation. It helped that he had a number of famous, often quoted, poems: 'The Whip', 'For Love', and so on, and a well-received novel, *The Island*, whereas Bukowski never wrote one single poem that made his reputation as a poet. There is no 'Howl' or 'Waste Land' or 'Prufrock', just an accumulated body of work. In this Bukowski is a modernist: just as Monet painted in series – waterlilies, haystacks, cathedrals – rather than producing a few set-piece masterpieces in the Renaissance tradition, so Bukowski worked on a limited number of themes, working and reworking the same stories from different angles, no version ever the final, definitive one.

Nonetheless, Bukowski felt very competitive towards Creeley and Hank's visitors had to prove their allegiance by decrying Creeley's work. The poet Steve Richmond described Bukowski checking him out: 'Creeley is Hank's real competing suitor for th' brass ring . . . if I've gone too far over for Creeley, then Hank has no choice but to forgo paying for the next two six-packs.'

Virtually all Creeley's work was about relationships; love and marriage in all its complexity, albeit a sceptical and sometimes sarcastic view about human relationships in general, but these were feelings that Bukowski did not want to deal with in his own life. Creeley's and Bukowski's poems have much in common: they are brief paintings, frozen moments of time, they particularise a moment and give an awareness of a precise thought set in time and place. (It is regrettable that Bukowski did not date his poems as the time is often important to the understanding, particularly when he refers to 'three years ago' or 'ten years ago'.)

Like most poets, the contemporary poets that Hank liked were the ones whose work most resembled his own; this included Steve Richmond, Doug Blazek, Al Purdy, Brown Miller and Harold Norse. In the public eye, Bukowski became most readily associated with the Beats but he found them very problematic. He was a natural loner and disliked their camaraderie. His biggest problem was with Allen Ginsberg because not only was he influenced by Ginsberg's work, he was jealous of his fame. He tried to use Ginsberg's homosexuality against him and even criticised him because his friend Burroughs came from a wealthy background, as if he were selling out by association. Bukowski tried to moderate his homophobia in later years but to dismiss Burroughs because his grandfather invented the adding machine was pointless (in fact Burroughs' family sold their shares in 1922 and Burroughs never received a penny from the company; his parents did give him a small allowance from their garden supply shop until the early 60s).

Ginsberg is the poet that Bukowski mentions over and over in his correspondence, even if he misspells his name as 'Ginsburg', but his literary criticism of Ginsberg is mostly fatuous. His Ginsberg-influenced poem 'I Shot a Man in Reno' revealed the truth: 'Bukowski thought Mickey Mouse was a Nazi; Bukowski made an ass out of himself at Barney's Beanery; Bukowski made an ass out of himself at Shelley's Manne-Hole; Bukowski is jealous of Ginsberg; Bukowski is jealous of the 1969 Cadillac; Bukowski can't understand Rimbaud . . .' Change the name to Ginsberg and it could have been a Ginsberg poem. There are many uses of Ginsberg's forms, including the catalogue style, adapted from Whitman and used in the 'Moloch' section of 'Howl', which was copied by Hank in the poem 'Fear and Madness':

San Pedro I will wring you out like a wet rag
San Pedro I will break you like a wild stallion.

Another aspect of Ginsberg that rankled with Hank was the way that his fame led to enormous crowds at his poetry readings, although Hank couldn't accuse Ginsberg of selling out because, until the late 60s, Ginsberg refused on principle to accept money for a reading in case it commercialised his work. He relented only late in the decade in order to get income for his poetry foundation, which basically kept a set of junkies and junkie-poets alive.

Ginsberg and Bukowski did meet but, like Hank, Ginsberg only really liked poets whose work was similar to his own and he regarded Hank's poetry as minor.

Meanwhile, Bukowski continued his dead-end job sorting letters at Terminal Annex, the main Los Angeles post sorting office near Union Station. He had memorised the streets served by the Sanford post office in Hollywood and his job was to sort their mail into street blocks and buildings for the delivery staff. He stood leaning back against an angled wooden board designed to take some of the weight off his legs, but the continuous action of grabbing letters from the long shallow tray and throwing them into slots for eleven and a half hours each night gave him tremendous cramps and pains in his shoulders and back. His poetry describes the physical effects on his fellow workers: people who got up to take a break and found they couldn't walk anymore or who suddenly developed speech defects or were shaken by tremors or rapid blinking of their eyes. They reacted by coming to work on drugs or drunk – as in Hank's case – or both. Nervous breakdowns occurred, people went to bed so tired that they set themselves on fire by dropping burning cigarettes on the mattress, and there were accidental shootings.

At work Hank did not speak unless he was spoken to, but he replied and was courteous when he was addressed. He listened to all the talk, about little personal tragedies, deaths in families, dismissals, shootings, families breaking up. He perched on his wooden rail and was friendly enough to be accepted by the largely black workforce. He put up with the boasting about Dionysian nights and prodigious drinking sessions. He was not a racist and was accepted by them in most things though one time he asked about a supervisor whom he had not seen recently and was told, ominously: 'He won't be around for a while.' He had been knifed in the parking lot on his way to his car; the black guys knew who did it but they weren't about to tell Hank.

The pressure of the job began to get to him. He wrote hardly anything during the month of September, then decided to take a thirty-day leave of absence without pay. He had been working at the post office for four years and was entitled to it. The job was unrelenting, it had him 'by the throat' and he told a number of his correspondents that he didn't know how much more he could take, but, as he had no special trade and was no longer young, he didn't know what else he could do. He spent much of his time off at Hollywood Park, his nearest racetrack, a favourite with TV and movie stars, where the summer season was followed by a trotting season. The 'track of the lakes and flowers' was landscaped with infield lakes, one of which featured a girl in a boat.

Hank had a hatred of Christmas; the enforced gaiety, the parties and the drunk drivers all depressed him. He got drunk on the night of 16 December, fell and twisted his ankle, and got thrown in jail for causing a disturbance. He missed two days of work and had to take a day off to appear in court. As it was by no means his first offence, he thought the judge might give him twenty days, which would have meant the loss of his job. He fell into a fit of depression. Whereas jail once meant little to him, he now hated and feared it, the idea of it almost drove him mad. He decided that he could no longer drink and complained to his correspondents that he had no trade and no future, was sick and depressed, 'blackly, heavily depressed'. But the judge was clearly filled with Christmas spirit and none of the forty or fifty people who came before him that day received even a day in jail; everyone was fined. Hank's drinking days were apparently not yet over after all. He spent Christmas day in bed just so that he didn't have to go outside and see the false joviality of his neighbours as they sped through red lights, shouting greetings to people they didn't know.

The highlight of the next year, 1963, came towards the end when Jon and Louise Webb (usually known as Gypsy Lou) published a beautiful hand-printed collection of his poems, *It Catches My Heart in Its Hands*. Before this could happen Hank was required to make a trip to New Orleans so that the Webbs could check him out and make sure that he was for real and not just putting it on. Jon Webb believed that most writers were detestable human beings when they were away from their typewriters.

The train left from Union Station just below the Terminal Annex of the post office where he worked all night. Hank sat in the bar car and drank scotch and water and watched America glide past the window. Jon and Louise met him at the railroad station. Gypsy Lou: 'All the different people were getting off, and Jon and I were hidden behind a post at the station, looking to see which one's Bukowski . . . Then a guy staggered, and I said, "That's got to be him!" Sure enough, it was.' They all three drank and talked for two weeks. One night Jon Webb told him: 'Hank, you have ruined poetry for me, because after reading your poems, I can't read anybody else's.' Hank replied: 'I have the same problem.' At the end of the two weeks Jon Webb told him: 'You're a bastard, Bukowski, but I'm going to publish you anyhow.' Hank returned to Los

Angeles, but it seems the Webbs had second thoughts and needed to confirm their decision. This time they came to Los Angeles and were soon ensconced, along with their two dogs, in a cheap hotel just off skid row; it was the only place that would take the dogs. There was a lot more drinking and talking. It turned out that Hank was still a bastard but they loved him and his work anyway. This time the farewells were more emotional, with Louise in tears and them both waving through the window as the train pulled away.

But first, in the spring, came the third issue of *Outsider* magazine. It was the usual lavish production on different types of paper and in different typefaces and contained work by Michael McClure, Robert Creeley, Carl Solomon, Harold Norse, Jean Genet, Kenneth Patchen, Henry Miller, Diane Wakoski, Gary Snyder, as well as a large selection of Bukowski. In it Jon Webb announced that Hank was the recipient of the 'Outsider of the Year Award' for 1962 and, to mark this singular honour, the cover bore a portrait of Hank. In the little magazine world this was like being on the cover of *Time* or *Rolling Stone* and gave Bukowski a much-needed shot of confidence in his work. He wrote a grateful letter to the Webbs, thanking them for the award – a wooden plaque that he displayed on his wall for many years – praising the magazine, and applauding their critical attack on Creeley. 'CREELEY CAN'T WRITE, nor can the rest of them,' he said, forgetting, perhaps, that this was a criticism of Webb's editorial judgement, as Creeley also featured in the issue.

Despite everything, Bukowski kept writing, pounding the keys late at night until the neighbour in room 203 banged on the ceiling with a broomstick and complained: 'It is like living below an arsenal.' Hank still needed to drink to write and told Arnold Kaye that he didn't think he had ever written a poem when he was completely sober, but that he had written a few good ones 'under the hammer of a black hangover when I didn't know whether another drink or a blade would be the best thing'.

It took Jon and Louise Webb four months, beginning in June 1963, to print *It Catches My Heart in Its Hands,* a title taken from a line in Robinson Jeffers' poem 'Hellenistics' that Hank found early one morning and said 'They've got to take it, they've just got to . . .' The summer months in New Orleans are hot and steamy and the Webbs were working without air conditioning in what used to be the slave quarters workshop in the back of a sagging, once beautiful, ramshackle mansion in the French Quarter. The yard was covered with dog shit and a walkway of boards led to the workshop behind.

The workshop's windows looked into a walled-in courtyard, the surrounding walls topped with broken glass, overflowing with rotting banana trees, stinkweed and vine. These were, in turn, inhabited by varieties of spiders, snails, ants, ticks, silverfish, lizards and huge cockroaches. The air above teemed with bats, gnats, wasps, flies, mosquitoes and moths, while rats galloped across the roof at night, loosening showers of ancient dust and plaster over the stacks of completed pages. Webb built an overhead platform they could sleep on so that there would be more room to stack completed pages. The high humidity meant that the ink would not dry, and rainwater dripping from leaks in the ceiling, combined with bugs getting into the ink, meant that some pages had to be done more than once. Mice copulating in the font scattered the alphabets, fuses blew, and on two occasions the wiring caught fire, but still the old letterpress kept rolling. All 777 copies were hand-bound in October 1963, and the job was finished. Jon and Louise were exhausted but they had loved the work. Louise felt that: 'He was real . . . He would write stuff about whores and race tracks and nobody but Bukowski would write [about] drinking and all that, like things that go on everyday.'

On 26 November Hank came back from the store to find that the mailman had left a package by his door. It was the book: an extraordinary fine-print production in seven colours of paper with a cork cover, an illustrated wraparound card binding so beautifully made that it became an instant collectors item. 'By god, you've done it, you've done it . . .' he wrote to the Webbs. 'I do not think there will ever be another event in my life like this book . . .' He felt buoyant, encouraged, delighted that someone should take so much time and effort to put his poetry into print for very little in the way of financial gain. He had a small, nagging feeling that the beauty of the book as an object threatened to overwhelm the poetry and even three years later wondered if maybe he should have had his books published in cheap editions of one or two hundred copies so that the writing alone could be judged rather than the lavish production. But *It Catches My Heart in Its Hands* was a remarkable achievement for all involved. It gave Bukowski's career an enormous boost, and lifted him from the depression that had dogged him since Jane's death.

The poet Kay Johnson, known as Kaja, corresponded with Bukowski in the early 60s from Paris where she was living at the Beat Hotel at 9 rue Git-le-Coeur. He told her that he admired Harold Norse's poems in *Evergreen Review* but complained that his own were always rejected. Norse was a friend of Kaja's and also resident in the hotel. Hank's next letter was addressed to both of them and he sent Norse a copy of It Catches My Heart in Its hands with a flattering inscription. Norse liked the work and recommended him to Fred Jordan, the editor of Evergreen Review, and Hank's poems were accepted. This was the beginning of a complicated, rewarding and at times tempestuous relationship that ended, as did most of Bukowski's relationships, with Norse feeling bitter and used.

Hank had a new system at the racecourse which seemed to be working. He began to win so much that he considered becoming a professional gambler, claiming to make $500 at the track, while only going two or three times a week. He applied for another leave of absence from the post office and was given ninety days without pay. His favoured track was a hundred miles south of Los Angeles, so he rented cheap motels nearby and drove back to the city a couple of times a week to collect his mail and sometimes sleep over. After a day at the track he would eat a decent steak and salad then drive around looking for a motel room. According to Post Office, on one of his winning days he was set up for a robbery by a girl he picked up at the track, but saw his attacker coming at him just in time.

Poems about gambling usually only make sense to fellow gamblers, and as the American betting system is different from the European ones, many of the poems are just not intelligible to non-racegoers. But, at his best, Hank could make the racetrack itself seem exciting even to someone who was totally non-sporty. One such is 'A 340 Dollar Horse and a Hundred Dollar Whore'. His descriptions of the expensive whores at the racetrack are hilarious, if only for the drooling wonderment he expresses: 'you wonder sometimes if nature isn't playing a joke/dealing out so much breast and ass and the way/it's all hung together, you look and you look and/you look and you can't believe it.'

His sex life, however, remained virtually nonexistent, but this was to change in the spring of 1963 with the beginning of his third important relationship. Frances Elizabeth Dean was born into a middle-class family in San Rafael, California, in 1922 and was shortly afterwards taken by her parents to Lexington, Massachusetts, home of her paternal grandparents, who raised her after her father died when she was eight years old. At Smith College she became a member of the poetry club but, after some initial success, she neglected her writing for twenty years in order to bring up four daughters. She had nothing published until 1963 but remained interested in literature and kept up an exchange of letters with other writers including the poet Stanley Kurnik, who ran a writers' workshop in Los Angeles. Kurnik knew Hank and would sometimes visit his apartment and select poems to read to his workshop. He sent copies of some of them to Frances who rapidly became a Bukowski fan. When her marriage ended she moved back west to stay with her mother in Garden Grove, in Orange County just south of Disneyland. It was here that she received a telephone call from Bukowski.

She had written to him about his work and asked if she might visit. Hank's routine in those days was to work for a ten-day stretch at the post office, then take a four-day weekend. This was to enable him to get really drunk and then have time to recover for work. During the week he moderated his drinking but on his days off he really let go. It was the evening of a spring weekend, he had had a few drinks and was feeling bored and lonely. He was reading through her letter so he picked up the phone and dialled her number. Her mother was using the car so she had no way of getting to Los Angeles, but Hank insisted that he had to see her right away. A Greyhound bus left Anaheim around midnight, but that would not get her to East Hollywood until about 2 a.m. 'I'll be awake,' he assured her. She certainly hoped he would be because she was acutely aware that she didn't have enough money to pay the cab fare from downtown to Mariposa Avenue.

Hank was waiting on the steps outside the apartment building with the car fare. He was not allowed female visitors at night so they had to sneak upstairs to 303 and talk in whispers lest someone heard them. They found it very amusing that they were both adults in their early 40s and yet they were creeping about like naughty children. They talked through the night. Frances was lonely, depressed and feeling suicidal because she had lost her children and her marriage had collapsed. Hank was still recovering from Jane's death and the guilt he felt for not looking after her. They shared their sorrows over a bottle or two and finally Hank pulled down the Murphy bed. When they woke up the next afternoon, Hank took her for a day out to the Santa Anita racetrack beneath the San Gabriel Mountains, a venue chosen perhaps because it was a place for celebrity spotting and also for the scenic view and the one million special Santa Anita giant pansies planted in the infield.

They began to see each other regularly, and Frances moved to East Hollywood to be close to him, taking a place on North

Vermont Avenue next to the Hollywood freeway, near where Jane had lived and died. Moving to Los Angeles and meeting Bukowski caused something of a transformation in Frances; she began writing poetry again, began to attend Stanley Kurnik's poets' workshop at the First Unitarian Church at 7th and Vermont, and changed her name to the more eye-catching FrancEyE.

Hank was very irritated by Kurnik, whom he calls Mosk in the hilarious poem 'Dogfight Over L.A.', and appears to have threatened to beat him up. But at the poets' workshop Frances soon got to know a group of artistic Hollywood types, and through the Unitarian church where the group met she became involved in political campaigns for world peace and in the Civil Rights movement in the Southern States, going on marches, collecting signatures on petitions and attending protest meetings. In the early days the love affair between Frances and Hank was intense, though he later disparaged their relationship, saying he never really loved her – she is called Fay in *Post Office* – but years later, in a contrite mood when he no longer had anything to lose, he wrote in 'One For Old Snaggle-tooth': 'we were once great lovers'.

Despite his new love interest, Hank continued to drink in prodigious quantities and in August he was thrown in the drunk tank at 6 a.m. on a Monday and bailed out at 8 p.m. that evening. Two days later the judge gave him a choice of three days in jail or a $30 fine. He paid the fine. He resolved to be more careful and do his drinking at home; it was when he went out that he got into trouble.

There was a side of Hank that was still bourgeois German; no matter how much he criticised the Beat Generation, he was never prepared to take that final leap and quit work and try and make it as a writer. (By 1963 Burroughs was earning enough to live on and had stopped his $200-a-month family allowance; Ginsberg had been able to scrape by on his poetry since 1958; Corso had never worked, preferring to demand money from admirers – usually female – or from Ginsberg; Kerouac had been self-sufficient since the publication of *On the Road* in 1957 and, as he lived with his mother, he had low overheads; Jack Micheline, Ray Bremser, Bob Kaufman and the other hard-core Beats all scraped by without jobs; others like John Clellon Holmes, Gary Snyder, Michael McClure and Jack Hirshman survived on a combination of teaching, translation work, readings and reviewing. Not for Hank. For decades he railed against the tyranny of the 9 to 5 job yet he always worked – contrary to the public image, he was rarely unemployed for long and some of his jobs he held down for years, even during the so-called 'ten-year drunk'. By working for the government he had a relatively secure job but it was driving him slowly insane as well as damaging his health. He suffered from insomnia and his right shoulder, arm and neck were virtually paralysed from the repetitive throwing action, but each evening he would 'go back moth-eyed and white to the spider mouth and they suck again . . .'

Sometimes he felt he could take it no longer. On 1 October he took a night off to write. He had been spoken to before about absenteeism and knew the danger of losing his job, but he just could not bring himself to get in the car and drive himself willingly to the torture chamber. Instead he settled himself down to create and enjoy the machine-gun rattle of the carriage jerking along its tracks. At least he no longer had to worry about the effect of the noise on his downstairs neighbour. The person in the flat below died and was replaced by someone who liked to play their television loud; so loud that Hank thought he would have to move. Hank didn't mind overhearing lovers' quarrels or fights but the quiz contests, the anodyne news broadcasts and mindless comedy shows really got on his nerves.

However, he soon had a very good reason to move because within nine months of Hank and Frances getting together she was pregnant. At 41 she had thought she was too old to have any more children and Hank disliked using condoms. She dreaded telling him, knowing that he very much did not want children, but when she screwed up courage he immediately offered to marry her, not because he wanted to be married again, but because he thought that was the right thing to do. He broke the news of her pregnancy to the Webbs, telling them: 'Frances is a good woman.' But he went on to complain that she had what he called a 'coffeehouse attitude' and appeared determined to save and understand all mankind. The idea of writers' workshops was obnoxious to him but he conceded that he had his racetrack and beer and his beer-drinking friends whom not everyone found to be the best company. Hank began to look for another place to live; they needed more space and their own bathroom in order to have a baby.

Number 1623 Mariposa had been an important address for Hank. He lived there for six years and the thought of leaving brought a rash of memories. In some ways he was sad to leave it. It was true that the landlords had made virtually no repairs during that time except when the water pipes broke and they had to rip open the walls. That had happened several times and the workmen were not pleased to find Hank lying in bed, hungover or sick, watching their every move. Nor were the landlords happy when he threw a few glasses of whiskey against the walls – where the wallpaper was already mended with scotch tape to prevent it from peeling further – or when he bled on the rug from broken glass or the times he almost died and required resuscitation, or the visits from the police. He told the Webbs: 'Old 1623 is gone and it was a magic number and a magic place.' Many times he had sat, beer in hand, and stared out of his window, three floors up, at night-time Hollywood with its ribbons of lights, and the palm trees silhouetted against the luminous sky. It had been home.

Los Angeles was his hometown and he knew it in all its moods: the Santa Ana winds whipping at the strands of plastic trapped in chain link fences tangled with weeds and torn supermarket bags, broken bottles glinting in the sun; the way the sun rose in a hot luminous red ball, painting the whole city a fluorescent orange after a fire in the canyons; the spectacular red and orange sunsets through the smog, colouring the concrete garages and white walls topped with razor wire; the waste lots filled with yellow palm leaves and crushed cigarette packs, the peeling billboards and broken neon; the earthquake zones and slide areas. It was his town and much as he railed against it, he secretly loved it. In his next major book the wonderful title poem, *Crucifix in a Deathhand*, gave the whole history of Los Angeles from its earliest days, opening with a surprisingly Olson-like line: 'this land punched-in, cuffed-out, divided,/held like a crucifix in a deathhand', then describing the period of Mexican rule; the 20s boosters and oilmen; up to 'and now/real estaters, subdividers, landlords, freeway/engineers arguing. This is their land and/I walk on it, live on it a little while/near Hollywood.'

Bukowski: 'I was raised in LA; I've always had the geographical and spiritual feeling of being here. I've had time to learn this city. I can't see any other place than LA. LA has a spiritual and geographical difference which, because I've been hanging around it, I've picked up on. I have an acquaintanceship with LA you might say.' In fact Hank was continually getting lost and all of his girlfriends experienced the phone call from a booth on some remote highway, asking them to look up the street and give him directions back to Hollywood. Why did he not pick up a free street map from a gas station for his glove compartment? Perhaps he liked the thrill of exploring new neighbourhoods while searching for a freeway on-ramp. He would find the right freeway then drive in the wrong direction, then realise his mistake and anxiously look for an off-ramp, feeling foolish among the other drivers who all knew what they were doing. He would get lost trying to get back on the freeway in the correct direction and take off into an unknown neighbourhood and lose himself among silent dark houses with no one in sight to help. Sometimes he would stop the car, turn on the radio and sit for a while.

Then would come the phone call to his girlfriend: 'Listen, baby, I'm lost, I'm in a phone booth and I don't know where I am!' They would tell him to go and look for a street sign and he would leave the phone dangling while he investigated. They would look it up and tell him calmly what to do, but he was not calm: he didn't understand or it was too complicated and he would end up screaming 'I can't do it!!'

One time he left the Santa Anita racetrack and took a side road to avoid the heavy traffic and before long found himself on a dusty unlit road, climbing up into the hills. He eventually reached a built-up area with shops but all the signs were in Chinese. Way below him he saw what he knew must be the Pasadena Freeway. It took him 45 minutes to reach it, driving carefully through an expensive residential area and when he got there he took the wrong on-ramp and finished up going the wrong way.

Another time, after driving around for hours, he stopped and rented a motel room which had a liquor store across the street. He got two fifths of vodka, some 7-Up and sat watching TV. In the morning, as he turned in the key, he asked the clerk which way to Los Angeles. 'You're in LA,' she told him.

On 1 May 1964, Hank and Frances moved to an apartment two blocks away in a small unfinished court at 5126 1/4 De Longpre Avenue just south of Sunset Boulevard. At just $85 a month, Bukowski described it as one of the last slum courts on De Longpre, but it was hardly a slum. It was a little shabby, with blistered white paint, cracked, peeling stucco and the glint of tiny shards of broken glass in the weeds growing from cracks in the pavement, but it had two good size rooms and all the amenities that one would expect. The low hazy Hollywood Hills with the giant Hollywood sign perched on top still held the view to the north but they were now surrounded by single-floor Spanish stucco boxes, low-rise and almost suburban but for the Twentieth Century Fox studios with the Daniel Boone sets still standing, a few blocks away on Sunset. This was old Hollywood, before the Fox studios were demolished to make way for a shopping mall. Even better, the landlords, Francis and Grace Crotty, were both friendly and accommodating.

Hank had blamed himself for Barbara's miscarriage, thinking that it was caused by his drinking, so he took every precaution to make sure that things went smoothly for Frances. He even made two practice runs to the hospital to be ready for the event, though, when it was time, he didn't know where to park. Marina Louise Bukowski was born on 7 September 1964. He wasn't present for the birth – it was a Catholic hospital and such things were not allowed – so he sat in the waiting room, reading the *Dialogues of Plato*. The doctor who delivered her came up and said, 'Still reading that highbrow stuff? Last time I read that I was in High School.'

'I read it,' Hank said. The doctor said Marina weighed 9 pounds 3 ounces: 'No trouble at all.' After a wait Hank was called upstairs and stood, staring through the glass at the red-faced baby. 'Hey, look at this, Plato: another broad!' he thought, and envisioned her in future years 'shaking it in a tight skirt'.

Hank loved his child and wrote lovingly about her to all his correspondents. She provoked some beautiful lines in his poetry, such as: 'a beautiful skunk of a child with pale blue eyes/who made me swallow my heart like a cherry in a/chilled drink'. However, life with a baby in the house was difficult: the child kept Hank awake in the day when he was trying to sleep, ready for his night shift, and his typing kept the child awake at night. He could have changed to a day shift but then he would have missed the racetrack. Things were not improved by Frances's friends. Hank would stagger in after almost twelve hours of back-breaking work and take hours to get off to sleep. Then he would be awakened by Frances's poetry workshop and church group friends giggling and making jokes in the other room. It seemed to him that they just couldn't spend enough time together, they were forever discussing civil rights freedom marches, marches for world peace, poetry readings and the gossip surrounding their poetry workshop. Hank felt they should have had the decency to wait until he had gone to work before meeting in his living room.

Marina and the workshop group took up most of Frances's time and Hank would arrive home exhausted to find nothing in the fridge. The sink would be blocked, filled with dirty glasses from a meeting, floating in murky water, while Frances sat on the couch eating chocolates and reading the *New Yorker*. One of her friends was a poet who, despite being forty years old, still lived with his mother. He had once had a poem published in Canada. Frances told

Hank how depressed this friend was because he had lost his job driving a delivery truck. When Hank suggested that the man get a job at the post office she reacted in a fury, saying that her friend was 'too sensitive to work at the post office'. Hank complained in horror to Douglas Blazek about the 'potluck' dinners she attended and the 'long church drools' on Sundays and how her group met for coffee and cakes at Fay's or Marty's. 'They all STINK,' he concluded.

It was when they tried to interest Hank in civil rights marches that he got really annoyed. Bukowski was regarded by his workmates as one of the least prejudiced whites in the sorting office. His choice of the night shift meant that he was one of about 500 whites among 3,500 blacks. He got along with those people he liked, whatever colour they were, and disliked the rest. It was probably Bukowski's refusal to become a knee jerk liberal that gained him respect at work, and his insistence on only treating people as individuals that irked Frances's workshop chums.

At De Longpre another change was that Hank no longer had to hide his drinking from his landlord, it was the landlords who were his drinking partners. They first visited six months after Hank and Frances moved in and Grace caused a fuss over the state of the kitchen and bathroom; Hank never bothered to clean up and Frances wasn't much of a housekeeper either, but Hank managed to calm her down and they were soon slugging it down so that even Hank confessed to being 'very drunk'.

In March 1965 Bukowski again visited the Webbs in New Orleans to work on his second book with them, *Crucifix in a Deathhand*, and to add his signature to 3,000 sheets as it was to be a signed edition. Hank could not believe the conditions they worked in. There was no room for a guest but they had arranged for Hank to stay with their friend Minnie Sedgate, who lived in a large house just a few blocks away and was the owner of the Country Kitchen restaurant on Chartres Street. Louise told her he was a great poet. Louise Webb: 'She didn't give a damn whether he was a great poet ... She liked men, you know. Oh boy! She got the right one.' Hank took over a six-pack and the two of them hit it off right away. 'She fed him that first night they were together, and he had the best of everything. He'd eaten like he'd never eaten before in his life. And she drank like he did, so everything was perfect.' Bukowski described Minnie as 'a fat, kind woman whose husband had died'.

Hank would wake up around 10.30 a.m., usually feeling quite sick and hungover. He would stagger up and down the long, narrow hallways of Minnie's house, hiding from the fierce New Orleans sun, as he conducted the ritual morning vomiting of a confirmed alcoholic. Then he would dress and walk round to 1109 Royal Street to see the Webbs, looking for a beer. The printing press was below street level and Hank would peek down at Jon before he knocked, watching him wrestle with the machinery. Webb would always ask if he had any new poems, and Bukowski never did, having only just got up. Hank would repeat his request for a beer but Webb would shake his head. Webb could be very fierce if Hank didn't produce a handful of poems each day and was not pleasant to be around when he was in that state. Hank would then shamble back to Minnie's and bang out a few on the typewriter. He would return in the evening with six or seven and Jon Webb would look them through, select two or three he particularly liked, then say: 'OK, go get a beer from the box,' and they all drank and talked until the early hours of the morning, seated around a small table in the kitchen, watching the cockroaches run up and down the wall next to them. The roaches particularly liked to circle around an unshaded lightbulb sticking out of the wall.

It Catches My Heart in Its Hands had been a retrospective and the Webbs had the pick of everything Hank had written up to that date. Rather than use poems rejected for that volume in the new book, they wanted new poems, but Hank didn't have nearly enough of the same high quality to make a book so he had to write them on the spot. The bulk of the poems were written during that one very hot month in Minnie's house. He describes handing a sheaf of ten or twenty poems to Jon Webb each day and Webb would keep a straight face and ask: 'Is that all?' and all the time, in what sounds like *Dharma Bums*-period Kerouac, Hank was 'struggling back with wondrous six-packs' to Royal Street for an evening's drinking. Hank had never focused so hard on his writing and it began to get to him; he would stagger as he walked down the street, even though he was sober, and when he was drunk, he behaved very badly.

Writing from New Orleans Hank told Al Purdy that he was sitting at Minnie's, sick, shaking and frightened, feeling cowardly and depressed. He had hurt almost everybody's feelings and recognised that he was not a very good drunk. He said he only wanted 'sweet peace and kindliness' when he awoke but there was always a finger pointing, telling him of some terrible deed committed during the night. It used to be his father's finger, now it was his editor's. But after a few bad days in New Orleans they all adjusted to each other and ignored each other enough to be comfortable.

Hank had hoped that Jon Webb would let him illustrate *Crucifix* himself and sent him a pile of early drawings, but Webb brought in a professional, Noel Rockmore, to do it. He didn't return Hank's drawings. Though Hank realised that, with a few obvious exceptions, the work was not as good as the previous book, he was not too disappointed and later described his period in New Orleans as his 'lyric period' when he pounded out 'fat rolling lines' and drank gallons of beer. The visit itself was of course used as material for later poems, particularly in 'How to Get Published' where Jon and Louise Webb become HR Mulloch and Honeysuckle, and Hank gives a very funny account of dogs, a parrot and lots of whiskey.

The biggest upset came when John William Corrington, who wrote the introduction to *It Catches My Heart in Its Hands*, drove over from Baton Rouge to finally meet the man with whom he had been corresponding for four years. Unfortunately he arrived with Miller Williams, another university professor, and the two of them spent the evening trying to outpoint each other in matters to do with degrees and how they were going to take over the university magazine, the usual academic power-play and intrigue that bored Bukowski. Hank claimed that they totally ignored him except when one suddenly noticed him, turned to him and said, 'My balls hurt!' Hank told him that was too bad, and they returned to their university conversation. Corrington was an overconfident, agreeable young man who expected everyone to be interested in his recent studies at the new University of Sussex in Brighton, in the south of England, where he had just taken his doctorate. There was also a lawyer present and Hank clearly felt alienated and out of his depth. When Corrington, a Southerner, began to defend the right-wing Republican Barry Goldwater, Hank launched into full verbal attack. Over the years their letters had achieved a greater and greater intimacy so that, although they had not met, they regarded each other as friends. This was the end of the friendship though they continued to correspond.

Hank was not paid by Jon Webb for publishing his books so Hank undersold him with the free copies he received in lieu of payment. He sold Henry Miller three copies of *Crucifix in a Deathhand* for $15 because Miller had a rich patron who didn't want to pay $7.50 for each. Miller wrote to Hank: 'I hope you're not drinking yourself to death! And especially not when you're writing. It's a sure way to kill the source of inspiration. Drink only when you're happy *if you can*. Never to drown your sorrows and never drink alone!'

As far as Hank was concerned the very *best* way to drink was alone, though he stuck to beer whenever possible because his stomach was in a perilous condition and he believed the doctors who told him that with the next haemorrhage he would be dead. Unfortunately, drinking was a central part of the self-created Bukowski myth; and it was already out of control. Publishers and editors magnified and glorified his achievements, making him into a romantic loner. Jon Webb added six inches to his height, and no doubt exaggerated his consumption, when he told the *Vieux Carre Courier*: 'Bukowski is a tough write, but in person he is very gentle – for a guy who is six foot six. He drinks about a case of beer a day, and that doesn't stop him from writing 30 poems a week. When he was down here visiting the other week he drank 30 beers at one sitting. He was still articulate.'

In July Hank finally got hold of a copy of *Journey to the End of the Night* by Louis-Ferdinand Céline; a book which had been a tremendous influence on Burroughs, Ginsberg and Kerouac in the 40s. Hank went to bed with the book and a big box of Ritz crackers. He read the book in one sitting and roared with laugher all the way through it. At the end the box of Ritz crackers was empty. He got up and drank gallons of water until he couldn't move. He told actor Sean Penn: 'That's what a good writer will do to you. He'll damn near kill you!' He was amazed. He told the rare book dealer Jim Roman: 'Finally reading Céline and it's about time. A master, no doubt of it,' and he described Céline to Steve Richmond and others as someone who could write better that he did, a rare admission. Hank was overjoyed; at last there was someone else to do 'the dirty work'. He told Richmond there were so few people he could read, listing Camus' *The Stranger*, the early novels of Sartre, the few poems of 'that homo' Genet, Jeffers and early Auden as work that was up to scratch. Hank said he could never get into Céline's other books, though *Death on the Instalment Plan* would surely have appealed to him.

In the summer of 1965 simmering resentment in the Watts area of Los Angeles at the racism and brutality of the LAPD finally erupted during a heat wave when a policeman used his baton against a crowd of bystanders during a routine traffic violation. Watts went up in flames and sometimes special arrangements had to be made to get post office personnel in and out of the building as smoke from the burning ghetto and sporadic street fighting erupted near the building. The five days of rioting left more than 34 people dead, almost all of them black, and at least 1,000 injured. An estimated $200 million in property was destroyed by looting and burning, including the whole Watts business district, which was razed to the ground. This gave rise to unpleasant tension at work; to most of the black workforce – those who didn't know him – Hank was just another white guy, and they reacted by spitting at him or cursing him. He sensibly ignored it, but when he got home he drank even harder.

He was encouraged by his landlords who showed up at his door about once a week to invite him over, invariably when he was in the middle of writing a poem. They liked to sing along to show tunes, particularly *Oklahoma*. He asked if they had *Guys and Dolls* at least, but they didn't, so *Oklahoma* it was. Hank liked a singalong and joined right in. Fortunately Frances and Marina, now a year old, would usually show up to rescue him before he became insensible. That November he had another haemorrhage and coughed up half a pint of blood. He was slowly killing himself with drink, though, as he saw it, it was someone else's fault: 'They beat you down with their factories, their booze, their women, until you are no longer any use to them or yourself.' Certainly racial tension at work had made the post office almost unbearable. The difficulties of sharing the small cottage with Frances and a baby while working nights and trying to write poetry, combined with the tiredness and exhaustion associated with alcoholism, conspired to make his life a misery and he frequently felt suicidal.

His drinking was gradually getting out of hand: in late May he drank so much that he fell down in the bathroom and vomited over himself. The next month he bragged to Blazek about how much he was drinking: he had a pint of Scotch to drink after he finished a dozen half-quart cans: 'so it figures to be a burning and perhaps ugly night, but maybe easy enough.' In an undated letter from 1965 to Douglas Blazek he wrote in a black depression that he badly wanted to kill himself and wished he had a gun, but this was exacerbated by a bad toothache. He took five days off over Labor Day and went on a bender, finishing up with bruises and scabs on each knee and elbow from falling over drunk in the streets. Naturally some of this activity resulted in his ending up in the drunk tank, which in Los Angeles had piped-in Muzak. After one party at an expensive apartment his last memory of the evening was of lifting some girl's dress up to her waist and kissing her legs. After that was a blank, though the police no doubt played their traditional role. Lying on the floor next to him in the cell was a young man whose arm had been broken by the police when they worked him over but he was not intending to complain to the judge as that would have only resulted in a longer sentence and another beating.

The only advantage to being an alcoholic was that it made it impossible for some people to deal with him. Hank had been engaged in a long correspondence with Sheri Martinelli, Ezra Pound's ex-girlfriend and biggest fan. Though she advertised this fact at every opportunity, whenever Hank mentioned her in a poem she was incensed by what she regarded as talking out of school. Hank had never met her but one of her boyfriends came down from San Francisco and informed Hank that they were going to sue him for using Sheri in one of his poems. Hank was there with Frances and was lying drunk on the floor at the time. 'OK,' Hank told him. 'If you're going to sue that's the way it works, only I don't have any money, I don't even have a jockstrap.' Then he turned on a tape he had made while drunk and lay on the floor listening to his witticisms, jokes, madness and singing. The man refused to join him in a drink and pretty soon gave up and went away. No law suit was forthcoming.

The drinking was beginning to affect Hank's relationships with his friends. He misbehaved so badly one night that autumn during a visit to the Webbs at their new home in Santa Fe that he was locked out of the house in an icy rainstorm. He was drunk and began banging on the doors until they finally relented and let him in but he was forced to listen to a long angry speech. On the train on the way back to Los Angeles his foot began to swell. Hank liked to walk around barefoot when he was drunk and some of the tiny shards of broken glass from his habit of smashing glasses and bottles had embedded themselves in his flesh. He found a German doctor who sliced open his heel and dug and probed without giving him a local anaesthetic. Bukowski reported their exchange to Douglas Blazek: 'Vell, vell, you took it like a man!'

Hank: 'You enjoyed it more than I did.'

'Nein, Nein . . .'

Back home his depression and drinking was exacerbated by Marina's crying in the other room, which disturbed his writing. He told Blazek: 'her cries cut through all my poems, all my writing, but she is a sweetie, they have not gotten to her yet, she is all eyes and skin, she bends, she bubbles . . . she wails.' Frances would bring Marina in when Hank was working and sit her in a chair at his elbow where she could watch him type; he adored her but living with them made it impossible for him to work.

Hank and Frances split up amicably at the end of November. Frances took a place at 5526 Carlton Way, about ten blocks away, that Hank helped to find, and he helped her move out. Hank continued to assume financial responsibility and always remained a reliable source of money and a loving father to his daughter. Hank paid the rent and Frances brought Marina to visit every day. He told Blazek: 'I am soft in the head for her, Marina. The other day Frances brought her over and I was in bed asleep and she crawled on my chest and looked at my face and smiled like crazy and then she kissed me on the mouth. Little wench. And then she laughed. She's all full of this kind of love and she makes me remember somehow how it once was.' It always tore him up when he left them after a visit at their place. Marina screaming, 'No, No, No!' and crying as he struggled into his old '57 Plymouth: ('as what is left of me gets into what is left of the car'.)

7. CHINASKI RIDES OUT

In the middle of an afternoon in March 1966, Bukowski was sitting on his couch, well into his second six-pack of beer, when someone knocked on the door. He opened it to find a balding, red-faced man with a high forehead and 'well-scrubbed' face wearing a faint, perpetual grin. He was dressed conservatively in a suit and tie. Somewhat suspiciously, for such people rarely visited his abode, Hank asked him what he wanted. His visitor's name was John Martin and he turned out to be a great admirer of his work. Hank invited him in and sociably offered him a beer, which Martin declined on the grounds that he was teetotal and a Christian Scientist. This made Hank even more suspicious.

John Martin was the manager of a furniture and office supply company who had encountered Hank's work in *Outsider* magazine. He was also a rare book collector. He asked Hank if he had any poems he could see. Hank pointed across the room and told him to 'Open the closet.' A mountain of paper was stacked haphazardly inside in front of a mannequin called Sadie that Hank had bought from a junk shop. He described her in several poems, 'she was a hot number'.

The poems began to tumble out onto the floor. Martin sat down.

'How long did it take you to write this?' he asked. Hank considered the question:

'Half a year, three or four months, a year and half.' Martin was astonished at the quantity and asked if he could read some of them. 'Go right ahead.' Hank told him.

Hank sat there on the couch, drinking his beer, while Martin sat on the floor in front of the cupboard and pored over the manuscripts. Bukowski re-created some of the dialogue. Martin would pick up one of the poems and say:

'Oh, this is *very* good.'

'Oh yeah?' Hank would reply.

'This is great. This is an immortal poem.'

'Oh yeah?'

'This one's not so good here, this one's not so good. Oh. Hey!' and then he would get very excited. He sat in front of the cupboard for a long time going through all the poems – they were mostly poems – then he told Hank:

'You know, I'm starting a press.'

'Oh yeah?' Martin asked if could take three or four of the poems with him to look over because he thought they would be suitable to publish as broadsides. Then Martin told him:

'There'll probably be some money in it for you, I don't know how much, we'll have to see.' This was a new development. Hank said:

'That's OK, just, you know, whatever.'

A few days later John Martin telephoned and offered an advance of $30 each for four of the poems to use as broadsides: 'True Story'; 'On Going Out to Get the Mail'; 'To Kiss the Worms Goodnight' and 'The Girls'. He published them in April, May, June and July of that year, handset on beautiful deckle-edged paper in editions of thirty copies each, all signed by Hank. Twenty-seven of each were for sale at $10 each, a price which reflected the expensive paper used and the fact that in theory Martin could have placed most of them with bookshops, who in those days took one third of the published price. In fact he says that the first broadside was given away, though the others were sold. They were the first four publications of the Black Sparrow Press, which grew to become America's most important publisher of poetry. Hank says that when they came out he took Sadie the mannequin and dumped her behind an old folks home. He no longer needed her because, as he said, the real Sadies began to come round right then. As for John Martin, the Black Sparrow Press became Bukowski's publisher for the rest of his life – and beyond. Bukowski was so prolific that there were many books' worth of poems remaining to be published at the time of his death.

John Martin was everything an author could want from a publisher. The previous April Hank's old typewriter had finally fallen apart; irreparable. It was like the death of an old friend after all they had been through together. He bought a cheap second-hand portable but it took some getting used to because Hank was used to pounding away at the keys of his 'typer', as he called it, and getting a satisfyingly loud sound from the carriage as it clacked along. Martin recognised his need and bought him a large heavy Underwood. Martin also sent him envelopes of stamps to enable him to mail copies of his poems to him and to little magazines and encouraged him to keep carbons of his work so that important poems did not get lost forever.

By the mid-1960s Bukowski had a large body of published work. After *Flower, Fist and Bestial Wail* in 1960, he had chapbooks published by Epos Quarterly, who devoted a special issue to his work in 1962; by 7 Poets Press in New York who published *Longshot Poems for Broke Players* that same year and *Run with the Hunted*, published by RR Cuscaden at Midwest Poetry Chapbooks also in 1962. Cuscaden has the distinction of being the first person to write a critical appraisal of Bukowski's work; his 'Charles Bukowski: Poet in a Ruined Landscape' appeared in the spring–summer 1962 edition of *Satis* though there had been previous reviews. After the two Loujon Press books came *Cold Dogs in the Courtyard*, published in Chicago by LiteraryTimes-Cyfoeth in 1965 and *Confessions of a Man Insane Enough to Live with Beasts*, mimeoed by Douglas Blazek at *Ole* magazine in Bensonville, Illinois (that is 'ole' as in 'hole', not the Spanish Olé). Blazek was one of Bukowski's great supporters and their correspondence gives a very accurate picture of Bukowski's state of mind and day to day activities during the years that Blazek published his work.

In December 1965 Hank's health had deteriorated and he began to get fainting spells when he was working. They were so bad that it was all he could do to keep from falling to the floor. It was very embarrassing; he felt very weak and had pain in the throat, the back, chest and shoulders, he had scratched both his legs raw with his fingernails and was sick to his stomach. Things got worse over the Christmas period when Hank was forced to work overtime during the rush and resented it. Unlike his fellow workers, he wanted a small amount of money and lots of time off. What he found was that it either worked one way or the other: no job and sleeping out in the alley, scavenging for food; or a job seven days a week, eleven hours a day, and no time to himself at all.

Then on 2 March he entered Queen of Angels hospital where he was operated on for a haemorrhoid condition so bad that they also had to remove part of an intestine which had been pushed out of shape. He was in considerable pain for many days, sitting on a pillow to ease his discomfort. He was confined to a ward with a fellow patient who never shut his TV off so Hank was condemned to watch hour upon hour of American television, which almost drove him mad. Typically, he wrote up the whole grisly episode as the humorous story, 'All the Assholes in the World and Mine', which Douglas Blazek published as a little chapbook from his Open Skull Press, later that year. The story is now included in *South of No North*.

It was 1966 when, in addition to meeting John Martin, Bukowski first began his correspondence with Carl Weissner who was to become his German agent and translator. Weissner edited a mimeographed literary magazine called *Klactoveedsedsteen* – named after the Charlie Parker number – from Heidelberg, publishing people like Harold Norse, Diane di Prima, Larry Eigner, Allen Ginsberg, William Burroughs and the cut-ups gang: Mary Beach, Claude Pelieu, Jeff Nuttall and Weissner himself, as well as a number of European writers less known in the States such as Simon Vinkenoog. It was clear that Hank was impressed at being regarded as a member of the international avant garde and his letters are rather self-consciously literary and, though he would have hated to admit it, Beat Generation-orientated. In a letter to Weissner dated 27 January 1967, reprinted in the September 1967 issue of *Klacto*, Hank wrote: 'Every now and then I fall into this real sheer depression bit, the rusty razorblade fog green sliding sides, vomit moon, cancer kiss of sheets, I AM THE PURPLE KID WITH LEPER LEG BRAIN SLIDING LIKE A LOOSE EGG YOLK ON TOP OF DIRTY STOVE IN MIDDLE OF JANUARY RAIN WHILE THE SPIDER SNEEZES the blues get so purple that my head hurts . . .' for four more lines, which, even if it was a parody of the Burroughs–Pelieu–Weissner collaboration in the previous issue, still came out as a pretty good example of the genre.

Hank's friend the poet Steve Richmond was an ex-lawyer who had given up the profession to live outside straight society. He once told Hank that he was due to inherit a lot of money when he was 25 so it was not quite the sacrifice that one might think. He was something of a loner, though he had many girlfriends. He ran a small bookshop called Earth Books at 244 Ocean Park Boulevard, in the run-down neighbourhood of Santa Monica, down near the beach bordering on Venice. The shop was dedicated to little literary magazines and poetry books and stocked everything by Hank. He published one issue of a literary newspaper called *Earth Rose* and there would have been more issues but on 1 November 1966 the shop was raided by the police. Four people were arrested and the newspaper and two dozen books, including some of Hank's, were seized as being obscene. They even took a letter from the typewriter that he was writing to Hank when they burst in. It was the headline in *Earth Rose* that aroused their ire: 'FUCK HATE whereby, on this day we able minded creators do hereby tell you, the Establishment: FUCK YOU IN THE MOUTH. WE'VE HEARD ENOUGH OF YOUR BULLSHIT.' That didn't go down well with the cops. Jim Lowell's Asphodel bookshop in Cleveland was raided less than two months later and Ed Sanders' Peace Eye bookshop in New York was raided earlier that year as the American establishment tried to contain the growing wave of underground and avant garde publications.

Bukowski was one of the authors who contributed to *A Tribute to Jim Lowell*, published in Cleveland in June 1967 to raise funds for his defence. One of the books seized at the Asphodel was Bukowski's *The Genius of the Crowd*, published in Cleveland in 1966 by DA Levy's 7 Flowers Press. (Levy had attracted attention by publishing an eccentrically hand-set literary magazine called the *Marrawanna Review*, also seized by the police.) Richmond's Earth Books remained open while he was out on bail and became a centre for anti-censorship activism. Hank kept in touch largely by letter as the store was some distance from where he lived though he sometimes made it to the coast to visit the Venice Café. Though Hank did not read there himself, he would attend readings and events; the owners kept him supplied with beer and wine as his presence was enough in itself to energise the whole scene. After one reading at the Venice Café there was a party at Steve Richmond's apartment in Ocean Park, where Bukowski lived up to his legend by pulling his pants down around his ankles and bending over, his head looking out between his legs while Steve Richmond's dog, a bitch, licked his balls and ass.

Hank's absenteeism began to cause him problems at the post office and he was officially reprimanded. There was no parking near the post office so he had to explore the area to find something nearby. He found a splendid spot on a dirt road behind a slaughterhouse. The downside of the spot – which no one else ever seemed to want – was that as he sat and smoked a final cigarette before clocking in, he had to watch the pigs being herded onto the runways which led to the killing floor where their throats were slit. Many evenings he was so dispirited after watching this slaughter that he finished his cigarette and drove home again instead of clocking in. He says that his absenteeism reached such proportions that he finally had to pay to park behind a Chinese bar where the view contained nothing more threatening than a neon sign for an Oriental drink.

On his way home from his shift at the post office Hank would often stop to visit his friend John Thomas in Echo Park. The walls and ceilings of the house were covered with a collage of newsclippings, photographs of Sitting Bull, Hitler, Lucky Luciano, Al Capone, gangsters on their deathbeds, transcripts of their last words. Thomas was a huge man, bearded, who according to Hank 'sat in his chair like a Buddha'. Thomas had a huge library, most of it rotting in his cellar. He was a brilliant chess player and a superb conversationalist and would listen calmly as Hank spouted off on the state of poetry and the world. Thomas recorded much of it and sometimes would play it back to him the next day and 'I would realise how pitiful, how cheap, how inept I sounded.' Their talks often lasted seven or eight hours, fuelled by amphetamines that Thomas kept in a big bowl on his coffee table. Thomas had other visitors, and on speed it seemed to Hank that they were also brilliant and interesting. It was a haven from the post office and his drab life in East Hollywood.

In December 1967, during the taping sessions, Thomas asked Hank to bring over some poems to read aloud. Hank was writing well during this period, having gone through what he called a two-year 'slump' from October 1964 until October 1966. Though he wrote plenty of poems, many of which were published, he did not care for them very much. Whereas, by February 1967: 'they come out full of butter and steel'. He took some of the new poems over to Thomas's house and they made a tape but afterwards he left the poems behind and forgot about them and they got thrown away. A few days later, Thomas phoned Hank and said: 'Those poems, Bukowski, would make a good book.'

'What poems, John?' he asked. Thomas had taken out the tape of Hank's poems and listened to it again. Hank realised that he had no actual copies of the poems and told Thomas: 'I'd have to type them off the tape, it's just too much work.' But Thomas generously offered to type them up for him, an offer that he naturally agreed to. Not long afterwards he had the poems back in typescript. Hank checked the transcriptions against the recording and found that Thomas had done a careful, accurate job. Hank showed them to John Martin, who took them home to look them over. A few days later he telephoned to say: 'You have a book there and I'm going to publish it myself.' Hank called it *At Terror Street and Agony Way*. John Martin published it in May 1968 at the Black Sparrow Press, at the same time issuing the tape recording of Hank reading the poems in a limited edition of fifty copies. There were 75 hardbound copies, signed, numbered and each with an original drawing or painting by Hank. He originally did sixty but John Martin called and said: 'Give me twenty more and I'll pick them up Monday' as if paintings could be turned out like a production line. Hank complained to Carl Weissner: 'Each painting must come from the balls like a fuck. Few men can fuck six times a night. Twenty is just impossible.' In the meantime John Martin had been busy and had published books by Paul Bowles, Diane Wakowsi, Robert Kelly, Denise Levertov and others, even Hank's old bête noir Robert Creeley, so it was time for a book from Bukowski.

At Terror Street and Agony Way sold extremely well, and only two weeks after publication Hank received a royalty cheque from Martin for $460. As he owed the post office 192 hours' work for sick leave this just about saved him from going under. Martin wanted to publish Hank's next book, and Hank wanted him to do it. The problem was that he felt indebted to Jon Webb who had suggested doing a third volume of Hank's work, but had not made any specific suggestions. The big difference being, of course, that John Martin paid and Jon Webb didn't. Hank struggled to find a way to extricate himself from the Webbs without upsetting them but in the end, on 4 June 1968, he bit the bullet and wrote to Webb, explaining how important the Black Sparrow royalties were to him and asking him to understand his situation, adding: 'And I hope that you don't get pissed and we have to go into one of our long dark silences. As crappy as I feel that wouldn't help much.'

Hank had also kept in touch with John Bryan, ever since he ran a poem called 'The Way to Review a Play and Keep Everybody Happy But Me' in the first issue of *Renaissance* magazine in July 1961. Hank had more in the third issue and Bryan published him again when he started *Notes from Underground* in San Francisco in 1964. After spending time as a music critic and reporter for the San

Francisco *Examiner* and then the San Francisco *Chronicle*, John Bryan started *Open City* in November 1964 with his $700 severance cheque from the *Chronicle*, hand-setting the headlines and printing it himself on an ex-US Army surplus multigraph printing press. Then called the *San Francisco Open City Press* it ran for fifteen issues. Bukowski had a story in issue 6 in January 1966.

To pay his rent Bryan became the editor of the Sunday Review section of William Randolph Hearst's Los Angeles *Herald-Examiner* but quit after two years because the management wanted him to remove a woodcut of the Madonna and child from his office wall because Jesus had his penis showing. This was the subject of his first column for the Los Angeles *Free Press*, Art Kunkin's new underground newspaper. Bryan decided to publish his own underground paper and revived the name *Open City*.

Hank had published several pieces in the Los Angeles *Free Press* but when *Open City* began in May 1967, he became a staff columnist, and for 87 weeks (*Open City* ran for 92 weeks before folding) he wrote the 'Notes of a Dirty Old Man' column, named for him by Bryan, between 1967 and 1969. Some of his friends were quite shocked to find that he was writing a column as he used to laugh at Lawrence Lipton for writing his Radio Free America for the Los Angeles *Free Press*, but Hank had a ready answer: 'Lipton writes a kind of left-wing Walter Winchell thing. I create Art. There's a difference.' He liked the immediacy of deadlines. He knew that once a week he had to hand in his copy. He would lie around, leaving it until the last minute, so that if he didn't write it then it would be too late. Then he would seat himself in front of the typewriter, staring at the white sheet of paper, often with no idea at all of what he was going to write: 'And it would come, 'cause the deadline was there. And you would just think, writing for a deadline, you get a piece of shit, right? And sometimes it's dead. But a lot of times, if the deadlines weren't there, I would never have written and come up with something really lucky.' 'I wrote one a week whether I felt like writing or not. It was good discipline.'

Bukowski felt ambivalent about the hippies at *Open City*, calling them 'Commie scum'. Most of the staff were not hippies; Mike Hodel, the office manager, was a pipe-smoking, short-haired academic-type with leather patches on his tweed jacket. There were some hippies there as *Open City* – like most underground papers – was typeset at the last minute in a frenzied all-night session at the IBM compositor, aided by vast amounts of amphetamine. The *Open City* office looked like a hard-core hippie pad but this was for the curious reason that the premises had actually once been a Hollywood movie set for an underground newspaper and had a huge, badly painted, psychedelic mural all across the back wall. It could only happen in Hollywood.

Bukowski was older than the parents of many of the people there and some, particularly the young women, didn't like the way he leered at their legs. John Bryan summed up their attitude: 'We knew the bastard was an asshole but we also knew that he was a GREAT asshole. Bukowski was born lucky. He had endless energy and style. He could produce unimaginable quantities of first-rate prose and poetry at a single sitting. He had a certain loathsome charm. How can you hate a talent like that?'

John Bryan lived near Bukowski and they saw a lot of each other. Bryan loaned Hank money, babysat Marina, worried with him over Frances's latest radical activities: 'listened to him scream and curse the world all night, screamed back, wiped up his treacly vomit, believed in the crazy bastard and trusted him with my life.' They shared intimacies; Bryan regarded him as a friend and told him everything.

Bryan should have realised that this was not a good idea from reading Hank's column. Nothing was immune from his gaze and he was prepared to write about anything. Jon Webb was one of the first people to feel betrayed by him.

In the 14 July 1967 issue of *Open City* Hank wrote a column thinly fictionalising his visit to the Webbs who were now in Tucson, Arizona, identifying Webb only as 'the great editor'. The Webbs had arranged for him to stay in a university-owned cottage but the temperature was 100–110 degrees every day, too hot to go outside, and it wore Hank down. He spent much of his time drinking with Louise's old father and playing cards for dimes with the Webbs. Jon Webb kept trying to get Hank to write an attack on the hippies but Hank had nothing against them; he was neither for nor against, whereas Webb was violently opposed. Jon had dyed his white hair red, which took some getting used to and despite being as broke as ever, they kept running off to Las Vegas where Louise played the slot machines – behaviour that Hank felt was 'a type of madness' considering their finances. Some of Hank's aggressiveness in Tucson may have been due to the fact that the Webbs were now heavily involved with publishing a Henry Miller book and Hank felt sidelined.

On his return to Los Angeles he let his vindictiveness run loose and Hank told the story of a few things that had happened in

Tucson on some very hot days and published it in his column. He mischievously sent a copy to a reporter on the *Tucson Daily Citizen*, causing a terrible falling out between them. Hank recognised his debt to the Webbs, but did not think his column was hateful or unjust. Jon Webb remained hurt and angry with Bukowski for the rest of his life. Hank didn't see why anyone should object to what he said when he wrote similar things about himself, often showing himself up to be foolish or describing embarrassing situations. He didn't realise that some people valued their privacy.

'Notes of a Dirty Old Man' finally made Bukowski famous, and in turn he made *Open City* a success. His columns were without doubt the best material in the paper. Every week Hank was promoted on the streets of Los Angeles. *Open City* was sent free to a select mailing list of writers, directors, producers, musicians, actors, artists and entertainment industry executives; everyone in the city who was creatively engaged saw a copy and it was mailed to people in New York, London, Paris and across the globe. Each week five to fifteen thousand copies were printed; half of which were given away. The other half were sold for ten cents from vending machines and street sellers on the Strip, near recording studios, publishing houses, the giant movie lots and television cities, on the beach at Santa Monica, some even sold in conservative Orange County. Suddenly Bukowski went from being known to a tiny subculture of small mimeographed literary magazines, to reaching the literate public of the media capital of the world. He became a Los Angeles celebrity. 'Ordinary people who despised all poetry and its effete creators took Bukowski to their hearts,' said John Bryan.

Bukowski's column began in the second issue of *Open City* in May 1967 and it was not long before an interfering busybody reported him to the post office enclosing a sheaf of newsclippings from his column with certain passages outlined in ink, in particular a column about the post office and one about sodomy. On 8 January 1968, someone contacted the FBI to inform them that he was 'allegedly writing obscene articles for the "Open City" newspaper at Los Angeles, California, and that he was not married to the individual shown as his beneficiary for his Life and Health Benefits Insurance'. The FBI began an investigation, gathering back issues of *Open City* as 'exhibits'. On 8 February 1968, Hank was called into an office to explain himself to a post office manager and an FBI agent. They sat there in a large, dark room with one tablelamp with a run of *Open City* on the table before them. They told him they were considering charging him with Conduct Unbecoming a Postal Employee and asked if he was going to write anything more about the post office. He told them he probably wouldn't, but reminded them of his constitutional rights. 'Are we to consider the postal authorities as the new critics of literature?' he asked them and also mentioned the American Civil Liberties Union (ACLU). The post office manager was confused and said that they hadn't had a case like this in ten years which made Hank wonder who the previous suspect was. The men were astonished to find that he had published a number of books and wanted to know how much he had had to pay to have them published. The solution proposed by the post office manager was for Hank to resign, but he refused. It seemed to be stalemate so Hank went back to his post.

Hank was broke, as usual, but with help from John Bryan he sold a collection of his columns in *Open City* to Essex House as *Notes of a Dirty Old Man* for $1,000 advance on royalties. Essex House was an erotic imprint, a subsidiary of Milton Luros's Parliament News empire. It was unusual among such publishers in that it required its authors to use their real names and among the fifty or so titles published were works by Philip Jose Farmer and Michael Perkins. Hank received a typical paperback deal for the time: 4 per cent of retail price up to 150,000 copies, 6 per cent after that. It was published some time later in January 1969.

One night in January 1968, when he was dropping off his column at *Open City*, John Bryan pulled Hank over and introduced him to Neal Cassady. Hank had a six-pack with him and offered one to Cassady who swallowed it down like water. Hank was impressed and gave him another one. Outside it was beginning to rain as Bryan, Hank and Cassady got into the car. Next they got to experience one of Cassady's famous car rides on the rain-slick streets, Cassady making split-second decisions and narrowly missing the other cars as he shot through impossible spaces. Bryan later claimed that Hank had soiled his pants. At Bryan's they all ate and had a few more drinks. Cassady died only two weeks later. The incident provoked one of Hank's more famous memoirs.

In August 1968 John Bryan asked Hank to guest-edit *Renaissance*, a literary magazine that Bryan had resurrected as an insert in *Open City*. Hank was given complete editorial freedom to choose the poems and stories. Hank told Steve Richmond that he could see why Bryan didn't want the job after he had ploughed through all the 'half-assed' submissions that Bryan already had. Hank began writing to people he knew to get some good stuff; to make a section that would be 'stone pure hard'. He only accepted three of Richmond's poems and told him that was more than he had accepted from anyone else; Blazek only got two in. Many of Hank's correspondents were irritated at being rejected. It was not all poetry, and Hank took a short story by the poet Jack Micheline called 'Skinny Dynamite', about a red-haired New York girl who liked to fuck. This proved to be the paper's undoing.

Renaissance, Open City's Magazine of the Arts, appeared as the second section of *Open City* volume 70 on 20 September 1968. Hank was angry because Bryan had slipped in some poetry by Diane di Prima without him knowing, poetry he didn't like.

Alerted by their investigation of Bukowski, the FBI was monitoring *Open City's* every move. The Micheline story was just what the FBI was waiting for. They tipped off the county and the Sheriff's deputies arrested Bryan for publishing obscenity, beating him up on the way to the jail. The legal fees bankrupted *Open City*, which closed down after a run just short of two years; Hank donated $100 to the bust fund but the lawyers charged $10,000. Bryan's wife Joan suffered an acute attack of paranoia about being in Los Angeles and persuaded her husband that they should move out. A year later the judge in Beverly Hills dropped the obscenity charges, but it was too late to save the paper and Bryan was long gone.

Now, just as he had written insensitively about Jon Webb, Hank turned his hand to John Bryan, the man who, more than anyone to date, had made his name in Los Angeles. Hank wrote the whole story of *Open City* and its demise in a thinly fictionalised short story called 'The Birth, Life and Death of an Underground Newspaper', which was published in the September 1969 issue of the wide circulation literary glossy *Evergreen Review*. *Open City* was called *Open Pussy* and all the main protagonists were easily identifiable, particularly John Bryan and his wife. Years later John Bryan wrote simply: 'He betrayed me and for twenty-five years I hated his guts but today forgave him.' The problem was that much of what Hank said was true. Bryan wrote: 'What hurt the most was that I went to Bukowski as a friend when I was fighting for my life and what I told him in strict confidence were my most hideous secrets and my darkest nightmares. I needed help. I was on the verge of self-destruct. Bukowski laughed and sneered and told the world.' Bryan's conclusion, after Bukowski's death, was that he was 'a great writer and a lousy human being'.

In fact, most people thought that Bukowski was exaggerating and fictionalising what went on. Then in the December 1969 issue of *Evergreen Review* there appeared a letter from Robert Igriega who had been the news editor on *Open City* who said:

> I can attest, though not many will believe me, that everything he says is true. (Which makes me wonder about his other fantastical stories – the three-hundred pound whore, and Jimmy Valentine who pissed in ladies' refrigerators – could it *all* be true?) Some considered Bukowski the flagship of *Open City*, a great rusting hulk riddled with torpedoes that ploughed on, the rest of us fluttering like pennants on him. (This ignores the stainless steel ego that keeps him afloat.) Bukowski was by no means the only good writer on *Open City*, though I would probably agree with him that he was the only great one.

Igriega was right, the stories *were* all true.

Bukowski: 'Those were great days writing a column for the hippie newspapers. I had total freedom to say whatever I wanted. *Open City* was the best of them all. It was a sad and terrible day when John Bryan had to close it down.'

The 60s were hotting up, but Hank was barely aware of the changes taking place all around him. In June 1967 he had to take another post office 'scheme' where he was examined on his knowledge of street numbers by blocks and intersections. He got a 98 per cent pass. But the post office was getting to him. In August he told Carl Weissner that he hadn't written a poem in four or five months and complained that at work they had installed an air conditioning system but it did not work, and people were falling off their chairs. He had dizzy spells and felt feverish. One night he could only work three hours before he almost passed out; he had to grab hold of the side of the letter case to prevent himself from falling. All his colleagues stared at him as he staggered out. He had been counselled that he missed too many days and had been given warnings. They genuinely thought he was faking. The post office doctor told him straight out: 'There's nothing wrong with you, Bukowski! Next patient.' Outside on the street the colours seemed harsh, the shadows too dark. He managed to drive home but, even there, the heat was nightmarish. He had a fan but it was ineffectual; he had the door of the fridge open and it had frozen solid into a block of ice but the ice didn't melt. It didn't even feel cold, more like a block of marble. He dared not drink in case he passed out. The radio barely played – this was nothing to do with the heat but because of Hank's habit of throwing it out of the window. One time he forgot that the screen was there so there was now a big hole in it. Sometimes, when his four-day weekend finally came round, he would pull down the shades, stuff the doorbell with rags, put the telephone in the refrigerator (when it was not blocked with ice) and go to bed for three or four days, depressed, exhausted, almost at the end of his tether.

All around him bungalows were being bulldozed and high-rise apartment buildings were going up at twice the rent. Construction workers in steel helmets holding claw hammers milled around in what were once suburban gardens. The noise of construction prevented him from sleeping when he got in from the night shift. But at least his landlord was in no hurry to sell. He and his wife continued to come over and Hank's depression would lift. Sometimes Hank threw enormous parties that lasted until the sun came up, or until his mood turned sour and he threw everyone out.

This was a side of Los Angeles he liked. People there had a way of minding their own business; he could have the isolation that he craved or, if the time seemed right, he could party. He could get on the phone and within an hour have a dozen people crammed into the house, drinking and laughing. 'But they won't come unless I phone them, unless I want them. You can have isolation or you can have the crowd. I tend to mix the two, with a preference for isolation.'

There was hardly room for a party. The living room was about twenty feet long by twelve feet wide, with the space occupied by a beaten-up sofa and an upholstered easy chair. A large wooden desk stood against the far wall, on top of which was a set of old wooden pigeonholes that Hank must have salvaged from the post office. There were thirty divisions in three rows and here Hank kept his typing paper and postcards, his paperclips, his envelopes, pens and pencils and stamps. Next to the sofa was a student-style bookcase constructed from three-foot-long wooden shelves, supported by housebricks and cement blocks that Hank had brought in from the street. It is an established fact that this type of bookshelf is not stable once it gets higher than five feet, which is how it was. Here Hank kept all his appearances in periodicals and copies of his books. In front of the window, next to the front door, stood Hank's typing table, and on that stood the big old Underwood. 'You can hit a big typewriter and hit it hard. Hate won't come through on a dinky portable. I literally dramatise the act of creating. I play powerful symphonies and smoke powerful cigars when I write.' In front of the sofa was a dirty rug. There was cigarette ash everywhere, dishes in the sink, and the place hadn't been cleaned since someone else last did it.

The walls held some of Hank's paintings. After his experience in the art class with Barbara he had continued painting and the best were now on display. At one point he had accumulated more than fifty paintings and in order to study them he had covered his walls with them. There were so many that he continued across the ceiling until the whole place was like being inside one of his works. Bukowski:

So one night I went to a bar and picked up a lady and brought her to my place. I opened the door, she walked in, looked around and said, 'Holy shit!' 'You like them?' I asked. 'I'm getting out of here!' she screamed and ran off into the night. A couple of nights later I took all the paintings and put them in a bathtub full of hot water. Then I took them out and painted over them. In the morning I looked at everything and threw the mass of it, totally, into the trashcans out back.

Despite his perpetual poverty, Hank took so many days off work that he often forgot payday. Come the next payday, everyone would be talking about what they planned to do with their money and he would chip in, 'Payday? Hell, is this payday? I forgot to pick up my last cheque.' His fellow workers would think he was kidding them, but he meant it. He would go down to the payroll office and there would be his cheque. When he returned and showed it to the other men – 'Jesus Christ, I forgot all about it' – they would fly into a rage with Hank's apparent disregard for money. They all had families and bills and car payments and every penny was important to them; some of them were working two jobs.

On another occasion he came to work in an old raincoat that he had not worn for months. He looked in the pocket for cigarettes and came up with a five dollar bill. He showed it to the guys, 'Look I found a five dollar bill I didn't know I had.' They would all react with annoyance. He was so used to being rolled when drunk that he would hide his money all over his clothes instead of keeping it in his wallet. As he spoke he searched through the other pockets. From an inside pocket he found a twenty. His co-workers did not find this funny. And then he found yet another twenty, a ten and a five. 'I'm rich!' he yelled as they cursed him. Their waves of hatred confused him. They believed he plotted the whole thing just to provoke them, to rub their noses in their poverty. The story, published in *Love is a Dog From Hell* as '$$$$$$' may be exaggerated, but probably has a solid basis in fact.

In the 60s Bukowski maintained an enormous correspondence with magazine editors, fellow poets, fans and friends. It was his way of, as he put it: 'screaming from my cage', along with the horse racing, the drinking, the poetry and short stories. Some of his correspondence became so extensive that it merited book publication: his letters to Ezra Pound's old girlfriend Sheri Martinelli, for instance, and his correspondence with the Canadian poet Al Purdy. A letter from Purdy always got his day off to a good start.

In September 1968 the University of California at Santa Barbara special collections library offered Hank a large sum of money for some of his papers but specified that they were particularly interested in his correspondence, if he could retrieve it from the people he sent it to. He wrote to all his regular correspondents and asked, begged, them for his letters back so that he could sell them. Carl Weissner, Doug Blazek, William Wantling and some others did, but many hung on to them, knowing that they would only increase in value. Some did not reply, many would not comply and John William Corrington told him bluntly: 'I am going to use your letters to help to send my son through college.' This particularly annoyed Hank because earlier, when he was still living at 1623 Mariposa, Corrington had asked Hank for *his* letters to be returned because Jim Roman, the rare book dealer in Fort Lauderdale, offered to buy them. Hank had carefully lined them all up on the rug and sorted them into chronological order before sending them off to him; it had not occurred to him to say no. He reminded Corrington of this but to no avail. Hank raged against those who refused, trying to explain that with the money he could take a year's leave from the post office; it would give him a year of freedom to write, to sit and stare at the typewriter or at the walls.

He still saw Marina and Frances regularly and Marina sometimes stayed over, sleeping in his bed. She brought out an unexpected tenderness in him. Instead of the usual boasting about beer and drunkenness he told William Wantling: 'She is a joy. I look at her and light goes all through me. I am soft, man, soft, and I don't mind a bit.' He loved having conversations with her, particularly at this age – three to four years old – because she said things of such brilliance that it stunned him: 'They're like ancient philosophers because they haven't been taught anything yet from the outside. They have this knowledge that's already there. They're born with it and it hasn't been tinkered with yet.' By now Frances's hair was white and hung in a long braid down her back. She wore a shapeless overall which hid her body and liked to wear one-thonged Japanese sandals. Hugh Fox encountered her in 1969 when he went to interview Hank and described her as being 'kind of hatchet-faced, red, oily-skinned, belligerent'. He described Hank as 'meek'. He thought Frances had him under control.

Hank was paying child support of $45 a month and thought he would have to find a cheaper place to live but never did. Then, in April 1969, Frances decided to move to New York, and naturally take four-year-old Marina with her. Hank was stunned and saddened, but he couldn't raise the child himself. Fortunately it was not long before Frances returned to the Coast.

Despite his growing fame, Bukowski still fluctuated wildly between suicidal depressions and enormous egotistical self-confidence. The former diminished as the 60s progressed, and one of the ways he resolved them was by writing his way out. His correspondents received frequent reports in gruesome detail of his perilous state of mind. Visitors to his bedroom were sometimes surprised to see a large kitchen knife taped to the back of his door; though that was there for self-protection rather than as a sword of Damocles. The suicidal impulse had been with him since childhood and his biography is riddled with lesser attempts at self-harm such as dancing on broken glass, smashing windows then leaning out, as well as his excessive drinking against doctors' orders, described by him as 'slow suicide'.

In 'The Old Gang' he describes how he walked about naked and barefoot, stepping on shards of glass which he sometimes felt and sometimes not, depending how drunk he was. Sometimes he tried to pick some of it out but he didn't want to get it all because he had read somewhere that the glass could work its way through the bloodstream to the heart and kill you. He wanted this possibility of death to be ever present with him. It was the thrill that comes with Russian Roulette: part death wish, part a desire to be shaken out of torpor, into life, to break through the carapace. He gives himself away in the title of the poem: 'These Mad Windows That Taste Life and Cut Me If I Go Through Them'. This was his reason given for lying drunk in the alley behind the bar in Philadelphia at lunchtime because there was a possibility that a truck making deliveries would run him over. He also used to purposely sleep in the middle of the road in Los Angeles. He had a favourite hill, Westview Street just above 21st Street, a steep hill with no street lights. He would get very drunk and lie down on the centre line near the top and pass out. He was never hit by a car, but there was always the possibility. As John Bryan wrote: 'It's ... pretty clear that Bukowski didn't like Bukowski much. It flavoured all he did and everything he ever wrote.'

He was more likely to kill himself by drinking; another haemorrhage could occur at any time. He did his best during the period shortly after Jane's death. His view was that 'drinking is a form of suicide where you're allowed to return to life and begin all over the next day. It's like killing yourself, and then you're reborn.' He became a master of resurrection.

One way to fight the suicidal impulse was to drive: when the thought of suicide would suddenly surface he would drive for several hours, choosing strange streets in unfamiliar neighbourhoods, driving up and down, at times slowing down carefully whenever children were playing in the street. He would find a coffee shop, park, enter and sit drinking coffee, reading the newspaper, listening to the staff and customers exchanging the usual dull banalities of everyday life. He would return to his car and start driving again: 'and at once/everything will lift.' This is also Bukowski as the *flâneur*; the distant, removed observer, seeing, reporting, not just other people, but watching himself.

Hank had quickly run out of material for his weekly *Open City* column and began a more thorough investigation of his own past experiences to use both for the column, and for the novel that he began in 1967. It was as Walter Benjamin wrote: 'Whoever seeks to gaze more closely at one's own buried past must proceed like a man who excavates. Above all, he must not shy away from coming back time and time again to one and the same fact – scatter it, just as one scatters earth, root it up just as one roots up the soil.' This is what Bukowski did, the same incidents are told time and time again, each time a little different, each time a new angle. He concentrated on the outrageous exploits: the embarrassing, the painful. It was a celebration of the low life.

In December 1966 Hank told Doug Blazek that he was working on a novel called *The Way the Dead Love* about the two years he lived in a faded hotel in the early 50s. He had so many addresses during this period, it is difficult to pinpoint which he is talking about as he gives contradictory information. In one place he gives a very detailed description, complete with room number, and in another he describes it as being a hotel at Vermont Avenue and Third Street where he only went now and then to see a girlfriend, usually staying for just two or three days and nights.

A section of the book appears in *South of No North* under its original title. The hotel in the book was near the top of a hill with just enough of a slope to make a run to the liquor store easy, and just enough to make the climb back up seem worthwhile. The hotel was once painted peacock green, but the Los Angeles rains and sun had faded it. He had room 309, a front room facing the street on the third floor. The phone was just outside his door in the hall. He had a hotplate in the window, a large sink with a little mirror over it, a small wall refrigerator, a table and a couple of chairs. The bathroom was down the hall. The building was old but it did have an elevator. His drinking partner 'Whitey' – an old man so called for his white hair – lived in the hotel on Vermont. One night at 4 a.m. Whitey came staggering out of his room with blood pumping from his mouth. He began to scream 'Help me! Help me! Help me!' in between vomiting blood. Hank helped him lie down in the hallway then ran and beat on the landlady's door. She screamed at him: 'You Polack bastard, are you drunk again?' Then she looked through the spy-lens and saw the blood on her floor. Calmly she called the ambulance while Hank hugged the wall to keep from keeling over. The ambulance attendants made Whitey stand up and walk down the steps and Hank never saw him again.

Everyone in the hotel drank, mostly cheap wine. They were living from day to day, one night until the next, never knowing if they would have a room next week. They ignored awful reality by remaining drunk as long as possible. There was one resident who Hank called 'Mr Adams'. Two or three nights a week, usually around 1.30 a.m. when he was attempting to reach the liquor store around the corner before it closed, he would go tumbling down the long, hard staircase. They could hear the sound of him banging on each step as he rolled past. Hank's girlfriend – presumably Jane – would say: 'There goes Mr Adams,' and they would be quiet to see if he would go through the glass doorway, which he did about half of the time. The next day the manager had somebody come and replace the doorway; he was used to it. Mr Adams was never badly injured though the fall would have killed him had he been sober. Bukowski: 'When you're drunk, you fall loose and soft like a cat, and there's no fear inside of you, you're either a bit bored or a bit laughing inside of yourself.'

Hank claimed to have had sex with very nearly every woman in that hotel including the sixty-year-old white-haired cleaning woman who lived in a tiny closet-like room. He had another drinking buddy in the hotel called Marty, in love with the attractive alcoholic waif who had to live in the cellar of the building because she couldn't pay her rent. One time Hank and Marty quarrelled and Marty kept pushing Hank back in his chair so he couldn't get up. Bukowski wrote: 'I got even: I fucked his/girl.' According to Hank, after Marty left, he took the elevator down to the ground floor and walked down to the cellar bringing a fifth of cheap whiskey with him. It was one or two in the morning. There was a light burning in her room so he knocked. If one can believe a story that a young attractive woman would let a strange man into her room and her bed just because he had some whiskey with him, then it is a believable story – after all, most of Bukowski's unbelievable stories have turned out to be true. He tells the story in 'Guts' and mentioned the incident in passing in a 1967 interview: 'I think that I made every woman in that hotel and there were four floor-fulls, and I even went down into the cellar and got one there.' She was evicted a week later and Hank took a job in a meat-packing plant. When Hank told Marty what he had done, his tormentor burst into tears. Hank went and bought a bottle of cheap port and they were soon friends again. They were all alcoholics, none of them had jobs, all they had was each other.

Hank told Blazek that *How the Dead Love*: 'ought to be a laugher. Starvation, drink, madness and fuck,' and said that he: 'Even screwed a guy in the ass by mistake one night.' This was the hilarious story that someone had clipped from *Open City* and sent to the postal authorities. Hank repeated the story in a number of forms and mentioned it in letters so it, too, has a basis in truth. At the Green Hotel, as he often called it, there was usually someone in his room, and a continuous party going on. For two dollars and some change you could have a roomful of talk and drinks for six or seven people that lasted all night. One morning he awakened in bed drunk, but clear-headed. The lights were all out and he leaned on one elbow and looked around at the empty wine bottles in the moonlight. Everybody seemed gone but then he noticed someone in bed with him. He was delighted by their bravery and love. As he told it: 'Anyone who could stand me had a lot of forgiveness of soul. I just had to REWARD this sweet, little dear deer for having the guts and insight and courage to stay with me. What better reward than to fuck her in the ass?' This was something he had never done, even though he had talked about it for years. Women were just not interested, probably because of the crude manner in which he suggested it, but this was his big chance. He got up and found a glass of wine with only a little bit of cigar ash in it and threw it back, then climbed back into bed and slipped it in. His partner moaned, and in the excitement the blanket slid off to reveal . . . his friend 'Baldy M'. A man. Hank achieved instant detumescence and fell back, limp, aghast.

In the morning Baldy said nothing. Hank kept waiting for him to leave but he stayed two weeks, three weeks. One evening Hank came home, limping from where a box of frozen fish had fallen from a boxcar onto his foot; his hand was cut and bleeding, his foot bruised. The house was a mess and a drinks party was in full swing. They had eaten all his canned food, used all the glasses, dishes and silverware and everything was piled in the sink. When all the plates were dirty they used paper plates and threw them in there too. The sink was clogged and someone had vomited into it. Hank poured himself a tumbler of wine, drank it down, then threw the glass against the wall and roared: 'That's it! Everybody out! Now!'

They filed out: the whores, the men, the scrubwoman with white hair that he had fucked, everyone but Baldy M who sat on the edge of the bed, mumbling 'Hank, Hank, whatza matta? Whatza matta, Hank?' Hank told him, politely, that if he didn't shut up he would knock him out. Then he went to the hall phone and called Baldy's mother. He was 32 years old but still lived at home. It turned out she had filed a missing person's report on him. 'Come and get your son,' he told her.

Hank intended the chapters in *The Way the Dead Love* to be short, filled with abbreviated action, clipped like the hard-boiled detective novels of his youth. There was to be no general plot, just a picaresque record of events in the hotel, of the tenacious survival of the beautiful, tragic people in his life, presented like his chapbook *Confessions of a Man Insane Enough to Live with Beasts*, only much longer.

It is likely that all his tales of drinking and flea-pit hotels are true, the one described in 'somebody else', for instance, where his friend Lou tries to commit suicide. Lou owes Hank $10 and when he goes to collect it, he finds Lou on the bed with the gas heater on and not lit. He turns the gas off, opens the windows and swings the door to and fro to make the gas escape. Lou awoke and gave Hank a sheepish smile, 'You saved my life, you're my buddy forever.' Hank returned to his room. Lou came knocking but all Hank wanted was his $10. Lou had five, which Hank took. Then he opened his last remaining bottle of wine and they drank it together. He found the book easy to write and had completed five chapters by February 1969, but seems to have gone no further. Most of the material was presumably used in other places such as *South of No North* and the published novels.

Nineteen sixty-nine was really the year that Bukowski became a full-time writer. Apart from the small problem of the post office he was writing a regular column for *Open City*, he was preparing a second volume for Black Sparrow, and Essex House published his *Notes of a Dirty Old Man* that January. He entered the literary world big-time by appearing alongside Harold Norse and Philip Lamantia in the British anthology *Penguin Modern Poets 13*. Carl Weissner became his German agent and translator, and he began a little literary magazine of his own.

By the end of the 60s, Hank and Harold Norse had established a mutual admiration society. Bukowski genuinely seems to have regarded Norse as one of the greatest poets alive and praised him wildly to his other correspondents, calling him Prince Hal, Prince of Poets. In the course of their letters, Norse attempted to interest Bukowski in the cut-up technique, being developed at the Beat Hotel by Brion Gysin and William Burroughs, with reluctant help from Gregory Corso, in which texts were sliced up and recombined then examined to see if any unusual or extraordinary phrases or meanings emerged. Norse was very keen on the new method but Bukowski was not having any of it. He did, however, give the Beat Hotel a name check in one of his poems, 'Down by the Wings', and in 'The Seminar' referred to Burroughs' cut-up technique, though he got it slightly wrong.

The Norse correspondence was long and stimulating. Five years later Hank told the Webbs that he considered Harold Norse to be a much better writer and a better person than himself – though he had not met him – and said that receiving a letter from him was always a big event. Norse, for his part, remained a great supporter of Hank's work, though he was a little irritated when Hank quoted more than 500 words verbatim from one of his letters in the middle of his *Open City* column in March 1968, attributing it to 'a well known poet – editor'. Hank's column was about 'the frozen man', the subject of Norse's letter, so it was apposite. Norse had recently moved to London and the letter was a report on his state of mind. Norse was homosexual but he saw beyond the casual homophobia expressed in much of Bukowski's writing and it did not disturb him, though he later annoyed many of Hank's friends by suggesting that Hank was a closet bisexual.

In London, Norse's friend, Nikos Stangos, the poetry editor of Penguin books, was looking for material for his Penguin Modern Poets series, described as 'a series designed to introduce contemporary poetry to the general reader by publishing representative work by each of three modern poets in a single volume'. *Penguin Modern Poets 1*, for instance, featured Lawrence Durrell, Elizabeth Jennings and RS Thomas; number 5 featured Allen Ginsberg, Gregory Corso and Lawrence Ferlinghetti; number 9 had poems by Denise Levertov, Kenneth Rexroth and William Carlos Williams. By suggesting that Bukowski should be included alongside himself and Philip Lamantia, Norse was doing Bukowski an enormous favour; introducing him to the poetry-reading public at large through one of the world's most prestigious imprints.

Harold Norse returned to the States in 1968, settling in Venice, California, to be close to his mother who had moved there from New York. He continued to correspond with Hank and they spoke regularly on the phone. Then, one day, during the most violent thunderstorm Los Angeles had experienced in 31 years, Hank suddenly appeared at his door, soaked to the skin. He was polite, respectful and from then on they were in close contact. Norse wrote: 'We fascinated each other but I had to deal with his mood swings, fuelled by alcohol. He admitted that he "tested" his friends – Bukowski-speak for offending them. I saw him as an American Céline, compelled to jeopardise his relationships.' It had probably not escaped Norse's attention that Hank even looked rather like Céline. In his autobiography, *Memoirs of a Bastard Angel*, Norse described Hank as being: 'a big hunchback with a ravaged pockmarked face, decayed nicotine-stained teeth and pain-filled green eyes. Flat brown hair seemed pasted to an oversize skull.' He said he had hips broader than his shoulders and grotesquely small, soft hands. His huge beer belly sagged over his belt.

Hank had been very nervous about meeting Norse, describing him as a great writer, and confided to Neeli Cherry that he didn't know what to say to him, but, as usual, after a few drinks, Hank found plenty to say. At first they were both respectful and a close friendship ensued, with Hank even trying hard to avoid making cracks about 'faggots'. Sometimes Hank got so drunk he had to stay over on Norse's couch. They walked on the beach together and at one point Hank told Norse: 'I don't want to sound like a goddamn romantic, but I got a real feeling of human warmth for a change. We're two old dogs, hooked on life.'

It couldn't last. After a few years Hank got careless and misbehaved at Norse's apartment. Then Hank wrote disparagingly about him in a poem that bordered on homophobia: 'I Meet the Famous Poet' where he also attempted to put down Philip Lamantia by pretending to forget his name. He ended the poem: 'and it also/isn't true/that without his/aid/I never would have/appeared in the/*Penguin Collection of/Modern Poets*/along with him/and who/ was it?/yeah:/Lamantia.' A feud developed between them and once more Hank managed to destroy a friendship with someone who had put themselves out to help advance his career. As usual Hank responded by writing mean things. In one piece, 'Twelve Monkeys Who Won't Copulate Properly', he said: 'Norse hasn't written a decent poem since 1955. His mother supports him,' and there was much worse.

Harold Norse:

He's an alcoholic and plays alcoholic games. His life and his work are based on a compulsion to humiliate people, to eliminate friends and enemies alike; to make a fucking mess of everything and then blame them all for his aggressions and hostilities. He feels like a shit afterwards and begs forgiveness. But he'll do it every time. If you're the patsy or the good Joe – the role in which I had cast myself – he'll try harder next time to doublecross or destroy you, till you tell him, finally, that you've had enough. That, of course, confirms his own feelings of self-hatred and gives him the chance to put you down for not being big enough to let him destroy you! ... Bukowski didn't mess around with me until we'd known each other for two years. He used to say, 'I love thee in my fashion.' He has got to play the Pig, I believe, in order to push way down and out of sight the intimacy he will never get in touch with – an intimacy for men. He hates women much more than the stereotype homosexual is said to.

Accompanying Bukowski on his first visit to Harold Norse was Neeli Cherry (Cherkovski), the son of Hank's friend Sam Cherry. Neeli spent a lot of time hanging out at Hank's place, and one night in February or March 1969 they came up with the idea of starting their own literary magazine. Hank wanted to call it *Laugh Literary and Man the Fucking Guns* but Neeli persuaded him to not get engaged in yet another censorship battle like that of Steve Richmond and they settled in the end on *Laugh Literary and Man the Humping Guns*. A rich backer was found and poems solicited. By the time the rich backer pulled out, Hank was having fun and liked the poems they had chosen so much that he decided to put the magazine out himself. It was his chance to rail against Creeley, Olson and the Black Mountain School and sound off about anything he damn well pleased: he wrote rude remarks on people's manuscripts before returning them, sometimes mutilating them in the process by smearing jam or wine on them. He loved the sense of discovery, that sometimes there would be something very good sent to him: 'I open these envelopes very reluctantly – and once in a while you get that surprise . . . there are some strange people out there who can write. I mean, they're not great writers but they write very well. So I have to keep accepting that fact and it's OK.' It ran for three issues.

After Carl Weissner ran his work in *Klactoveedsedsteen*, Hank began a correspondence and sent him a copy of *Notes of a Dirty Old Man*. That year, 1969, Carl had collaborated with Claude Pelieu and William Burroughs on *So Who Owns Death TV?* which he also translated into German. He was so impressed by Hank's book that he offered to translate it and find a publisher in Germany. Hank was delighted and told Carl that he was honoured. He said it gave him chills to think of it: 'crawling back to the Fatherland like that – my own tongue cut out – but you've got a good tongue, Carl, you speak for me'. It was the beginning of Weissner's distinguished career as a translator: in 1971 he translated William Burroughs' *Electronic Revolution* followed in 1973 by Burroughs' *Ali's Smile*; he translated Ginsberg: *Indian Journals* (1972), *Iron Horse* (1973), *The Fall of America* (1975) and *Howl and Other Poems* (1979); as well as Claude Pelieu's *Amphetamine Cowboy* (1976), Frank Zappa's lyrics and many other underground texts.

Hank was being drawn inexorably into the literary world but it was using up all of his time. He was ticketed for absenteeism often that year, and in August the post office suspended him without pay. He was about to lose his job but even then he took three days off one week in September. When his workmates asked where he'd been he told them: 'Drunk'. He probably was; his landlord had recently given him an extra garbage can, just for the beer bottles. The alcohol fuelled his writing. One night he didn't go to work, and instead he sat at the typewriter and in 45 minutes had written a seven-page story called 'The Copulating Mermaid of Venice, Calif'.

One of the sex magazines he had been writing for told him they would pay him $150 for it on publication. But, he told Weissner, more than the money the beautiful thing was the fact that he did not have to *compromise* his style. It was a story about necrophilia and was eventually used as the basis of *Crazy Love*, a film by Belgian filmmaker Dominique Deruddere made in 1987.

Since Hank was still listed in the phonebook, he was plagued by admirers and poets; the admirers were the worst, giving him no time to write, no time to take out the garbage, go to the store, buy stationery supplies (the housework he always neglected). The two or three hours free time a day he normally had was taken up by fans who always arrived bearing gifts of alcohol and accompanied by their girlfriends or wives. No matter how rude or vile he was to them, they laughed, insults washed right over them because this was what they came for and they hung on every word. Hank had become a cult figure.

8. YEARS OF FAME

John Martin continued to support Hank in his work throughout 1968 and 1969, sending him notes of encouragment saying 'Send me some of the stuff you're writing. Let me have a look at it', planning the next book. Hank would mail him a few things, and Martin became more and more convinced that Bukowski was a great writer. One day in December 1969 Hank received a telephone call from him: 'I'll tell you what, Hank. If you quit the post office, I'll give you a hundred dollars a month for life.'

Hank was astonished.

'Yeah. Even if you don't write anything, even if you never send me anything, if you never write anything ever again, I'll give you a hundred dollars a month for life.'

Hank was reeling and needed time to take it in. He sat, considering his options for the space of two more beers. The fact was, unknown to Martin, the post office had written to tell Hank that he was about to be fired for persistent absenteeism but that he would have a chance to appeal. Hank knew that even if he won this appeal it would not be long before he was absent again and he would be thrown out for good. The problem was that over the years Hank had become a wage slave. He thought he couldn't make it without the 'big mother' there giving him his pay cheque. He was almost fifty years old and without a trade. Even with Martin's $100 a month he couldn't live on the income he had made from writing to date. However, as he well knew: 'I would have died if I had stayed.' Everything was conspiring to push him into becoming a full-time writer. He called John Martin back and told him it was a deal.

$100 a month was one-quarter of Martin's own income. It was an act of supreme faith and confidence in Bukowski's genius. Martin sold his collection of DH Lawrence first editions to the University of California at Santa Barbara (UCSB) for $50,000 which left him with $30,000 after tax for the Black Sparrow Press. Hank resigned from the post office just days before they would have fired him. He told no one at work what he had done, and on 9 January 1970, when he worked his last day he said goodnight to everyone casually, as if it were an ordinary workday. He had been there for eleven and a half years which entitled him to a pension fund. Contrary to his carefully fostered public image, Hank never drifted lazily from job to job, working only when he was broke. He was very careful with money and always put away some of his post office wage into his savings account, which already contained the majority of the money from the sale of his father's house and money from selling his papers to the UCSB. Financial insecurity was a constant worry for Hank, perhaps occasioned by his experience in Atlanta, and he was regarded by his friends as a bit of a tight wad. He was not materialistic; he had no need for an expensive kitchen, a new settee or rug, but he needed a safety net. Another concern was Marina; Frances was not very good at controlling money and they were frequently broke even though Hank was regular with his child support money.

For the first week after his resignation he was almost paralysed with fear. He lay in bed thinking that the walls would fall in on him while he slept. He was not helped by the attitude of his friends, who all knew what he'd done and issued dire warnings. His landlords, Francis and Grace Crotti, could not believe it. Grace told him: 'You're crazy, man. You gave up a lifetime profession?' She left and Hank sat and fretted: 'Geez, maybe I am crazy. What have I done?' In the morning he found that Grace had left a brown paper supermarket sack on the porch with a selection of tomatoes, oranges, radishes, green onions and cans of soup; intimations of impending penury.

Then Jon Webb's son came round to drink and hang out. As Hank said: 'He messed me all up.' He said: 'Well, you quit the post office, Bukowski, you're going to need this thing around,' and he pulled out a glass jar.

'What's that?' Hank asked.

'It's a human heart,' he told him. 'I stole it from a laboratory. I've got a nurse girlfriend.'

Hank quickly hid it in the closet, thinking: 'We could get put in jail for this, you fool.' It was his first week as a professional writer and he had a human heart in his closet. Each morning he would get up after drinking all night and open the closet door and take a good look at the heart. Then he would run to the bathroom and puke up the beer: 'I'd go Blauaagh! That was a beautiful puke. The human heart gave me heart.'

He told Carl Weissner that for the first ten days he nearly went out of his skull with worry. He didn't know what to do with his hands, his feet, his mind. With unlimited free time he almost cracked. A series of drunken New Year parties had clogged up both the bathroom and kitchen sinks and Hank ended up in bed with the shades down, sweating, staring up at the ceiling, unable to sleep, feeling deathly sick. He was shivering, depressed and suicidal. He had not eaten in three days and his stomach was raw from all the alcohol. Outside the January rain pounded on the roof. Then some friends arrived, bringing their guitars. They gathered up all the empty wine bottles, beer bottles and whiskey bottles, and took out the garbage. They made him laugh and pulled him up, out of his depression. He went out into the rain with them and ended up drunk again but feeling better. The next day he began work.

His anxiety made him drink more than ever. At the post office, his starting time had been 6.18 p.m. So each night, he sat down at 6.18 p.m. with his pint of scotch, two six-packs of beer, some cheap cigars and the radio tuned to KFAC, his favourite classical station. There was a bright light on overhead and lots of typing paper. He set himself a goal of ten pages, single-spaced, a night but he never knew until the next day how many pages he had written. He was used to working the night shift but he never remembered going to bed. He would wake up in the morning feeling sick, go and puke, and find pages of manuscript scattered all over the couch. 'I'd say, "Let me see if I made my ten pages last night. I'd pick them up. 10 ... 12 ... 14 ... 18 ... 23 pages!! Good God. If I just do ten tonight I'll be thirteen ahead!" I always kept exceeding. Of course, what I'd have to do the next morning, you know, some of these end pages ... when I got very drunk the writing got out of hand, sort of. I'd have to tighten that up a little bit! The last pages, I'd say,

"Wow, what was I saying there?" ' The novel was finished in twenty nights. 'It was the good fight, at last. My whole body, my whole spirit, was wild with the battle.'

After a few discarded titles, Hank decided to simply call it *Post Office*. Bukowski: 'It's about fourteen years of hell. But I didn't write it in – what shall we say – a bitchy style. It's mostly humorous, but there's a lot of pain in there – I tried to keep from getting emotional about it – just tried to record it as it happened. Some very funny and tragic things happened in those years.' He and John Martin had discussed what kind of writing Hank would do, now that he had free time, and Martin had suggested that a novel would be more saleable than poetry. Now, only three weeks into January, Hank called him and said, 'It's done, come and get it.' Martin had not even known that Hank was at work on a novel, and for him to have written it so quickly was astounding. Hank had written 120,000 words, 30,000 of which he pulled out on re-reading. There was to be no advance on royalties for it until publication.

It was scary to try and live off a writer's income. Hank's column at *Open City* died with the newspaper, though the Los Angeles *Free Press* was keen to take it on. For a $10 reduction in rent Hank helped out around the court, taking the garbage cans out one day, bringing them back in the next day. It all helped reduce his living costs. On the plus side, he was out of the post office that he had been complaining was killing him for years: it was 'crucifying' him, he was 'on the cross'. He also had a publisher who believed in him. Bukowski: 'It opened all the doors. I didn't take it for granted. When John sent the hundred, it was like the whole sky opened up and brightened and the sun came through. It was like he sent me five million.' This was also the time when John Martin replaced Hank's battered portable typewriter. He asked him what kind he wanted and Hank told him: 'A big one I can beat the shit outa.'

Bukowski was far and away Black Sparrow's bestselling author and John Martin was delighted to have a novel to publish; however, he was worried about some of the content of *Post Office,* also disturbed by what seemed to him to be grammatical sloppiness. Some parts were written in the present tense and other parts in the past. Hank told Carl Weissner that though he was pretty drunk when he wrote it, it was not sloppy or lazy writing: 'It was written as it fucking well came out, and that meant turds and blood and the rest of the wash.' However, since it meant so much to Martin, Hank allowed him to cast the whole book in the present but insisted the rest must stay; he didn't want swear words or obscenities to be replaced by anodyne substitutes. Martin told him that he didn't want to detract from his style, but inferred that he would be happier if Hank wrote something safer. Hank told Weissner that he would have preferred *Post Office* to be published in its original raw form and he was worried by Martin's attitude. 'He's a nice guy but he does treat me too much like an idiot.' Just discussing it made him feel depressed. As Weissner was already translating the book from a manuscript supplied by Hank, the German edition is presumably based on the original draft. Martin, for his part, claimed that very few changes were made grammatically in *Post Office* but, for Hank, even those were too many.

In *Post Office* Bukowski continued the form he had used in his columns; that of autobiographical fiction, using the experiences of his life as the basis of the narrative which is presented as a picaresque novel; no overall story except in the broadest sense, no character development, no development and no dénouement. It is the oldest storytelling form: used in Chaucer's *Canterbury Tales*, in Boccaccio's *The Decameron* – one of Bukowski's favourite books – in Rabelais' *Gargantua and Pantagruel* – which Bukowski surely enjoyed – by de Sade, Swift and many others. In Japan the principal form of novel is the *shishosetsu* or 'I-novel', which is essentially autobiographical but contains some invented episodes: also a definition of Bukowski's work, particularly the novels: 'I do cheat a little, I brighten it up. It may be mostly true but I can't help improving it with one thing that will make it sparkle more. The idea is the story need not be about me.' Bukowski creates a distance between himself and the narrator by naming the protagonist Henry Chinaski, giving himself a margin of freedom where his imagination can run wild and real events can be distorted and changed for literary or personal reasons. Bukowski: 'Bukowski would be too holy, anyway. You know, "I did this." Especially if you do something good or great or seemingly great, and your own name is there. It makes it too holy. Now if Chinaski does it, maybe I didn't do it, see, that could be fiction.'

This places Bukowski in one of the mainstream twentieth-century literary traditions. Proust drew heavily on his experiences, as did F Scott Fitzgerald, Ernest Hemingway, Nathanael West, Graham Greene, Aldous Huxley, George Orwell and many others, but they tended to fictionalise the material into something more universal. Bukowski is closer to Denton Welch, Henry Miller or Knut Hamsun where the raw autobiography is little changed. Many of Bukowski's contemporaries, the Beats, were autobiographical writers: Burroughs' *Junky* and *Queer* (though not the other major novels); all of Kerouac with the exception of *The Town and the City* and *Pic*; Alexander Trocchi's *Cain's Book*; John Clellon Holmes' *Go*; John Rechy's *City of Night*, and so on. Henry Miller and Jack Kerouac both stated that their complete works would add up to autobiographies if the fictional names were changed to the real names of the persons depicted. Kerouac's Duluoz is about as fictionalised as Bukowski's Chinaski; which is to say, more than most people think. Hank told Arnold Kaye (speaking about his poetry) 'Almost all [the work is frankly autobiographical]. Ninety-nine out of a hundred.' Seventy-five per cent would be a better estimate.

Post Office is rightly regarded as one of Bukowski's most successful books. Everyday dead-end repetitive work in a factory is not a subject that very many authors have ever attempted to depict, despite this being the most common experience of the majority of the population. Hank brings to it a combination of empathy and humour which transforms it into an American classic. Not since Steinbeck had anyone described the lot of working people with such objectivity. Hank is not sentimental, in fact the book is filled with violent, brutal images directly presented in the German tradition. That is its great value; it is honest and unromantic about the daily grind; written from direct experience.

In a letter to Ruth Wantling he described watching the clock, counting the hours as he did the same repetitive action, throwing the letters, over and over, minute by minute, hour by hour: 'I die a minute at a time. All those minutes that I could be Shit Shit using for myself!!! . . . never to be gotten back again.' It is this understanding and feeling for the human lives wasted by most work that gives his writing its rock solid credibility. His readers knew that despite the bragging, the egotistical posturing, his heart was right there. That he meant it when he was asked his opinion about the death of President Kennedy and said:

I see men assassinated around me every day. I walk through rooms of the dead, cities of the dead: men without eyes, men without voices; men with manufactured feelings and standard reactions; men with newspaper brains, television souls and high school ideals . . . How can I be over concerned with the murder of one man when almost all men, plus females, are taken from cribs as babies and almost immediately thrown into the masher.

This was his raw material, the centre of his work: 'I'm just discouraged that men and women have to live their lives the way they do. It's painful to them, and it's painful to me, but I don't know the way out. So all I can do is write about the pain of it.'

More importantly, Hank also wanted these people to be his audience, and to a certain extent they were. Because of his subject matter and his straightforward, honest descriptions of life in the underclass, he had readers in factories and jails, in bars and brothels: 'I am a very common, simple man. I do have genius, but with a very low common denominator. I'm simple. I'm not profound. My genius stems from an interest in whores, working men, street-car drivers – lonely beaten-down people. And these are the people I'd like to see reading my stuff, and I don't want to see too many learned comments, too much criticism, or too much praise get between me and them.'

He was enormously pleased when prisoners wrote to him, saying how his books were passed from cell to cell; and flattered when the madam of a high-class Las Vegas brothel invited him to come by for a drink and a visit on the house, saying that all the girls admired his work.

Weissner's translation of *Notes of a Dirty Old Man* was published by Kiepenheuer & Witsch in Köln. To ensure extra sales, Weissner made up a Henry Miller quote for the back of the jacket: 'Each line in Bukowski is infected by the terror of the American nightmare. He articulates the fears and agonies of that vast minority in the no-man's land between inhuman brutalisation and helpless despair.' Hank was not too happy with the fake quote but he did regard it as 'quite accurate' as a description of his work. He was prepared to go along with it if it would help sell more copies of the book but did worry what Martin's reaction would be. Making money became of paramount importance to him now that he no longer had a regular income from the post office. He began writing for the sex magazines, beginning with the *New York Review of Sex and Politics*, a spin-off from the New York underground paper *East Village Other*, which had started up to emulate Richard Goldstein's *Screw*. Meanwhile, on Melrose Avenue in Los Angeles, Calfornian pornographers had discovered Hank. They liked his *Open City* column and asked him to write for them which is why sex featured in so many of his stories from this period. Bukowski: 'So what I would do was write a good story, and then in the middle I had to throw in some gross act of sex ... And I kept writing the story. It was okay.' He would mail in the story and back would come a cheque for $300. Sometimes there was no place in the story for sex so he couldn't sell it to the sex merchants. The ironic thing was that Bukowski hadn't actually had sex with anyone for two years; his stories were either fantasy or happened back in the 50s.

With his new-found time and energy Hank wrote fifty poems in three weeks, most of them quite good from his point of view, and he soon found that he was running out of magazines to submit them to. He was in *Evergreen* and even managed to penetrate Creeley territory and have one published in *Stonybrook*. Hank now sent carbon copies of everything he wrote to John Martin and the manuscripts began piling up.

Another way of making money was to give poetry readings. Hank thought that writing had nothing to do with getting up and reading from your work in front of a crowd. To him it was a form of vanity, it was acting and had nothing to do with the creative act. Bukowski: 'The creative act is when it comes out of the typewriter.' So, though he read, he only ever did so because he needed the money and he disliked every minute of it and disliked the audience that came to see him do it and disliked everything to do with it. He told William J Robson and Josette Bryson: 'I've become what you'd call a literary hustler. I do things now that I wouldn't have done before – one of them is giving poetry readings. I don't like to do it at all.'

His first public reading was on 19 December 1969, before he'd even worked out his remaining days at the post office. His friend Peter Edler persuaded him to do a reading at The Bridge, a bookstore off Hollywood Boulevard that held literary events. Though they only expected a few dozen people, the store was packed, with over two hundred people jostling to get in. Hank didn't know how to present himself and was terrified at the idea of sitting on the small stage with a spotlight on him, but he was surrounded by friends and had chosen a good selection of his best, most accessible poems. As the evening progressed he grew more confident and the reading was such a success they asked him back the next night. This was probably one of the straightest readings he ever gave.

His anxiety about reading combined with his dislike of it, quickly coalesced into an aggressive stance against the audience: 'I feel like they're the enemy. That they've come to see the sacrifice.' Even though he was doing the reading, he was opposed to the whole thing, a contradiction that gave rise to much abusive conduct, many drunken insults and, later, much bad behaviour, such as the time he spat in the face of a fan who asked for a signature. He quickly realised that this was what the audience wanted to see: an act. He noticed the positive reaction of the audience whenever he raised a bottle of beer to his lips, so the bottle of beer became a prop. He didn't need it but the audience wanted to see it. It was a game that they both played; an image that he had built up that they related to. It was the persona of The Dirty Old Man. A pattern emerged, he would get drunk, read his poems, insult the audience, collect his money and leave. It was just another job.

His second reading was in May, at a college in New Mexico, followed the next day by one in Seattle. He went to New Mexico by train but to Seattle he had to fly. He was too embarrassed to ask the stewardess how to tighten his seat belt so left it dangling loose. He was nervous and frightened and arrived at the Bellevue Community College drunk. Fortunately the reading was not until the next day, though he managed to insult his hosts pretty thoroughly before retiring for the night. After the reading he was surprised by the applause. It was heavy and enthusiastic and it continued until he was embarrassed. He felt the poems weren't good enough to merit that much approbation and that they were applauding for something else, his image perhaps or just the fact that he was still alive after all he'd been through.

Now, in public, at readings, at the parties afterwards and at parties in general, Hank protected himself by assuming the carapace of The Dirty Old Man: this came complete with an idiot dance, crude sexual advances towards any woman in the place, vomiting and, of course, extreme inebriation, aided by his major prop, the never-to-be-seen-without bottle of beer. Unlike Churchill's cigar, which was rarely alight, Bukowski really did pour the beer straight down his gullet, just like the photographs show.

Another key part of his image was the face. Whereas he used to be too ashamed of his looks even to approach a woman until he was in his twenties, now it suited him. It gave interviewers something to write about: Don Strachan in 1971 described his face as being: 'a great pulpy, pitted receptacle of bad karma, self-pity and vengeance, capped by the beeriest, most bulbous nose ever to guide uncertain steps through the darkness. The face hung down between his shoulders, giving him the appearance of a massive troglodyte.' In fact he was nowhere near as ugly as he made out. His face showed his experience in the world, rather as Auden's deeply lined visage did. It also attracted women, now that he was becoming a well-known poet. Bukowski: 'I get all sorts of remarks about it. They say things like, "You've got a face more beautiful than Christ's." . . . I find women like ugly faces. Yeah, I'll make that statement flatly. They wanna mother you back to heaven. I have no complaints.' Hank knew that the shot of him that City Lights later used on *Erections* did a lot to sell the book; the face on the cover is so eye-catching, horrific and destroyed-looking that people stopped and wondered who he was. He welcomed the hard living that made him look as he did: 'Now I have this mug that sells books.'

Nineteen seventy was a difficult year for Hank: *Post Office* was not published until the following year; the German edition of *Notes* was hardback only and did not bring in much in the way of income; he had Martin's regular stipend, whatever he could sell to girlie magazines, a column in the Los Angeles *Free Press*, and fees for readings. The problem with readings was that by the time he had paid for his travel, taxis, his drinks and partying afterwards, there was very little profit in it. However, he told Neeli Cherry that he 'got laid a few times by sweet young things, tho,' which made it worthwhile. He told Cherry he wished he were back at the post office; there his mind was dulled; as a freelance the world came at him with knives out.

In June he had three weeks of problems with his neighbours, more than a dozen Islanders who lived in rotating shifts in a house in the court. Hank parked on the front lawn but the Islanders continually blocked him in, hoping to make him park somewhere else and make room for their own cars. He sent off three dollars for a nine-inch switchblade and though he liked to brandish it, there is no record of him ever actually using it. Another, unforeseen problem was that without the discipline of having to go to the post office, there was nothing to stop Hank from drinking all the time. He was proud of the amount he drank and would sit by the window when the garbage men drove up. They would begin to empty the garbage cans and he would listen for his. There was no mistaking it: the powerful sound of breaking glass, bottles smashing and shards of glass tinkling. He overheard one of the garbage men say to the other 'Man, they got one *powerful* drinker in there!' and glowed with pride.

Once he finished *Post Office*, his drinking sessions with his landlords increased in frequency so that he was now drinking beer with them every other night until about 4 or 5 a.m., usually until Francis passed out. Then Hank would give Grace a kiss and sit holding her hand for a while. They were good friends. Francis was a cheerful man, given to playing practical jokes. Just after Christmas, 1971, Hank came home to find a pair of legs sticking out from under the covers. His mind flashed through a dozen scenarios: a dead body, that drunken woman in the back court . . . he threw back the covers. It was just two mannequin legs, put there by Francis. It almost gave him a heart attack.

Linda King first saw Bukowski when she and her sister Geraldine attended a poetry reading at the Bridge in the summer of 1970. Hank was in the audience; he listened to three poems then got up and loudly walked out with a group of friends. A few weeks later, again at the Bridge, there was an evening of poetry with a flute accompaniment. Linda was bored and turned to Peter Edler, the owner, and said: 'God, doesn't anything ever happen here? Where's something exciting? Some action?' Edler made a phone call, then told her: 'I'm taking you to Charles Bukowski's.' She wondered if she was ready for that and made sure she took her own car. Her first impression was of how overgrown his court was, with bushes obscuring the door and windows. Peter introduced her as Morona, a name she was using at the time. Her sisters had been telling her that she was stupid and this was her humorous way of admitting it. Her first impression was not good: 'Bukowski was old . . . too old. Fat . . . too fat . . . and rather drunk.'

After a while the conversation turned to poetry and Peter told Hank that Morona wrote as well as sculpted. 'So you write poetry?' Hank asked, cynically. She told him yes, she did. She said she had been going up the walls at the Bridge because the poetry was delivered in such a quiet and timid way and there was a flute tootling along. 'Doesn't anybody scream in this city?' she asked. 'I like to scream mine,' and she began to declaim. Edler pushed between her and Hank yelling: 'No, no, not to Charles Bukowski! Not to Charles Bukowski!'

'Why not?' she yelled and climbed on the wobbly coffee table to continue her poem which was about the electroshock treatment she had received in the mental hospital; she began to act out the madwoman in the poem. Hank turned the radio on full volume to drown her out, but enjoyed watching her young body gyrate as Edler screamed obscenities at her, trying to cover her mouth with his hand. She finished her poem. 'It's a goddamn rhymer,' said Hank. 'I knew it. Nobody rhymes anymore.'

Right then Peter's girlfriend called from the reading, demanding that he come back to the Bridge. He left, after pushing Linda onto the busted down old couch next to Hank. They talked, she gave him a couple of kisses and rose to go.

'You're a tease,' said Hank

'Yes, I'm a tease,' she told him.

She bought some of his books. They made her laugh out loud but they also made her furious, disgusted and indignant. She couldn't believe his attitude towards women; he clearly didn't understand the first thing about them. Her father, who had recently died, had been an alcoholic so she was not keen on becoming involved with a drunk, but Hank intrigued her and she began dropping by De Longpre to see him. In July, Hank wrote to Neeli Cherkovski saying that Morona had been by, as had Liza Williams (soon to be Linda's rival), but all they did was talk, and all that Hank did was look. Hank got to know all three King sisters and in his usual way, engaged them in correspondence. In October 1970 he wrote a letter to all three, suggesting that they read the *Decameron*, saying that his writing on sex was nothing compared to Boccaccio's explicit, humorous understanding of the subject. He told them he would rather just talk to women or listen to them than fuck them, but if he did have to have sex, then it was up to them to do most of the work.' He asked: 'Maybe I am queer?'

Just before Christmas he told John Martin that one of them wanted to sculpt his head and he had told her to call him in January or February and he would come on over. One night, at 9 p.m., Linda arrived at De Longpre to take photographs of him to use for the sculpture. She took the pictures and they sat and talked for about two or three hours by her reckoning. She opened the door to leave and was astonished to find the sun rising. They had been talking all night.

She made an armature and, using the photographs, rendered a rough approximation of Hank's head. Then the sittings began. He would come over to her house in Burbank and sit for her in the kitchen breakfast nook where she had set up a sculpture stand. She would stare into his eyes, teasing him, flirting, pretending she was only looking at him professionally. She was only thirty and their twenty-year age difference meant that she couldn't imagine getting involved with him. She didn't like his negative attitude and he was a drunk. However, she kept flirting, each day getting him hotter and hotter, so that Hank would back her against the refrigerator or the stove for long kisses and each evening he would write her a love letter. He wore clean new shirts and went on a diet to lose weight. Linda had to scrape away clay as his weight went down. Linda perched on her stool, studying his head and told him: 'My husband said when I divorced him that he hoped I would meet a real crud, and now I have.' Hank laughed, he was delighted by her. 'I've got to have this woman,' he thought.

She said that she knew that Hank didn't do oral sex because it wasn't in any of his books and if he did it he would have written about it. She told him 'I'll never get mixed up with a man again who doesn't like to eat pussy. Uh-huh. Never again. If a man doesn't like it, he doesn't like it. There's no way.' Her two children, a boy and a girl, were playing outside. Hank locked the door, picked her up and carried her to the bedroom, kicking and screaming. Afterwards he sent her a poem, saying: 'I have eaten your cunt like a peach.' To her surprise she found herself falling in love with him; she loved his wry humour and the look in his eyes, his sardonic comments and his kisses, but still felt he was too old for her. She suggested that he tried out his new-found skills on other women.

The sculpture had taken several months to make, but as they had always worked at her house she had been protected by the presence of her children and her sister, who dropped in on her all the time. Now Hank was about to publish a third issue of *Laugh Literary and Man the Humping Guns*, and early in March he invited her over to the collating party where a few of his friends gathered to staple the pages of the magazine together. After everyone had left, Linda and Hank went to bed together for the first time. She had told him that she was not on the pill, but he got over-excited and came inside her. She leapt out of the bed screaming in anger, convinced he had made her pregnant while Hank sheepishly mumbled his apologies, telling her he had not been with a woman for four years and had been too aroused to stop himself.

The claim of not having had a woman in four years directly contradicts many of his other statements about groupies, one-night stands at readings and prostitutes met at bars; he claimed both in so many interviews, poems and stories that we cannot tell which to believe. He had certainly not had a proper relationship since he was with Frances, if that is what he meant. He did not feel bad about it, he didn't want the strain of a relationship and the huge amount of time it took up. In order to get his writing done he had needed as much time as possible as during most of those years he was still at the post office. He masturbated a lot and got a lot of writing done. He told Glenn Esterly: 'Writing, after all, is more important than any woman. But I will make this concession: jerking off runs a distant second to the real thing. When you're with a woman you like, and the sex is good, there's something that takes place beyond the act itself, some kind of exchange of souls that makes all the trouble worthwhile.'

There certainly was a lot of trouble when Linda was around. Hank described being with her as like trying to hold on to the tail of a female tigress. She was volatile, unpredictable, intense, with bright penetrating eyes and a wicked giggle. She was still fighting against the idea of falling in love with Hank but he had already become involved. In April he told Weissner 'I'm hooked in – her delicious mind, body, et al. And the way she makes love . . .'

Hank had to stop drinking because she was so demanding as a lover and that was the only way he could keep it up. Three months later he was still on the wagon and told Weissner that he had had to learn how to talk all over again now that he was sober, like a baby learning to speak, but he stayed off the drink: 'That's what keeps the pecker hard.' For the first month off alcohol he couldn't sleep and when he did drift off he was plagued by demons. Five times a night he would leap up, convinced there were intruders in the room. His weight dropped from 240 pounds to 160. He grew a longer beard and allowed his hair to become fashionably long. He bought new clothes, even flared trousers; his colleagues at the post office would not have recognised him.

Linda taught him how to be a good lover. He had a lot of inhibitions to get over. Bukowski:

I'm just not a dirty guy. There is a lot of Puritan in me. That's what my girlfriends tell me 'God, you're almost a Puritan, and you write that stuff.' . . . In the sexual act, in making love, I tend not to be too forward. I even hate to make love in the day time; you know, you're looking into her eyes, she's looking into yours. It's kind of embarrassing. There's a great deal of Puritan in me. Luckily I've met a woman now who's taught me a great deal about lovemaking, you know, what a woman wants. I've complied and I've enjoyed it. So I'm learning at a late age. I guess I've been a bad fuck to a lot of women for two or three decades.

Linda told Vanessa Engle: 'He had a puritan streak on him this wide, like a skunk. A puritan streak right down his back.'

Linda could be exhausting. According to Hank she didn't think anyone was having fun unless they were on their feet, making a lot of noise and dancing. She didn't understand that some people preferred to spend their time quietly, engaging in more introspective activities. He loved her, but he didn't expect it to work out. They were too different and she had too much youthful exuberance. Inevitably there were arguments. They both say they fought like tigers; Hank would storm out, never to return and they would call each other all night long, yelling abuse and hanging up. She hurt his pride. He would call in a drunken rage and scream: 'I'm Charles Bukowski. You don't know who you're with!' She accused him of making arguments as an excuse to go and get drunk. They argued every week, ferocious, theatrical shouting matches that often ended up in bed, though one time he hit her and broke her nose; one of the few known examples of him hitting a woman. Bukowski: 'In my life, of all the women I've known, I have hit two of them. And that's a pretty good record with all the women I've known. They got to me twice. Generally I'm very gentle, very tolerant. I try to understand what's bothering them.'

Their arguments were loud, and in the month of November 1971, the police were called to Hank's place three times, but they always made up. Jealousy was the usual cause. Linda was a flirt and a tease. When she danced she liked to do what she called the White Dog Hunch, named after a hound in her home town who rubbed itself against everyone's leg. It drove Hank wild with jealousy to see her grinding up against other men. They split up constantly, ir- revocably; forty times in their first year together. Each time they split, Hank would take the sculptured head, which she had given him, and return it to her; she would find it on her doorstep in the morning. Their friends soon got to know the precise state of their relationship by whether or not Hank had his sculpted head at his house or not. It was a mad, passionate love affair such as Hank had never had before. With his previous relationships he had been too drunk most of the time for there to be much of a sexual element.

Linda had only recently broken up with her Italian–American husband of ten years and no longer believed in marriage. He had been of the old school who thought that women belonged in the kitchen with a broom in their hands. Along with tens of thousands of other American women Linda had embraced the ideas of the evolving women's liberation movement and had seized control of her own life. She devoted her time to her two children, to her sculpture, her poetry and to writing a novel. Nonetheless, Linda often found it best to act the country girl around men as that was what they expected. Raised as a Mormon in Utah, she knew nothing about drugs. When Don Strachan passed Hank a hash pipe, he showed her how to use it, explaining to Strachan: 'She's from the hills. She don't know nothing.'

Hank was fascinated by her and wrote about her a lot. She is 'Lily' in many of his stories, 'Lydia' in *Women*. They became very much a couple, going to the park together, to restaurants, to the racetrack. He took her to meet his friends. They spent an afternoon with Harold Norse in Santa Barbara – Hank was still friends with him then – and Hank sat back and let them talk for hours about ghosts and visions and the meaning of dreams and the Astral Dome of Revelation.

In January 1972 Hank went on a winter holiday with Linda and sister Geraldine to the desert near Phoenix, Arizona. Hank couldn't see the attraction of the saguaro cactii forests or the untouched desert, it looked to him like something that wanted to give up, but didn't know how. He borrowed Linda's polka dot painted car, with its California licence plates, and drove to Turf Paradise, the local racetrack, ignoring the quizzical looks the car drew from the locals. He went three times and did pretty well.

Back in the city, all was not well, and they split up once more. This time it looked serious. Hank drove out to Burbank to deliver the sculpted head and found she had moved out. He had a key but found the place empty except for his air conditioner that she had borrowed and a note telling him she had gone for good. Linda had returned to her family in Escalante, near Boulder, Utah. Though there were endless telephone calls and letters back and forth between Utah and East Hollywood, Hank did not wait long to replace her.

He had run into his friend Liza Williams when he was dropping off an article and she slipped him her phone number and told him she was looking for a new boyfriend. Liza Williams was then president of the West Coast office of Island Records and Hank had known her for some time because they both had columns in the Los Angeles *Free Press* and she had visited De Longpre a few times, usually with her boyfriend. Liza was 43; she knew everyone on the movie and rock and roll scene. She was an integral part of the Laurel Canyon music colony and drove the requisite black Mercedes. She shared her house in the Hollywood Hills with a friend, with Liza taking the bottom floor. To Hank it looked like a palace. Liza took him to shows and receptions as well as home to her bed. He mined all of it for material, and even the most mundane occurrence was likely to appear later in a poem. At a party Hank was introduced to a number of underground cartoonists. He got on very well with Robert Crumb, and later worked with him on a number of projects. But when he was introduced to Spain Rodrigues, the creator of *Trashman*, the hero of a regular strip in the *East Village Other*, Hank told him he liked his name but he didn't like him and invited him to step outside. As Spain ran with the New York Hell's Angels it was probably a good thing that their hostess intervened, but Hank still got a poem out of it: 'Trouble with Spain'.

Liza also introduced Hank to a television documentary maker named Taylor Hackford who worked for KCET, the local public television station, and wanted to make a film of him. He filmed Hank at the racetrack with Liza and later with Linda. The resulting film won the award for the best cultural programme of the year from the Corporation For Public Broadcasting and as a result the National Endowment For the Arts gave Hackford a $10,000 grant to cut the film down to half an hour for transmission nationally, introducing Hank to a much wider US audience.

Liza liked to leave town and took Hank to the mountains, to country hotels up and down the coast, and to endless music-related events, most of which he hated. In July she took him on a vacation, paying for him to accompany her to Catalina Island where they stayed at the Hotel Monterey in Avalon, the harbour town. Santa Catalina Island is only 22 miles offshore and a classic tourist trap: they were greeted by the Avalon song as they stepped off the 35-year-old red seven-seater amphibious flying boat, about which Hank had serious misgivings, and watched as young boys dived for coins thrown off the jetty by the tourists. Hank described his week's vacation in the amusing story 'No Neck and Bad As Hell'. Guessing, correctly, that Hank would not be remotely interested in seeing the sights, Liza brought along her portable electric typewriter for him to use in the hotel, telling him 'It's not good for you not to write.' He stayed in his room drinking cold beer while she went for walks, and did the tourist sights. To Hank, the highlight of their trip to Catalina was watching *Jesse James*, a 1939 movie with Tyrone Power, Randolph Scott and Henry Fonda. Hank had no television of his own.

Liza quickly fell in love with Hank and told him so, but, though he liked her, he did not reciprocate. He told Carl Weissner that it just didn't seem the same as with Linda. Hank called Linda, sometimes from Liza's place, running up enormous phone bills. Eventually he decided that he had to see her and told Liza he was going to Utah to try and sort things out. Liza reacted to the news by taking an overdose of sleeping pills. Hank had to push his fingers down her throat to make her vomit them up. In doing so he dislodged her dental plate which came out as well, much to Hank's delight. She knew right then that he would write about it, to her acute embarrassment. He called her Dee Dee Bronson in *Women*.

Though he had officially broken with Linda, she called him on 29 August the moment she got back from Utah and asked him to meet her a block away from De Longpre outside the Pioneer Chicken joint on Western, Hank's favourite eating place, a block away from his cottage. He told Liza he would be back in five minutes, climbed into the Volks – he was a true Los Angelino, no one walks if they can drive, even one block – and there she was parked by the outside tables, with two cups of coffee waiting on the dashboard. She told him 'You are the only man who can make me laugh, you're really funny and I miss that.' He told Carl Weissner that her face and eyes looked strangely hard after the four-month separation: 'I'm afraid something has gone out of it for me.'

But Linda had a magnetic charm over Hank. He had been corresponding with an airline hostess called Patricia Connell and told her that Linda had an immense pull on him; all she had to do was walk in the room and he was finished. He felt very bad about Liza, whom he described as a fine person who should never have put her trust in someone like him, and had no excuses for dropping her except that he didn't love her, and he did love Linda. He told Liza that he was going back to Linda. She took it hard. They talked for seven hours about it, during which time she physically attacked him five times. He told Connell: 'I let her beat on me because I felt bad about what I was doing to her. But she'll make it.'

For Linda King, it was 'Marvelous, two weeks straight of love . . . two, three times a day. We couldn't get enough of each other. I felt like rolling all over him . . . in every direction. Soak up those feelings.'

To help promote the recent publication of *Erections, Ejaculations, Exhibitions and General Tales of Ordinary Madness* by City Lights Books in San Francisco, Bukowski gave a reading at the Telegraph Hill Neighborhood Center in North Beach on 4 September 1972.

After throwing up a few times, Hank climbed on stage where he was amazed to find a refrigerator full of beer. He reached in and took one. He read some poems. He introduced Linda King to the audience. She stood up and waved her arms. He began to get more interested in the beer than the poetry and launched into long rambling asides between the poems, while the audience yelled at him to read poetry. He jeered at them. It was a great success. It was described by Lawrence Ferlinghetti: 'During the course of the event, he drank all the beer in the refrigerator onstage, read pugilistically from his works, and roused the huge audience to cheers, sneers and insults, all of which bounced off him as off an old boozer in a skid row saloon.'

They stayed in the small guest apartment above the City Lights bookshop where Ferlinghetti kept overstock and old paperwork. There was a roaring party afterwards in the apartment during which Jack Micheline fell and cut his head and someone broke the window. Hank finally threw everyone out and went to bed. Linda went off into the night but reappeared some hours later, kicking in the panels of the door to gain entrance. After a huge argument in which Hank accused her of going off with one of the guests, Linda attacked him. She scratched his face and bit a hole in his arm and together they tumbled down the steep narrow staircase after which she grabbed her air ticket and suitcase and ran. Hank poured a half bottle of iodine over his wounds. The *San Francisco Chronicle*, ever the small town paper, reported the quarrel, quoting Linda as saying: 'I think I would kill him if he wasn't so good in bed.' Bukowski's reputation soared ever higher.

Hank returned to Liza's bed and, while he was being solaced in the Hollywood Hills, Linda broke in and stole her sculpture back. However, it was not long before Hank, Linda and her two children, Clarissa and Gaetano, set up house together. Linda took a mortgage on 2440 Edgewater Terrace, a short road next to the Silver Lake reservoir in Silver Lake. It was an attractive detached house with a terrace above the garage, a stone chimneystack and a large backyard for the children to play in filled with trees and stands of bamboo. Frances and Marina were now living in Santa Monica, so Marina often came to stay the weekend and Hank would attend her school functions like the proud dad that he was. It was domesticity on a level never before known to Bukowski – or desired by him. He kept De Longpre on as a bolthole and a place to take other women but he enjoyed family life; it appealed to the romantic in him.

Jane had been the first person who made him understand the nature of love and through her he discovered pleasure in the little things that people do that make them care about each other. He loved lying in bed with her on a Sunday morning reading the paper or fixing a meal together. In 'Pretty Boy' Hank wrote of his sentimental attachment to these moments with women: he loved to see her pillow next to his on the bed and listening to the rain together from the bed. He remembered with enjoyment sitting in his car, pushing her stalled car down the street. In the poem 'Yes' he described the pleasure he took from someone with fingers more nimble than his getting the knots out of his shoelaces, and how he liked hairpins on the floor and table and to have her drive the car on dark nights, smoking cigarettes together and talking as they drove through the silent streets, and even the insane and useless fights. There were fewer fights with Linda now because Hank had agreed not to drink in the house. He did his share of the housework and played with the children in the garden like the all-American family he once despised.

The year Hank and Linda were at their closest was 1972. They even published a book together called *Me and Your Sometimes Love Poems*, from the KissKill press; one hundred copies illustrated with drawings by both of them on the cover in the best small press manner. It joined a whole series of books and chapbooks that Hank now had behind him. After *Notes of a Dirty Old Man* had come *A Bukowski Sampler*, edited by Douglas Blazek, which included appreciations from old supporters like Al Purdy, William Wantling and Steve Richmond. This was followed on the last but one day of 1969 by *The Days Run Away Like Wild Horses Over the Hills*, a massive Black Sparrow collection of poems. Black Sparrow did *Post Office* in February 1971 followed by another enormous collection of poems, *Mockingbird Wish Me Luck*, in June 1972. City Lights had been about to approach Bukowski when Black Sparrow originally stepped in and so they waited in the wings for any droppings. John Martin did not like the overtly sexual material that Hank wrote in his *Open City* and later his Los Angeles *Free Press* column, and certainly did not like the stuff he wrote for the sex magazines. In fact this was the most commercial material so City Lights was very happy to publish Black Sparrow's rejects. In April 1972 it published *Erections, Ejaculations, Exhibitions and General Tales of Ordinary Madness*, the book that Hank's San Francisco appearance was designed to promote. It was an enormous book of 480 pages and they later broke it into two: *Tales of Ordinary Madness* and *The Most Beautiful Woman in Town*. *Erections* . . . was so successful that they bought *Notes of a Dirty Old Man* from Essex House to make a prose trilogy, paying Hank a $10,000 advance. Hank commented: 'All my books are Black Sparrow, except now and then when Martin loses his mind, City Lights gets lucky.'

His work was also beginning to take off in Germany. In the early 70s, the rise of the erotic avant-garde in the USA and Britain was mirrored in Germany and France. The censorship battles in those two countries helped publicise the books: William Burroughs's *Naked Lunch* was banned in Boston; Allen Ginsberg's *Howl* was banned in San Francisco; Hubert Selby Jr's *Last Exit to Brooklyn* was banned in Britain; Henry Miller's *Tropic of Cancer* and *Tropic of Capricorn* were banned all across America, and so on, making the fight for a free press an international issue. The works of the Marquis de Sade were published freely for the first time, so was the erotic classic *The Story of O* by Pauline Reage. Carl Weissner, the German translator of William Burroughs, Allen Ginsberg and the Beats had long hoped to find a German writer of the same power and promoted Bukowski's work tirelessly. Charles Bukowski's work fitted right into this category of free-speaking, no-holds-barred, earthy, radical fiction. The fact that he was German helped make him a cult hero among students and the intellectual left in his homeland where there were no comparable authors. Weissner's third translation, *Notes Written Before Jumping Out an 8 Story Window*, paid off and it eventually sold more than 50,000 copies, a poetry bestseller that made Bukowski's name in Germany. Bukowski was unusually modest about his appeal there: 'It wasn't that I was so good, it was just that they were so goddam bad.' He was their own, home-grown William Burroughs. The image of Bukowski, with the beer bottle and the hangover, the whores and the horses, was in some ways more important than the writing, and German fans began to show up at his door, some of them young women.

It didn't take long for the sniping to start. Jealous of his success, Steve Richmond accused him of selling out because he made his living at the typewriter and was writing for magazines like *Vogue*. But Richmond had a private income and as Hank wrote to Bill Robson: 'Richmond lays in the sun outside his beach cottage, claiming to be worth only $300.' Hank thought that the mimeo revolution had run its course; whereas it was once cutting-edge, hard, pared-to-the-bone, exciting stuff, it had become a way for talentless writers to pretend to themselves and their girlfriends that they had an audience.

There were just too many temptations now that Hank was becoming famous and he began seeing a fan referred to in *Women* as 'Nicole', whom he visited two or three times a week in the mid-afternoons. One evening, while drunk, he told Linda all about her, including where she lived. Why he did this was not quite clear to him afterwards: 'But when one drinks one sometimes thinks unclearly.' Hank's feeble excuse was usually that he was going to the supermarket. He and Linda had one of their regular fights and Hank had decided to spend the night with Nicole. Hank had already visited her and had gone out to replenish the supplies of alcohol when Linda found him. He was already quite drunk and was carrying two six-packs of bottled beer and a pint of whiskey. He recognised Linda's orange Volkswagen parked out front on Santa Monica Boulevard and, in a moment of aberration, thought: 'Oh, jolly. I'll take her up and introduce her to the other one, and we'll all be friends and have drinks.' This was not to be. Linda rushed him, grabbed the bottles and started smashing them on the pavement, one by one, including the pint of whiskey, yelling 'Ho! So you were going to get her drunk on this and fuck her!' The other woman was watching the action from her doorway and Linda ran up the stairs and began hitting her with her handbag, yelling 'He's my man, he's my man! You stay away from him.' Then she leapt into her car and roared off. The afternoon rush hour traffic was just beginning to build up. Hank took a broom and began to sweep up the broken glass. Then he heard a sound. He looked up just in time to see Linda driving her car along the pavement, rushing straight towards him. He flattened himself against the wall and she missed him by inches. He finished sweeping but as he walked up the stairway Linda reappeared with a bottle which she threw at Hank with such force that it went through the windowpane in the door leaving a round hole behind it like a bullet instead of smashing the whole pane. 'For God's sake, Bukowski, go with her,' screamed the other woman, worried that Linda was going to demolish the place. Hank climbed into the orange Volkswagen and Linda sped off triumphantly.

Soon afterwards, as Hank once more began making suspicious visits to the supermarket, Linda found his car parked near the woman's house. She left a note under the windscreen wiper telling him she had gone; she went home and packed her bags then took the children and drove to Boulder, Utah, where she took a job working at her sister Margie's bar. Hank continued to live on at Edgewater Terrace because he had by now given up De Longpre and eventually Linda gave in and invited him to visit.

The King sisters threw a huge party to welcome him, where he was surprised to find that the mountain men were even crazier than he was and could party louder and longer than him. Hank, Linda and the children, and sister Geraldine and her family drove out to the thirty acres of land the family owned outside Boulder. Boulder is between the Capitol Reef National Monument and the Bryce Canyon National Park, a wild, undeveloped area of rugged cliffs, bare mountainsides and thick pine forests. July and August are prone to thunderstorms in these mountains, many of which are above ten thousand feet. Linda and Hank camped out but it rained so hard they had to squeeze into the family trailer home with Geraldine and her family. After three days of this the beer ran out and, frustrated beyond belief, Hank stamped off into the woods, perhaps looking for a friendly liquor store. He was safe enough as long as he stayed on the King sisters' land, but he foolishly climbed a fence. In one of the funniest passages Hank ever wrote, he describes in *Women* how he got completely lost and panicked; was attacked by hornets and finally fell in a swamp; and how Linda was forced to use the tracking skills of her youth to find him. 'I felt fear, real fear. Why had I let them take me out of my city, my Los Angeles? A man could call a cab there, he could telephone. There were reasonable solutions to reasonable problems.' Linda drove him to the airport. It was agreed that he would leave Edgewater Terrace by 29 July. He moved to 151 South Oxford Avenue, one block east of Western but a little further south than he usually lived, between 1st and 2nd Streets. It was more expensive than his usual lodgings; perhaps living on Edgewater Avenue had given him a taste for a more comfortable life.

He remained embroiled with Linda. It was the usual rocky road, enlivened with fights and scenes. He couldn't resist other women when they presented themselves but flew into a jealous rage when Linda saw other people. He told Carl Weissner that she fucked two other guys in one week to spite him for going back to Liza Williams again. Then in June 1974 she took off for Utah for her usual three months in the summer, telling Hank that she would get a summer man but that he was her winter man and not to forget it.

In December 1974 Hank did the 2nd Annual Santa Cruz Poetry Reading with Allen Ginsberg, Gary Snyder, Lawrence Ferlinghetti and others including Linda King. There was an audience of 1,600. Bukowski went on first, while he was still relatively sober, followed by Linda who was introduced by Jerry Kamstra as 'Bukowski with a cunt but a fine poet regardless of sex'. Compère Jerry Kamstra, knowing he had a full line-up, kept her time on stage restricted and pulled her from the stage just when she was getting hot. Her raunchy, sexual poems had the audience roaring with approval. Kamstra apologised afterwards: 'It was my fault. She was one of the best received poets and I should have given her half an hour.' At the reception following, Hank finally met Allen Ginsberg. The drunken Bukowski grabbed Allen and bellowed: 'Ladies and Gentlemen, we have Allen Ginsberg as guest of honour tonight. Can you believe it? Allen Ginsberg, a man of genius, the first poet to cut through light and consciousness for two thousand years and these bastards don't even appreciate it. Have a drink, Allen,' and he thrust a drink into Ginsberg's hand. But then Hank's pride got the better of him: 'God, it's good to see you Allen, really,' he continued. 'I don't care if you are a fake. Did you hear that folks? Washed up. Everybody knows that after *Howl* you never wrote anything worth a shit. How about that folks, a vote? Has Allen written anything worth a shit since *Howl* and Kay-dish?'

Hank was unfamiliar with the pronunciation of the word and slurred it. Ginsberg quietly corrected him having had decades of experience of dealing with abusive drunks: from Jack Kerouac's late-night anti-Semitic ravings to Gregory Corso, who so routinely disrupted Ginsberg's readings that he didn't even notice any more. Ginsberg's own lover, Peter Orlovsky, was at times dangerous to both himself and others when in an alcohol frenzy. Bukowski's insults were routine to him. Hank later wrote: 'Ginsberg was all right, he seemed a good sort.' He had been impressed by Ginsberg's reaction to a bomb threat, which was to go on stage and improvise a poem about it.

'Come on you bastards, let's party,' Hank yelled and began to dance. Linda King described the event: 'It was the first of many times after that that Bukowski did his dance . . . He added dancing to the Bukowski show. It was still a one-man show. I doubt if he could ever perform as a couple.' Bukowski: 'I did my Indian dance, my Belly dance and my Broken-Ass-in-the-Wind dance.' The crowd were of course amused, particularly when he slipped and fell flat on his back in the middle of a puddle of wine that he had spilled. When someone who had not been at the reading asked Linda: 'Who is that ass making such a fool of himself?' she said she didn't know. Later Hank had his cock sucked by a groupie in the bathroom. Linda was used to it, she knew he wouldn't even remember in the morning. As she put it: 'I knew that creepy, ugly, cockroach slime who inhabited Bukowski when he got too drunk.'

Bukowski:

I feel that I'm an ass a lot of the time. If I'm an ass, I should say so. If I don't, somebody else will. If I say it first, that disarms them. You know, I'm *really* an ass when I'm about half smashed. Then I look for trouble. I've never grown up. I'm a cheap drunk. Get a few bottles in me and I can whip the world ... and I want to.

He was actually unable to binge as much as he used to. If he drank two or three days in a row his body overheated and his skin got very hot to the touch. He recognised these as danger signs so every few days he took some days off. He tried to improve his physical condition and had even bought a set of barbells to work out when he was at De Longpre. He was still a powerfully built man, even with the massive beer gut. Bukowski: 'Sometimes I throw them. I put a whopping big hole in the wall of one apartment once, which I thought improved the place but the landlord didn't. I don't know if you realise it but a 20 lb barbell weight makes a great discus if you're drunk and feel like sending something sailing.'

Hank found himself in middle age, more satisfied with life than ever before, on the brink of financial success with already a significant reputation as a poet and novelist. His mind was not at rest, but he was working hard to find some peace:

I care for many things and that's what bothers me. But I don't know how to line them up. I can't find any guiding element to tell me how to set these things up I care for into a fashion that will make them more durable, or grow better ... I have to figure it out alone. I can't have any help. But I'm moving very slowly. The writing helps, and the drinking. That's about it.

9. BOOGIE IN THE MUD

The Louisiana swamp-rock guitarist Danny James once released a record called 'Boogie In The Mud': 'Get on down in this mud with me ...' a reference to the French expression, *nostalgie de la boue*, a longing for the low life (*boue* literally means mud), the call of bohemianism, the sporting life. In June 1974 Hank moved back to East Hollywood. The low life was important to him; he was very conscious that this was his subject matter, an area that he had made his own, and one that he had to keep in touch with. He had used up virtually all his stories from the 40s and the 50s in his *Open City* and Los Angeles *Free Press* columns and needed a constant supply. If he was to write about the low life, he had to live it. It was a very conscious decision. In 1975 he said: 'I have to keep living in order to write ... I have to get burnt in order to write at all, to intermingle. And that means women, jails, various strange spots, you know, whatever happens. I have to taste it before I can write. I can't lose contact. Just memory alone I can't work on.'

He returned to his old neighbourhood between Sunset and Hollywood boulevards, this time to 5437 2/5 Carlton Way, in the seedy section east of the Hollywood Freeway which cuts diagonally through the locality. It was one of a group of eight bungalows in a court. He paid $105 a month. There were cracks in the ceiling from the last earthquake. He set up his metal-rimmed, formica typing table, the same one that his parents had given him when he studied journalism at college, and built his rickety plank and housebricks bookcase, hung the walls with his own paintings and tacked his mother's best lace tablecloth over the window. He dragged his cigarette-burned, wine-stained mattress into the blue-painted bedroom and installed a large, noisy fan for the summer heat. At night he could hear the distant muted roar of the freeway, particularly in the early morning, when it was still pitch dark but when the birds were already up, chirping, and the early risers were heading for another day at the office. Then he would hear cars starting everywhere on the streets, just as he was thinking of turning in from his night's work at the typewriter.

A block to the north ran Hollywood Boulevard, the apartment blocks with their skimpy lawns illuminated in pastel spotlights, skinny palms black-silhouetted above; and a block west was Western Avenue. Where they crossed was the centre of the sleaze industry; a neighbourhood of fast-food takeouts, massage parlours and porno movie houses; the late night bars with their tawdry neon, the beckoning doorways leading to brothels, the liquor stores and the endless passing traffic. Hank had ambivalent feelings about it. In one poem, written about driving along Hollywood Boulevard in the rain, he described it as: 'the most depressive of all the streets, jammed glass nothing of nothing, it was the only street that really made me angry.' But most of the time the area delighted him: the seedier it got, the better he liked it:

My idea of life is where the black pimps are, where the music is playing, where the jukeboxes are playing in the bars, where the lights are on, that's where life is . . . you're in a lively joint and something is happening. I think degradation, black pimps, prostitutes, are the flowers of the earth. I think those joints where this is going on, I think there's great happiness. And terror and horror too, but that all counts as adding up when you walk into a place to get a drink. It's a liveliness, when you clean up the city you kill it.

He lived just a block from it all, easy walking distance to the liquor store or fast food joints. He told Al Purdy that he lived in the 'whorehouse district' of east Hollywood and said: 'I was walking down the street today when one of the girls in a love parlor hollered, "Hey, come on in!" I didn't even blush, man. Gave her an easy wave and moved on. At age 54 I've developed a minor smooth.' That he could still write about such a minor incident betrays the old German puritan streak that Linda complained about.

His next-door neighbours were a stripper and the manager of a pornographic bookshop; another managed the massage parlour across the street. Where he lived pleased him; he was happier in the squalid surroundings. He had large palms, and plenty of birds flying about and wrote a magnificent Los Angeles poem about the area: 'A Little Sleep and Peace of Stillness'. It is as if he was writing to one of his many correspondents; he tells them about the view and how good the parking is and how a religious maniac lives in the next house on the court who drinks cheap wine and has visions and plays the religious stations on his radio as loud as he can so that everyone else gets the message. Bukowski:

> It was beautiful, always action. This is an action-place. We had a great hotel next door. Most of the lesbians lived there and they started beating each other up. One would say: 'You fucking whore . . . I'll kill you!' All of a sudden you'd see glass breaking, flying through the night. You'd hear screams. But you know the cops never came, it could go on for two or three hours. And suddenly there would be silence. So you knew somebody either would be dead or reamed up the ass with a telephone-pole. But they got what they wanted.

The police helicopters would circle overhead, their spotlights shining down, exploring the alleys and backyards, the heavy throbbing of their rotors beating down through the night air. Hank and his various girlfriends would go outside naked and stare up at them; it was like living in a cyberpunk novel.

He loved walking to the end of the block and seeing the pimps and whores hanging around the corner eating hot dogs with mustard dripping down their chins. In 'The Death of a Splendid Neighborhood' he wrote about a brothel off Western Avenue just above the Philadelphia Hoagie Shop where he ate: 'where you went up a stairway/to get head'. The door was guarded by a big Hell's Angel who sat there in the heat, wearing his swastika-emblazoned leather jacket. He was there to decide if you were the vice squad and to protect the girls if things got rough. The man who ran the sandwich shop hated the girls but he was too afraid of the biker not to serve them. Hank went by one day and there were bullet holes in the door above the stairway and everything was boarded up. The sandwich shop man was happy but a few days later his window was broken and the shop set on fire.

Hank had always written a lot about Los Angeles, stories about garages and auto repair shops, nothing was ever too insignificant. In Taylor Hackford's documentary he said: 'You get the stink of LA in your bones, you know it. I didn't even want any other town, I couldn't write.' Hank wrote a well-observed poem about the garbage collectors, called 'The Trash Men', about the freeways: 'I can hear cars on the freeway, it's like a distant sea/sludged with people/while over my other shoulder, far over on 7th street/near Western/is the hospital, that house of agony.' He could write a long poem about appearing in court for public drunkenness. In 'The Drunk Tank Judge' he describes where the courthouse is, on San Fernando Road, among the junkyards, who is there, the judge's complexion, what the average fine is and the terrible state of everyone's car as they drive away. His work was written in everyday speech, recording small, commonplace events and using them to reveal often brutal facts of life and nature. But most of all the poems were hymns to Los Angeles, celebrating its low life: 'L.A. is a wonderful town. I like the way the streetlights shine, I like Sunset Boulevard. I like this town, it's great.'

It was at Carlton Way that he gathered the material used in *Women*: a succession of groupies, junkies, hangers-on, girlfriends, poets and drug dealers passed through the house, providing a wealth of stories for his book. He was famous as the chronicler of the dead-beats and drunks of 40s and 50s West Lake from his days with Jane. Now he was in the middle of the Hollywood punk scene; the burgeoning pornography industry, the cocaine dealers and the addicted girls who called him in the middle of the night, and had him wrapped round their little fingers.

He now clearly aspired for success. In a revealing story, 'The Shipping Clerk With a Red Nose', written sometime before 1973, he gives a third person view of his own career. Though many elements are fictionalised, it shows his attitudes towards Jon Webb and his various girlfriends, his daughter, his 'Notes of a Dirty Old Man' column, and much else. Towards the end of the story the girls get younger and his financial position improves. At the end, Bukowski is living in a mansion high in the Hollywood Hills and the butler informs the writer of the piece that Mister Bukowski cannot be disturbed.

Although his reputation as the hard-drinking, belligerent, wild-man of literature was an important aspect of his success, Bukowski was concerned that it might have isolated him and complained about the limited scope of his writing: 'All I can write about is drinking beer, going to the racetrack, and listening to symphony music. That isn't a crippled life, but it's hardly all of it either. How did I get so limited? I used to have guts. What happened to my guts? Do men really get old?'

This restriction to just a few closely observed subjects is perhaps more common in the visual arts. The photographer Alfred Stieglitz maintained that an artist only needs the minimum of subject matter to work with. He was thinking of painters and photographers, of course, and his own pictures were virtually all taken in the surroundings of his house on Lake George, New York. Cézanne painted endless versions of Mont St Victoire, Giacometti endlessly reworked his club-footed women, Moriani devoted his whole life to painting groups of bottles. Rarely, however, has a writer focused as intensely on such a small body of experience as Bukowski: the daily grind in the factory or warehouse, the racetrack, bars and bar fights, tempestuous relationships with women, drinking. There are no memorable characters other than himself, the setting is almost always Los Angeles, the action more or less predictable. It is a restricted pallet, but the formula is infinitely variable.

In the past Hank had been ashamed to revise or correct a story. He felt that if it came out like that, *that* was how it was meant to be. He would write it and leave it, but in 1974 he began a process of revision. He would take out bad or unnecessary lines that detracted from the story but hardly ever added anything; he did this especially when he had written the story or poems drunk the night before. By 1975 he said that he was taking out whole lines or paragraphs: 'and when I get sober I insert a new line. I buck it up.' He sometimes felt the work could use some help but he never did extensive rewriting because, as he said: 'I'm lazy.'

He liked a certain amount of interruption when he was writing. He did a lot of his writing at Linda's Edgewater Avenue house, when he and Linda were on good terms, and her children would often run into the room. 'I like interruptions, as long as they're natural and aren't total and continuous.' At De Longpre he purposely put his typewriter next to the window so that he would see people walking by: 'Somehow that always worked into what I was doing at the moment. Children, people walking by and classical music are all the same that way. Instead of a hindrance, they're an aid.' Classical music was his preferred background sound, it did not engulf the work but had a certain presence. He had no records; it would have been a distraction to have to choose what to play and to turn the records over. He listened to the classical music station on the radio and hoped it would bring him something that he could 'align with' as he was writing. He didn't listen consciously; it was background music, but he did have his favourite composers, many of them German: Bach, Beethoven, Mahler, Mozart, Wagner, Handel, Gluck, Bruckner, Franck, Shostakovich, Sibelius and Stravinsky, but he was less fond of Brahms and Tchaikovsky.

He continued to write straight onto the typewriter which kept the work strict and confined. He had tried to write longhand but it just didn't work. For Hank it was too intellectual, too soft, too dull. He needed the machine-gun sounds of his Royal. Critic Ron Blunden suggests that it is almost possible to tell by the rhythm of the stories how many drinks he had had when he wrote them. Too early in the evening, they are a bit stiff, aggressive, too late they are 'runny, redolent with self-pity, and often incoherent'. In between they are perfect, funny and pathetic, raw and ribald, with a sense of purpose and pace. In fact he found it very hard to write prose when he was drinking, because for him prose was much harder work than poetry so it tended to be written while sober, or early in the evening.

Poetry was another matter. He started with a feeling in mind that he wanted to put on the page: to 'lay down the line that startles'. He always got a bit dramatic and corny when he was drunk. The symphony music would fill the room, and he would be puffing at a cigar, lifting the beer high to pour it down his throat, knowing he was going to tap out some great lines. Sometimes he would write poems all night and find them lying on the floor in the morning. He would delete all the bad lines, and have a handful of poems. 'About sixty percent of the lines are bad; but it seems like the remaining lines, when you drop them together, make a poem.' An evening would produce ten or fifteen, and the next morning he would look through them. Six of them he would discard, six he would accept only after certain lines had been deleted, and three were alright the way they came out.

He quickly assembled a huge stock of poetry for John Martin to use in selecting poems for his next book. Hank always gave Martin complete editorial control in matters like this and made no suggestions what to include. *Burning in Water Drowning in Flame* was published by Black Sparrow in June 1974. It was a fat book, but still represented a fraction of the amount that Hank had written. It was powerful stuff; Hank had not succumbed to the pleasantries of the Black Mountain School. Hank's work is a shout of recognition, more suited to a poetry slam than quiet musings in a book-lined library. Writer Victor Bockris once proposed an event where a boxing ring be set up and poets slugged it out – verbally – from each corner, topping each other with aphorisms, cunning twists of meaning, unexpected insights. Hank would have been a contender.

If his poetry was forceful, it was nothing compared to his prose, beginning with *Erections* . . . in 1972, which reprinted columns from *Open City* and the *Los Angeles Free Press*, as well as stories written for sex magazines, that John Martin rejected. Columns and stories that Martin did like appeared the next year in *South of No North*. Hank was getting more of a reputation as a hard-hitting prose writer than as a poet. And, as was the case with Jack Kerouac, his readers were beginning to confuse the heroes of the stories with the writer himself. The pieces Hank wrote for porn magazines are purposefully shocking, containing bizarre sex and violence often written to order. Sometimes the story was given to him by a friend, for example, 'The Man', about a dishwasher who hits his woman and puts a cigarette out on her wrist. Bukowski: 'This isn't totally imaginative. There was a guy like that. So I just took off on the memory of him and wrote him up. It wasn't me. I'm very gentle with my women.' An example of a newspaper story that Hank used is 'The Murder of Ramon Vasquez', which he prefaced with a note to say that the story was fiction and that 'any events or near-similar events in actual life which did transpire have not prejudiced the author toward any figures involved or uninvolved.' In fact the story is based directly on the Ramon Navarrow murder, which is treated in a rather different way by Joan Didion in her collection *The White Album*.

The story which upset most people was 'The Fiend', about a little girl on roller skates getting raped, which first appeared in the Los Angeles *Free Press*. The editor Art Kunkin foresaw trouble and prefaced it with a long editorial which explained that Hank was not advocating such behaviour, that he was a good man and had a daughter of his own, and so on. The story caused a good deal of controversy because it was written in the first person. He was trying to get into the mind of a man who would do such a thing, and to write his viewpoint. Bukowski: 'I wrote a short story from the viewpoint of a rapist who raped a little girl. So people accused me. I was interviewed. They'd say, "You like to rape little girls?" I said, "Of course not. I'm photographing life." I've gotten in *trouble* with a lot of my shit. On the other hand trouble sells some books. But bottom line, when I write, it's for me.'

Some of Hank's readers wrote to tell him that they were aroused by some of his writing, especially by 'The Fiend' and Hank thought it was perhaps because he described her clothing and what happened very slowly and in detail and that was what excited them. But, he told Silvia Bizio: 'I didn't get a hard-on while I was writing it.' Douglas Howard suggested that some of Bukowski's stories were written for the sheer excitement of playing with strange ideas and Bukowski agreed: 'I get my kicks out of exploring those areas. You know when I write the poem I tend to stay pretty close to the source of things. In the stories I kick up my heels; I rather enjoy myself in the stories; I get my natural kicks, as you might say. It's a relaxer. Sometimes I might even write stories that might upset people, deliberately, just to do it.'

Bukowski wrote stories about murderers, rapists, all types of lowlife. It did not mean that he was a murderer or a rapist, nor did it mean he was advocating murder or rape, but the public did not appear to understand. Bukowski: 'I like to explore what this man might be thinking and that a murderer can enjoy a cup of hot cocoa or enjoy a comic strip. This is rather fascinating to me, you know, to explore these things.' It was a problem that writers have had for a long time: 'Shall I be accused of approving these things because I describe them?' wrote Henri Beyle Stendhal.

Many of the stories in *South of No North* have a similar genesis in news stories or articles. 'Stop Staring at My Tits Mister' was written in response to a story in a sex magazine that someone mailed him. The story was so bad that Hank decided to rewrite it with a better ending. 'Maja Thurup' came out of a newspaper story of a woman explorer who went into the jungle and found a savage and brought him home with her. Hank read it in the paper, and the story took off naturally from there. Bukowski: 'There is one in which imagination and reality do mix up. A lot of people didn't like that story. It upset them.' Most of the stories in *South of No North* had little autobiographical content, being 'found' rather than from his experience. Some were pure fiction of the traditional kind; 'No Way to Paradise', for instance, about miniature people, was a piece of automatic writing. He was up against his weekly deadline for the *Los Angeles Free Press* and had no idea what to write. So he sat down and just started typing, and the story of the little people was what came out of his unconscious.

* * *

Ever since 1972 Hank had been working on a new novel called *Factotum* but it was proving difficult; whereas the first one took twenty days, the second one took four years. He found it hard work, like working in a factory, and he found that the only way he could do it was to write very short chapters, like Fante: one in each sitting. It was a curious choice of title; a factotum is not someone who has had a lot of jobs, it refers to someone hired to perform a wide variety of jobs: a servant who is a chauffeur, carpenter, gardener and general handyman for instance. Bukowski was a few degrees off in meaning. He got the idea for the book from George Orwell's *Down and Out in London and Paris*, which had made him feel competitive, regarding his own hard times as much tougher than those described. His original idea was to write about all the jobs he had had, but there were too many, and many of them were very similar. He had quite a bit of it written but when the selection of stories was made for *South of No North*, he found that many of the stories were similar to sections already written for *Factotum*, so he had to take those chapters out and patch it back together without them. This made life difficult because he had naturally chosen the most interesting stories for his short stories.

Writing *Factotum* was not the smooth, easy ride he was used to with the poetry. He described his methodology. First he had to fight the urge to do something other than write, then to prepare himself for the ordeal. He said that he felt bad, he felt a tightness as if he were about to get into a fight. Then came a period of distraction involving the chair, the typewriter, the table, paper and so on but finally he would seat himself down, drawn to the machine against his will as if by a magnet, and begin to type. Bukowski: 'I always throw the first draft away, saying "That's no good!" Then I enter into the act with a kind of fury, writing madly for four, five, even eight hours. Next day I'll write for two or three. Then I'm spent and exhausted and won't touch the typewriter again for at least a week, then the whole cycle starts over.'

It was slow going and for the last period the manuscript sat in a drawer, stalled. He had two or three chapters to finish and the ending but he couldn't bring himself to open the drawer. Sometimes he would take it out, flip through the pages and say: 'Shit, I don't know.' Then one night he came home from the track, walked in, had a few beers, and typed up two or three pages. Suddenly it was all done. 'It was so easy.'

It was another existential view of his own life. Bukowski:

I'm not so much a thinker as I am a photographer . . . I have nothing to prove or solve. I find that just photographing is very interesting. Especially if it's people you see and then you write it down; it can get a little bit holy here, but there's a message or sense of direction after you've written it down. It says something which you didn't even quite know. So that works better for me.

This is the literary phenomenon of giving form to your own unconscious. In *Factotum* Bukowski was doing just this. He told Nanda Pivano that it was 95 per cent truth and 5 per cent fiction: 'It's just polished up a bit around the edges.' To Marc Chénetier he suggested that the figures were more like nine-tenths fact, one-tenth fiction. He said that he improved his life with creative fiction by shining up the areas that need to be shined up and leaving out the parts that he didn't want known. It was a process of selectivity. It was mostly fact but it was adorned with a bit of fiction: 'a turn here and there to make it separate. I guess it's cheating in a way, but you could call it fiction . . . I mix fact with fiction . . . I take all the advantages, that's what.' To Sean Penn he confirmed: 'What I've tried to do . . . is bring in the factory workers aspect of life . . . the screaming wife when he comes home from work. The basic realities of the everyman existence . . . something seldom mentioned in the poetry of the centuries.'

In 1975 Hank was seeing five different women, but Linda King was keeping most of them at bay. He was vacillating between thinking he was the best writer alive and feelings of deep insecurity, as if the praise and success was all a joke and someone would suddenly take his typewriter away and everyone would laugh. But most of the time he found himself happy. He loved his daughter, his monthly stipend from Black Sparrow had been increased to $300, his fee for a reading was now $1,000, he was doing what he loved best, he loved life, at last. He described the peace he felt driving his battered blue '67 Volkswagon through the streets like a teenager, the radio tuned to 'The Host Who Loves You Most', feeling the sun on his back and the solid hum of the rebuilt motor as he wove his way through traffic. He was receiving a lot of fan mail: poets wanting an introduction to John Martin or for Hank to read and comment on their poems; letters from prisoners or factory workers; letters from people who told him that without his writing they would have killed themselves, that he saved their life, that he made them see things that transformed their lives. And of course there were the letters from young girls who wanted to fuck him, often accompanied by explicit photographs.

Hank's neighbours, Brad and Tina Darby, the manager of Le Sex Shoppe and a stripper, became good friends. They went to clubs and parties together and spent a lot of time just hanging out, drinking, smoking pot and talking. Whenever Linda showed up unexpectedly, Hank would quickly usher any visiting girlfriend or girlfriends into Brad and Tina's bungalow while he dealt with her.

Hank could not help but flirt with Tina, who was very attractive, and friends reported that they would sometimes visit Hank and locate him in the Darby's house, sitting on the bed naked while Tina teased him. Tina had thirty pairs of high-heeled shoes on the floor in the bathroom that the unwary stumbled over, and specialised in clothing from Frederick's of Hollywood. She often did her strip act for Hank and Brad, coming out in a skimpy outfit while Hank betrayed his 30s upbringing by hollering: 'Jesus, Jesus, look at that!' and then when she appeared in an ever skimpier outfit, with more breast showing and even higher heels, he would mop his brow and gasp: 'Jesus! Oh my God. I can't *stand* it!' and Tina would sit on his lap and Brad would take pictures.

One time a number of Polaroid pictures were taken of Tina sitting on Hank's lap, completely naked, laughing as he felt her up while wearing only his shorts with an open fly. Brad and several visitors posed with her as well but the next day, while they were all looking at the pictures, Linda came charging into the room – Hank's front door did not lock – grabbed the pictures in both hands and ripped them to pieces, screaming at the top of her voice. In the subsequent fight, Tina's finger was injured. It was already in a splint and Linda pulled it right back, necessitating a visit to the emergency ward. After yet another break-up, Linda suddenly appeared and attacked one of Hank's girlfriends who was sitting quietly in the living room. She kept him on his toes.

Linda knew that she could not allow things to stay as they were. She recognised that the relationship was almost over and began to see other men, but the bond with Hank was so great that they continually gravitated towards each other, with explosive results. Taking the initiative, she decided to move to Phoenix, Arizona, and make a clean break. She put the house up for sale and began packing up her possessions. It was then she found that she was pregnant. She had been seeing two other men, one called Frenchy, and another from Flo's Cocktail Lounge on Sunset Boulevard where she had been working as a hostess; any three of her lovers could have been the father. Early in December 1975, as she moved the furniture and packed her things into boxes, she began bleeding badly. A friend took her to County Hospital where she miscarried.

Meanwhile, Hank had developed a crush on a 26-year-old he dubbed Cupcakes, but who was largely indifferent to his advances. It was Hank's habit to telephone Linda and tell her about his other woman; he thrived on the drama and adrenaline rush of fights and screaming arguments. His relationship with Jane had been like that and it was as if this was the only way he knew how to relate to women. He called Linda when she was recuperating from her miscarriage to tell her that Cupcakes had finally agreed to have sex with him, on condition that he buy a new mattress to replace the filthy old one. When she told him about her miscarriage he expressed no sorrow or sympathy with her ordeal; the purpose of the call had been to get her riled up. As he was sure it had not been his child he was indifferent and said he was on his way out of town for a reading and didn't have time to come over and see her. Linda brooded over his callous phone call and the next day, when someone brought her a bottle of rosé wine to build up her iron, she drank the whole thing, leapt into her Volkswagen and headed for Carlton Way.

Hank came back from the reading to find that Linda had broken in and that all his books were gone, along with his typewriter, radio, paintings and other items. He found her outside, crouching beneath a bush. As soon as she saw him she began breaking things and screaming. She smashed his typewriter on the road, the parts flying in the air, and when he protested that he must have his books, she threw each one through his windows, breaking them all and ruining his valuable first editions. Some items he never did find. Tina Darby came out of her house to see what was happening but Hank pushed her back inside; Linda seemed so out of control that Hank feared she might attack Tina again, as she did after the Polaroid incident. Not knowing what else to do, he called the police. A prowl car pulled up and Linda was taken to the station, sobbing uncontrollably, claiming that she had lost their baby.

Hank did not press charges, but the incident shook him up pretty badly. He bought new glass and replaced the windows, puttying them back in place himself. He wrote to John Martin enclosing the receipt for a new typewriter for $143.10, tax included, telling him: 'I am putting things back together and trying to start over again. I am in a semi-state of shock so please don't expect too much literary work until after Xmas, OK?'

Hank clearly did not want to end their sex life, though life as Linda's lover was becoming increasingly dangerous, and the relationship dragged on a few months more. The attraction between them was so great that, when he was interviewed by Rolling Stone six months later, Linda was his companion at a reading in Long Beach, and even spoke to their reporter. Confusingly, Linda told BBC interviewer Vanessa Engle that after throwing all Hank's books through his windows: 'The sex that night was pretty good,' which suggests that there may have been several such destructive incidents since she couldn't have been describing the night of that incident as she was with the police. Perhaps with no one else did he feel so relaxed and self-confident, able to try new things, to innovate and have fun. Linda King told Glenn Esterly: 'He's a very creative lover. I've stayed with him five years, and if he wasn't good I could certainly find someone else.'

Hank added:

I may as well admit it, I'm a good lover. But I think Linda's probably talking about sexual exploration, working down below there with the tongue and also getting in some creative movements you haven't tried before. It's like writing a story or a poem, you don't want to do it the same way every time or it gets boring . . . it's just an instinctive thing to keep things fresh and exciting. Like maybe doing it standing up as a change of pace. I can do that with these goddam legs of mine.

Hank was inordinately proud of his tree trunk legs; his balls also delighted him. He told Esterly: 'The legs are dynamite. And . . . I have genuinely magnificent balls.' But he confided that sexual imagination was the key. Ultimately sex was a creative act.

But Hank was being creative with too many other women and the fights were stupendous; the periods of break-up began to exceed the time together. Linda and her two children moved to Phoenix, and after Hank spent a week with them there the relationship finally ended.

Hank complained that his time was taken up by fans but he remained listed in the Pacific Bell telephone directory for anyone to call. His rationale was that he didn't have sex until he was 23, and didn't have much after that until he was 50. He thought he should stay listed: 'until I get as much as/the average man has had'. At the age of 55 he appears to have already exceeded his quota. One of his favourite, and often told, tales concerned his postman who arrived each day just before noon. This was about the time Hank's girls were leaving. One day, as the postman turned into the court, Hank was sitting on his porch with three young women, drinking beer. Having spent so many years working for the post office, Hank gave him a big friendly smile as a greeting. The next day the postman asked him: 'Hey bud, mind if I ask you something?'

'Go ahead, friend.'

'Well,' he said. 'I wondered why all these beautiful young women are drinking beer with you 'cause you ain't exactly what I'd call a pretty boy.' Hank laughed with him.

'Go ahead baby, it's all right. I know I'm ugly – the secret is availability.'

Two young German women called him, asking to see him. One was 20 and the other 22. He told them his heart was broken and he was giving up women; they laughed, smoked some pot and went to bed with him. The younger one was having her period so Hank settled down with the 22-year-old 'and/ate her up'. They stayed two days and two nights, then he drove them to Sherman Oaks and dropped them at the bottom of a long driveway leading to a grand mansion. He was on the tourist route. Another time John Martin found two young Dutch girls sitting on the rail of his porch, waiting for him. When asked what they wanted they said: 'We've come from Amsterdam to fuck Bukowski.'

Hank had become a lady's man. Just when he thought one of his loves had gone forever, she would appear again. The problem was that they sometimes showed up two or three on the same day and that was when the trouble started. Hank could not believe what had happened to him: 'I've got this big pot belly; I'm fifty-four years old; my shoulders are slumped; my nerves are shot. All of a sudden I'm a lady's man. It's weird.' It was terrific material for the book, and it also fitted the image, and he was very concerned to maintain that, telling interviewer Marc Chénetier:

Here's a guy with a bottle of beer in his hand, a cigar, and he's just banged a 25-year-old girl in the ass and they've had a big fight and there's a broken window and she runs out of the door and he goes up and he turns on Mahler. Maybe it does fit, I believe it fits, but from the standard concept of a person put together as a total person, it doesn't fit.

Cupcakes became the new woman in Hank's life: her friends called her that because of her size 38D chest. She had long, flaming red hair and worked as a cocktail waitress at the Alpine Inn in Hollywood, where her attractive figure ensured good tips. She started dropping by Carlton Way after her shift. She was born Pamela O'Brien, but Hank refers to her as Pamela Brandes, her married name. She was also Miss Pussycat Theaters of 1973 when she worked for a chain of movie houses showing sex films. Hank described her as 23, with brains, a great body and spirit, but it was the mane of red hair that obsessed him. A couple of months after he began seeing her, he told John Martin: 'She's a speed freak, pill-head and on the smack. You just don't understand how HARD people can get until you've met one of those. And, of course, I got sucked in early.' He told Carl Weissner that she would be the death of him, but it was worth it. He fell for her hard, just as he had done with Linda King. Bukowski: 'That's why I have trouble with women, I get attached. All my women all say, "Oh you write this hard stuff, but you're soft, you're all marshmallow inside." And they're right. I don't have it.'

Pamela's Irish father abandoned her and her mother when she was two, she had a child at fifteen, and her interest in Hank, who was twice her age, seemed to be more as a father figure than anything else. She had little interest in him as a writer, and thought his poetry was mere doggerel. She liked him because they could go to the racetrack or the boxing matches at Olympic Auditorium together and have fun drinking. Hank's interest in her was almost entirely sexual. He liked to lie back in the bed and watch her comb her hair in the mirror, staring at her in wonder. He celebrated her in the book *Scarlet*, published by Black Sparrow in April 1976 in a limited edition and consisting of four poems inspired by her, but she was unmoved, and barely glanced at it. She was very flirtatious and often disappeared for days on end, leaving Hank racked with anxiety. She drove around in a beaten-up, blood-red Camaro with the doors hanging from broken hinges, the side windows missing, and out-of-date licence plates, the seats piled with make-up, empty soda cans, bottles, cigarette packets, boxes of Kleenex, magazines and children's things belonging to her daughter Stacey. The only space in the car not piled high with junk was the driver's seat.

Hank's crushing obsession for Pamela ensured that she distance herself from him but when she vanished he would drive aimlessly around the streets, 'an inch away from weeping', looking for her beaten-up Camaro. His own '67 Volkswagen was not in such good shape, either, particularly after Cupcakes kicked a hole in the windscreen. He would visit her bungalow and leave a note, returning hours later to find it still there. In one of the poems in *Scarlet*: 'I Made a Mistake' he described how he left the Maltese cross from his car rear view mirror, the one given to him by his grandfather, and books of poems tied to her doorknob with a shoelace. Typically the poem is also funny in a self-deprecating way: he takes a pair of blue panties from the top of the closet and asks Cupcakes if they are hers. 'No,' she says, 'Those belong to a dog,' and leaves. She was evicted for non-payment of the rent and Hank persuaded his landlord to allow her to take one of the bungalows in the court. Now she lived right behind him and could watch him through his kitchen window. The hilarious daily minutiae of their lives is described in *Women*, where she is called Tammie.

Hank and Cupcakes flew to New York City for a reading at the St Mark's Church Poetry Project. On the way over Cupcakes passed out from drugs, her head on Hank's shoulder. At first he was contented, loving the intimacy of it, staring at her enormous breasts. Then he noticed they were not moving and panicking he found a stewardess to try and revive her. In Manhattan they stayed at the Chelsea Hotel in Janis Joplin's old room 1010 on the top floor. It was 104 degrees and they had the window open, perhaps not realising that air conditioning units had to be rented separately from the desk (as were televisions in those days). Cupcakes was now on speed and was sitting on the windowsill, one leg over the edge. She leaned out and almost fell ten floors to her death, just catching herself in time. She pulled herself back in and went over to the bed, flopped down on it, rolled over and off on to the floor. When Hank reached her she was fast asleep. She had been pestering Hank to take her to see the Statue of Liberty, which they could see in the distance from the window, but she was too out of it. It could never come to anything and he knew it. In September he still saw her but according to Hank she had gone back on the game and he foolishly cashed a cheque for $100 from one of her johns. Shortly after that she began going out with a medical student of her own age and left Hank. Hank told Carl Weissner that it was going to take a long time to get over her even though he had three new girlfriends to try and replace her. There was 'none so vicious, so evil'. He missed her long hair and her witchy ways.

In October 1976 Hank made his first-ever trip outside the United States, to give a poetry reading at the Western Front in Vancouver, BC, organised by Ted Laturnus. Thinking that Hank might

encounter trouble at customs, Laturnus sent him a plane ticket to
Seattle and arranged to drive him the rest of the way, a two-hour
car ride. The story of the reading appears at the end of *Women*.
There were more women than men in the audience and many
people could not gain admission because it was sold out. Hank was
besieged by women wanting to have sex with him and he eventually
left with one whom he called Iris Hall in his book. They got along
well and on three occasions he sent her tickets to fly down to Los
Angeles to visit. She got to know his friends Brad and Tina, but
though she liked Tina she described Brad as a 'slime ball'. At this
point Hank was avoiding bars and Iris says he didn't drink more
than anyone else, preferring good German white wine, 'Mostly
what we did was laugh. He was so funny. Devastatingly funny.'
This is what sets Bukowski apart from Kerouac and the others
(except Burroughs); he is very, very funny. His books and poems
have a wry humour, self-deprecating, but hilarious.

There were many, many women. In *Bukowski in Pictures*,
Howard Sounes tracks down many of the literary ones among them
and prints their pictures. They are young, pretty, willing to
experiment and try new things, even with a borderline alcoholic
twice their age. Hank put them all in *Women*. But the poetry fans
were gradually displaced by a much harder crowd. Hank fell in with
a gang of young female junkies who took up a good deal of his time
and who used him unscrupulously to drive them around, to buy
them food, and give them money for drugs. They robbed him when
he went to the bathroom and allowed him just enough sex to keep
him stringing along. He got poems out of it, of course, such as
'Hunk of Rock', about two girls who came over to have sex in front
of him for $25. He was good company in the early hours. They
introduced him to a night-time world of uppers, downers, cocaine
and other drugs. In 'Junk' he describes sitting in a dark bedroom at
1.30 in the afternoon, surrounded by bags of garbage, hanging out
with three young women who are all waiting for a fix. None of
them work, they all rely on food stamps and handouts, some of
them have children who are at school. Days and nights ran together,
an anaesthetised haze of pills and alcohol, uppers and downers,
vodka, wine, beer and brandy, it didn't matter what they took as
long as they were numb: 'petrified/out of existence'.

Hank thought he knew what he was doing; gathering material for
Women: 'I fooled myself pretty well, I even/got myself to thinking
that I loved/one of them, the worst one.' This one exploited him
mercilessly, getting him to buy her $143.63 worth of goods in a

department store just before Christmas, promising, 'You buy me this stuff and I'll fuck you like you never been fucked before.' Naturally he paid, more than a month's rent, but then she met her friends, a couple, and it was arranged that they would all go to Hank's place. He saw the girls whispering, arranging for the one he loved to leave with them without fucking him: 'She was a young girl/and I was an old/man.' She had been to bed with him two or three times but now thought that it was enough just to show up, high on speed, and spend the night playing Scrabble for eight or ten hours at a stretch. One time she showed up at 3.45 in the morning and had to have sex with the cab driver because Hank refused to pay her fare.

Hank became friendly with a spaced out brother and sister, who were both on drugs. The girl's brother was always stealing her purse, taking all her money for drugs, and she would mumble her complaints to Hank through her own foggy, drug-induced haze. One time she called to say she had a prescription that her brother was trying to get off her; she had hidden it in her mouth. Hank had to tell Eddie (as he is called in the poem) to leave her alone or he'd come and kick ass. The girls fell about on their high heels, giving Hank drugs, and he drove them around to pharmacies and doctors, flattered to be allowed in their company. Stories of this late-night, drug-fuelled scene began to appear in his poems: 'Chicken Giblets' or 'The Lover' in *Betting on the Muse*, 'Girls' in *War All the Time*. The shabby burned-out scene at Western and Hollywood re-enacted in Carlton Way.

As he described it, the word got out that there was an easy touch living in the back court, who provided free booze and wasn't very demanding sexually. They usually visited in twos. It was something for them to do in between scoring for drugs. The young women were the subject of many poems. In 'Ladies' Man' he described their knocks on his door at 3 or 4 a.m. and how he was always charmed by them, even though they were drugged, drunk or crazy and obviously had little or no feeling for him. They would drink and talk until 5 or 6 a.m. then go to bed: 'those vicious children of the night'. They would rise at noon, paint on their brilliant red lipstick then get on the phone.

Hank was buying coke, terrible low-grade cocaine cut to pieces and was sniffing it with beer and scotch. He had no regular woman and became mentally very depressed and physically sick. At his age, his body couldn't stand the abuse. He couldn't eat. All he did all day was snort coke and down scotch and beer. One morning he awoke trembling and having hallucinations. He couldn't even drink a glass of water. He thought he was dying. He was kicking cocaine. The story is told in 'Overhead Mirrors':

Brad and Tina Darby stopped by.

'Listen, this is it,' he told them, 'I'm dying.'

The poem continues:

' "we'll fix you up," said the porno bookstore/guy (who was also selling me/the watered-down coke)./the nudey dancer shacked up with him.

'He came back with something pink in a/bottle.'

Unfortunately his friends couldn't stay with him; they were booked into a hotel with a mirror ceiling where there were planning to spend a weekend taking drugs and fucking. Hank was left alone, up all night, turning lights on and off, running the water taps and turning them off, flushing the toilet and waiting for the cistern to refill, turning the radio on and off. It was a night when he felt he was fighting against death itself: 'If you don't fight death it will/just move in.' He knew he had to get out of the neighbourhood for his own good. He was being sucked in. The area was growing more violent every day, and someone was killed right outside his house. The problem was that he loved the area: the taco stand and the pawn shops and cheap bars, the crazy people who slept on the bus stop benches or in the dusty bushes. In all the years he lived there he had no trouble, but he felt that the place was getting too dangerous for visitors and for himself as he grew older. Fortunately, it was at this time he met Linda Lee Beighle.

10. SAN PEDRO

On 29 September 1976 Hank read at the Troubadour, the well-known rock venue on Santa Monica Boulevard. In the audience was Linda Lee Beighle, a long-time fan of his work. She had read all of his books and had attended all his readings within a hundred miles or so of Los Angeles. Hank was not yet earning enough to live on from Black Sparrow and was doing a lot of readings to make up. The Troubadour had a separate bar next to the front door, and during the intermission Hank, surrounded by his entourage of young women, left the main room and pushed his way through the crowd to a table in the bar. Linda decided that it was about time she introduced herself to him and waited until most of the women had gone to take their seats for the second set before introducing herself and telling him how much she loved his work, and how she had seen him read so many times. She passed him a note with her phone number. Hank saw an attractive, petite, bright-eyed young woman with a good figure and a mass of wavy red-blonde hair and immediately wrote a note with *his* phone number, a short poem, one of his characteristic drawings of a little man with a bottle and a little sun shining in the background. Two days later he called and a few days after that he drove out to see her. Linda: 'He was doing research at the time on a novel called *Women*. And so he was stuffed with experience researching women. And so I found I was part of that in the beginning.'

They had arranged to meet at the Dew Drop Inn, a natural-food restaurant that Linda owned in Redondo Beach at 211 avenida del Norte, a couple of blocks from the Redondo County Beach Esplanade. It was only open Tuesday through Saturday and from 11 a.m.–4 p.m. for lunch only. It was a friendly place, like a big living room with a couch, magazines on the tables, a row of poetry books including many well-worn ones by Hank, paintings on the walls and a big photograph of Meher Baba. Linda had been celibate for six or seven years when she met Hank because one of the tenets of her guru, Meher Baba, was that unmarried people should not have sex. She remained technically celibate for the first six or seven months after they met, and in the meantime Hank had lots of other girls. Bukowski:

> Before Linda came along I'd take them in. Those were the days when the more screwed-up critics started to call me 'Genius Bukowski'. So you'd get these women sending me nude photographs and saying they want to come and clean house. Hell yeah! But I'd meet them at the airport and I was always lucky. I'd be thinking, 'Oh no, I bet that's her, the one with the not-so-nice face, like mine.' But then this fresh young 25-year-old would bounce up and say 'Hi, Hank!' And I'd say, 'Well, hi there! – yeah, beautiful baby, beautiful!'

Linda: 'Then his book was finished, and so were they, and I stayed.' First Cupcakes left him and then another girl went, and the junkie girls didn't find him so much fun anymore, and finally they were all gone. Linda said: 'I am the only one to have the guts, the courage, and the humour to stay. Ha ha ha!' Hank had finished his research and was in grave need of recuperation; the junkie girls had left him enervated, depressed and on the point of cracking up. Bukowski: 'When Linda met me I was a broke, dead-arse living in a hole in the wall. I was near the big burn-out but she's looked after me real well.'

Linda came from Penn Valley, a small town on the Main Line, the row of wealthy communities on the west side of Philadelphia beginning with Bryn Mawr, and extending through Haverford and Penn Valley to Merion. Penn Valley was situated between Bryn Mawr and Bala Cynwyd; an area settled by the Welsh and now filled with colleges and institutions including the famous Albert C

Barnes Foundation. Linda's father, James Beighle was of Welsh and German ancestry. Her grandfather OJ Snyder founded what is now the Philadelphia College of Osteopathic Medicine; the library carries his name and the OJ Snyder Memorial Medal is that institution's highest award. Linda was born in 1943 and had a brother, Peter, and two sisters, Gwendolyn and Jhara. She reacted against the constraints of this privileged background by running away, first at the age of eleven, then at the age of fifteen when she managed to live for four months, working as a waitress and living in a cheap rooming house, before her parents found her. In the 60s, attracted by the burgeoning counterculture, she went to California where she became involved with an artist who was a follower of the self-proclaimed avatar Meher Baba. Meher Baba became her guru. After a trip to India, she settled in Redondo Beach and set up Dew Drop Inn using her life savings from her many jobs.

Hank had drunk mostly beer up until this point; he was a relatively benign beer drinker, most of the time. It was the whiskey that got him into trouble. When he drank whiskey in company he used to get silly, or pugnacious or begin to act really wild, all of which could cause problems. He used to drink beer and scotch together in the evenings but he found that he could only write for an hour, or maybe an hour and a half that way before he became too drunk. He would continue to write but he threw away the results the next morning. Linda was concerned about his health and persuaded him to cut out all hard liquor and switch from beer to wine. This was much better all round and he found that he could write for three or four hours. Bukowski: 'With beer, you have to go to the bathroom every ten minutes. It breaks your concentration. So the wine is best for creation. The blood of the Gods.' With the expertise gained from running a health food restaurant, Linda put Hank on a regime of up to 35 vitamins a day and forbade him red meat. His weight dropped and he began to feel much more healthy.

Having finished his research on women just before they finished him, it was now time for Hank to write up his findings. *Love Is Like a Dog from Hell* and *Women* are two parallel texts; one poetry, one prose; both confessional to an unprecedented degree. They are central to the Bukowski canon. He began *Women* with some trepidation:

> I want to write one more novel, but I don't think I'm mature enough to write it. Maybe it'll take twenty more years. I'll call

it *Women*. It should be a laugher if I write it. It really should
be. But you have to be very honest. Some of the women I know
now must not know that I write this. Some things I really want
to say . . . but I'm not going to report it! It would get me into
all kinds of trouble.

He finished *Women* on 21 September 1977. The manuscript was
433 pages. He told Carl Weissner that he thought it was 'all right',
a rather tentative description for him, but that it would 'confuse'
some people. Others, he knew, would hate it. He began to make
changes almost as soon as he sent it to John Martin. One of the first
was a request that Martin change Ruth Wantling's name to Cecilia
Keesing. There had been some unpleasantness with her, with
Bukowski at his most boorish. William Wantling was one of Hank's
tough guy poet correspondents, an ex-marine who had spent time
in prison including five years in San Quentin. Hank admired his
hard, uncompromising writing; stark brutal poems about dealing
heroin, Korea, cracking people's skulls for small change. Wantling
was writing about an infinitely harder life than Hank had ever
experienced, but when he finally made his escape and was offered
a job teaching poetry at college, Hank accused him of selling out.
Considering how outraged Hank himself was when his readers
demanded that he continue to write about bars and whores long
after he had left that life behind one wonders if he felt any regret
for his treatment of Wantling. Wantling arranged for Hank to give
a reading in Illinois and Hank flew out there. He was drunk, read
poorly and was abused by the audience who felt ripped off. At the
party afterwards Hank was rude to everyone, including Wantling,
who had idolised him for years, and then he flew back to California.
   Wantling regretted ever meeting him; his image of the man was
shattered, he took Hank's put-downs to heart and he began
drinking heavily. Hank, meanwhile, did his usual hatchet job; just
as he had attacked John Bryan and Jon Webb, he now wrote a
vicious put-down of Wantling in his Los Angeles *Free Press* 'Notes
of a Dirty Old Man' column, thinly disguising him as Howard
Stantling, saying he had once been a great but now he was washed
up. Wantling entered a deep depression, telling friends that he
wanted to drink himself to death. Less than two weeks after Hank's
column appeared, Wantling suffered a heart attack and died.
Wantling had always been an unstable personality, but Hank's
column almost certainly contributed to his death. Worse was in
store; when Ruth Wantling came through Los Angeles not long

after her husband's death she stayed with Bukowski who expected her to have sex with him. He was so insistent and abusive that Brad Darby, who, along with Tina, had gone to the beach with them, had to warn him to back off. The next day Hank refused to speak to Ruth. Though he didn't actually rape her, Ruth Wantling told Howard Sounes that it was 'the ugliest experience I ever had in my life. He was unbelievable.' The version of the event in Women absolves Hank from any culpability in her husband's death and ends, callously, ' "No wonder Bill died," I said. "He starved. She never gives it away." '

It would be a mistake to expect an honest account of his relationships with women in that book; his attitudes towards women were formed in the 30s and, like many of his generation, he failed to comprehend what the women's movement was about. Add to that his enormous ego and capacity for reinvention of situations and it's clear that this is a work of fiction and should be taken as such. The unfortunate models for the characters have already, in some cases, written their own versions of the stories. Hank, of course, said that he also makes himself look foolish, but that has nothing to do with his portrayal of the women who thought they were close to him and who were aghast when they read his version of their relationship.

One example was Frances, who wrote in 'Christ I Feel Shitty': 'At least it's clear now/He hated me/for being somebody I never was . . . I thought he would want to hear amazing stories/when all he wanted was somebody to clean up the kitchen, just like he said all along.' Perhaps John Bryan was right when he wrote: 'He loved to fuck but was a total misogynist . . . He despised and mistreated all his women and attracted nothing but full blown masochists.' It was a view many people held, including some of his friends.

As fiction Women is one of his most popular works. He was right to be concerned about the book's reputation, and told his old friend AD Winans: 'I may get killed on this one. It's written as some type of high-low comedy and I look worse than anybody but they're only going to think about how I painted them.' However, he said, 'It's a jolly roaring blast.' The book had been quite easy for him to write and was the product of three bottles of white wine a night.

It was written in a spare, economical style which lent itself to his dry humour. Bukowski: 'A good style is important. Style is what makes you different from the run.' Hank's style takes a lot from his acknowledged mentors Hemingway, Céline, Fante and Hamsun, but in his considerable use of direct speech he owes a lot to the masters of everyday American vernacular: Chandler, Cain, Hammett and Spillane. His approach is close to that of James M Cain. For example, consider the words of Cain on the use of American speech, written in 1945:

> I make no conscious effort to be tough, or hard-boiled, or grim, or any of the things I am usually called. I merely try to write as the character would write, and I never forget that the average man, from the fields, the streets, the bars, the offices, and even the gutters of his country, has acquired a vividness of speech that goes beyond anything I could invent, and that if I stick to this heritage ... I shall attain a maximum of effectiveness with very little effort.

It is this same vividness that characterises Bukowski's prose and his ear for narrative.

Bukowski's ideas are expressed by actions and events in his slow, spare, Los Angeles drawl: 'no ideas but in things' as William Carlos Williams demanded. It was spelled out in detail by Raymond Chandler in an essay contrasting British and American English. Of the latter he wrote:

> It is a fluid language, like Shakespearean English, and easily takes in new words, new meanings for old words, and borrows at will and at ease from the usages of other languages, for example the German free compounding of words and the use of noun or adjective as verb ... It is more alive to clichés. Its impact is emotional and sensational rather than intellectual. It expresses things experienced rather than ideas.

His method while writing *Women* was to alternate between prose and poetry. *Women* is episodic, essentially a collection of short stories like the *Decameron*, which he used as a model. Both books are divided into short sections. Those in *Women* are numbered 1–104 (the original manuscript had 99), and those in the *Decameron* numbered by day: the storytelling takes place over ten days, with ten stories each day, plus a foreword, an introduction and an afterword making 103 sections in all. (Hank had to have one more, though his chapters are much shorter.)

He alternated between writing the prose for *Women* and the poems which appeared in *Love Is Like a Dog from Hell*. He found writing the short stories easy, they were relaxing. After that he would return to the poetry: 'I jump back and forth. One helps the other. . . . [stories] just come straight on out. I'll change a line or two that's awkward. I revise poems much more. Stories they just come out.'

Love Is Like a Dog from Hell is as confessional as *Women*; we are spared no detail of his personal hygiene or that of his guests, or the exquisite details of his sex life. He describes everything from finger-fucking a 19-year-old groupie in his bed, to the freaked-out young girl who leapt onstage at a reading in the redwoods outside Santa Cruz screaming 'I want you! I want you! Take Me! Take Me!' tearing off her clothes and grabbing his balls, almost twisting them off, until two women wrestled her offstage.

Love Is Like a Dog from Hell was published first, in September 1977, a huge undertaking of more than 300 pages in hardback, paperback and the usual special signed editions with paintings by Hank tipped in. Hank was anxious to see *Women* in print, and told John Martin that he was awaiting it more than any other book he'd had published. As he wrote it he felt that it was different from his other work, that it was really happening: 'that certain carving into the page with certain words in a way that you feel the power and the magic and the luck'. He recognised that Martin was taking a gamble on this title as it contained considerably more erotic material than Black Sparrow was used to, but he thought he was risking his own reputation with it too. He told Martin to expect rancour and bitterness as well as hatred when it was published and admitted that he had given the feminists a few extra little titbits, just to make them mad. He recognised that he and Martin would hang from the same branch and congratulated him on his courage in bringing it out.

There were longer delays than usual in preparing *Women* for publication and Hank began to get irritated, feeling that John Martin was beginning to take him for granted. When it was finally published on 15 December 1978, Hank was even more miffed. As usual he had told John Martin to go ahead and correct any grammatical errors he saw, but this time Martin had gone too far. Hank did look at the proofs but he was lazy about things like that and didn't examine them closely or else he would have found that Martin had rewritten numerous passages to make it, as he thought, more literate. Whereas Bukowski always liked to keep to the simple 'he said', 'she said', Martin had changed instances of this to 'he retorted', 'he said cheerfully', 'I shrugged', 'she seemed to be sore'. There was even one passage where Martin had changed the colour of a woman's dress from green to blue. 'I guess he thinks I can't write,' Hank told his old friend and fellow writer Gerald Locklin. Hank came down hard on Martin over this tampering with his text and insisted that all the changes be returned to his original wording and that the second edition have a notice stating: 'Second edition, revised'.

The book was greeted with derision by feminists because it was sexist, but in terms of literature it was a considerable development from the crude sexism of *Post Office*. Bukowski had matured as a writer; up until then he had only ever written about himself, Henry Chinaski, the protagonist. In *Women* he attempted for the first time to give a rounded portrait of another character, Linda King. There was also considerable irony in his portrayal of the male protagonist who, though holding the traditional American male view of sex roles, is continually subverted in this role: he often cannot achieve an erection, he is seen as an out-of-control libido, he lets people down and tramples over their finer feelings, he is seen as pathetic rather than macho. In a remarkable passage towards the end of the book he wonders if he could continue to justify his behaviour as merely a matter of research, a study of women for the book. He realised that he was simply allowing things to happen without thinking about them, he was being careless of other people: 'I wasn't considering anything but my own selfish, cheap pleasure.' He thought he was like a spoiled high school kid, that he was worse than any whore because there was never any pretence of feelings there, they just took your money and provided a service. 'I tinkered with lives and souls as if they were my playthings. How could I call myself a man? How could I write poems? . . . I didn't want *my* soul played with, mocked, pissed on; I knew *that* much at any rate. I was truly no good.' The worst part was that he passed himself off to these unsuspecting women as a *good* man, someone who cared and had feelings. 'I was able to enter people's lives because of their trust in me. I was doing my dirty work the easy way.' He begins to cry, his brain whirling.

This recognition of his attitudes and behaviour undoubtedly occurred in real life; it couldn't have happened to the author of *Post Office* or the protagonist of that book. It shows how far Bukowski had advanced in seven years.

Meanwhile things were developing slowly with Linda. Her initial refusal to have full sex with him meant that he had continued to see other women but more and more he had found himself longing for her calm demeanour and intelligent conversation while the junkie girls demanded money and stopped him from writing. More and more often he took refuge in Redondo Beach and found himself falling, inexorably, in love with her. He told AD Winans: 'Linda Lee is a good woman. I was due some luck. She is a stayer with a gentle courage and doesn't play man against man as if she were some golden cow.' Hank's recognition of something like love at first sight shows through in his poem 'Mermaid' where he walks into the bathroom to find Linda in the bath, playing, looking like a girl of five or eight years old: 'You were not only the essence of that/moment/but of all my moments/up to then.'

Back in 1965 Hank's Uncle Heinrich had written to him from Andernach, and Hank had remained in touch with him ever since. Hank fantasised about returning to the town of his birth. He just wanted to spend a few days there, to walk around and see the house where he was born. Bukowski: 'I'm a very romantic fellow, I'm very sentimental. I am a softie . . . If I could only know the corner it was.' He expected that the whole place had been flattened by bombing during the war and rebuilt, but the idea persisted. A visit to Germany was proposed early on by Carl Weissner, who, as Hank's German agent and translator, was responsible for his enormous popularity in Germany. His book sales there, and his income, were far higher than in the USA. His book *Stories and Novels*, consisting of sections taken from *Post Office* and *Factotum*, and known familiarly to German readers as *The Blue Book*, had sold a hundred thousand copies; three other books of short stories, all taken from the original City Lights collection *Erections, Ejaculations, Exhibitions and General Tales of Ordinary Madness*, had sold over eighty thousand copies each. Even the collection of poems, assembled by Weissner under the title *Poems Written Before Jumping Out of an 8 Storey Window*, had rapidly sold fifty thousand copies; Hank was a star in the land of his birth. By March 1977, Hank was already telling Carl Weissner that Linda was learning a bit of German because she thought they were going to go there.

Hank, Linda and their friend Michael Montfort, a German photographer who had recently moved to Los Angeles, left LAX on 8 May 1978 at 8.15 in the evening. It was a long-haul overnight flight and because of the time difference they did not set foot in Frankfurt until 3.20 in the afternoon. In the course of the flight, Hank drank the Lufthansa drinks trolley dry of white and rosé before starting on the red wine. Carl Weissner was there to meet them at the airport. Hank felt slightly embarrassed by this, as he told Weissner in a letter two months earlier when arrangements for the trip were being made. When Weissner had visited him in Los Angeles, some years before, Hank had made excuses not to meet him at the airport. He now revealed that the reason was fear. At that time Hank had never been to an airport and he didn't know the procedure of meeting someone from a plane and thought he would get it wrong so he chickened out.

They were to stay three weeks but had asked Carl to organise only one reading. Hank told him he was off beer and only drank wine, mostly German white. He ate only poultry and fish, no red meat. No more sirloin steak special dinner for $1.35 sitting at the counter at Norm's. As a consequence his weight had dropped from 223 pounds to 196 but he drank more than ever. In fact, that February he had appeared in court on a drunk driving charge.

Carl Weissner had booked them into a hotel in the centre of Mannheim, where he lived. He also took them on a sightseeing trip through Germany but Hank was as uninterested in German nature as he was in the natural beauty of America. Bukowski: '[He was] showing us all the hills, the hills, and the greenness and I started nodding off . . . Trees, greenness, it's OK, it's OK, but I mean it can finally be deadening. What are you going to do with it?' Hank also had little interest in man-made sights; coming from Los Angeles, which has no history and where the built environment barely exists, Hank did not know how to read ancient towns and cities. The castles and cathedrals meant nothing to him because he did not know the context in which they were built, nor understand the idea of a town or city as a living thing, a palimpsest of layers of human activity and meaning. There were many things that did not interest Hank, and he listed them all in a hilarious passage in *Shakespeare Didn't Do This*. 'That which interests most people leaves me without any interest at all.' Among the things which were of no interest to him were: 'social dancing, riding roller coasters, going to zoos, picnics, movies, planetariums, watching tv, baseball games, going to funerals, weddings, parties, basketball games, auto races, poetry readings, museums, rallies, demonstrations, protests, children's plays, adult plays . . . I am not interested in beaches, swimming, skiing, Christmas, New Years, the 4th of July, rock music, world history, space exploration, pet dogs, soccer, cathedrals and great works of art.' He said he wrote about what was left over: 'a stray dog walking down the street, a wife murdering her husband, the thoughts and feelings of a rapist as he bites into a hamburger sandwich; life in the factory, life in the streets and rooms of the poor and mutilated and the insane, crap like that.'

On 18 May Hank read at the Hamburg Markthalle (followed the next day by Gerry and the Pacemakers). The official capacity was 800. They allowed in 1,300 before turning 300 more away. People had travelled from Denmark and Sweden to see him. Fans were sitting in the aisles and perched on the roof girders. Hank surveyed the crowd and felt weak and frightened. He held Linda's hand and asked Carl Weissner for a drink. As they pushed down the aisle to the stage people thrust bottles at him, he took a swig from each. The crowd chanted 'Bukowski! Bukowski!' like a big rock and roll concert. His fear left him, the performer took over and he hit the wooden stage as a star. Uncorking a bottle of *Qualitätswein b.A*, he lit an Indian *sher bidi*, took a sip of wine, leaned into the mike and said, 'Hello. It's good to be back.' Almost immediately a skinny young man ran up to him and yelled: 'Bukowski, you fat bastard, you swine, you dirty old man, I hate you!' Hank at once felt at home and relaxed.

The audience was very different to those he was used to; in the States a nightclub crowd expected – and received – humorous poems. In Hamburg the crowd laughed at the funny poems, but applauded the serious ones. Hank had been concerned that they might not understand his English but they did. Afterwards he signed books for about twenty minutes until he begged for mercy as the crowd seemed to be getting larger rather than diminishing. Then there was champagne backstage and a drive in a sleek black Mercedes to an exclusive party where Hank drank and smoked and snorted the night away, just like a big rock and roll star.

Carl hired a Mercedes and drove Hank, Linda and Michael Montfort to Andernach to see the town of his birth and visit his mother's brother, Uncle Heinrich, whom he had not seen since he was three years old. They took a hotel overlooking the Rhine and even Hank was impressed by the beauty of the town. Heinrich Fett was ninety years old and was taking a nap when they arrived, but he soon came bounding down the stairs like a fifty-year-old, dressed in sharp suspenders and highly polished shoes. Louisa, his companion for fifty years, brought cakes and coffee but Heinrich had read Hank's books and soon produced a bottle of wine, telling him there were many more bottles. Hank spoke no German but his uncle still remembered a lot of English from the war and its aftermath and had no trouble telling them about events of the past. The house where Hank had lived as a child was across the street, but the house he was born in on Aktienstrasse was a short car ride away. They all piled into the Mercedes and went to see it. It was a tall, narrow house of yellow brick built on a triangular corner site. It was for sale and Linda immediately wanted to buy it. Hank was particularly pleased to find that until recently it had been a brothel.

Back at the house, Heinrich Fett produced a suitcase of letters and photographs sent by his sister Katherine from America. Heinrich never saw his sister again after Henry took her away to the United States. They went through the old black and white photographs of Hank's parents as a young couple, the pictures of the houses, trips to the beach, Hank as a toddler and as a young man. Hank found tears running down his cheeks. That evening, back at the hotel, he drank seven bottles of wine. The memories brought on by the photographs were too powerful for him to handle but, try as he did, he could not drown them out.

Everywhere they went there were photographers and film units; Hank was a big celebrity, and everyone wanted to interview him and have him sign their books. In the hotels, the parties went on until the early hours but, though there were complaints, they were never thrown out. Hank later commented that he thought it was 'real class' that they had not called the police.

Hank regarded Michael Montfort's photographs, taken during the German trip, as rather staid: 'they need a drink or a goose in the ass.' He had agreed to write a commentary to them but he put this off by writing a dozen poems about the trip, half of them 'pretty fair'. Nonetheless he was determined to save the book somehow. He told Weissner that if his planned trip to France came off then there would be no photographers along, planning picture opportunities on boats, in front of castles and visiting markets. He knew that Montford meant well but: 'I think slowly . . . I felt as if I were tied with ropes and drugged most of the German trip.' He wrote a commentary, basing his text on the photographs, but was dissatisfied with it. He discrded the first fifty pages and wrote it over again without looking at the pictures. It was looser and had more energy.

Shakespeare Never Did This reads, presumably intentionally, like a school 'What I did on My Holidays' essay, written in a slightly begrudging manner, as if he would rather not be writing it at all, persuaded to write it against his better judgement. He was reasonably happy with it, but the pictures were still pedestrian. Bukowski conflates his two foreign trips into one – he made a second trip four months later, to France – and writes about fictitious train journeys to try and make the narrative sound more authentic.

The French trip was in October 1978. Hank had been asked to appear on the most prestigious of French literary programmes, *Apostrophe*, on Channel 2 TV. There was nothing like it in any other country, a prime-time, ninety-minute programme watched by millions in which intellectuals and writers engaged in high-flown discussion about books and issues of the day under the watchful eye of host Bernard Pivot. The subject of that day's discussion was 'Writers on the margin' and there were five or six guests including the psychiatrist who administered Antonin Artaud's shock treatment. Hank was nervous, and consequently had become very drunk; he had requested two bottles of good white wine and the first was brought to him while he was in make-up. He had a simultaneous translation earplug so that he could understand the questions and the other guests.

Pivot spoke to Hank first as he was the star guest. They did not get off to a great start because Hank poured him a glass of wine and pushed it in front of his face. Pivot waved it away, a disdainful look on his face. Pivot asked him how it felt to be fêted in Europe and be on French television. 'I know a great many American writers who would like to be on this programme now,' Hank drawled. 'It doesn't mean so much to me.' Hank was having trouble with his translation plug and was getting confused so Pivot turned to another guest, a woman. Hank wanted to stay the centre of attention and interrupted what was being said. He turned to the woman and said: 'Well, I can't tell if you're a good writer or not. Lift your skirt and let me look at your legs and I'll tell you if you're a good writer or not.' Then he began gulping his wine straight from the bottle. Hank kept talking and interrupting the other guests and Bernard Pivot was at a loss as to how to control him. Exasperated, he finally put his hand over Hank's mouth yelling: 'Shut up! Shut up!', but Hank pulled his hand away and went right on talking. The other guests were all angry at being upstaged and eventually Pivot said 'That's enough, that's enough. If you don't shut up now . . .' At that Hank stood up, ripped the simultaneous translation speaker from his ear and threw it on the ground, grabbed his bottle of wine, finished the whole bottle in one long draft, and lurched off the set.

The audience was cheering and yelling, Pivot had lost control, the other guests were jeering good riddance: 'Get rid of him so we can talk.' Pivot turned to the camera: 'Ladies and Gentlemen, America sure is in bad shape, isn't it?' Hank and his rowdy entourage of about ten people left. At the door there were armed security guards and Hank foolishly pulled a knife on them. They responded by picking him up and giving him the bum's rush out into the street; meanwhile photographers were taking pictures and newspaper men clamoured to get quotes. Overnight Hank was famous in France. It was a big scandal, every major newspaper reported it, virtually all of them positive. It seemed that people enjoyed seeing the air of pomposity and elitism of *Apostrophe* deflated a little. The literary critic from *Le Monde* called the hotel the next morning to tell him how great he had been. Hank was instantly famous. The French people ran to their bookstores and bought all of his books; they had all sold out within hours. France was divided between those who were insulted by his behaviour, and those who saw it as a way to *épater le bourgeoisie*.

It had been arranged that Hank and Linda would take the train down to Nice to stay with her uncle who lived in Saint Paul de Vence and visit with Linda's mother, Honora, who had already arrived there. But rich old Uncle Bernard had watched the programme and had been outraged at Hank's behaviour. He told Linda's mother: 'I will never let Bukowski through my door, never.' He allowed them make the long trip to the south of France for nothing, refusing his hospitality only when Linda called for directions. Bukowski: 'But a very nice thing happened in Nice. It was the next day. We were sitting at a café having coffee and one of the waiters came over from this ultra-chic restaurant across the road and he said, "Excuse me, are you the great writer Bukowski?" I said, "You bet." He clicks his fingers and these five guys appear from nowhere. They're dressed in fancy waiter gear and they stand in line in front of me and then, cool as anything, they bow. Then they turn on their heels. No need for words. Beautiful!'

Bukowski did not like travelling abroad. This was a man who had been scared to meet someone at the airport for fear of getting it wrong. The opportunities for making mistakes in countries where he did not know the language or local customs were just too many. Carl Weissner thought he was tense throughout his visit, and his account of travelling to Paris and Nice shows that he felt very uncomfortable. He never went abroad again.

Shortly after returning from France, in November 1978, Hank and Linda moved to San Pedro, a working class community on a hill overlooking Los Angeles Harbor. Hank's income was now substantial, mostly from German and French sales. It was enough for his tax accountant to advise him to spend as much as he could on tax deductible items: a house, a new car, an electric typewriter, office equipment. He even tried to get the tax officials to allow alcohol but they were not having that one. Hank and Linda drove around looking at places but nowhere seemed suitable. Topanga Canyon seemed a possibility, but everyone in the bars there knew who he was and Hank hated the hippie ambience.

They decided on a large two-storey house with blue awnings in San Pedro, at the extreme southernmost extension of the City of Los Angeles, built on the east side of the Palos Verdes Peninsula, overlooking Los Angeles Harbor and San Pedro Bay. It is not the place for a long term investment as Palos Verdes has the dubious distinction of being the fastest rising piece of land on the earth's surface, with thirteen successive terraces marking ancient shore lines, and is famous for its minor earth tremors. The house was on Santa Cruz Street, high on the ridge overlooking the harbour with a second bedroom upstairs that made a superb study for Hank to write in. The house was sheltered from view by hedgerows and had a garden filled with fruit trees giving them lemons, tangerines, walnuts, figs, guavas and oranges. At midday Hank would pick a pail of oranges, take them to the kitchen and squeeze them in an electric juicer, then call Linda down to breakfast. The garden had a Jacuzzi and a pool and plenty of room for Hank to lie down on the grass and look at the sky, disturbed only by their two cats and the bees humming in his rose garden.

The kitchen floor was laid with dark red tiles. The large living room had a sliding glass door to the garden, an open fireplace and a thick green wall-to-wall carpet. There were black lacquered rattan chairs, a pair of love seats, and eventually a stuffed wolf in sheep's clothing appeared on the settee. Framed birthday and valentine cards made for Linda by Hank hung on the walls. In the bathroom a large photograph of Meher Baba smiled down at Hank while he moved his bowels.

The view from Hank's balcony looked east and north. In the harbour below, huge container ships moved slowly up and down the main channel, passing beneath the enormous span of the Vincent Thomas Bridge, one of the highest in the United States. Far in the distance, beyond Terminal Island and the Long Beach Middle Harbour the *Queen Mary* was moored. Some people might not have regarded a view of Mobil Oil's giant storage tanks and the Evergreen container terminal on Terminal Island as a particularly beautiful prospect, but Hank thought it was fine. They had an end-on view of the Harbor Freeway curving round the container terminals of the West Basin on its way to Long Beach and San Pedro. At night, there was a constant flickering moving band of red taillights and the white headlights of on-coming traffic on the elevated section of the freeway a mile away to the north.

Hank's study was lined with books, most of them by him. There were photographs and memorabilia on the walls including a two-by-three-foot colour photograph of a 1916 German Fokker tri-plane, one of Baron Manfred von Richthofen standing with his buddies, his tri-plane in the background; a photograph of Céline wearing a large overcoat, carrying a cane and a basket, was pinned to the bulletin board. There was a small refrigerator for beer and white wine. There were office supplies, and piles of manuscripts, mostly his own. About three times a week he received manuscripts from young poets hoping that Hank would comment favourably on them or recommend them for publication to Black Sparrow. Virtually all of them were 'astonishingly bad'. Next to his desk was a steel waste basket, bought for him by Linda after he set his wastebasket on fire late one night, dropping cigarette ash into it while drunk. (Hank got a four page poem out of it.)

Hank liked San Pedro; the blacks, whites, Mexicans and Yugoslavians mixed together without the trouble or tension he saw in other parts of Los Angeles, perhaps because it was a port with a transient population from all over the world meant that the local working people were more tolerant of difference. It had none of the madness and excitement of East Hollywood, but there was fresh fish each day at the harbour, and it was easy to get to the racetracks from there. Junkie girls no longer stole his money; now it went to the vet, who charged him $200 for medicine for Butch the cat, injured while fighting. Hank got a poem out of that too. The house cost $80,000 and the mortgage was $400 a month, a sum which gave Hank considerable worry even though his monthly cheque from Black Sparrow was currently for $500 and he had recently received a royalty cheque from France for $9,000. Hank was very organised about paying his bills and keeping his accounts.

He decided that it was time to regularise his financial arrangements with John Martin and asked for a six-monthly accounting, showing exactly what the sales figures were. They had signed contracts on each book and Martin paid him his regular amount as an advance on royalties. Hank resented the fact that Martin had increased his percentage on money from overseas sales from 10 to 20 per cent and he also realised that the hundreds of paintings he had done for the special editions were now worth tens of thousands of dollars. He still felt loyal to Martin for all he had done for him, and easily fended off the New York publishers who were now sniffing around his door, offering big advances, but he recognised that it was his books that kept Black Sparrow afloat, just as Allen

Ginsberg kept City Lights books going, and that he should be making sure that he received proper payment for his work. After some sharp words in June 1978, things were settled amicably.

When the Italian journalist Nanda Pivano asked why he lived in such a beautiful house surrounded by trees and flowers Hank laughed and told her it was for tax purposes. If he didn't buy a house like that then the money would go to the government and he would still be living in a small apartment. 'I would never live in a place like this of my own choice. I have lived through all my life in tiny rooms. A house gives you a tax write-off.' It did seem an odd choice of location, a distant suburb, far removed from any action. Hank could have stayed near Hollywood but moved into the hills; a secluded house in a woody glade off Beachwood perhaps. It was true that his hero, John Fante, had attended junior college in nearby Long Beach, and had used the 1933 Long Beach earthquake, where buildings collapsed and more than one hundred people died, as the central and most memorable scene in *Ask the Dust*, but this was hardly reason to move there. (Fante took most of his characters and settings from real life, though fictionalised them far more than Bukowski ever did.) More likely it was Linda's influence. She had always lived in this part of Los Angeles: her restaurant was at Redondo Beach just the other side of the Palos Verdes peninsula.

When Hank and Linda first moved in the neighbours were friendly and helpful. Bukowski: 'We were here about a week and there was screaming and drinking and crushing the bottles and it was seven thirty in the morning – the sun was just coming up – and Linda is running out there and I am naked with my balls and my cock, I was throwing dirty clothes out and saying, "You whore, I'll kill you." So after that . . .' The neighbours remained friendly but a little more distant. They told Hank that they heard things, but that was Hank's business, they did not believe in calling the police. He thanked them.

In May 1979 the front wheels finally fell off his '67 Volkswagen and Hank accepted that the car was finally dead. His tax accountant informed him that he would get a 52 per cent write-off on a new car so, after researching the specifications and deciding exactly which model he wanted, he shambled into a BMW showroom, looking like he couldn't afford a tank of petrol. The salesman ignored him, then treated him with disdain, just as Hank knew he would. Part of the pleasure of buying the car was in seeing the salesman's reaction when he pointed to a black $16,000 320i with a sunroof and all the extras and said he would pay for it with a cheque. Hank didn't need to pay by instalments. When the man called the bank he was told there were funds to cover the amount.

Hank was now a successful author with money coming in from many different sources. An Italian film group paid City Lights $44,000 for the film rights to Hank's stories in *Erections* – released as *Tales of Ordinary Madness* in 1981 – another film group optioned *Factotum*, and in 1980 the filmmaker Barbet Schroeder paid him $10,000 to write a screenplay of his own life. This was to become *Barfly*. Hank insisted that a clause be added to his contract that disallowed any dialogue changes without his consent.

For *Barfly*, Bukowski took one of his favourite books as a model: *The Catcher in the Rye* by JD Salinger. He had already made a pun on the title with his autobiographical novel *Ham on Rye*; now he took Salinger's structure, three or four days in the life of the hero, and applied it to his own hero. The influence may be deeper than that, certainly with his travel memoir, *Shakespeare Never Did This*, he uses the same breathless first person 'then I did this and then I did that' technique that works so well in Salinger's masterpiece. The difference is that, in Salinger, the narrator is speaking, not writing (a distinction that Mark Twain warned should always be very clear to the reader). The film was set in Los Angeles and based on real episodes from Hank's life: his period as a barfly in Philadelphia in the 40s; his meeting with Jane in a bar and their living together in a seedy apartment house in downtown Los Angeles; the fights with the bartender in the alley out back and his brief affair with Liza Williams are conflated to make a narrative. He finished the *Barfly* screenplay in October 1979 but it was not made and released until 1987.

Bukowski's greatest influence remained John Fante, and, though Hank had never met him, a few lines in *Women* were to cause enormous changes in Fante's life. Beginning in December 1979, Fante had been visited by the Los Angeles poet Ben Pleasants, who, over the next two and a quarter years, would tape-record five long interviews with him. In the course of their conversations, Pleasants asked Fante if was interested in getting *Ask the Dust* back into print and told him that his friend Charles Bukowski had offered to write a preface for it. Fante had never heard of Bukowski, even though he was by now quite well known in literary circles. When Pleasants suggested asking Lawrence Ferlinghetti if he would re-issue *Ask the Dust* through City Lights Books, Fante happily agreed. Ferlinghetti was keen to do it, but, before he could prepare a contract, John

Martin, who was still in the course of preparing *Women* at the time, came upon the lines:

'Who was your favourite author?'

'Fante'

'Who?'

'John F-a-n-t-e. *Ask the Dust, Wait Until Spring, Bandini*' . . .

'Why did you like him?'

'Total emotion. A very brave man.'

Martin telephoned Hank to ask if Fante was a real writer. If so, he would be interested in reading him. Hank assured him that Fante was real and described him in glowing terms as one of the greatest unrecognised writers of the century. The same battered 40-year-old copy of *Ask the Dust* that Hank had originally read in the Los Angeles Public Library was photocopied and Martin was bowled over. He told Bukowski that he would be honoured to publish it at Black Sparrow. He contacted Fante and signed him up.

Hank had never dared to approach Fante even though he knew that he lived in Los Angeles, but now that they were both involved in the re-issue of *Ask the Dust*, Linda suggested that Hank go and visit him. Hank sent a selection of his work to his idol including the album from his German reading tour and a copy of *Love Is a Dog From Hell* inscribed: 'For John Fante – who taught me how. Hank.' By this time Hank was in the middle of writing the screenplay of *Barfly* for Barbet Schroeder and was feeling uncomfortable with the strict screenplay format and the fact that Barbet insisted on overseeing every page of the script. It provided the perfect reason for him to write to Fante to ask the old pro's advice. Grateful for Hank's interest in getting his work republished, Fante replied to Hank's letter immediately, saying:

> Your French director who stands over your shoulder measuring the screenplay at one minute per page sounds like a kook to me. It seems to me that subject matter determines style and time. Maybe you might want to break some rules . . . You need limitless horizons and distances. You cannot be bound by the Frenchman's rules. You are the writer, so write a unique, an unorthodox screenplay.

In May 1979 Fante received Hank's first draft introduction to *Ask the Dust*. By this time Fante was a patient at Motion Picture Hospital with an infected ulcer on his right foot. He was already blind and his left leg had been amputated, piece by piece, as the doctors had been unable to check the spreading gangrene.

Hank and Linda visited. Fante was in a small neat private room, lying flat on the bed 'like a grounded seal'. Hank felt embarrassed, he didn't know what to say. He only knew Fante through his books, not as a person. Fante was drugged to kill the pain but Hank and Linda's visit did him a world of good. He had been the subject of blackest despair and paranoia; now he spoke of the future, of baseball and writing and the idea he had for his next novel. For Hank it must have been extraordinary to find himself in a position where he could actually help the man most responsible for his writing style. Hank liked to think of him in the 30s, living in the cheap hotel next to Angels Flight, struggling to be a writer, being encouraged by Mencken. 'The scream came from the gut. I heard it.'

Hank had some burning questions to ask him, like 'What ever happened to that Mexican girl in *Ask the Dust*?' Fante growled: 'She turned out to be a goddamned lesbian.' One bizarre side of their visit was the nature of the hospital, filled as it was with Hollywood veterans: actors, directors, cameramen, all making theatrical entrances and exits, framing shots, speaking with the deep gravitas of the old-time Hollywood pro. One of the patients was Johnny Weissmuller, the most famous of all the actors who played Tarzan, who was running up and down the halls giving his jungle mating call, and, in the middle of it all, lay Hank's hero, his body being slowly chopped away.

Inspired by Hank's support, Fante dictated his final novel, *Dreams from Bunker Hill*, to his wife, Joyce. It was a time when Hank was suffering a rare writer's block: 'an impotent period'. Oddly Fante's book could easily have been written by Hank, it reads just like him, as if Hank had somehow given Fante his energy for one last final book. Joyce read the last chapter to Hank over the phone and it stimulated him to begin writing again. He told Fante: 'You have meant, do mean more to me than any man living or dead. I had to tell you this. Now I am beginning to smile a little.'

In June 1980 Fante was back at home in Malibu, having been released from Motion Picture Hospital after further operations on his right foot. Hank and Linda drove out to have lunch with him. Fante was in terrible shape and in great pain. He cracked a lame joke about Joyce having to hold on to him on trash collection day in case the garbage collectors threw him in the truck along with the rest of the rubbish. No one laughed and he excused himself from the table and rolled his wheelchair into the next room. The next thing they heard were terrible groans of pain. In July, Fante's right leg also had to be operated on; his right toe was amputated and nine days later, the leg was cut off at the knee. His body was being chopped away piece by piece, yet tenaciously he hung on to life. When Hank published *Dangling in the Tournefortia* in September 1981 it was dedicated simply 'To John Fante'.

As Fante lay dying in and out of hospitals, Black Sparrow reissued all of his books to great acclaim. Hank told him he was in the big time now, and Joyce would not have any money troubles when he was gone. 'You wouldn't shit an old blind man, would you?' Fante asked. It must have been a source of great personal satisfaction for Hank to know that he had helped his mentor in his time of need. Fante talked enthusiastically to Hank about a further novel he intended to dictate to Joyce, about a woman baseball player who made it to the big leagues. 'Go ahead, John, do it,' Hank told him, but he knew it would never happen. Bukowski: 'He was a little bulldog, just brave without trying. But he was going . . . He was a writer to the end.'

Fante died on 8 May 1983. Hank and Linda attended the funeral on 11 May at Our Lady of Malibu where Mass was said in the traditional Latin. They sat by themselves to one side. Fante was buried at Holy Cross Cemetery in Fox Hills. For Hank, Fante remained an inspiration and a series of poems about him were published over the years: 'Fante', 'The Wine of Forever', 'The Passing of a Great One', 'Result', 'Suggestion for an Arrangement'. Bukowski wrote: 'John, meeting you/even the way it/was, was the event of my/life.' Fante's simple, clean line lived on in Hank's poetry and prose.

11. THE OLD MAN AND HIS CATS

L ife with Linda in San Pedro started well. Hank told Detroit poet
  Hank Malone, 'I've been with one almost three years, basically
a good sort, although some of her ideas on the Hereafter and her
particular god seem to me to be pretty assy, her other qualities seem
to overcome most of that.' They settled into a routine. Hank always
tried to stay in bed until midday, if he had to rise earlier he didn't
feel good all day, even if it was only a few minutes before twelve.
He would breakfast then go straight to the racetrack. He would
spend the afternoon at the races then come home to a meal prepared
by Linda. They would talk awhile, then at about 9.30 he would go
to his study with a couple of bottles of German Riesling and type
until 1.30 or 2.30 in the morning. He was still drinking too much.
Shortly after Christmas 1978 he fell into the fireplace, drunk,
burned himself and tore a few muscle sheaths. Linda patched him
up with cat medicine. What worked for Butch worked for Hank.

Hank still needed the stimulus of the track; he got a lot of stories
and poems there. One day, for example, sitting at the end of the
upper grandstand was a violinist; a short, fat, bald man in his sixties
playing classical music. Hank watched him through all eight races
and stayed behind as the crowd pushed they way to their cars. He
continued playing and Hank sat listening until they were the only

ones there. When he finished Hank applauded. The man stood, faced him and bowed. Then he put his violin in its case and made his way to the exit. Hank gave him time to get ahead of him before walking to his car. This was a meticulously observed vignette, carefully recorded in 'The Violin Player'.

He even managed to get a long poem out of being cut off in valet parking at the track by a red Mercedes. He ran to the rich man's car and tried to open the door. It was locked, the man and his girlfriend looked straight ahead, but Hank saw her slip him a .32 from the glove compartment so he walked away.

Hank felt ambivalent about the track and the amount of time he spent there: 'Racetracks are horrible places. If I had my way I'd have them all burned down, destroyed. Don't ask me why I go because I don't know. But I have gotten some material out of all that torture.' He once estimated that he had seen 70,000 races, which, at eight races per meet, would be 24 years of going to the track seven days a week. He went regularly for forty years so that was probably about right. Ultimately it was just another eight-hour job: 'It's just repeat and/repeat and/repeat,/the grinding hours,/the routine . . .'

It is likely that elements of fiction creep into Bukowski's racetrack stories more than any other; like fishing stories, they are open to more exaggeration than most. For example, in the story 'A Nickel' – did he really advise a gangster's girl to play horse number 6, and did she really search him out afterwards and slip him $500 under the nose of her boyfriend? Every element is exaggerated: the phone number she gave him, the fact he was down to his last 35 cents, had two gallons of petrol and one day's rent left on his room. But stranger things have proved to be true in his work.

In October 1979 Hank and Linda flew to Vancouver for a reading. The hall held 500, and 650 drunks showed up. Hank himself was spectacularly drunk: he had been drinking all afternoon and drank three bottles of wine during the reading itself. At the party afterwards he did his dance act and kept falling over; everyone got what they expected and Hank got the money: $1,000 plus air tickets and hotel. But he paid a dear price; back at the hotel Hank staggered about the room demanding more wine until he finally fell and cut his head open on the radiator. Linda did her best to clean up the room in the morning but there was blood everywhere, so it looked like a murder crime scene.

Linda began to get restless. Apart from the few trips to readings or events in Los Angeles, Hank was at the track all day, and every evening she sat alone in the living room while Hank typed and drank in his study. She had closed Dew Drop Inn in 1978 and missed having lots of people around. Hank encouraged her to see her friends: 'I tell her, you must go talk to your friends. She says, is it another woman?' But when she did begin to see her friends, Hank was immediately jealous.

They did see quite a bit of Barbet Schroeder, who had rented Linda's old house in Redondo Beach and was now looking for financial backing for *Barfly*, a story told in hilarious and painstaking detail in *Hollywood*, Hank's account of the making of the film.

Hank was reasonably content. He wrote to Louise Webb, complaining that Linda was religious, but said that most women were and that it was her business and certainly none of his. He told her he was: 'Finally living with a woman who isn't a whore.'

This telling line explains many of Hank's problems. In his interviews and stories he continually talks about living with whores and madwomen, but of his four previous relationships only Jane could possibly be described as a whore. Certainly Barbara was not, nor Linda King. He claimed that Cupcakes was one but she denied it, saying it was all paranoid fantasy on his part and that she had been faithful to him until she began sleeping with the medical student for whom she finally left Hank. His insistence that all his women were whores was an absurd exaggeration, a way of pre-empting the possibility of being cuckolded.

The jealousy and anxiety induced by Jane's behaviour appeared to colour his view of women for the rest of his life. He was insecure, and sexual betrayal was one of his greatest fears despite his macho image. He fantasised that Linda was having affairs even though he knew that her devotion to Meher Baba forbade extramarital sex; the relationship with Hank counted as marriage. Another follower of Meher Baba was Pete Townshend, guitarist with the Who, and he attended a number of Meher Baba-related events while playing Los Angeles with the band. Linda met him on a few occasions and went to the Who's gigs, causing Hank to falsely accuse her of having an affair with Townshend. At that time Townshend was strung out on heroin and an alcoholic, unlikely to have an affair with anyone.

The best thing to come out of the *Barfly* movie project was *The Bukowski Tapes*. As the months went by, and still no money was forthcoming for the film, Barbet Schroeder began a small interim project and began making a series of videotape interviews with

Hank, mostly shot in his garden, but some of them on location in East Hollywood, at Carlton Way and at his parents' old house at 2122 Longwood Avenue. He edited the results down to four hours of tapes, divided into short numbered segments, and sold it to French television. Each night they ran a short segment, three to six minutes long, on prime time beginning 7 January 1985. Hank was clearly drunk and sweating profusely in some of the episodes, but he was at his most drunk and belligerent in episode six, where he was interviewed with Linda sitting at his side. Linda had also had a few drinks. Hank was talking about his relationships with women, and how he felt hard done by.

Hank: 'I've always been used because I'm a good guy. Women, when they meet me, they say, "I can use this son of a bitch, I can push him around. He's an easy going guy," so they do it. Do you know, finally I got to resent it a bit?'

Linda fell for his gambit: 'What do you resent?'

Hank pounced, ready to return to what was obviously a frequent on-going argument: 'Just being pushed. Just being pushed . . . I've told you a thousand times to leave. You won't leave. I'm going to get an attorney to tell you to leave . . . because I'm kind-hearted, I give the other person another chance . . . I've given you dozens of chances but you keep pushing and pushing and you keep laughing at me. That's why I'm telling you I'm getting an attorney. I'm getting your ass moved out of here.'

Hank addressed Barbet: 'She thinks I don't have the guts, she thinks I can't live without her.' He returned to Linda and how he was going to move her out and then began complaining about her 'Meher Baba bullshit' and 'All your goddam staying out every night bullshit.' When Linda objected that she was not out every night the true scale of his paranoia was revealed:

Hank: 'You were out five nights in a row last weekend. You came in 5.30 one night, 3.30 the other. The night before last you came in 2.01 a.m.'

Linda: 'There was a reason for every one of those nights, and I told you about them and you simply wouldn't accept them.'

Hank: 'Of course not, would you accept my nights out?'

Linda: 'Yes I would. I invited you along every time. You can see nothing is happening . . .'

Hank: 'I don't want a woman out six nights a week after 2 a.m. in the morning . . . The month of May you were out fifteen nights past midnight.' The situation was now so ridiculous that Linda began laughing. Hank was acting the role of the authoritarian father or Victorian husband. It was revealed that he had marked the calendar with her coming home times.

Linda: 'Why are you so offended by me doing something else?'

Hank: 'Because I live with a woman or she lives with me, she doesn't live with other people.'

Linda: 'I *do* live with other people and I'm going to for the rest of my life.'

Hank: 'I know. I'm going to turn you over to them, don't you see?' At this, Hank twisted round on the settee and with his powerful legs began kicking and pushing Linda, knocking her on the floor. 'You shit! You fucking cunt! You think you can walk out on me every fucking night? You fucking whore! You bitch! Who do you think I am? Just "I'm going to do this, live with other people ..." You fucking shit.' Here he lunged at her, throwing himself out of the camera's range. The episode ended.

In a BBC-TV interview with Vanessa Engle Linda said: 'He was extremely verbally abusive and he was so good at it, he was a man of words, he could crush you into a little tiny piece of dust.' She said that the filmed incident was the only time he physically attacked her. Her tactic was not to fight back, not to play his power games. So when he ranted and raved she would go upstairs and leave him to it. The film shows beyond any doubt Bukowski's fundamental misogyny. All his deep-seated patriarchal values are revealed in this horrible and compelling piece of film as Hank re-creates the role his father played with his mother. The next day he had no memory of the incident, which came after a whole day of drinking and filming; he had had an alcoholic blackout.

Hank and Linda stayed together throughout 1981, during which time Hank worked on his latest book: *Ham on Rye*, the story of his childhood. His visit to Longwood Avenue, and the questions about his youth all brought up more memories that were hard to deal with. He found writing the book very difficult and in February 1981 told John Martin that it was depressing him. He was going to rewrite the whole thing, then decided that he couldn't do that as it would be too much like working for the post office. He did, however, rewrite certain portions: the bits he didn't like or that read without verve or energy. Despite his complaints about Martin's editing work on *Women* he again asked him to check it for syntax, grammar and spelling but told him not to make it *too* smooth. What Hank liked about his writing was its roughness, and lack of literary qualities. By April he had written 240 pages of manuscript, which meant it was almost done.

Hank turned down well-paid trips to Italy, France and Spain. They would have meant more interviews which he disliked after being made to do six in one day by the French who woke him out of a vicious hangover at 9.30 and thrust a microphone in his face. He no longer needed to do readings. Though he was only receiving $500 a month from Black Sparrow (in fortnightly cheques) which, as Hank told Martin, would probably make him eligible for food stamps if he relied on that to live on, his royalty cheques from Germany and France were bringing in more than $100,000 a year, enough to buy Linda a new $10,000 sports car to drive around in, though when she did go out in it he still objected.

Meanwhile Martin was readying another huge collection of poetry, *Dangling in the Tournefortia*, for publication in September 1981, which Hank dedicated to John Fante. (A tournefortia is a large flowering tree from the tropics, found in many southern Californian gardens.) While Hank and Linda were visiting Fante in hospital Hank had a seven-day writer's block. It was the first hot night of summer and Hank paced the room and fretted, looking at himself in the mirror, wondering what he would do if he couldn't write any more. John Martin assured him that he had so many poems on backlog that even if Hank died that day, he could bring out five or six more books and all of them would be good. Hank modestly amended the figure to three.

January 1982 arrived and Hank and Linda were still together but their problems continued. Their household now included a third cat in addition to Butch and Piranha. The white Manx cat had arrived at their door almost dead and they took him in. Almost immediately a friend of theirs came by drunk and ran him over. Hank took him to the vet for X-rays. It turned out he was not a Manx; someone had cut off his tail. He had also been shot, the vet found a pellet still lodged in him, and he had been run over before and hurt his backbone. The vet doubted he would ever walk again. Soon he was up and running about, tongue hanging out, eyes crossed. Hank liked his guts.

Hank always carried a knife. He pulled it every time he entered his house in case a burglar was waiting for him inside. He would unlock the door, then kick it open and rush in, searching the place for intruders, looking behind the shower curtain, behind the couch. Such tactics had probably been necessary in Carlton Way, but not in San Pedro. Unfortunately he carried it with him everywhere. After a friend's wedding reception the bride and groom took everyone to the Polo Lounge at the Beverly Hills Hotel. Hank was drunk, he pulled his blade on the maître d' and threatened the waiters and, had it not been for some fast talking on the part of Linda and the wedding party, Hank would have been arrested. The party had continued at a film cameraman's house in Marina del Rey. When it came time to leave Hank insisted on driving and smashed the front of his BMW because he could not find reverse and rammed a telephone pole before giving up. The hosts insisted they stay the night. Hank awoke the next day in a strange bed; they left before anyone else got up; Hank scraped the car on a cement wall before driving off the wrong way down a one-way street. He was always embarrassing Linda. He was used to going to pick up the newspaper from the porch in his shorts, for example, bending over and his balls falling out while the rich neighbours looked on, aghast.

While Barbet Schroeder pursued the saga of finding finance for *Barfly*, Marco Ferreri, director of *La Grande Bouffe*, finished filming *Tales of Ordinary Madness*, starring Ben Gazzara, shooting much of it in Venice, California. Hank got drunk with Ferreri and Gazzara and enjoyed their company but when he saw the film he didn't recognise the poet as anyone he knew, he was such a mild, friendly fellow, not the sort of person who ever fell through a window; no one like himself. At the premiere, held at the Encore Theater in Hollywood, Hank drank from bottles of wine that he had smuggled in and screamed 'against the whole atrocity' while members of the audience tried to silence him. Hank's opinion was that the film was 'ridiculously bad' and that 'almost all of it was worse than bad'. Disgusted, he drank heavily afterwards with an entourage of hangers-on, first in a bar then in Dan Tana's restaurant where he insulted the staff. He was pulled over for erratic driving on the way back to San Pedro, and made to lie face-down in the street in the rain while the cops handcuffed him. Naturally he got a poem out of it, the image was too good to pass up: here he was, a drunken poet in the gutter having just attended the premiere of a film about a drunken poet; himself.

In May 1982 *Ham on Rye* was published. Cleverly, not only is ham on rye the typical sandwich in the American working man's lunch pail, but it is also a definition of a ham (Hank himself) on rye whiskey, and finally it is a terrible gastronomic pun on Salinger's *Catcher in the Rye*, one of Bukowski's favourite books. Arguably Bukowski's finest novel, this is his *bildensroman*, dealing with his childhood, his tortured relationship with his father, all through high school and up to Pearl Harbor and Bukowski's first break from home. It is moving, poignant, sometimes funny, sometimes ugly. As the *Times Literary Supplement* said: 'It offers grim insights into the construction of masculinity and American life between the wars'; a masculinity that Hank was still trying to come to terms with.

The arguments continued and in September Linda moved out though they continued to see each other on a regular basis two or three times a week. This was a hard time for both of them but Linda had the worst of it. Hank immediately contacted old girlfriends and carried on with his old routine of visits to the track and typing late into the night whereas she had to find an income and somewhere to live.

They were apart for most of 1983. Linda came by two or three times a week; otherwise the only people Hank saw, apart from occasional girls, were his neighbours and the people at the racetrack. By February 1983 he seemed resigned to their break-up, telling Al Fogel that he no longer had an old lady and that she had found him restrictive so he had set her free, but said she was never around anyway. When he did go out, he often got into trouble. Though he was now in his 60s, he still caroused like a man in his 20s.

That summer he attended a birthday party for Michael Montfort's wife held at Spago where, completely drunk, he lurched up to Arnold Schwarzenegger who was seated with his new wife Maria Shriver and berated him: 'You little piece of shit! You and your big shitty cigar, who do you think you are? Just because you make these shitty little movies, you're nothing special, you megalomaniac piece of shit . . .' Schwarzenegger got this sort of thing all the time so he didn't make a big thing of it. If Hank thought that he could take Arnold, the ex-Mr Universe, in a fight he might have had an unpleasant surprise. He would have been better off discussing poetry or classical music: Schwarzenegger was a friend of Harold Norse from his body-building days and, though he kept quiet about it, he was an avid reader of modern poetry and a lover of Bach.

By the end of 1983 Hank was becoming concerned about Linda's state of mind. He told John Martin that she appeared to be getting worse, and said he didn't think he would ever be able to write 'that novel', a reference, perhaps, to a book about his days subsequent to those covered in *Women*. Though they were still arguing badly, Hank proposed marriage to Linda. She was 41, he was 64. One of the problems had been her biological clock ticking away: she knew that Hank did not want any more children, but if she was to have some with anyone else she had to decide soon to leave him for good and find a new partner. After considerable thought she decided to marry Hank; she essentially made him her child. Hank, for his part, seeing that Linda was having a hard time dealing with an unsettled future decided to give her some measure of financial security and, in April 1984, without informing Marina, who at that time stood to inherit everything, he changed his will to give Linda one-third of his estate with the rest going to his daughter. In subsequent changes he divided his estate between the two of them and after his marriage he left everything to Linda. That year he earned more than $110,000 and was able to pay off his mortgage, something that had always worried him.

He instigated improvements to the house: a fence around the garbage cans; a hot tub in the garden with a new doorway in the wall leading to it; an extension with a room for Honora Beighle, Linda's mother, so that she could stay with them for the wedding. After his parents' criticism of his writing Hank now had Linda's mother. He overheard her asking Linda: 'Why does he have to write that way? Why does he do it?' He knew that, as long as the mothers-in-law protested, he was on the trail of something living and lively. Hank got so worried about the cost of the renovations and the wedding, especially since the dollar was strong against the European currencies, which meant a drop in his overseas income, that he began writing for *Hustler* and the porn magazines again.

The wedding was held at the Church of the People in Los Feliz on Sunday, 18 August 1985. It almost didn't happen because Linda was struck down by flu at the last moment and was told by her doctor that she was not in a fit state to attend the ceremony. Hank was left to make all the final arrangements, which he did not relish doing, and when Linda asked him to pray for her recovery he screamed at her: 'Fuck it all! Don't you realise that there isn't a God!' and smashed a full length mirror in his frustration. The house filled with guests: Linda's mother, John Martin and his wife Barbara, who designed all the Black Sparrow books, Marina and her boyfriend Jeffrey Stone, Michael Montfort and his wife, Steve Richmond, Gerald Locklin, and other friends from way back. Hank insisted that John Martin, as best man, drink a glass of champagne to celebrate even though Martin was a lifelong teetotaller. He got dizzy after the first sip and thought the room was spinning.

Hank was resplendent in a creamy white tuxedo, complete with a floral tie, snakeskin shoes and a corsage. Then, by a miracle of modern medicine, Linda appeared at the top of the stairs in her wedding dress with a huge lace-trimmed hat and Hank was able to announce: 'Ladies and Gentlemen! The bride!' A white Rolls-Royce sped them up the Harbor Freeway to the church with Handel's *Water Music* playing on the speakers. After a reception for eighty people at a Thai restaurant, during which they cut a wedding cheesecake – Linda's aversion to unhealthy food extended to wedding cake – a select group of friends returned to San Pedro for a night of drinking. There was no fighting, no blood, no screams in the night. Hank felt positive about it. He dismissed the idea that marriage would affect his writing, telling William Packard, editor of *New York Quarterly*, one of his favourite magazines: 'If this destroys me as a writer then I deserve to be destroyed.'

Some of the problems clearly were not yet resolved and it does not sound as if married bliss reigned immediately. In January 1986 Hank complained: 'My home life here has developed into nightmare proportions. I'm unable to write about this portion of my life now and may never be able to but if I ever get the space to, I've got a novel that will make *Post Office*, *Factotum* and *Ham on Rye* look like kindergarten stuff.' However, by February he was feeling pretty good and: 'My five cats and my wife and the walls soothe me, smooth me.' He told the German writer Guindolf Freyermuth: 'I don't know whether I do Linda any good, but without her I wouldn't be here.'

Hank had become very friendly with Barbet Schroeder, and carefully followed the wheeling and dealing as he attempted to get the money for *Barfly* promised by Menahem Golan and Yoram Globus, the owners of Cannon Films. At one point, exasperated by the devious Hollywood ways of doing business, Schroeder decided on an expedient of his own: he bought a chainsaw, walked into the chief executive's office, started it up, and declared: 'Right, I'm going to cut off one of my fingers for every ten minutes you don't give me the money for my Bukowski movie.' They must have thought he meant it because Schroeder finally got his money.

Casting placed Hank in an ethical dilemma. Sean Penn wanted to play the role of Hank so badly that he offered to do it for one dollar, but only on condition that his friend Dennis Hopper directed it. Schroeder had worked so hard to get the money, staking everything on his dream to make the film, that Hank remained loyal to him. At one point Schroeder was living in the Black section of Venice, $60,000 in the hole, and so depressed that Hank offered to give him back his $10,000, but he was not going to give up. Schroeder was offered good money to become the producer in order to let Hopper direct but he refused. It was his film, he commissioned

Hank to write it, and he was determined to direct it. Hank had very little option but to go along with him. Hank did not like Dennis Hopper when they met; he was wearing a lot of chains around his neck and he seemed to Hank to be the most pretentious type of hip Hollywood character. He did, however, like Sean Penn who at that time was married to Madonna.

Bukowski: 'I got to like Sean, especially when he came over with Madonna. She's talking about Swinburne! I'm making my usual cracks about Madonna trying to be hip. Sean gets angry. He stands up, but I say quietly, "Sit down Sean, you know I can take you baby." When he sits down I think, "I like this guy."' Sean Penn and Hank became good friends despite the disagreement over *Barfly* but Hank never got on with Madonna. In January 1992 she approached Hank to appear with her in her book of sex photographs but he refused.

There were rewrite problems with *Barfly*, and Hank had to go over and fix it up since he had a clause in the contract that the screenplay could not be touched. One character in particular was wrong and had to be rewritten. Hank did not study screenwriting method before writing the script as he thought it would take away some of his natural energy and he preferred it rough to polished. He liked working with Schroeder and got closely involved with the making of *Barfly*, selecting and advising actors, reworking scenes, suggesting some final cutting or changes, and appearing in a cameo: the camera pans past him sitting among the other barflies.

Eventually the role of Hank went to Mickey Rourke and that of Jane to Faye Dunaway, who was attempting a career comeback. Shooting began on 19 January 1987. Bukowski: 'Mickey Rourke is a real human guy, on and off the set. And in *Barfly* he really came through with the acting. I felt his enjoyment and inventiveness. Faye Dunaway just can't match his talent or humanness but she filled her role.' But both were badly miscast: Faye Dunaway was far too glamorous for the role of the drunken slob the script called for, and Mickey Rourke overacted, exaggerating his speech and his walk to make a parody of the character. He was not a convincing drunk; even leaving a half-finished bottle of beer on the bar when he departed, something no real alcoholic would do. Hank would much rather have had Sean Penn do it, but he had no choice: 'Sean was alright! I knew he had the wildness to do it, much more than Mickey Rourke who doesn't touch a drink anyway!'

Hank watched some of the shooting, and sat in on the dailies and at the time he thought Mickey Rourke was doing an '*excellent* job

. . .' Hank liked him both on and off camera. There was one thing Hank didn't like – Mickey Rourke's wardrobe. The baggy pants dragging along the pavement, the unkempt hair, the filthy shorts and T-shirt. Even though Hank was a bum at the time, he would still get home drunk to his rooming house and wash his blue jeans, underwear, shirt, shorts and socks in the bathtub, take them back to his room and put them over the chairbacks to dry. He had a second set of clothes to wear while the first set dried. 'My clothing was wrinkled but clean.' Of course Rourke was playing a role that was not necessarily a portrait of Hank, but it upset him. His other objection was to the fight scenes which in his opinion were much too brutal. In reality, by the time Hank and his adversary had reached the alley, they were barely able to stand up, let alone deliver a powerful punch.

The sense of *déjà vu* was overwhelming as shooting progressed. Some of the shots were filmed in a building on Alvarado Street where Hank had actually lived, briefly, with Jane, more than thirty years before. It was the same building he had been thrown out of for having three women in his room one night. The place looked about the same but with a new set of residents. He found it strange and chilling to sit and drink beer in the same building, now filled with cameras and lights and the crew.

Things became stranger as filming continued. One night, thirty years before, Jane had drunkenly scrambled onto a vacant lot where someone was growing corn, yelling: 'I want some corn!' and gathered up an armful in a drunken frenzy, intending to cook and eat it. The police arrived and they escaped, giggling to their hotel as the cops yelled: 'Halt or we'll fire!' They knew the cops couldn't see them. The production team had scouted for a suitable location and they finished up using the exact same lot that the corn had originally been stolen from. It was now owned by a rehabilitation centre for Alcoholics who charged them $5,000 to use it. Corn was planted and stolen, rather unconvincingly, by Dunaway. The large building next to the vacant lot had originally been a popular ballroom thirty years before and Hank and Jane had very much resented the people who went there; their chauffeurs waiting outside while the glittering couples whirled to the live orchestras under the revolving mirror globes that scattered moving points of light over their evening clothes. The hotel where they had lived at the time was still standing but it was now a home for the aged. It was as if each physical site was telling him something.

It was in the course of making *Barfly* that Hank got to meet author Norman Mailer. One of Yoram Globus and Menahem

Golan's other projects was a screen version of Mailer's *Tough Guys Don't Dance*, which he was directing himself. Mailer was staying in the penthouse suite of the Chateau Marmont, the West Coast version of the Hotel Chelsea, and Hank met Mailer there on their way to a birthday party for one of the producers. When they shook hands, Hank greeted him, saying: 'The Barfly meets the Heavyweight Champ.' Mailer liked that. At the reception Hank requested so many drinks that in the end the waiter brought him the bottles. At one point in the evening he caught Mailer staring at him. Hank winked at him and laughed before going to the kitchen to tip the bus boys before they left. While he was away, Mailer told Linda: 'It was nice of Hank not to say anything about my writing.' Hank thought that was pretty funny.

Hank saw all the various edits of the movie and concluded that in some ways it didn't work and that some of the fault was his. He gave in too easily to suggestions that the film needed a love interest and that they should show that the man was a writer. Hank didn't want the love interest or the writer. He concluded that *Barfly* was not a great film but it kicked along. It is an attractive film to look at, each shot looked like an Edward Hopper, but ultimately it was a bad film. Bukowski: 'It's pepped up enough to keep everybody eating their popcorn. It's entertaining. I'm trying to record what happened thirty years ago, with splendour. And it's an original story. I have never written anything about this. It's about three or four nights in my life, at the age of 24. Ninety-three per cent of what really happened.' Predictably the film had a better audience reaction in Europe than in the USA; viewed from abroad, the Los Angeles underbelly, particularly when filmed in such gorgeous colour, seemed appealing and romantic. Also Bukowski was better known there.

The après-premiere gathering was one of the worst events Hank had ever attended. He felt ghastly surrounded by such a pretentious crowd but was cheered when Barbet Schroeder walked up to him and said: 'God, these people are horrible! I feel like my whole body is covered with shit!' Hank and Linda left early – and for Hank to leave somewhere with free drinks it had to have been pretty bad. Hollywood left him with a bad smell; a perfect subject, therefore, for a book. Hank talked a lot in his writing about being famous, but it wasn't really until after *Barfly* that he had any real celebrity. As the Hollywood publicity machine ground into action, Hank turned down invites to appear on *20-20*, *60 Minutes* and the *Late Night Show* with Johnny Carson. He did agree, however, to let Sean Penn interview him for *People* magazine.

Until the late 80s Hank was famous only in Europe. Had he walked down the street in Hamburg or Paris, many people would have recognised him. He had no such problems in the USA. There had always been cult fans, of course, who bombarded him with letters and poems, asking to come and drink a few beers with him, but he was adept at avoiding them. One couple had camped outside his door in their Winnebago for days, but that kind of behaviour was exceptional. Now he had fans appearing at his door, in his yard, tapping on the window asking for autographs. He called them 'Chinaski freaks'. Hank bought a doormat that said 'go away' but Linda hid it, thinking her mother would be offended. He told Donald McRae in 1991: 'The availability's gone now, but they keep sending their Xeroxes. It's strange, lying butt-naked on a Xerox machine so you can send the copy to some 71-year-old guy. But to them, I'm "Bukowski – the poetic genius".'

The 80s was a period when poems flowed from him like water; many are in the posthumous volume *Bone Palace Ballet* as well as a series of fat books published in his lifetime: *War All the Time: Poems 1981–1984* (1984); *You Get So Alone at Times That It Just Makes Sense* (1986) and *Septuagenarian Stew: Stories and Poems*, published in 1990. (That period also saw the publication of *The Roominghouse Madrigals: Early Selected Poems 1946–1966* (1988). He was like an old fox, the master, the poems appear with no effort, just roll out with no trouble at all, an old pro. Everything that happens around the place gets incorporated: he sees his first owl in the garden, sitting on a telephone pole, illuminated by Linda's flashlight; his cat Craney who sleeps on his back with his legs in the air gets a mention, as do all five cats, Ting, Ding, Beeker, Bleeker and Blob, who sleep on their bed, carried upstairs by Linda; going to the bank merits a poem, classical music on the radio, overheard conversation, buying a sandwich, giving a beggar money, and becoming one of his most frequent themes: the Los Angeles freeway system.

Hank always used to avoid the freeways, preferring to take the highways with their stop signs, buildings and people. But San Pedro is thirty miles from Hollywood, and the only fast way in and out is the Harbor Freeway. He managed a 41–line poem, 'Driving Test', about how he gave the finger to someone who pulled out in front of him from a supermarket exit without waiting; a 93-line poem about a traffic jam on the Harbor Freeway; there are poems about changing a flat tyre as the huge rigs thunder past, shaking the earth; about cars stalled in the fast lane, overheating in a traffic jam, their hoods up, steam boiling out; and about the drivers gawping as they pass an accident, staring at the bloodstains, the twisted metal and the flashing lights. There's 'Drive Through Hell' in which the freeways are described as 'a circus of cheap and petty emotions', and many more, but sometimes one can't help but feel that he's scraping the barrel a bit particularly with 'The Freeway Life': three pages about having a leaky petrol tank. Hank still got lost on the freeways, even coming home from the track, a trip that he made hundreds of times.

Sometimes he would stand out on his balcony in the cool night air in his slippers, shorts and T-shirt, to clear his head from hours of typing. He would smoke a *bidi*, watching the giant ships in the harbour and the never-stopping headlights of the cars on the Harbor Freeway and muse on his life, how he had reached such a position with millions of readers, a comfortable middle-class life, and the freedom to write anything he pleased. From the tone of some of his poems it seems that he sometimes could not believe it really happened. He would listen to the sound of tyres on the wet street, the distant ships' sirens, and the strange muffled crashing sounds that came from the container docks, way below, brilliantly illuminated by their security lights.

Sometimes he also wrote love poems to Linda, like 'Confession' where he says the hardest words he could ever bring himself to say, 'I love you.'

By January 1988 Hank was working on *Hollywood*, and he had finished it by October. There are readers who regard this as Bukowski's finest work: a searing indictment of Hollywood that cuts to the core of the deceit, the mendacity, the hypocrisy. It does do all this, to a certain extent, but it would have been a great deal more powerful had it been presented as a straightforward memoir. The transparent pseudonyms used in the book – Friedman and Fischman for Golan and Globus for instance or Jon-Luc Modard for Jean-Luc Godard – are no defence against libel when everyone in the book is easily identifiable and the narrative corresponds in virtually every detail to the actual making of *Barfly*. In fact there is nothing libellous in the book. Like Kerouac's 'fiction' we can assume that most of the dialogue is reproduced verbatim, or at least as verbatim as Bukowski's memory allowed, since he rarely carried a notebook. In fact he managed a sly dig at Jack Kerouac in the book where he calls him Mack Derouac and scoffs at the name of the film made from Carolyn Cassady's book *Heartbeat*, which he calls *The Heart's Song*.

In *Hollywood* Hank was not the central character, he was mostly an observer of others, a big change for him, but it was not a difficult book for him to write. Bukowski: 'Wrote it straight through, without a word change. With a poem, I will tend to drop a line or two out of each poem as I rewrite it. So I do rewrite the poem, but not the novel or the short story. Why? I don't know.' Hank certainly used the book as a way to express his true feelings about The Industry, as it is known in his home town. He told the *New York Times*: 'I guess I never believed in Hollywood – I heard it's a horrible place – but when I went there, I found out how really horrible, horrible, horrible, horrible it was, black and cut-throat . . .'

The day after he finished *Hollywood* he woke up with a temperature of 103 that lasted all week. He felt terrible, he couldn't eat or sleep. His temperature dropped sometimes, generating false hope, but it always came back. One night he experienced severe chills, shuddering with cold in bed, his teeth chattering, for two and a half hours. He went to two doctors, but neither could figure out what was wrong. He lost 22 pounds. The bouts of fever continued, three attacks in four months, leaving him enervated and frail, sometimes too weak to even brush his teeth. His weight dropped from 217 to 175 pounds. The doctors ran tests, connected him to machines, analysed his blood. He had a low haemoglobin count. He was always tired. He was unable to write, instead he retired to bed early. He developed a hacking dry cough which was relieved to a certain extent by a herbal mixture administered by Linda. By late April he even accepted her suggestion of acupuncture. His weight dropped to 133 pounds, a tremendous weight loss for someone of his size. He was unable to type, and could only handwrite in bed.

Harold Norse had finally given up his correspondence with Hank because of Hank's continual bad-mouthing. Then, in April 1989, Norse received letters handwritten in large print in capitals from what seemed a broken man. Hank told him he could no longer write, he had 'more hospital tests, some not so good. Totally drained. Just to sit down and attempt to pay a gas bill takes a great act of will.' Norse was forgiving. He believed that Linda made Bukowski's last years worth living and was happy to see his old friend relatively content.

Finally, after six months of debilitating illness, Hank's vet suggested a chest X-ray. As he suspected it revealed the obvious: a shadow on the lungs. Hank had TB. He was placed on a six-month course of antibiotics, during which time he could not drink. He stopped coughing and began to gain some weight, but the antibiotics did something to his brain and he couldn't write, though this might have been the body's shock at his withdrawal from alcohol. He slept upright on two pillows to keep from coughing. TB is contagious so they had no visitors for almost a year, and the phone stopped ringing. He tried to watch TV but the soap operas and talk shows were a nightmare and for the lack of anything else to do he watched baseball games. After three months he began to write a little, but it came slow. His weight stabilised at 170 pounds, good for a man of his height approaching his seventieth birthday. He was still weak and found it hard to get out of bed, to walk downstairs, to type. He longed for 14 November 1989; the day he would be able to take his first drink in six months.

When Hank was going through a difficult period with his tuberculosis he was unable to go to the racetrack. He was weak and depressed and sat around the house doing nothing so Linda gave him a copy of *The Wall*, Jean Paul Sartre's short stories; he could not concentrate for any length of time so short stories were the best thing for him. The collection of five stories, in Linda's words, 'blew him away'. She told Jean-François Duval, author of *Bukowski and the Beats*: 'He said, "I should have read him before, I should have met him in Paris . . . But it was too late." Then he regretted it.' They had been unable to meet because when the message came that Sartre would like to see him they had only had two hours' sleep the night before and Hank was completely drunk.

Hank had had a previous health scare in May 1988 when his doctor diagnosed skin cancer, but he was able to have it successfully burned off by a dermatologist who told him: 'It's like arc welding. Same principle.' His mood was lifted on this occasion when he received *Roominghouse Madrigals*, a collection of his pre-1966 poetry, which arrived in his mailbox at just the right time to cheer him up. He was still elated when he saw a new book of his work, or even his work in a magazine; each time it was an affirmation of his worth. During his illness John Martin had begun working on another book, *Septuagenarian Stew*, using poems from his backlog folders and others Hank wrote during his illness. Though Hank had not written as many as usual, those that did appear were on target; no tricks, just honed skills. At one point he wrote to ask John Martin to find and withdraw the poem 'The Dinner' from *Septuagenarian Stew*, which was about dining with Sean Penn and Madonna and how they let him pick up the tab. Irritated that millionaires would let him pay, he had dashed off a poem about it, but, since then, they had paid for meal after meal, sent limos for him and generally paid for everything, so he felt the poem was mean-spirited. Hank didn't want to hurt Penn. It was withdrawn. *Septuagenarian Stew* covers not only his usual beat: the racetrack, manual workers, bums and whores, but also charts his new life: his large house, his pool, his cars and, inevitably, his approaching old age and death. Bukowski: 'The writing's not bad for an old guy I guess, and yeah, maybe now I fear the loss of my soul.'

In an earlier interview he'd talked about the influence of alcohol on his writing: 'I always used to write while drinking and/or drunk. I never thought I could write without the bottle. But the last five or six months I have had an illness that has limited my drinking. So I sat down and wrote without the bottle, and it all came out, just the same. So it doesn't matter, or maybe I write like I'm drunk when I'm sober.'

After nine months Hank was able to resume his normal way of life: smoking cigars and *bidies*, drinking wine and going to the track. He slowed down a bit, writing only two or three nights a week. Ideal writing conditions for him were between 10 p.m. and 2 a.m., equipped with his usual cigars, cigarettes, and his radio tuned to classical music. He drank slowly as he typed and he found it took him about two hours to drink a bottle of wine. Good work continued for about a bottle and a half. 'After that I am like any other old drunk in a bar: a repetitive and boring fool.' He still only wrote at night: 'I never write in the daytime. It's like running through the shopping mall with your clothes off. Everybody can see you. At night . . . that's when you pull the tricks . . . magic.'

He was strong enough to return to the track. In *The Bukowski Tapes* he told Barbet Schroeder: 'If I don't go to the track for two or three days I just wilt like a flower without water. I can't name it, it's just there.' But even before his illness he thought the tracks were becoming sadder and sadder places: there were fewer blacks, because they preferred to play the lottery; there were many more old and infirm people, whiling away their days; and the newly arrived from South and Central America who could barely speak the language, who were desperately betting the rent money, the food money, the clothing money on an impossible dream. Hank remembered the track in the 50s, when the bars were crushed full of people laughing and wisecracking, and there were fist fights and enormous crowds of fifty and sixty thousand people on the weekends. Everybody seemed to have enough money to get by. If you lost your job you could get another one, life was not desperate.

Now everything had changed. There were no crowds, maybe seven thousand people at a major racetrack on a sunny afternoon. There was nobody at the bar, just the lonely barkeeper holding a damp towel, the TV blaring. Before TV sets people used to talk to one another, they were the entertainment. Now people were sad and broke and the track was beginning to lay off people at the concession stands, the parking lots and in the business office and in maintenance.

Hank still needed the track as a fixed point in his life, for the routine, even though he had little interest in the horses themselves. Now he went to the Club House, had his 1989 Acura Legend valet parked instead of preferred parking – $3 extra plus a $2 tip for the one who drives the car. Santa Anita Turf Club parking was for the big shots, he was one of the big shots. But he could still see how pointless it was. Bukowski:

> One time I was sitting way down at the curve. There were twelve horses in the race and they all got bunched together. It looked like a big charge. All I saw were these big horses' asses going up and down. They looked wild. I looked at those horses' asses and I thought, 'This is madness, this is total madness.' But then you have the other days where you win four or five hundred dollars, you've won eight or nine races in a row, you feel like God, you know everything. It all fits together.

Marina and Linda bought Hank a Macintosh IIsi computer for Christmas 1990 running system 6.0.7 and using the MacWrite II word processing programme. Marina, who studied engineering at CSC Long Beach in the 80s, was a computer expert so she installed it for him and Hank went on a course to learn how to use it. He loved playing with typefaces, usually settling on Palatino, and the fact it had a spell checker delighted him as his own spelling had always been terrible. Bukowski: 'When I wrote my first computer poem I was anxious that I would be suffocated by these layers of consumerist suffering. Would old Dostoevsky have ever used one of these babies? I wondered, and then I said – "hell, yeah!" ' Hank couldn't stay away from his computer and he wrote hundreds of poems on it; it doubled his output. By the May of 1991 he was having trouble finding new places to send them. Hank still got a tremendous kick out of seeing his work in the 'littles' but there were few left that had not already accepted something. Any time he saw a new magazine listed he would shoot off a few poems to it, just to try them. Bukowski: 'I used to get drunk one night to write the stuff then get drunk the next night to correct it. Now I do it all in one night.' All the carbon paper, the whiteout ink, new ribbons, erasing tape for the IBM Selectric, were all packed away. How Hank would have loved the Internet and the ability to send his words straight to John Martin within seconds of completing them.

Linda fished Hank's wedding ring out from the bottom of the swimming pool where he had lost it, swimming drunk the night before with Barbet Schroeder. Hank had kidded Schroeder about his big house and enormous Hollywood salary and reminded him that he knew him when he lived in the ghetto and there were fresh bullet holes in his front door in the morning. Had he sold out, did he worry about his soul? 'Oh no,' said Barbet. 'You see, I don't have a swimming pool.' Hank not only had a swimming pool and a Jacuzzi, he now had a lap pool installed in the garden.

Two kittens were added to their growing menagerie, inspiring Hank to write his first cat poem, 'An Animal Poem'. He expected them to piss off his readers who all wanted poems about bums and whores. More stray cats turned up and were brought in until there were now nine cats; some were disdainful of each other, some required different diets or preferred different eating arrangements. They delighted and calmed him. Hank had become an old man fussing with his cats . . . just like William Burroughs.

In 1991 Hank began work on another novel, called *Pulp*; this time it was a work of fiction, a new departure for him. He thought that in the real sense his previous works couldn't legitimately be called novels because they were factual; this, however was to be a detective story in the grand Los Angeles tradition of the hard-boiled private eye. Hank had grown up with the pulps – large format magazines, usually 128 pages of text between lurid colour covers containing a novel of anything up to 60,000 words supported by a number of shorter stories, all for a dime. They had enormous print runs and were literally made from wood pulp paper, the cheapest available. There were usually about 250 titles on the newsstand at any given time, most of them quarterlies. Street & Smith's *Detective Story Magazine* and *The Shadow Magazine* were good examples of Hank's reading matter in the early 30s.

In July he lost two chapters on his Mac and, in searching for them, erased the rest of the novel. But by mid-August John Martin had an early draft of the book. Hank continued to send him deletions and changes and, unusually for him, thought that he would do a rewrite because at that moment he didn't even like the first page. Bukowski: 'Right now I'm trying something new. I call it *Pulp* and its easily the dirtiest, weirdest thing I've written. It's about this private detective, Nicky Belane, and for a change, he's not me. The publishers are getting anxious, for this one's way over the edge. Maybe they're starting to like me too much out there so I'm gonna test them a little with *Pulp*.'

Pulp took him several years. He never knew what would happen next, just nudged the story along, bit by bit, getting his detective into situations where he found it almost impossible to envisage a way of getting him out. He had exhausted the store of personal material: each story, no matter how minor, had been written, often many times, and it was time to find some new subject matter. Hank was having fun. *Pulp* was not thought of as a literary work, and it isn't one, the dedication page simply says: 'dedicated to bad writing'. He was presumably not thinking of his own, but was acknowledging the masters of hard-boiled detective fiction: James Cain, Raymond Chandler, Jim Thompson, Dashiell Hammett and, the most reviled of all, Mickey Spillane, whom Nicky Belane, the hero of *Pulp*, is named after. Spillane was so hard-boiled that he was almost a parody of the genre: 'The bullet went in clean, but where it came out left a hole big enough to cram a fist into.' In keeping with this, and although it wasn't autobiographical, Hank gave Nicky Belane all of his own 'most fucked up qualities. In fact, he may even be a bigger asshole than I am.' Elements from all parts of Hank's life were in there: John Martin, Sholom 'Red' Stodolsky who ran the Baroque Bookshop specialising in rare Bukowski first editions, Céline, the Harbor Freeway, Black Sparrow; in fact the story, if there can be said to be one, is the search for the Red Sparrow (like the Maltese Falcon) and the outwitting of death. The language is terse and acerbic; the wisecracks – essential in hard-boiled language – came thick and fast and are sometimes witty. Bukowski is a master of the laconic, throwaway line and there are plenty here. It was to be his last book. He signed the limited edition copies shortly before his death but the official publication date came a few weeks after.

At John Martin's suggestion, Hank began to keep a journal, beginning 28 August 1991. He used it to ruminate about his life and it contains some of his most insightful prose. Published in 1998 as *The Captain Is Out to Lunch and the Sailors Have Taken Over the Ship* he talks at length about how his writing was inseparable from his life. He knew he could always write about the racetrack, where he goes each day to 'murder' and 'mutilate' the hours. The hours have to be killed while he waits for the perfect hours; those at the machine. He needs imperfect hours to get perfect hours. Ten hours need to be killed to make two hours live, but warns the reader to take care not to kill *all* the hours, *all* the years. He goes to the track because he feels guilty about simply lounging about in the garden at home, even though the track bores him. Many of his readers thought he loved the horses, that the gambling action excited him and that he was a big-time gambler. They sent him books about horses, and horse racing, short stories about the track and gambling. He had no interest in them, he didn't give a damn. He went to the track reluctantly, fearfully, because, in his words, he was too idiotic to figure out any other place to go. In a real city he could watch the passing show but Los Angeles has nothing like that, no Parisian sidewalk café culture, no Barcelona Ramblas, no Italian piazzas where he could observe humanity and charge up his batteries, where he could be the *flâneur*, the invisible spectator.

He found that if he stayed away from the track then he got nervous and depressed, he became irritable and when he came to sit before the Macintosh, there were no juices there to fuel the writing. He needed to look at humanity: 'and when you look at Humanity you've GOT to react. It's all too much, a continuous horror show.' He was bored at the track, he was terrorised by the people there as he genuinely hated crowds, but he was a student: 'a student of hell'. And so he continued to point the Acura Legend towards Hollywood Park and its seething masses.

He writes that writers set themselves up to be writers by doing the instinctive things which feed both them and their work. Things that protect against death in life. These things are different for every one and they continually change. For Hank it meant alcoholism, drinking to the point of madness so that the drunkenness shook him violently out of his shell, provided that jolt needed to create life. It sharpened his words, gave them an edge. Another way of receiving that necessary jolt was to put himself into dangerous situations: bar fights, stormy relationships with women, driving dangerously, almost starving to death, the thrill of gambling. For many decades all of it fed the word, his word.

In old age his needs changed. What he needed was more subtle, an intangible something, a feeling in the air. His poems became more like those of his hero, Chinese poet Li Po, about overheard conversations, observed situations, little events, his cats playing, words spoken, words heard, subtle nuances and fleeting shadows. 'I am fed words by things that I am hardly aware of. This is good. I write a different kind of crap now. Some have noticed.' People told him that he had broken through. He was aware of it, he knew it was true. 'The words have gotten simpler yet warmer, darker. I am being fed from different sources. Being near death is energising.'

He was still the existentialist, the self-conscious observer of his own life – the things most people do without thinking: read a newspaper, fill the car with petrol, buy a sandwich in a coffee shop – he had to force himself to do, to plan it, to push himself to do. He said he still felt like the 'frozen man'. These are the observations which coalesce in his unconscious, ready to be revealed in his dreamlike state before the computer:

> When I sit down at the machine, I have no idea what I am going to write. I never liked hard work. Planning is hard work. I'd rather it came out of the air or some place behind my left ear. I have found that I am in a trance like state when I write. Sometimes my wife will walk into the room and ask me something while I am typing and I will *scream*! Not because the work is so precious or because I am precious but because I have been shocked awake.

In the meantime he was to see one more large poetry collection. Hank continued to send poems to John Martin, who filed them until he had enough for a book. Then he made his final selection and sequenced them. It was not until the book was actually published that Hank got to see what was in it; a system surely unique in publishing where poets usually fret over the selection and the running order until the very last moment. In March 1992 Black Sparrow published *The Last Night of the Earth Poems*. There are Bukowski enthusiasts who much prefer his early work, but for the sheer clean power of his writing and his ability to universalise even the most mundane object or experience, this is one of his most accomplished books. He knew it himself, saying: 'Inside I feel the same – only stronger with the writing getting better as I get older.'

In a fascinating interview with journalists David Andreone and David Bridson in 1990 Bukowski discussed his approach to writing:

> I am not sure that I explain anything in my writing but I do feel better for having written it. To me, creation is just a reaction to existence. It's almost, in a sense, a second look at life. Something happens, then there is a space, then often, if you

are a writer, you rework that happening out in words. It doesn't change or explain anything but in the trance of writing it down, a rather elated feeling occurs, or a warmth, or a healing process, or all three, and maybe some more things, depending. Mostly when I write something that works for me, I get a very high feeling of good luck. And even in purely inventive work, ultra fiction, it is all taken from basic factuality; something you saw, dreamt, thought or should have thought. Creation is one hell of a marvellous miracle, as long as it lasts.

The Last Night was filled with poems dealing with old age and death: in 'Hello, Hamsun', he describes himself as an old man, in 'Death Is Smoking My Cigars' the message is even more obvious. Death is mentioned in seven poems in the first section of the book alone; it was becoming one of his grand themes, as it was in *Pulp*. He knew what his readers wanted, though: stories about drunks and bars, whores and pimps, so he gave them a bit of what they wanted. A good example was 'The Unaccommodating Universe', which combines all four, along with some gratuitous violence. He wrote enough of those for Martin to always satisfy Hank's lowlife readers. Even this demand was subject matter for a poem in which Hank mused that some of his readers wanted him to go on writing about whores and puking, even though he was in his 70s and living in middle-class comfort. He said he didn't miss the whores but thanked them for becoming 'fodder' for his writing. He had no idea that those roaring drunken nights and screaming arguments would produce so much writing. Hank's writing remained belligerent, insulting and scornful but he was no longer on the attack.

Everywhere there were intimations of mortality. The 96-year-old man who lived next door fell and broke his hip. His wife had died the week before in a nursing home. They had been married 47 years. He would tap on the window with his cane when he saw the Bukowskis and blow kisses to Linda. Hank liked him and would sometimes visit him. Now the old man asked what Hank would trade him for his house as he was obviously going to die soon. 'I don't know if you can give me what I want for it,' he said. Hank couldn't guess the price. 'I'll trade for a new set of testicles!' he roared. Hank hoped he would have this man's verve at that age.

Hank continued to be plagued by medical problems. In May 1992 he had a cataract operation on his right eye and it was seven weeks before the doctor removed the stitches, making it hard for him to see the computer screen. After the operation he got an eye infection, followed by a nasty bout of flu. But sometimes his maladies were of his own making. In November 1992 he returned home in a limo from a U2 concert at Dodger Stadium where Bono had announced to 25,000 people: 'This concert is dedicated to Linda and Charles Bukowski', and everybody had screamed, as if they knew who he was. The free drinks backstage afterwards got the better of him, and he slammed down huge double shots of vodka-7 (vodka and 7-up) for hours while hanging out with the band. On his way into the house he staggered and fell down the brick steps he had recently had installed to replace the cement porch. He gashed the right side of his head, sprained his knee, twisted his back and bruised his right hand. The next day, seeing the brick steps baptised with his own blood, Hank decided to cut down on seeing celebrities. He always got too drunk and regretted it afterwards. Honora, Linda's 82-year-old mother, 'who can barely walk or think but remains full of stubborn ways', came to visit for Christmas. He now saw more old people than young.

Hank fell ill early in 1993 and was diagnosed with leukaemia. He was in hospital for 64 days, tended by an anxious Linda seated at his bedside. He was allowed home in mid-April for two weeks but he was still on a full programme of chemotherapy and antibiotics. The chemotherapy caused him to lose his luxuriant hair and he took to wearing a hat. He lost weight and his movements slowed down, he hunched forward, suddenly an old man. He stopped smoking, choosing to quit cold from one day to the next. He also had to stop drinking, and substituted herbal tea and bottled mineral water instead. He spent his days in the garden under the walnut tree. The cancer was declared in remission but he was due for another round of chemo beginning 1 June. In August, after some hopeful signs, the doctors had to give Hank the bad news that the leukaemia had returned. He was told that he had about a year to live. Hank was so ill that Carl Weissner came over for a week to see him for the last time. 'You have no idea what a God damned surprise it was to see you!' Hank wrote him, but it depressed him that people were preparing for his death.

He continued to write. The last poems, many of which were published in Betting on the Muse are about waiting for death; he is calm, placid: 'I've reached the pause before the full/stop.' The hair he lost to chemotherapy was slowly growing back, but his feet were numb, making it difficult to walk because it threw him off balance. The poems are about his restricted everyday life, sitting in his sauna, playing with his nine cats; poignant, beautiful poems. Rumours of Hank's death appeared on four different occasions while he was ill.

On 25 August Hank began studying Deepak Chopra's Aryuvedic healing method of mind over matter, thinking he had nothing to lose, and tried the healing methods of Deepak Chopra. He was willing to try anything and on 19 September had his first Transcendental Meditation session and received his mantra. It turned out that his TM instructor had lived in the same town as Hemingway. She heard the shot on the morning he killed himself. She was also a good friend of Aldous Huxley's second wife. On 3 November he returned to the hospital and after a long stay was back home just before Christmas with more blood transfusions, more chemo, more antibiotics. He had virtually no bone marrow left. The chemotherapy left Hank open to infection and he developed pneumonia, weakening him even further.

Charles Bukowski died of cancer on 9 March 1994, aged 73. At his request he was not buried in the family plot in Altadena, but in his own, in Green Hills Memorial Park overlooking his adopted home of San Pedro. The funeral was held on 14 March. He entered his grave dressed casually, with a row of pens in his pocket. He was once more half a block from Western Avenue, but a long way from Carlton Way. Near the end he had become interested in Buddhism and had begun practising Buddhist meditation, following his breath, learning how to let go. The funeral ceremony in the chapel was performed by three Buddhist monks. It was described by Gerald Locklin as being in two languages, neither of them understandable, but with much bowing and chanting. In attendance were Linda and Marina, John and Barbara Martin with other friends and colleagues from the Black Sparrow Press, Carl Weissner, Gerald Locklin, John Thomas and Philomene Long, Red and Mina Stodolsky from the Baroque Bookshop, Sean Penn, and many friends and neighbours from San Pedro. Then Hank was taken in his simple poplar coffin to his grave, high on the ridge.

On the way, his coffin almost got away from its handlers, and, at the grave itself, one of the monks stood before it for a photo opportunity. Hank would have seen the humour in it.

INDEX OF SOURCES

Abbreviations used:

Charles Bukowski	CB
interviewed by	int.
William Carlos Williams	WCW
Allen Ginsberg	AG
William Burroughs	WSB
Confessions of a Man Insane Enough to Live With Beasts	*Confessions*
Dangling in the Tournefortia	*Dangling*
You get So Alone at Times That It Just Makes Sense	*Alone*
The Days Run Away Like Wild Horses Over The Hills	*The Days*
Notes of a Dirty Old Man	*Notes*
Tales of Ordinary Madness	*Tales*
Love Is a Dog From Hell	*Love is*
The Last Night of the Earth Poems	*Last Night*
The Roominghouse Madrigals	*Madrigals*
South of No North	*No North*

Bone Palace Ballet: New Poems   Bone Palace
Burning in Water, Drowning in Flame: Selected   Burning
  Poems
The Night Torn Mad With Footsteps: New Poems   Night Torn
Mockingbird With Me Luck   Mockingbird
What Matters Most is How Well You Walk   What Matters
  Through the Fire: New Poems
The Most Beautiful Woman in Town, and Other   Beautiful
  Stories
New poems 2   NP-2
New Poems 3   NP-3

HOUSE OF TORTURE

3   'I'm Buke . . .' 'Buke'; 'Suckerfish', Dangling, p187

11   'Every Sunday it was death and gas.' 'Gas', NP-3

11   One evening, when she was 87 . . . 'Emily Bukowski', Alone, p153

12   'Kindergarten was mostly . . .' Ham On Rye, pp20–21

13   'The horses were more real . . .' The Days, p30

13   'I'll take you back inside . . .' Ham On Rye, pp20–21

14   Henry wound it up too tight 'A Gold Pocket Watch', Love Is, p302

14   'what are they doing' Pivano, p50; CB int. Jean Francois Duval, 1986

14   'I've never felt good with the crowd . . .' CB to Steve Richmond, 11 June 1965

15   It was the school yard . . . 'Luck Was Not A Lady', Last Night, p270

15   He noisily slurped his coffee . . . 'Dinner 1933', Last Night

15   'it all turned to glue inside.' 'Poop', NP-3, p23; 'Painting: To Miles Payne', quoted in CB to Sherri Martinelli, 2 July 1960

15   'Oh Henry, your father is so disappointed . . .' 'Education', Alone, p29

16   'Those aren't my parents . . .' CB int. Jean-Francois Duval, 1986

17   'The smaller boys took their beatings . . .' Ham On Rye, p22

18   For some inexplicable reason . . . 'Panties', Betting On The Muse, p35; Ham on Rye, p42

18   Henry ordered the man . . . 'The Monkey', Betting On The Muse, p19

18   His favourite topics included . . . 'Retired', Alone, p17

18 'Eenie, meanie, miney, mo . . .' 'My Non-Ambitious Ambition', *Alone*, p27

19 'She never had much of a chance . . .' CB int. David Andreone and David Bridson, 1990, collected in Calonne

19 'Between the imbecile savagery . . .' CB to John William Corrington, 14 January 1963

19 Every Saturday morning his houseproud parents . . . Love Is title poem, p229

19 'Silverfish!' 'Silverfish', *NP-2*, p48

20 'Nothing I could think of . . .' 'Magic Machine', *Alone*, p251; 'My Secret Life', *NP-1*, p4

20 Hank and his friends sat there . . . 'Our Big Day At The Movies', NP-1

20 To advertise the film . . . 'The World War One Movies', Betting On The Muse, p46

21 There were lots of crashes . . . Tales, p191

21 Hank and his friends built models . . . 'The World War One Movies', Betting On The Muse, p46

21 Red and Hank went swimming . . . '2 Buddies', Open All Night, p17

21 'Here I was, with my German accent . . .' CB int. Ron Blunden, 1978, collected in Calonne

21 They would pretend to hang him . . . 'Fun Times: 1930', *NP-2*, p55

22 He would take peanut butter sandwiches . . . 'Those Marvellous Lunches', *Betting On The Muse*, p30

22 'The afternoon light hurt my eyes . . .' *Ham On Rye*, p25

22 'Don't you hit my boy!' 'Me Against the World', *Betting On The Muse*, p39; 'We Ain't Got No Money Honey, But We Got Rain', *Last Night*, p282

23 After a fierce argument the other woman left . . . *Ham On Rye*, p50

23 'Come on Henry, let me have a couple of bucks.' 'The Women', *Betting On The Muse*, p15

24 'Rags! Bottles! Sacks!' 'Rags, Bottles, Sacks', *Septuagenarian Stew*, p13

25 'If somebody looked at you wrong . . .' 'The Lady In Red', *Dangling*, p13

26 'You're a small creature . . .' 'I Was Born To Hustle Roses Down the Avenues of the Dead', *Madrigals*, p227

26 'I'd say one thing they taught me . . .' CB int. Robert Wennersten, 1974, collected in Calonne

27   'I guess that's where it all started . . .' CB int. Donald McRae, 1991, collected in Calonne

27   'I was BORN into the Frozen Man Stance . . .' *Notes*, pp188–90

27   'Shame!' 'Practice', *Alone*, p221

28   He often exaggerated these fights . . . CB int. William Childress, 1974, collected in Calonne

28   Eugene, who was a year older . . . 'The Bee', *Love Is*, p214

28   'I just made the whole thing up.' Pivano, p91

29   'That makes it all the more remarkable . . .' *Ham On Rye*

29   'So that was the first recognition . . .' Pivano, p92

29   'I had become a man.' 'Depression Kid', *Bone Palace*, p30

29   Hank and Baldy walked ten or twelve feet behind them . . . 'Those Girls We Followed Home', *Alone*, p253

29   that his first thought of suicide came at age 13 . . . 'On and Off,' *Last Night*, p258

30   'What the hell you staring at?' 'The Bully', *Last Night*, p247

30   Hank had long ago concluded . . . 'The Bully', *Last Night*, p247

30   Katherine escaped into her own . . . CB int. Silvia Bizio, 1981, collected in Calonne

30   'Why did he do that?' 'The Snails', *Betting On The Muse*, p42

30   Hank thought that his father made him . . . 'My father', *Septuagenarian Stew*, p283

31   'the terrified talk of our parents' 'Rogues' Gallery', *Night Torn*, p82; 'Waiting', *Last Night*, p107

31   Once inside he hid behind . . . 'My Secret Life', *NP-1*

32   His interest in sex was also stimulated . . . 'Classical', *Bone Palace*, p23

32   Rosalie was the best stripper . . . 'Love Poem to a Stripper', *Alone*, p223

32   The place was raided . . . 'Burlesque', *Bone Palace*, p34

33   She was the only person in the hospital . . . *Ham On Rye*, p148

33   He would sit for hours . . . 'Now', *Burning*, p155

33   'You toughen up to physical pain . . .' CB int. Sean Penn, 1987, collected in Calonne

33   The tears and pain remained . . . *No North*, p170

33   'It was my hatred of my father . . .' Quoted by Glenn Esterly, collected in Calonne

33   Hank was 15; he had been out of school . . . CB to John William Corrington, 14 January 1963

HIGH SCHOOL NAZI

34   Maybe the neighbourhood . . . James Ellroy, *My Dark Places*, p11
35   'I hadn't heard crap . . .' CB int. William Childress, 1974
35   At least an army uniform . . . *Notes*, p194
35   'Then without rancour . . .' *Notes*, p195
36   'Meanwhile the poor and the lost . . .' *Ham On Rye*, p168
37   'On the slum streets of LA . . .' CB int. William Childress, 1974
37   'It's not nice to be followed home . . .' CB int. Jean-Francois, *Drink*, 1986
37   At the age of seventeen he tried . . . 'Whorehouse', *Alone*, p113
38   'God, look at the balls on that guy.' Pivano, p88
38   Lawrence was always there . . . CB to Douglas Blazek, 11 December 1966
38   He liked writing that created . . . CB to Neeli Cherkovski, early 1962
39   'He wrote a very serious melodrama . . .' CB int. Marc Chénetier, 1975, collected in Calonne
40   Bukowski's competitive feelings . . . 'Class', *No North*, p65
40   He compared it to buttoning a button . . . CB to Jon and Louise Webb, 28 July 1963
40   The Bukowski household went . . . *Ham On Rye*, pp168–71
40   He felt that without those books . . . 'The Luck of the Word', *Betting On The Muse*, p259
41   He read later that Sanderson . . . 'Crime and Punishment', *Last Night*, p290; 'Stages', *Betting On The Muse*, p52
41   'Henry, I am going to FLUNK you!' CB to Carl Weissner, 28 April 1967
42   Hank went to the bathroom . . . CB to William Wantling, 1965
42   They drank and sometimes slept . . . 'The Rat', *Mockingbird*, p78
43   '"Have you finished?" I asked.' *Notes*, p193
44   '"I have often let shackjobs and whores . . ."' 'Whorehouse', *Alone*, p113
44   '"What you have done is worse than murder!"' CB to Layfayette Young, 1 December 1970
45   'I love this town . . .' CB int. Glenn Esterly, 1976

45   'Mr Bukowski, there isn't any use . . .' CB int. William J Robson and Josette Bryson, 1970, collected in Calonne

45   Hank had one teacher for three units . . . Pivano p92; CB int. Jean-Francois Duval, 1986; 'The Lisp', *Dangling*, p15

46   Hank enrolled in the . . . CB int. William Childress, 1974

46   'I even made a study of the operation . . .' CB int. Robert Wennersten, 1974

47   'He had a great influence on me . . .' CB int. Douglas Howard, 1975, collected in Calonne

50   They would sit in the malt shop . . . 'Glenn Miller', *Alone*, p152

51   '. . .There were these guys . . .' Ben Pleasants, 'When Bukowski Was a Nazi', Hollywoodinvestigator.com, 8 April 2003

52   There is some confusion . . . *Ham On Rye*, p276; CB int. Alden Mills, 1989; CB int. David Andreone and David Bridson, 1990; *War All The Time*, p205; CB intro to *Hitler Painted Roses* by Steve Richmond, Santa Monica, 1966

52   'This is a great short story.' 'My Old Man', *Love Is*, p292

ON THE ROAD

53   Hank continued to take courses . . . CB int. William J Robson and Josette Bryson, 1970

53   They sent their stories to *Atlantic Monthly* . . . 'Self-Inflicted Wounds', *Night Torn*, p343

54   To Corrington he claimed that he knew . . . CB to John William Corrington, 14 January 1963

55   This was the neighbourhood where Fante . . . 'The Burning of the Dream', *Septuagenarian Stew*, p42

56   He finds a dark alley and follows it . . . 'Training For Kid Aztec', *War All the Time*, p22

56   There was a large whore . . . 'Long Sad Story', *Night Torn*, p207; 'The Theory of the Leisure Class', *Night Torn*, p209

56   . . .who complained that Hank read . . . *War All the Time*, p77

56   He learned quickly that the workplace . . . 'The Novice', *NP-3*, p84

57   'Bukowski, about half of what you say is bullshit.' 'Self-Inflicted Wounds', *Night Torn*, p343

57   All I wanted to do was . . .' Bukowski Tapes

57   There were a lot of troops on the bus . . . *War All the Time*, p79; 'Life In a Texas Whorehouse', *Beautiful*, p15

58   He met up with the redhead . . . *Notes*, p12
58   He could see into the bar from his window. 'Drink', *Betting On The Muse*, p83
59   'Wine gives a man nothing . . .' Dr Johnson, quoted in *Boswell's Life of Johnson*
59   He drank his money up and got a job . . . CB to John William Corrington, 14 January 1963
59   Next he worked in the composing room . . . 'We the Artists –', *Burning*
59   He goes to Miami Beach . . . CB to John William Corrington, 14 January 1963
59   He thought that he would be working . . . CB int. Jean-Francois Duval, 1986
60   . . . Hank had not eaten in sixty hours . . . 'Death Sat On My Knee and Cracked With Laughter', *Alone*, p141
61   'At the worst of times, in the worst of cities . . .' CB int. Alden Mills, 1989, collected in Calonne
61   . . .about picking up a couple of six packs after work . . . *Dangling*, p21
61   He put on the symphony and played it . . . 'We the Artists –', *Burning*, p208
62   In Philadelphia Hank took an attic room . . . 'Fhe Fish With Yellow Eyes and Green Fins Leaps Into the Volcano', *Night Torn*, p21
62   To Hank they were like creatures . . . *The Captain*, entry for 9 October 1991
62   He was wanted because . . . *Mockingbird*, p91
63   At first Hank let his beard grow . . . *Mockingbird*, p91
63   After lights out the cook arrived . . . *Mockingbird*, p18
63   Each day the cook whispered his thanks . . . *Tales*, p11
63   The psychiatrist had been reading through his short stories . . . CB int. Pivano, p34; 'Remember Pearl Harbor', *No North*, p82
64   Once you hit *Story* you were supposed to be "ready" . . .' CB int. William J Robson and Josette Bryson, 1970
65   This was when he still thought . . . CB int. Robert Wennersten, 1974
65   Hank was disgusted by what he says he saw . . . CB to Tom McNamara, 9 April 1965
65   'I was a sucker for Art movies' 'Schubert', *Open All Night*, p300

65   They quickly conned him into buying a suit ... *Notes*, p34; *Factotum*, p39

66   'it made me feel filth ...' CB to Tom Mcnamara, 6 May 1965; *Factotum*

66   He had to cross two or three third rails ... *Notes*, p37

67   He lived on loaves of bread ... CB int. Sean Penn, 1987; *War All the Time*, p51

67   He hated New York ... CB to Al Purdy, 25 January 1965

67   He passed by a corner drugstore ... CB to Al Purdy, 25 January 1965

67   'A hell of a feeling, believe me ...' CB to Jim Roman, 26 September 1965

67   But he turned her down ... CB int. William J Robson and Josette Bryson, 1970

68   'In New York you've got to have all the luck ...' *Notes*, p37

68   'Maybe the next day when I wasn't so tired ...' *Notes*, p37

68   He would get a cheap room ... CB to Douglas Blazek, 4 November 1964

69   The rent was due that day ... 'An Honest Lovely Lady', *War All the Time*, p89

69   'I worked not so much with craft ...' 'The Beautiful Lady Editor', *Alone*, p208

70   Then to finally undress ... 'You Don't Know', *Betting On The Muse*, p113

70   Hank was particularly careful ... *Tales*, p89

70   At each of these jobs he entered ... 'My Best Friend', *Septuagenarian Stew*, p72

71   It was in Philadelphia that Bukowski ... *Alone*, p94

71   '... But I wasn't gathering that experience to write it ...' CB int. Robert Wennersten, 1974; for opposite view: 'Master Plan' *Alone*, p94

71   It was about one in the afternoon ... Bukowski Tapes number 3

72   There was an early barkeeper called Jim ... Pivano, p74

72   'I was the only one who stayed ...' CB to Douglas Blazek, 2 June 1965

72   He became a neighbourhood character ... Pivano, p73

72   He ran errands for sandwiches ... CB int. Robert Wennersten, 1974

73   The whitewash in the alley was a problem. CB to Douglas Blazek, 14 July 1965

73   He was not at the bar all the time . . . CB to Al Purdy, late May 1965

73   He was evicted from room after room . . . 'Strange Luck', *Betting On The Muse*, p347

74   '. . . People have no sense of humour . . .' 'My Madness', *Betting On The Muse*, p335

74   'Hey, what the fuck is this? I want a drink!' CB to Douglas Blazek, 2 June 1965

74   Hank walked to another bar . . . 'Poem For Lost Dogs', *Septuagenarian Stew*, p98; CB to John William Corrington, 3? Dec 1961

75   His love of brawling sometimes got him into trouble. *Alone*, p96

75   Often his opponents were well-fed . . . 'Eddie and Eve', *Burning*, p179

75   'I think violence is often misinterpreted . . .' CB int. Sean Penn, 1987

75   "Jesus, you move slow man . . ." CB int. Sean Penn, 1987

76   His face was never completely healed . . . 'Looking Back', *NP-1*, p126

76   Beating was that recognition . . . CB int. William Childress, 1974

76   The desire to pick a fight . . . CB int. William Childress, 1974

76   'The crowd is his domain . . .' Charles Baudelaire, 'The Painter of Modern Life', in *Selected Writings On Art and Artists*, University of Cambridge, 1972

76   He felt sorry for them all . . . '59 Cents a Pound', *Piano*, p115

76   And so, just when the myth suggests . . . Baudelaire, *Selected Writings on Art and Artists*, Penguin, 1972, quoted in Keith Tester introduction to *The Flâneur*

77   One day he did not show up at the bar . . . CB int. Jean-Francois Duval, 1986

77   Hank made several trips to Atlanta . . . 'A Strange Horse Poem', *NP-1*, p86

78   Hank had always been in love . . . 'Black Sun', *Open All Night*, p77

78   He had a loaf of sliced bread . . . CB to John Martin, 29 June 1990

78   Then he saw the newspapers on the floor . . . 'Contemporary Literature, One', *Dangling*, p261

78   'It's no good quitting . . .' CB int. Alden Mills, 1989

79   He had no girlfriends . . . CB to John Martin, 30 June 1991

79   The other letter was from his father ... 'The Beautiful Lady Editor', *Alone*, p208; CB to Douglas Blazek, April 1965

79   Bukowski gives various accounts ... CB int. Michael Basinski, 24 January 1993, collected in Calonne

79   The railroad transported the men ... 'Hot', *Mockingbird*, p80

DRINKING WITH JANE

83   The rooms had a sink ... Edward Bunker, *No Beast So Fierce*, 1973 No Exit Press, Harpenden, 1993

84   She was obviously an alcoholic. 'Love For the First Whore', *Open All Night*, p31

84   'She had a kind of mad sensibility ...' Bukowski Tapes

85   She claimed to have almost won ... *Confessions*

85   Hank found her physically very attractive ... *No North*, p168

85   She was at a stage ... Quoted in CB int. Glenn Esterly, 1976

86   They truly were the neighbours from hell. 'Piss', *Betting On The Muse*

86   Suddenly she would sit up ... 'Sloppy Love', *What Matters*, p200

86   To save on petrol ... 'Empties', *NP-1*, p135

87   Hank was a slow starter ... *Betting On The Muse*

88   Hank made three or four trips to the yacht ... *No North; Confessions; Factotum*, p73

89   One of the neighbours had clumps of corn ... *Most Beautiful*, p58

89   'Oh God almighty!' Jane gasped ... '3 Women' Bukowski Tapes

89   'I was doing much more drinking then ...' Pivano, p80

89   One day, while he was having coffee ... 'Coffee', *Alone*, p126

89   They reinforced each other... 'The Summing Up', *Septuagenarian Stew*, p53

89   'We were very close to freedom.' 'The Summing Up', *Septuagenarian Stew*, p55

89   Somehow they always found money ...' 'Bumming With Jane', *Alone*, p44

90   The whiskey roaring through his blood ... 'Downtown LA', *Alone*, p32

90   'Los Angeles, the only city in the world ...' *Tales*, p88

90   Then the horse would start flapping its wings ... *Beautiful*, p75

90 Hank and Jane sat in silence ... '40 Years Ago', *Night Torn*, p66
91 'I tried to make a woman out of you ...' *Factotum*, p110
92 In the poem he takes out a butcher's knife ... *The Days*, p18
92 Castration was the theme in at least two stories ... CB int. Douglas Howard, 1975
93 They were on the fourth floor ... *Notes*, p157
93 It was a great release ... 'Sunbeam', *NP-3*, p156
94 'I can hear the sound of human lives ...' 'The Sound of Human Lives', *Burning*, p214
94 ... Jane had been joined by two of her girlfriends ... *Beautiful*, p65
94 All she had to do was suck off his wife ... 'Good Times', *Open All Night*, p35
95 When he did get a round his tiredness ... 'Torched-Out', *Last Night*, p381
95 Another feature of the Coronado Street apartment ... 'A Radio With Guts', *Piano*, p71
96 One day they went on a picnic together ... 'Some Picnic', *Piano*, pp24–5
96 He first knew heartache with Jane ... 'A Place To Hang Out', *Open All Night*, p40
97 Hank's health was beginning to break down ... *Beautiful*, p130
97 On an examination table they began asking questions ... *Beautiful*, p133
98 He was put in the terminally ill ward ... 'Longshot', *Alone*
98 The priest was around all the time ... 'Longshot', *Alone*
98 'That's not true ...' *Alone*, p168
98 The most he witnessed was eight ... 'Like Lazarus', *NP-2*, p35
98 Hank asked him if he had a cigarette. *Alone*, pp169–70
99 The best thing about the ward ... 'The Mexican Girls', *Madrigals*
99 The Mexican nurse clearly had a profound impact ... CB to Jon Webb, 4 September 1962
99 'When I came out of that hospital ...' CB int. Robert Wennersten, 1974
100 He had two weeks on the rent and no job. 'Reunion', *Tales*, p58
100 'I got out of the hospital ...' CB int. Silvia Bizio, 1981
100 ... he says that the first drink ... *No North*, p174

101 It was that night he decided . . . *War All the Time*, p40

101 He was always treated kindly by Mexican bartenders . . . *Hollywood*

101 'Bravado and glory . . .' *The Captain*, entry for 3 October 1991

102 'Horse racing does something to you . . .' CB int. Robert Wennersten, 1974

102 'I went to the tracks as a chance of life.' *Shakespeare*, section 20

102 His memory which was once good . . . CB to John William Corrington, 14 January 1963

102 'I found my fingers making the poem.' CB to Jon Webb, 4 September 1962

102 'You do not understand the true meaning . . .' CB to Jon Webb, 1 October 1962

103 'No ideas but in things' WCW, *Paterson*

103 Williams himself never delivered this . . . WCW in a letter to Kay Boyle, 1932; *The Selected Letters of William Carlos Williams*, edited by John C Thirwell, New York, 1957

103 'American is an ill-at-ease language . . .' 'Notes On English and American Style', from Chandler's Working Notebook, in *Raymond Chandler Speaking*, University of California Press, Berkeley, 1997

103 'You get in a kind of trancelike state . . .' Pamela Cytrynbaum, *New York Times Book Review*, 11 June 1989

103 'The typewriter imagination tells the writer what to write.' AG to WSB, 'The Ugly Spirit', in Lotringer, *Burroughs Live*, XX, p809

104 'So I was writing again . . .' CB int. Robert Wennersten, 1974

104 It ran for two years . . . 'I Didn't Want To', *Dangling*, p37

104 He learned little tricks . . . Pivano, p54

104 'Gee, Hank, what happened?' 'The Fool', *Bone*, p146

104 'I only loved one woman . . .' CB to William Wantling, 11 November 1965

WRITING AGAIN

105 He liked the camaraderie . . . 'Sparks', *War All the Time*, p27

106 With Jane not there to talk to . . . *Notes*, p121

106 'And they published forty of them . . .' CB int. William J Robson and Josette Bryson, 1970

107 'my whole soul would shake and scream' *Notes*, p122

107 'Here comes this cute sexy blonde . . .' *Notes*, p122

107 She had told him she was a nymphomaniac . . . *Notes*, p122

107 This is a recurring point in his writing . . . *Notes*, p121

108 He did, however, have some memorable experiences . . . 'The Weather is Hot On the Back of My Watch', *Burning*, p143

108 She enjoyed the company of artists . . . CB int. Robert Wennersten, 1974

109 His neighbours in the front building . . . *Notes*, p124; *Post Office*, p53

110 The instructor took Hank's painting . . . *Notes*, p126

110 Hank continued to paint at home . . . CB to William Packard, 23 March 1989

110 By now Hank was working a 44 hour week . . . 'Fragile!', *Madrigals*, p234

110 He was writing a lot himself . . . CB to CE Harper, 13 November 1956

110 The problem was that he didn't love Barbara. CB to John William Corrington, 23 February 1961; CB int. William Childress, 1974

111 By his own definition he was an alcoholic . . . CB to John William Corrington, 14 January 1963

111 . . . Hank found out that his mother was in hospital. 'Cancer', *Septuagenarian Stew*, p49; CB to John William Corrington, May 1963

112 It was a quiet Catholic funeral with a closed coffin. *Notes*, p112

112 At work in the sheriff's office Barbara met a Turkish gentleman . . . *Post Office*, p71

112 Barbara began to cry. *Madrigals*, p41

112 She later moved to Aniak . . . Notes, p129

113 He was forty years old . . . CB to EV Griffith, 14 October 1960; 'My Madness', *Betting On The Muse*, p334

114 His father lay there . . . *War All The Time*, p205

114 A boy soprano . . . *Bone Palace*, p98

114 'Good for what?' 'In One Ear and Out the Other', *NP-2*, p15

114 . . . he dated his father's girlfriend . . . 'Father, Who Art in Heaven', *Burning*, p191

114 'It's no good:/I can't keep him alive . . .' 'Dear Pa and Me'

115 Worst of all was the family resemblance . . . *Madrigals*, p177

115 The neighbour and his wife came over . . . *Notes*, p114

115 After about a month he sold the house . . . 'The Death of the Father I', *Hot Water Music*

115 He let them take ... *Burning*, p191

115 Naturally the death of his father ... 'Father who art in heaven', *Burning*, p191

115 Hank realised that he needed a more secure form of employment ... CB int. Mary Ann Swisler, 1990, collected in Calonne

116 The flâneur needs the city and its crowds ... Priscilla Parkhurst Ferguson, 'The Flâneur On and Off the Streets of Paris' in *Tester*

116 'Nothing is quite real to me ...' CB to Jon Webb, 1 October 1962

116 'I am a camera ...' Goodbye to Berlin

116 'It says something which you didn't even quite know ...' CB int. Marc Chénetier, 1975

116 He used vile language ... CB to Jory Sherman, 22 August 1960

117 He already had more than a dozen arrests ... CB to John William Corrington, 8 June 1961; CB int. Arnold Kaye, 1963, collected in Calonne

117 'You work a goddam lousy job ...' Bukowski Tapes

117 'When I came in from the slaughterhouse ...' CB int. David Andreone and David Bridson, 1990

117 Nonetheless he does seem to have contemplated ... CB to Carl Weissner, 13 May 1967

118 'We slept without touching.' *Post Office*, p79

118 Hank told him not to light a match ... *Alone*, p177

120 'I went back to my whore ...' CB to John William Corrington, 14 January 1963

120 Hank bought a cheap black suit ... 'Uruguay or Hell', *The Days*, p40; *Post Office*, p109

121 'I had love/and love died ...' *The Days*, p65

121 He tried but they didn't come out right. AD Winans, *The Holy Grail: My Friendship With Charles Bukowski*

121 'I remember your bones ...' *War All the Time*, p186

121 He drowned himself in alcohol ... CB to John William Corrington, 24 June 1962

121 'In Sept he described his mood ...' CB to Ann Bauman, 4 September 1962

122 He sat on the couch and tried to read ... 'Eulogy to a Hell of a Dame –', *The Days*

OUTSIDER OF THE YEAR

124 The second issue of the *Outsider* . . . 'Chummy'; CB int. Marc Chénetier, 1975

124 This was a time when Bukowski . . . CB to Jon Webb, 21 December 1962

125 Going to the track was the first thing . . . CB int. Douglas Howard, 1975

125 When the magic happened . . . CB int. Michael Perkins, 1967, collected in Calonne

125 They would often all be on different subjects. CB int. William J Robson and Josette Bryson, 1970

125 Being at the track helped to focus the line. CB int. John Thomas, 1967, collected in Calonne

125 At the end of 1962 . . . CB to Raymond Federman, 6 December 1962

125 He described his early poetry . . . CB int. William J Robson and Josette Bryson, 1970

126 Though he often presented himself . . .' CB int. Ben Pleasants, 1975, collected in Calonne

126 Ezra Pound made quite an impression . . . *Madrigals*, p70

126 'He influenced me a great deal . . .' CB int. William J Robson and Josette Bryson, 1970

126 Jeffers' influence was defined . . . CB to Jory Sherman, 1 April 1960

127 Jeffers took an extreme isolationist position . . . 'Quia Absurdum', *Collected Poetry* vol 3

127 Bukowski liked Jeffers . . . 'Lonely Blood', *Mockingbird*, p102

127 'where everything is up against the knife . . .' CB to John William Corrington, 14 January 1963

127 This was also the reason . . . CB int. to Joseph Conte, 27 June 1966

127 'Once I was lying in bed . . .' CB int. Robert Wennersten, 1974

127 'I liked a lot of Auden . . .' CB int. Robert Wennersten, 1974

128 'let's admit it, the giants have gone . . .' *Tales*, p179

128 He often mentioned William Carlos Williams . . . *Burning*, p132

128 One thing he may have taken from Williams . . . 'Hot', *Burning*, p161

128 Naturally Hank could not keep quiet . . . *Tales*, p177

129 Nonetheless, Bukowski felt very competitive . . . Steve Richmond, 'Beer and Poets and Talk'

129 He tried to use his homosexuality against him . . . CB to Jon and Louise Webb, 1 October 1963

130 Ginsberg is the poet . . . *Tales*, p147

130 There are many uses of Ginsberg's forms. *Dangling*, p194

130 Bukowski continued his dead-end job . . . 'Transformations and Disfiguration', *War All the Time*, p162

131 Nervous breakdowns occurred. *War All the Time*, p162

131 The pressure of the job began to get to him. CB to Jon Webb, 1 October 1962

131 The job was unrelenting . . . CB to Ann Bauman, 8 October 1962 and 22 November 1962

131 Whereas jail once meant little to him . . . CB to Ann Bauman, 18 December 1962

132 The judge was clearly filled with Christmas spirit . . . CB to Jon Webb, 19 December 1962

132 Hank's drinking days were apparently not yet over . . . CB to Jon and Louise Webb, 27 December 1962

132 'All the different people . . .' Gypsy Lou, in 'The Outsiders' by Julia Kamysz Lane

132 'Hank, you have ruined poetry for me . . .' CB int. Pivano, p111

132 But first, in the spring . . . CB to Jon and Louise Webb, 17 March 1963

133 Despite everything, Bukowski kept writing . . . CB int. Arnold Kaye interview, 1963

133 'They've got to take it, they've just got to . . .' CB to Jon and Louise Webb, 18 October 1963

134 The summer months in New Orleans . . . Edwin Blair, in 'The Outsiders' by Julia Kamysz Lane.

134 'He was real . . .' Gypsy Lou, in 'The Outsiders' by Julia Kamysz Lane

134 'By god, you've done it . . .' CB to Jon and Louise Webb, 26 November 1963

134 He had a small, nagging feeling . . . CB to Douglas Blazek, 6 April 1966

135 Poems about gambling usually only make sense . . . *Burning*, p47

137 Hank was very irritated by Kurnik . . . *Open All Night*, p46

137 Despite his new love interest . . . CB to Ann Bauman, 14 August 1963

138 By working for the government . . . CB to Jon and Louise Webb, 18 December 1963

138 Sometimes he felt he could take it no longer. CB to Jon and Louise Webb, 1 October 1963

138 The person in the flat below died . . . CB to John William Corrington, 18 October 1963

138 'Frances is a good woman.' CB to Jon and Louise Webb, 1 March 1964

139 'Old 1623 is gone . . .' CB to Jon and Louise Webb, 1 May 1964

139 Many times he had sat . . . CB to Ann Bauman, 10 May 1962

139 'this land punched-in . . .' *Burning*, p52

139 'I was raised in LA . . .' CB int. Robert Wennersten, 1974

140 One time he left the Santa Anita racetrack . . . 'Houses and Dark Streets', *NP-1*, p76

141 'I read it,' Hank said. 'Birth', *The Days*, p144

141 'a beautiful skunk of a child . . .' 'These Mad Windows That Taste Life and Cut me If I Go Through Them', *The Days*, p139

141 Hank felt they should have had the decency to wait . . . CB to Douglas Blazek, 3 February 1965

141 When Hank suggested that the man get a job . . . *Post Office*, p120

142 At De Longpre Hank no longer had to hide . . . CB to Jon and Louise Webb, 1 November 1964

142 Hank would wake up around 10.30am . . . CB to Al Purdy, 23 March 1965

142 The bulk of the poems were written . . . *Alone*, p227

142 Writing from New Orleans . . . CB to Al Purdy, 14 March 1965

142 But after a few bad days . . . CB to Douglas Blazek, 25/26? March 1965

143 Hank had hoped that . . . CB to Douglas Blazek, mid June 1965

144 Though Hank realised that . . . *Alone*, p227

144 The visit itself was of course . . . 'How To Get Published', *Hot Water Music*, p149

144 The biggest upset came when . . . CB to Tom McNamara, April 16, 1965; CB to Kirby Congdon, March, 1966

144 As far as Hank was concerned . . . CB to Al Purdy, 3 January 1965

145 'Bukowski is a tough write . . .' *Vieux Carre Courier*, Vol 2, 14, 28 May 1965

145 'That's what a good writer will do to you . . .' CB to Jim Roman, 23 July 1965

145 He told Richmond there were so few people . . . CB to Steve Richmond, 23 July 1965; CB int. Jean-Francois Duval

146 Hank liked a singalong . . . 7 September 1965

146 That November he had another haemorrhage . . . CB to Douglas Blazek, 23 November

146 'They beat you down . . .' CB to William Wantling, 11 November 1965

146 His drinking was gradually getting out of hand . . . CB to Tom McNamara, May 1965

146 The next month he bragged to Blazek . . . CB to Douglas Blazek, 2 June 1965

146 He took five days off over Labour Day . . . CB to the Webbs, 7 September 1965

146 After one party at an expensive apartment . . . CB to Douglas Blazek, 23 February 1965

146 Lying on the floor next to him . . . CB to Douglas Blazek, 12 June 1965

147 On the train on the way back . . . CB to Douglas Blazek, 23 October 1965

147 'her cries cut through all my poems . . .' CB to Doug Blazek, 1 December 1964

148 'I am soft in the head for her . . .' CB to Douglas Blazek, 4 December 1965; *Post Office*, p133

148 'It always tore him up . . .' CB to Jon and Louise Webb, 28 February 1966

CHINASKI RIDES OUT

149 In the middle of an afternoon in March 1966. . . 'Moving Up the Ladder', *Septuagenarian Stew*, p227

150 'That's OK, just, you know, whatever.' CB int. Neil Gordon, 1992

151 In December 1965, Hank's health . . . CB to Douglas Blazek, 4 December 1965

151 Things got worse over the Christmas period . . . CB to Douglas Blazek, 31 December 1965

152 He was confined to a ward . . . CB to Jon and Louise Webb, 8 March 1966

154 On his way home from . . . 'The Strong Man', *Betting On The Muse*, p136

154 'they come out full of butter and steel.' CB to John William Corrington, 11 February 1967

155 'You have a book there . . .' *Burning In Water*

155 '. . .Few men can fuck six times . . .' CB to Carl W May, 1968

155 '. . . As crappy as I feel that wouldn't help much.' CB to Jon and Louise Webb, 4 June 1968.

156 'Lipton writes a kind of left-wing . . .' 'Beer and Poets and Talk', *Tales*, p141

156 'And it would come . . .' CB int. Jean-Francois Duval, 1986

156 'I wrote one a week . . .' CB int. William J Robson and Josette Bryson, 1970

157 'a type of madness' CB to John Corrington, 15 November 1967

158 On his return to Los Angeles . . . CB to John Corrington, 15? November 1967

159 The men were astonished to find . . . CB to Jon and Louise Webb, 25 February 1968

159 It was unusual among such publishers . . . Farmer: *A Feast Unknown. Vol IX of the Memoirs of Lord Grandrith*, North Hollywood, 1969; Perkins: *Blue Movie*, 1968; *Queen Of Heat*, 1968; *Evil Companions*, 1968; *Down Here*, 1968; *Estelle*, 1969; *Terminus*, 1969

159 One night in January, 1968 . . . CB to Jon and Louise Webb, 25 February 1968.

160 Hank began writing to people he knew . . . CB to Steve Richmond, 23 July 1968

160 He only accepted three of Richmond's poems . . . CB to Steve Richmond, 25 July 1968

160 Now, just as he had written . . . *Evergreen Review*, September 1969

161 'Bukowski was by no means . . .' *Evergreen Review* 73, December 1969

161 'Those were great days writing a column . . .' Ace Backwards, 1987

161 The 60s were hotting up . . . CB to Jon and Louise Webb, 24 June 1967

161 In August he told Carl Weissner . . . CB to Carl Weissner, 8 August 1967

161 One night he could only work three hours . . . Michael Forrest, 20 August 1967

162 One time he forgot that the screen was there . . . 'Night Streets of Madness', *Tales*, p162

162 Sometimes, when his four day weekend . . . 'Escape', *Alone*, p235

162 'But they won't come unless I phone them . . .' CB int. Robert Wennersten, 1974

163 'You can hit a big typewriter . . .' CB int. William Childress, 1974

163 There was cigarette ash everywhere . . . Steve Richmond, 'Spinning Off Bukowski'

163 The walls held some of Hank's paintings. CB int. William Packard, 23 March 1989

164 In the 60s Bukowski maintained . . . *Purdy*, p12

164 Some of his correspondence became so extensive . . . *The Bukowski/Purdy Letters* 1964–1974

164 Hank had carefully lined them all up . . . 15 October 1968

164 He reminded Corrington of this but to no avail. CB to Douglas Blazek, 23 September 1968; CB to Carl Weissner, 14 October1968

164 Hank raged against those who refused . . . CB to Carl Weissner, 23 October 1968

164 'She is a joy . . .' CB to William Wantling, February 1967

165 'They're like ancient philosophers . . .' CB int. William J Robson and Josette Bryson, 1970

165 He thought Frances had him under control. CB int. Hugh Fox, 1969

165 Then in April 1969 . . . CB to Jim Roman, 14 April 1969

165 In 'The Old Gang' he describes . . . 'The Old Gang', *War All the Time*, p184; *The Days*, p139

166 He was more likely to kill himself . . . CB int. Robert Wennersten, 1974

166 He would return to his car . . . 'We All Live in the Same World', *Last Night*, p259

166 'Whoever seeks to gaze more closely . . .' Benjamin: 'Excavate and remember'

166 In December 1966 Hank told . . . CB to Douglas Blazek, 11 December 1966

167 His drinking partner 'Whitey' . . . 'The Night They Took Whitey'

167 . . . Hank never saw him again. *Madrigals*, p37

167 Everyone in the hotel drank . . . CB int. Michael Perkins, 1967

167 'When you're drunk, you fall loose . . .' CB int. Alden Mills, 1989

168 'I got even: I fucked his/girl.' 'Bad Times at the 3rd and Vermont Hotel'

168 According to Hank after Marty left ... 'Guts' *No North*

168 She was evicted a week later ... CB int. Michael Perkins, 1967

168 They were all alcoholics ... *Alone*, p92

168 Hank told Blazek that *How the Dead Love* ... *Notes*, p146

169 'Come and get your son,' he told her. *Notes*, p147

169 Hank intended the chapters ... CB to Douglas Blazek, 11 December 1966

169 It is likely that all his tales of drinking ... *Betting On The Muse*, p67

170 He found the book easy to write ... CB to Jon Webb, 29 February 1969

170 He did, however, give the Beat Hotel a name ... *The Days*, p127

170 ... though he got it slightly wrong. 'The Seminar' *The Days*, p163

170 The Norse correspondence was long and stimulating. CB to Jon and Louise Webb, 25 February 1968

171 Norse described Hank ... *Memoirs*, p420

172 'Norse hasn't written a decent poem ... *Beautiful*, p85

172 'He's an alcoholic and plays alcoholic games.' Harold Norse to Winston Leyland, *Gay Sunshine* 18; Tapes April 1973, pub June 1973

173 'I open these envelopes very reluctantly ... ' CB int. William J Robson and Josette Bryson, 1970

173 He said it gave him chills to think of it ... CB to Carl Weissner, 27 May 1969

173 But, he told Weissner ... CB to Carl Weissner, 16 September, 1969

174 Hank was still listed in the phonebook ... CB to Carl Weissner, 16 September 1969

YEARS OF FAME

175 He thought he couldn't make it ... CB int. Marc Chénetier, 1975

176 Everything was conspiring to push him ... CB int. Neil Gordon, 1992

176 He told no one at work what he had done ... CB int. William J Robson and Josette Bryson, 1970

177 He told Carl Weissner ... CB to Carl Weissner, 20 January 1970

177 A series of drunken new year parties ... CB to Carl Weissner, 20 January 1970

177 His anxiety made him drink more than ever. *Women*, p7

177 There was a bright light on overhead and lots of typing paper. CB int. Alden Mills, 1989

177 He set himself a goal of ten pages ... *Women*, p7

177 'I'd say, "Let me see if I made my ten pages last night" ... CB int. Marc Chénetier, 1975

178 'It was the good fight ...' CB int. Alden Mills, 1989

178 After a few discarded titles ... CB int. William J Robson and Josette Bryson, 1970

178 'It's done, come and get it.' CB to Neeli Cherry, 1 September 1970

178 This was also the time when John Martin ... CB int. Neil Gordon, 1992

179 Martin told him that he didn't want to detract ... CB to Carl Weissner, 23 July 1970

179 As Weissner was already translating the book ... CB to Carl Weissner, 18 September 1970

179 'I do cheat a little ...' CB int. Marc Chénetier, 1975

179 'Bukowski would be too holy, anyway ...' CB int. Marc Chénetier, 1975

180 'Almost all [the work is frankly autobiographical] ...' CB int. Arnold Kaye, 1963

180 'die a minute at a time ...' CB to Ruth Wantling, 11 September 1965

180 'I see men assassinated around me ...' CB int. John Thomas, 1967

181 'I'm just discouraged that men and women ... CB int. Ron Blunden, 1978

181 More importantly, Hank also wanted ... CB int. Ron Blunden, 1978

181 Hank was not too happy with the fake quote ... CB to Carl Weissner, 23 November 1970

181 'So what I would do was write a good story ...' CB int. Silvia Bizio, 1981

182 Hank now sent carbon copies of everything he wrote ... CB to Neeli Cherry, 10 May 1970

182 Another way of making money was to give poetry readings. CB int. Ben Pleasants, 1975

182 He only ever read because . . . CB int. Jean-Francois Duval, 1986

182 'I've become what you'd call a literary hustler . . .' CB int. William J Robson and Josette Bryson, 1970

182 His anxiety about reading combined with his dislike of it . . . CB int. Ben Pleasants, 1975

182 Even though he was doing the reading . . . David Barker, 'Charles Bukowski Spat In My Face', in *Drinking With Bukowski*

183 He quickly realised that this was what the audience . . . CB int. Robert Wennersten, 1974

183 A pattern emerged . . . CB int. Jean-Francois Duval, 1986

183 His second reading was in May . . . *Tales*, p32

183 Another key part of his image was the face. CB int. Don Strachan, 1971

184 'I get all sorts of remarks about it . . .' CB int. Glenn Esterly, 1976

184 'Now I have this mug that sells books.' CB int. Glenn Esterly, 1976

184 'got laid a few times by sweet young things . . .' CB to Neeli Cherry, 4 June 1970

184 'Man, they got one *powerful* drinker in there!' *Tales*, p188

184 Francis was a cheerful man . . . CB to John Martin, 6 January 1971

185 'Bukowski was old . . .' Linda King, 'Bukowski', *Small Press Review*, 1973

186 In July, Hank wrote to Neeli Chinowski . . . CB to Neeli Chinowski, 12 July 1970

186 He asked: 'Maybe I am queer?' CB to the King sisters, 30 October 1970

186 Just before Christmas he told . . . CB to John Martin, 23 December 1970

187 'I've got to have this woman,' he thought. CB to Patricia Connell, 16 August 1972

188 'Writing, after all, is more important than any woman . . .' CB int. Glenn Esterly, 1976

188 'I'm hooked in . . .' CB to Carl Weissner, 10 April 1971

188 'That's what keeps the pecker hard.' CB to Carl Weissner, 13 July 1971

188 'I'm just not a dirty guy . . .' CB int. Douglas Howard, 1975

188 'He had a puritan streak on him this wide . . .' CB to Vanessa Engel, BBC television

188 Linda could be exhausting. CB int. Don Strachan, 1971

189 'I'm Charles Bukowski. You don't know who you're with!' Linda King, 'The Liberated Billie and the Old Troll'

189 'In my life, of all the women I've known, I have hit two of them . . .' CB int. Douglas Howard, 1975

190 In January 1972, Hank went . . . CB to John Martin, 17 January 1972

191 As Spain ran with the New York Hells Angels . . . *Burning*, p204

191 Liza liked to leave town and took Hank to the mountains . . . Vacation 23–30, July 1972; 'Co-operation', *Play The Piano Drunk*, p65

191 Hank described his week . . . 'No Neck and Bad As Hell', *No North*; *Women*, p58

191 To Hank, the highlight of their trip to Catalina . . . *No North*

191 He told Carl Weissner that it just didn't . . . CB to Carl Weissner, 20? June 1971

192 'You are the only man who can make me laugh . . .' 'Free Coffee', *Dangling*, p103

192 'I'm afraid something has gone out of it for me.' CB to Carl Weissner, 30 August 1972

192 He felt very bad about Liza . . . CB to Patricia Connell, 13 September 1972

192 'I let her beat on me . . .' CB to Patricia Connell, 13 September 1972

192 'Marvelous, two weeks straight of love. . . ' Linda King, 'The Liberated Billie and the Old Troll'

193 'During the course of the event . . .' Lawrence Ferlinghetti and Nancy J Peters, *Literary San Francisco*, City Lights and Harper & Row, San Francisco, p210

193 There was a roaring party afterwards . . . 'On the Vircuit', *Burning*, p200, revealed to Connell, 22 September 1972

193 Hank poured half a bottle of iodine over his wounds. 'This Is What Killed Dylan Thomas', *No North*, p129

193 Hank returned to Liza's bed . . . 18 September 1972

193 Jane had been the first person who brought him any love . . . CB int. Glenn Esterly, 1976

194 In the poem 'Yes' he described . . . *Dangling*, p138; same poem repeated as 'Yes, I Am', *Open All Night: New Poems*, p110

194 'All my books are Black Sparrow . . .' CB int. Pivano, p70; Weissner's third translation, *Notes Written Before Jumping Out an 8 Story Window*

195 'It wasn't that I was so good . . .' CB int. GlennEsterly, 1977
195 It didn't take long for the sniping to start. CB to Bill Robson, 11 July 1972
196 He recognised Linda's orange Volkswagen . . . CB int. Robert Wennersten, 1974
196 This was not to be. 'Hell Hath No Fury . . .' *Burning*, p220
196 He flattened himself against the wall and she missed him by inches. CB int. Robert Wennersten, 1974
197 'I felt fear, real fear . . .' *Women*, p84
197 He told Carl Weissner that she fucked two other guys . . . CB to Carl Weissner, 25 July 1974
198 'Ginsberg was all right . . .' CB to AD Winans, November 1974
198 'I knew that creepy, ugly, cockroach slime . . .' Linda King, 'The Liberated Billie and the Old Troll'
198 'I feel that I'm an ass a lot of the time . . .' CB to Robert Wennersten, 1974
199 If he drank two or three days in a row . . . CB to Robert Wennersten, 1974
199 'Sometimes I throw them . . .' CB int. William Childress, 1974
199 'I care for many things . . .' CB int. Marc Chénetier, 1975

BOOGIE IN THE MUD

200 'I have to keep living in order to write . . .' CB int. Marc Chénetier, 1975
201 He returned to his old neighbourhood . . . 'Nobody Home', *What Matters Most*, p245
201 At night he could hear the distant muted roar . . . 'Long Distance Drunk', *Hot Water Music*
201 'the most depressive of all the streets . . .' 'A Rain of Women', *Tales*, p154
201 'I was walking down the street today . . .' CB to Al Purdy, 6 November 1974
202 'A little sleep and peace of stillness' *Burning*, p137
202 In 'The Death of a Splendid Neighborhood' . . . *Alone*, p274
203 'You get the stink of LA in your bones . . .' Bukowski Reads Bukowski
203 Hank wrote a well-observed poem . . . 'The Trash Men' *Burning*, p156
203 'I can hear cars on the freeway . . .' 'Working It Out', *Alone*, p19

203 In 'The Drunk Tank Judge' he tells us ... *Play The Piano Drunk*, p88

203 'LA is a wonderful town ...' Bukowski-archiv

203 At the end, Bukowski is living in a mansion ... 'The Shipping Clerk With A Red Nose', *No North*

204 'All I can write about is drinking ...' *No North*, p137

204 In the past Hank used to be ashamed to revise or correct a story. CB int. Robert Wennersten, 1974

204 'and when I get sober I insert a new line. I buck it up.' CB int. Marc Chénetier, 1975

204 'I like interruptions ...' CB int. Robert Wennersten, 1974

205 Classical music was his preferred background sound ... CB int. Robert Wennersten, 1974

205 He didn't listen consciously ... CB int. Robert Wennersten, 1974

205 ... but he was less fond of Brahms and Tchaikovsky. CB to John William Corrington, 14 January 1963

205 He needed the machine-gun sounds of his Royal. CB int. Robert Wennersten, 1974

205 In between they are perfect ... CB int. Ron Blunden, 1978

205 'About sixty percent of the lines are bad ... ' CB int. Robert Wennersten, 1974

205 An evening would produce ten or fifteen ... CB int. William J Robson and Josette Bryson, 1970

206 'This isn't totally imaginative ... ' CB int. Douglas Howard, 1975

206 In fact the story is based directly ... *Beautiful*, p213

206 The story which upset most people was ... 'The Fiend', *Beautiful*, p207

207 'I wrote a short story from the viewpoint of a rapist ...' CB int. Sean Penn, 1987

207 'I didn't get a hard-on while I was writing it.' CB int. Silvia Bizio, 1981

207 'I get my kicks out of exploring those areas ...' CB int. Douglas Howard, 1975

207 'I like to explore what this man might be thinking ...' CB int. Douglas Howard, 1975

207 The story was so bad that Hank decided to rewrite it with a better ending. CB int. Douglas Howard, 1975

207 'There is one in which imagination and reality ...' CB int. Douglas Howard, 1975

207 He was up against his weekly deadline ... CB int. Douglas Howard, 1975

208 He found it hard work ... CB int. Ben Pleasants, 1975

208 He got the idea for the book ... CB int. Robert Wennersten, 1974

208 His original idea was to write ... CB int. Marc Chénetier, 1975

208 'I always throw the first draft away ...' CB int. William Childress, 1974

208 'Shit, I don't know.' CB int. Marc Chénetier, 1975

208 'It was so easy.' CB int. Marc Chénetier, 1975

209 'I'm not so much a thinker ...' CB int. Marc Chénetier, 1975

209 To Marc Chénetier he suggested that ... CB int. Marc Chénetier, 1975

209 'What I've tried to do ...' CB int. Sean Penn, 1987

209 He described the peace he felt ... 'One for the Shoeshine Man', *Love Is*, p305

210 And of course there were the letters ... CB int. Marc Chénetier, 1975

210 Hank's neighbours, Brad and Tina Darby ... 'A Good Show', *Open All Night*, p132

210 After yet another break-up ... Christy, p52

211 Hank did not press charges ... 10 December 1975

212 'He's a very creative lover ...' CB int. Glenn Esterly, 1976

212 'The legs are dynamite ...' CB int. Glenn Esterly, 1976

212 Hank complained that his time was taken up ... 'How Come You're Not Unlisted?', *Love Is*, p133

213 'Go ahead baby, it's all right ...' CB int. Robert Gumpert, 1991; 'Working', *Alone*, p293; 'The Lover', *Betting On The Muse*, p194

213 The younger one was having her period ... 'Waving and Waving Goodbye', *Love Is*, p184

213 'I've got this big pot belly ...' CB int. Douglas Howard, 1975

213 'Here's a guy with a bottle of beer ...' CB int. Marc Chénetier, 1975

214 Hank described her as 23 ... CB to Carl Weissner, 13 February 1976

214 'She's a speed freak ...' CB to John Martin, 28 March 1976

214 'That's why I have trouble with women ...' CB int. Marc Chénetier, 1975

215 He would visit her bungalow ... 'I Made a Mistake', *Love Is*, p200

215 When Hank reached her . . . 'Liberty', *Love Is*, p186; *Women*, p135

215 In September he still saw her . . . CB to AD Winans, 13 September 1976

215 There was 'none so vicious, so evil'. CB to Carl Weissner, 16 October 1976

216 She got to know his friends . . . 'Iris Hall', quoted by Ted Laturnus, in Christy, p74

216 'Mostly what we did was laugh . . .' Christy, p74

216 He got poems out of it, of course . . . 'Hunk Of Rock', *Last Days*, p86

216 In 'Junk' he describes sitting . . . 'Junk', *Play The Piano Drunk*, p102

216 Days and nights ran together . . . 'War All the Time', *Poems 1981–1984*, p231

218 'If you don't fight death . . .' 'Overhead Mirrors', *War All the Time*, p235

218 In all the years he lived there . . . 'Hard Times on Carlton Way', *What Matters Most*, p184

SAN PEDRO

220 'And so I found I was part of that . . .' Jean-Francois Duval, 1986

220 'Before Linda came along . . .' CB int. Robert Gumpert, 1991

220 'I am the only one . . .' CB int. Jean-Francois Duval, 1986

220 'When Linda met me . . .' CB int. Robert Gumpert, 1991

221 When he drank whiskey . . . CB int. Glenn Esterly, 1976

221 'With beer, you have to go to the bathroom . . .' CB int. Jean-Francois Duval, 1986

221 'I want to write one more novel . . .' CB int. Marc Chénetier, 1975

222 Others, he knew, would hate it. CB to Carl Weissner, 22 September 1977

222 One of the first was a request . . . CB to John Martin, 9 October 1977

223 'It's a jolly roaring blast.' CB to AD Winans, 2 November 1977

223 'A good style is important . . .' CB to Neeli Cherkovsky, early 1962

224 'I make no conscious effort to be tough . . .' James M Cain, preface to *Double Indemnity*, 1945

224 'It is a fluid language . . .' From Chandler's working notebook, 1949, in *Raymond Chandler Speaking*, ed Dorothy Gardiner and Kathrine Sorley Walker, Houghton-Mifflin, Boston, 1977

225 'I jump back and forth . . .' CB int. Douglas Howard, 1975

225 He describes everything . . . 'My Groupie', *Love Is Like a Dog From Hell'*, p231

225 Hank was anxious to see *Women* in print . . . CB to John Martin, 16 July 1978

225 'I guess he thinks I can't write' CB to Gerald Locklin, 15 March 1979

226 He begins to cry, his brain whirling. *Women*, p236-7

226 Meanwhile things were developing slowly with Linda . . . CB to AD Winans, 2 November 1977

227 Hank's recognition of something like love at first sight . . . 'Mermaid', *Play The Piano Drunk*, p112

227 'I'm a very romantic fellow . . .' CB int. Marc Chénetier, 1975

227 By March 1977, Hank is already telling Carl Weissner . . . CB to Carl Weissner, 3 March 1977

228 He now revealed that the reason was fear . . . CB to Carl Weissner, 12 March 1978

228 Carl Weissner had booked them into a hotel . . . Bukowski Tapes, Barbet Schroeder, 1985

228 'That which interests most people . . .' *Shakespeare* section 13

230 Hank later commented . . . CB int. Kevin Ring, 1990

230 'I think slowly . . .' CB to Carl Weissner, 1 August 1978

230 It was looser and had more energy. CB to Carl Weissner, 3 November 1978

230 In *Shakespeare Never Did This* . . . CB int. Kevin Ring, 1990

232 Then they turn on their heels . . .' CB int. Robert Gumpert, 1991; CB int. Pivano, p65

234 Hank's study was lined with books . . . 'Swivel Chair', *Open All Night*, p290

234 About three times a week . . . 'The Gods', *Betting On The Muse*, p360

234 Next to his desk . . . '3 a.m. Games', *Alone*, p284

234 Hank liked San Pedro . . . CB to William Packard, 31 December 1978

234 It had none of the madness . . . CB to Carl Weissner, 11 November 1978

235 'I would never live in a place like this . . .' CB int. Pivano, p37

235 They told Hank that they heard . . . CB int. Jean-Francois Duval, 1986

235 When the man called the bank . . . CB to Carl Weissner, 21 May 1979

238 Hank and Linda visited . . . 'Result', *War All the Time*, p156

238 Hank liked to think of him . . . 'Epilogue', *Betting On The Muse*, p371

238 'You have meant, do mean more to me . . .' Quoted in Cooper, p314

239 'You wouldn't shit an old blind man . . . 'Fante', *Betting On The Muse*, p373

239 'He was a little bulldog . . .' CB int. Kevin Ring, 1990

239 Fante died on 8 May 1983 . . . 'The Wine of Forever', *Alone*, p149

THE OLD MAN AND HIS CATS

240 'I've been with one almost three years . . .' CB to Hank Malone, 15 October 1979

240 They settled into a routine. CB int. Pivano, p78

240 One day, sitting at the end of the upper grandstand . . . 'The Violin Player', *Play The Piano Drunk*, p61

241 He even managed to get a long poem . . . *Alone*, p14

241 'Race tracks are horrible places . . .' CB int. Robert Wennersten, 1974

241 He went regularly for forty years . . . *Betting On The Muse*, p204

241 'It's just repeat . . .' 'An Evaluation', *Betting On The Muse*, p204

241 It is likely that elements of fiction . . . 'A Nickel', *Betting On The Muse*, p103

241 In October 1979 . . . CB to William Packard, 25 October 1979

242 Hank encouraged her to see her friends . . . CB to William Packard, end July 1979

242 'Finally living with a woman who isn't a whore.' CB to Louise Webb, 9 January 1981

243 Each night they ran a short segment . . . CB to Stephen Kessler, 15 January 1985

244 What Hank liked about his writing . . . CB to John Martin, 4 February 1981

244 By April he had written 240 pages . . . CB to Gerald Locklin, 2 August 1981

245 Though he was only receiving $500 ... CB to John Martin, 16 April 1981

245 It was the first hot night of summer ... 'I Don't Care', *Open All Night*, p257

245 Hank modestly amended the figure to three. CB to Gerald Locklin, 2 Aug 1981

245 Their household now included a third cat ... CB to Louise Webb, 27 January 1982

246 Hank scraped the car ... 'Token Drunk', *Open All Night*, p271

246 He was always embarrassing Linda ... 'I Don't Want Cleopatra', *Open All Night*, p276

246 Hank got drunk with Ferreri and Gazzara ... CB to Joe Stapen, 8 August 1981

246 ... but when he saw the film ... CB to Gerald Locklin, 13 August 1983

246 'against the whole atrocity' Suzy?, 1 March 1984

246 'almost all of it was worse than bad.' Suzy?, 1 March 1984

246 ... here he was, a drunken poet ... 'The Star', *War All the Time*

247 Linda came by two or three times a week ... CB to Gerald Locklin, 6 January 1983

247 By February, 1983, he seemed resigned ... CB to Al Fogel, 5 February 1983

247 He told John Martin that she appeared to be getting worse. CB to John Martin, 11 October 1983

248 'Why does he have to write that way? ... 'The Barometer', *Bone Palace*, p 276

249 'If this destroys me as a writer then I deserve to be destroyed.' CB to William Packard, end August 1985

249 'My home life here has developed into nightmare proportions ... 'CB to Al Bedrlinsky, 8 January 1986

249 'My five cats and my wife and the walls ...' CB to William Packard, 23 February 1986

249 'Right, I'm going to cut off one of my fingers ...' CB int. Robert Gumpert, 1991

250 In January 1992 she approached Hank ... CB to John Martin, 24 January 1992

250 One character in particular was wrong and had to be rewritten. CB to John Martin, 21 July 1986

251 It was the same building he had been thrown out of ... *Hollywood* p164–5, p167

252 Hank thought that was pretty funny. CB to David Reeve, 13 November 1991

252 Hank didn't want the love interest or the writer. CB to John Martin, 29 March 1987

252 He concluded that *Barfly* was ... CB to Gerald Locklin, 10 December 1986

252 'It's pepped up enough to keep everybody eating their popcorn ...' CB to Silvia Bizio, 1981

253 Everything that happens around the place gets incorporated ... 'Owl', *Bone Palace*, p307

253 ... his cat Craney who sleeps on his back with his legs in the air gets a mention ... 'Cool Fur', *Bone Palace*, p348

253 He managed a 41-line poem ... 'Driving Test', *Alone*, p38

253 ... a 93-line poem about a traffic backup on the Harbor Freeway 'Jam', *Last Night*

254 ... particularly with 'The Freeway Life' ... 'The Freeway Life', *Alone*, p80

254 Hank still got lost on the freeways ... 'We're Gonna Make It', *Open All Night*, p93

254 From the tone of some of his poems ... 'Cool Black Air', *Last Night*, p310

254 Sometimes he wrote love poems to Linda ... 'Confession', *Last Night of Earth*, p138

254 By January 1988 he was working on *Hollywood* ... CB to Jeff Weddle, 26 January 1988

254 ... and he had finished it by October. CB to William Packard, 22 October 1988

255 'Why? I don't know.' CB int. Alden Mills, 1989

255 'I guess I never believed in Hollywood ...' Pamela Cytrynbaum, *New York Times Book Review*, 11 June 1989

255 He lost 22 pounds. CB to William Packard, 22 October 1988

255 He was unable to write, instead he retired to bed early. CB to William Packard, 12 March 1989

255 By late April he even accepted her suggestion of acupuncture. CB to John Martin, 11 April 1989

255 Now in April 1989 Norse received letters ... *Bastard*, p93

255 Hank told him he could no longer write ... 'Twelve Monkeys Who Won't Copulate Properly', *Beautiful*, p85

256 He tried to watch TV ... 'TB', *Night Torn*, p303

256 After three months he began to write a little, but it came slow. CB to William Packard, 21 August 1989

256 They had been unable to meet ... Jean-Francois Duval, p119–120

256 'It's like arc welding. Same principle.' CB to William Packard, May 1988

256 His mood was lifted . . . CB to John Martin, 13 May 1988

256 Though Hank had not written as many as usual . . . CB to William Packard, end Oct 1989

257 Hank didn't want to hurt Penn. It was withdrawn. CB to John Martin, 3 January 1990

257 'The writing's not bad . . .' CB int. Robert Gumpert, 1991

257 'So I sat down and wrote without the bottle . . .' CB int. Alden Mills, 1989

257 'After that I am like any other old drunk in a bar, a repetitive and boring fool.' CB to Luciana Capretti, 6 February 1990; CB int. Kevin Ring, 1990

257 'At night . . . that's when you pull the tricks . . . magic.' CB int. Sean Penn, 1987

257 But even before his illness . . . CB to John Martin, March 1988

257 If you lost your job you could get another one, life was not desperate. 'Finis', *Betting On The Muse*, p339

258 Now people were sad . . . *The Captain*, entry for 3 October 1991

258 Hank still needed the track . . . CB int. Sean Penn, 1987

258 Marina and Linda bought Hank a Macintosh IIsi computer . . . CB to John Martin, 1 February 1991

258 '. . . Would old Dostoevsky have ever used one of these babies?' CB int. Robert Gumpert, 1991

258 Hank still got a tremendous kick . . . CB to Gerald Locklin, 1 May 1991

259 How Hank would have loved the internet . . . CB to Ivan Suvanjieff, 20 February 1992

259 Linda fished Hank's wedding ring . . . CB to William Packard, 12 January 1992

259 He expected them to piss off his readers . . . 'An Animal Poem', *Night Torn*, p328

259 They delighted and calmed him. 'Quiet', *Alone*, p307

259 In 1991, Hank began work on another novel . . . CB to Ed of *Explorationsa*, Alaska, 21 June 1991

259 In July he lost two chapters on his Mac . . . CB to John Martin, 14 July 1991

259 Hank continued to send him deletions and changes . . . CB to John Martin, 21 August 1991

260 'Maybe they're starting to like me ...' CB int. by Robert Gumpert, 1991

260 He had exhausted the store of personal material . . . CB to Jon Cone, 8 May 1992

260 '. . . In fact, he may even be a bigger asshole than I am.' CB to Maxwell Gaddis, 14 March 1992

261 He needed to look at humanity . . . The Captain, 31 October 1991

262 'The words have gotten simpler . . .' The Captain, 23 June 1992

262 He was still the existentialist . . . CB to William Packard, 5 March 1992

262 'Sometimes my wife will walk into the room . . .' CB int. Alden Mills, 1989

262 'Inside I feel the same – only stronger with the writing getting better as I get older.' CB int. by Robert Gumpert, 1991

263 "Creation is one hell of a marvellous miracle, as long as it lasts." CB int. David Andreone and David Bridson, 1990

263 A good example was 'The Unaccomodating Universe,' 'The Unaccomodating Universe', Betting On The Muse

263 He had no idea . . . 'Thank You', p229

263 He would tap on the window . . . 'Old', Bone Palace, p349

263 Now he asked Hank . . . CB to William Packard, 3 November 1991

264 The free drinks backstage . . . CB to Carl Weissner, 19 November 1992

264 . . . Hank decided to cut down on seeing celebrities. CB to Jon Cone, 4 November 1992

264 'who can barely walk or think but remains full of stubborn ways.' CB to Jack Grapes, 28 December 1992

264 . . . but it depressed him that people were preparing for his death. CB to Carl Weissner, 5 September 1993

265 He was willing to try anything . . . CB to William Packard, 14 August 1993

265 She was also a good friend of Aldous Huxley's second wife. CB to William Packard, 22 September 1993; CB to John Martin, 19 September 1993

BIBLIOGRAPHY

BOOKS BY CHARLES BUKOWSKI

Aaron Krumhansl lists 159 broadsides, chapbooks and books up until March 1999 so this list is only a selection of the more important titles.

Flower, Fist and Bestial Wail, Hearse Press, Eureka, Calif., 1960
Poems and Drawings, Epos, Crescent City, Florida, 1962
Longshot Pomes for Broke Players, 7 Poets Press, New York, 1962
Run with the Hunted, Midwest Poetry Chapbooks, Chicago, 1962
It Catches My Heart in Its Hands, Loujon Press, New Orleans, 1963
Crucifix in a Deathhand, Loujon Press, New Orleans, 1965
Cold Dogs in the Courtyard, Literary Times-Cyfoeth Press, Chicago, 1965
Confessions of a Man Insane Enough to Live with Beasts, Mimeo Press, Bensonville, Ill., 1965
The Genius of the Crowd, 7 Flowers Press, Cleveland, Ohio, 1966
All the Assholes in the World and Mine, Open Skull Press, Bensonville, Ill., 1966
At Terror Street and Agony Way, Black Sparrow, Los Angeles, 1968

Poems Written Before Jumping Out of an 8 Story Window, Poetry X/Change, Glendale, Calif., 1968

Notes of a Dirty Old Man, Essex House, North Hollywood, Calif., 1969

A Bukowski Sampler, Quixote Press, Madison, Wisc., 1969

The Days Run Away Like Wild Horses Over the Hills, Black Sparrow, Los Angeles, 1969

Post Office, Black Sparrow, Los Angeles, 1971

Erections, Ejaculations, Exhibitions and General Tales of Ordinary Madness, City Lights Books, San Francisco, 1972

Mockingbird Wish Me Luck, Black Sparrow, Los Angeles, 1972

Me and Your Sometimes Love Poems, KissKill Press, Los Angeles, 1972

South of No North, Black Sparrow, Los Angeles, 1973

Burning in Water, Drowning in Flame: Selected Poems 1955–1973, Black Sparrow, Los Angeles, 1974

Factotum, Black Sparrow, Santa Barbara, 1975

Scarlet, Black Sparrow, Santa Barbara, 1976

Love Is a Dog from Hell: Poems 1974–1977, Black Sparrow, Santa Barbara, 1977

You Kissed Lily, Black Sparrow, Santa Barbara, 1978

Women, Black Sparrow, Santa Barbara, 1978

Play the Piano Drunk Like a Percussion Instrument Until the Fingers Begin to Bleed a Bit, Black Sparrow, Santa Barbara, 1979

Shakespeare Never Did This, City Lights Books, San Francisco, 1979

Dangling in the Tournefortia, Black Sparrow, Santa Barbara, 1981

Ham on Rye, Black Sparrow, Santa Barbara, 1982

Bring Me Your Love, Black Sparrow, Santa Barbara, 1983

Hot Water Music, Black Sparrow, Santa Barbara, 1983

The Bukowski/Purdy Letters, Paget Press, Sutton West and Santa Barbara, Calif., 1983

The Most Beautiful Woman in Town and Other Stories, City Lights Books, San Francisco, 1983

Tales of Ordinary Madness, City Lights Books, San Francisco, 1983

There's No Business, Black Sparrow, Santa Barbara, 1984

War All the Time: Poems 1981–1984, Black Sparrow, Santa Barbara, 1984

The Wedding, Brown Buddha Books, San Pedro, 1986

The Day It Snowed in L.A, Paget Press, Sutton West and Santa Barbara, Calif., 1986

You Get So Alone at Times That It Just Makes Sense, Black Sparrow, Santa Barbara, 1986

The Movie: 'Barfly', Black Sparrow, Santa Rosa, 1989

The Roominghouse Madrigals: Early Selected Poems 1946–1966, Black Sparrow, Santa Rosa, 1988

Hollywood, Black Sparrow, Santa Rosa, 1989

Septuagenarian Stew: Stories & Poems, Black Sparrow, Santa Rosa, 1990

The Last Night of the Earth Poems, Black Sparrow, Santa Rosa, 1992

Run with the Hunted, HarperCollins, New York, 1993

Screams from the Balcony: Selected Letters 1960–1970, Black Sparrow, Santa Rosa, 1993

Pulp, Black Sparrow, Santa Rosa, 1994

Living on Luck: Selected Letters 1960s–1970s (Volume 2), Black Sparrow, Santa Rosa, 1995

Betting on the Muse: Poems & Stories, Black Sparrow, Santa Rosa, 1996

Bone Palace Ballet: New Poems, Black Sparrow, Santa Rosa, 1997

The Captain Is Out to Lunch and the Sailors Have Taken Over the Ship, Black Sparrow, Santa Rosa, 1998

Reach for the Sun: Selected Letters 1978–1994 (Volume 3), Black Sparrow, Santa Rosa, 1999

What Matters Most Is How Well You Walk Through the Fire: New Poems, Black Sparrow, Santa Rosa, 1999

Open All Night: New Poems, Black Sparrow, Santa Rosa, 2000

Beerspit Night and Cursing: The Correspondence of Charles Bukowski & Sheri Martinelli 1960–1967, Black Sparrow, Santa Rosa, 2001

The Night Torn Mad with Footsteps: New Poems, Black Sparrow, Santa Rosa, 2001

Sifting Through the Madness for the Word, the Line, the Way: New Poems, Black Sparrow, Santa Rosa, 2002

New Poems Book 1, Virgin, London, 2003

New Poems Book 2, Virgin, London, 2003

The Flash of Lightning Behind the Mountain, Ecco, New York, 2004

New Poems Book 3, Virgin, London, 2004

BOOKS ABOUT CHARLES BUKOWSKI

Calonne, David Stephen (ed), *Charles Bukowski, Sunlight Here I Am, Interviews & Encounters, 1963–1993*, Sun Dog, Northville, Michigan, 2003

Cherkovski, Neeli, *Hank, the Life of Charles Bukowski*, Random House, New York, 1991

Cherkovski, Neeli, *Whitman's Wild Children*, Lapis, Venice, CA, 1998

Christy, Jim, *The Buk Book, Musings on Charles Bukowski*, ECW, Toronto, 1997

Dorbin, Sanford, *A Bibliography of Charles Bukowski*, Black Sparrow, Los Angeles, 1969

Freyermuth, Gundolf S, *'That's It': a Final Visit with Charles Bukowski*, Xlibris, privately published, np. 2000

Harrison, Russell, *Against the American Dream, Essays on Charles Bukowski*, Black Sparrow, Santa Rosa, 1998

Krumhansl, Aaron, *A Descriptive Bibliography of the Primary Publications of Charles Bukowski*, Black Sparrow, Santa Rosa, 1999

Leyland, Winston, *The Gay Sunshine Interviews, Volume 1* (with Harold Norse interview), Gay Sunshine, San Francisco, 1978

Locklin, Gerald, *Charles Bukowski, A Sure Bet*, Water Row, Sudbury, Mass., 1996

Malone, Aubrey, *The Hunchback of East Hollywood, a Biography of Charles Bukowski*, Headpress/Critical Vision, Manchester, 2003

Morrow, Bradford and Seamus Cooney, *A Bibliography of the Black Sparrow Press, 1966–1978*, Black Sparrow, Santa Barbara, 1981

Norse, Harold, *Memoirs of a Bastard Angel*, William Morrow, New York, 1989

Pivano, Fernanda, *Charles Bukowski, Laughing with the Gods, an Interview*, Sundog, Northville, Michigan, 2000

Smith, Jules, *Art, Survival and So Forth: The Poetry of Charles Bukowski*, Wrecking Ball, North Cave, Yorks, 2000

Sounes, Howard, *Charles Bukowski, Locked in the Arms of a Crazy Life*, Grove, New York, 1998

Sounes, Howard, *Bukowski in Pictures*, Canongate, Edinburgh, 2000

Weizman, Daniel (ed), *Drinking with Bukowski, Recollections of the Poet Laureate of Skid Row*, Thunder's Mouth, New York, 2000

LOS ANGELES OR RELATED

Where a second date is given in square brackets, this is the date of the original edition.

Banham, Reyner, *Los Angeles, The Architecture of Four Ecologies*, Allen Lane, Penguin Press, London, 1971

Brown, James, *The L.A. Diaries*, Bloomsbury, London, 2003

Bunker, Edward, *No Beast So Fierce*, No Exit, London, 1993 [1973]

Cain, James M, *The Postman Always Rings Twice*, London, Jonathan Cape, 1934

Cain, James M, *Serenade*, London, Jonathan Cape, 1938

Cain, James M, *Mildred Pierce*, London, Robert Hale, 1943

Cain, James M, *Double Indemnity*, London, Robert Hale, 1945

Cain, James M, *The Butterfly*, London, Robert Hale, 1949

Chandler, Raymond, *The Big Sleep*, Penguin, London, 1970 [1939]

Chandler, Raymond, *Farewell, My Lovely*, Penguin, London, 1949 [1940]

Cooper, Stephen, *Full of Life: A Biography of John Fante*, North Point, New York, 2000

Davis, Mike, *City of Quartz, Excavating the Future in Los Angeles*, Verso, London, 1990

Didion, Joan, *The White Album*, Simon & Schuster, New York, 1979

Ellroy, James, *The Big Nowhere*, Mysterious, London, 1989

Ellroy, James, *My Dark Places*, Alfred Knopf, New York City, 1996

Fante, John, *Ask The Dust*, Panther, London, 1985 [1939]

Fante, John, *Dreams from Bunker Hill*, Panther, London, 1985

Fisher, Carrie, *Postcards from the Edge*, New York, Simon & Schuster, 1987

Hiney, Tom, *Raymond Chandler, A Biography*, Chatto & Windus, London, 1977

Huxley, Aldous, *After Many a Summer*, Chatto & Windus, London, 1939

Jacobs, Jane, *The Death and Life of Great American Cities*, Vintage, New York City, 1961

Lambert, Gavin, *Inside Daisy Clover*, Viking, New York, 1963

Layman, Richard, *Shadow Man, the Life of Dashiell Hammett*, Harcourt Brace Jovanovich, New York, 1981

Lurie, Alison, *The Nowhere City*, William Heinemann, London, 1965

Maynard, John Arthur, *Venice West, the Beat Generation in Southern California*, Rutger University, New Brunswick, 1991

Miles, Barry, *Frank Zappa*, Grove, New York, 2004

Miller, Henry, *The Air Conditioned Nightmare*, London, Secker & Warburg, 1947

Murphet, Julian, *Literature and Race in Los Angeles*, Cambridge University Press, 2001

Pepper, Laurie and Art, *Straight Life*, Schirmer, New York, 1979

Polito, Robert, *Savage Art, a Biography of Jim Thompson*, Vintage, New York, 1996

Pynchon, Thomas, *The Crying of Lot 49*, JB Lippincott, New York, 1965

Rayner, Richard, *Los Angeles Without a Map*, Secker & Warburg, London 1988

Rechy, John, *City of Night*, Grove, New York, 1963

Rechy, John, *The Sexual Outlaw*, Grove, New York, 1977

Sitton, Tom and William Deverell (eds), *Metropolis in The Making, Los Angeles in the 20s*, University of California Press, Berkeley, 2001

Spillane, Mickey, *I, The Jury*, EP Dutton, NY, 1947

Spillane, Mickey, *My Gun is Quick*, EP Dutton, NY, 1950

Spillane, Mickey, *Vengeance Is Mine!*, EP Dutton, NY, 1950

Thompson, Jim, *A Hell of a Woman*, Creative Arts, Berkeley, 1984

Ward, Elizabeth and Alain Silver, *Raymond Chandler's Los Angeles*, Overlook, Woodstock, NY, 1987

West, Nathanael, *Collected Works*, Secker & Warburg, London, 1957

Willett, Ralph, *The Naked City, Urban Crime Fiction in the USA*, Manchester University Press, 1996

Williams, John, *Into the Badlands, A Journey Through the American Dream*, London, Paladin, 1991

OTHER WORKS CONSULTED

Allen, Donald M (ed), *The New American Poetry 1945–1960*, Grove, New York, 1960

Benjamin, Walter, *The Arcades Project*, Belknap, Harvard University, Cambridge, 1999

Brian, Denis, *The True Gen, an Intimate Portrait of Hemingway by Those Who Knew Him*, Grove, New York, 1988

Crosby, Caresse, *The Passionate Years*, Ecco, New York, 1979 [1953]

Daumal, Rene, *A Night of Serious Drinking*, Boulder, Shambala, 1979 [1938]

Frank, Robert, *The Americans*, New York, Aperture, 1978

Glessing, Robert J, *The Underground Press in America*, Bloomington, Indiana University, 1970

Hamill, Pete, *A Drinking Life*, Boston, Little Brown, 1994

Hamsun, Knut, *The Wanderer*, Souvenir, London 1975

Hamsun, Knut, *Hunger*, Canongate, Edinburgh, 1996

Hunt, Tim (ed), *The Collected Poetry of Robinson Jeffers*, Stanford University, Stanford, 1991

Jeffers, Robinson, *Selected Poems*, London, Carcanet, 1987

Lynn, Kenneth, *Hemingway*, Simon & Schuster, New York, 1987

Newlove, Donald, *Those Drinking Days, Myself and Other Writers*, London, Junction, 1981

Polsky, Ned, *Hustlers, Beats and Others*, Pelican, Harmondsworth, 1971

Tester, Keith (ed), *The Flâneur*, Routledge, London, 1994

INDEX

alcohol 41–4, 48, 54, 59, 69, 70, 71–2, 73–7, 85–6, 116–17, 118–19, 121–2, 137, 142, 144–5, 146–7, 177, 184, 188, 198–9, 246, 261
'All the Assholes in the World and Mine' 152
Allen, Donald 133
Anderson, Sherwood 38–9
Andreone, David 262
'Animal Poem, An' 259
Apostrophe (TV prog) 230–2
appearance 30, 38, 44, 68–9, 76, 171, 183–4, 188
art 109–10, 163
Artaud, Antonin 127
At Terror Street and Agony Way 3, 155
Atlantic Monthly 53, 64, 69, 73
Auden, WH 127

Baker, Craig 84–5
Baker, Jane Cooney 83–93, 94–6, 97–104, 115, 117–22
Barfly 84, 90, 92, 236, 237, 242, 249–52, 254

Barrett Browning, Elizabeth 26
Bauman, Ann 121
Baume, Robert Stanton 51, 53, 54, 57
Beach, Mary 152
Beatles, The 1–2
'Bee, The' 28
Beighle, Linda Lee *see* Bukowski, Linda Lee (wife)
Benjamin, Walter 76, 166
Betting on the Muse 217, 264
'Birth, Life and Death of an Underground Newspaper, The' 160
Bizio, Silvia 100, 207
Black Sparrow Press 1, 122, 150, 170, 176, 194, 205, 214, 225, 234, 239, 245, 261
Black Sun Press 68
Blazek, Douglas 79, 130, 142, 146, 148, 151, 160, 164, 166, 168, 194
Blue Book, The 227
'Blue Collar Solitude' 61
Blunden, Ron 205
Bockris, Victor 206

Bone Palace Ballet 253
Bowles, Paul 155
Boyle, Kay 78, 79
Bradbury, Ray 34–5
Brandes, Pamela (Cupcakes) 211,
  214–15
Brautigan, Richard 2
Bremser, Ray 137
Bridson, David 262
Brothers Karamazov, The (Dostoevsky)
  27
Bryan, John 124, 155–6, 157, 158,
  159–60, 166, 223
Bryson, Josette 182
'Buddies' 21
Bukowski, Barbara (wife) 106, 107–13
Bukowski, Ben (uncle) 6, 23–4
Bukowski, Charles (uncle) 6
Bukowski, Eleanor (aunt) 6
Bukowski, Emilie (grandmother) 6,
  10–11, 12, 32
Bukowski, Emma (aunt) 6
Bukowski, Henry (father) 6, 7–8,
  13–14, 18–19, 80–1, 99
  death of 113–14
  and Hank's drinking 42–3
  on Hank's Nazism 51
  and Hank's writing 52–3
  letter to Hank 79
  unemployment 31
  violence 16–17, 23, 25–8, 30
Bukowski, John (uncle) 6, 24, 62
Bukowski, Katherine (mother) 7, 11,
  30–31, 33, 56, 80–1
  death of 111–12
  domestic violence 25–6
  and Hank's drinking 42–4
  Hank's education 16
  Hank's perception of 17, 19–20
  and Hank's writing 51
  homesickness 18
Bukowski, Leonard (grandfather) 6,
  10, 14
Bukowski, Linda Lee (wife) 219–21,
  226–39, 240–9, 254, 255–6, 258,
  259, 264, 265
Bukowski, Marina Louise (daughter)
  141, 147–8, 164–5, 176, 193, 248,
  258, 265

Bukowski in Pictures 216
Bukowski Junior, Henry Charles (Hank)
  alcohol 41–4, 48, 54, 59, 69, 70,
    71–2, 73–7, 85–6, 116–17,
    118–19, 121–2, 132, 137, 142,
    144–5, 146–7, 177, 184, 188,
    198–9, 246, 257, 261
  appearance 4, 29, 32, 38, 44, 68–9,
    76, 171, 183–4, 188
  art 109–10, 163
  and Barbara Frye 107–13
  birth 7
  death 265
  divorce 112–13
  domestic violence 92, 189
  drugs 216–18
  dyslexia 15
  early life 11–53
  education 4–5, 14–17, 28–30, 34–5,
    40–41, 44–6, 48–9, 50–52, 53
  fighting, love of 17, 18, 28, 74–6
  finance 56, 67, 68–9, 70, 77, 88,
    100, 115, 155, 159, 163–4, 175–6,
    209, 234–5, 236, 245
  and Frances Elizabeth Dean 135–42,
    147–8, 165
  health 15–16, 30, 32–3, 35, 77–9,
    97–100, 138, 144–5, 146, 151–2,
    199, 241, 255–7, 263–5
  and his father's abuse 16–17, 22,
    25–8
  horse racing 101–2, 112, 114,
    115–16, 125, 135, 240, 241,
    257–8, 261
  and Jane Cooney Baker 83–93, 94–6,
    97–104, 115, 117–22
  and Linda King 185–90, 191–7,
    209–12, 226
  and Linda Lee Beighle 219–21,
    226–39, 240–9, 254, 255–6, 258,
    259, 264, 265
  and Liza Williams 190–2, 193, 197
  Nazism 36–7, 47–51, 63
  and Pamela Brandes (Cupcakes) 211,
    214–15
  poetry readings 182–3, 192–3,
    197–8, 215–16, 222, 229, 241
  sexuality 64, 69, 85, 87, 88, 94, 107,
    168, 187–8, 212–14, 216–17

suicide attempts 30, 96
Bukowski Sampler, A 194
Bukowski Tapes, The 242–4, 257
Burning in Water Drowning in Flame 92, 205–6
Burroughs, William 116, 124, 129–30, 137, 145, 152, 170, 173, 180, 195

'Cacoethes Scribendi' 68
Cain, James M 224, 260
Caldwell, Erskine 47
Captain Is Out to Lunch and the Sailors Have Taken Over the Ship, The 260
Cassady, Neal 159
Céline, Louis–Ferdinand 104, 145
Chandler, Raymond 9, 103, 224, 260
Chénetier, Marc 209, 213
Cherkovski, Neeli 38–9, 51, 54, 84, 171, 172, 184, 186
'Chicken Giblets' 217
'Chickens' 91
City Lights Books, San Francisco 192, 194, 236
'City of Brotherly Love, The' 72
City of Night (Rechy) 9
'Class' 40
Coburn, Bill 34
'Coffee' 89
Cold Dogs in the Courtyard 151
Collegian, The 51
Confessions of a Man Insane Enough to Live with Beasts 151, 169
Connell, Patricia 192
'Copulating Mermaid of Venice, Calif, The' 173–4
Corrington, John William 54, 119, 120, 121, 144, 164
Corso, Gregory 124, 137, 170, 198
Coughlin, Charles E 49
Crazy Love (1987) 174
Creeley, Robert 128–9, 133, 155
Crosby, Caresse 68, 78, 79
Crucifix in a Deathhand 139, 142, 144
Crumb, Robert 191
cummings, e.e 104
Cupcakes *see* Brandes, Pamela
Cuscaden, RR 151

Dangling in the Tournefortia 239, 245
Darby, Brad and Tina 210, 211, 216, 218, 223
Day of the Locust, The (West) 9
Days Run Away Like Wild Horses Over the Hills, The 194
Dean, Frances Elizabeth 135–42, 147–8, 165, 223
death 265
'Death Is Smoking My Cigars' 263
'Death of a Splendid Neighborhood, The' 202
'Death of the Father I, The' 114
'Death of the Father II, The' 115
divorce 112–13
'Dogfight Over L.A.' 137
domestic violence 92, 189
Doolittle, Hilda 38
Dorn, Ed 124
Dostoevsky, Fyodor Mikhailovich 27, 46, 80
'Down by the Wings' 170
'Drive Through Hell' 254
'Driving Test' 253
drugs 216–18
'Drunk Tank Judge, The' 203
Dunaway, Faye 250, 251
Duval, Jean–François 3, 256
dyslexia 16

Earth Rose 153
Edler, Peter 182, 185
education
    Los Angeles City College 44–6, 48–9, 50–52, 53
    Los Angeles High School 4, 34–5, 40–41, 44
    Mount Vernon Junior High, Los Angeles 29–30
    Virginia Road Grammar School, Los Angeles 15–17
'Education' 15
Eigner, Larry 128, 152
Ellroy, James 34
Engle, Vanessa 188, 212, 244
Epos Quarterly 151
Erections, Ejaculations, Exhibitions and General Tales of Ordinary

Madness 184, 192, 194, 206, 227, 236
Essex House 2, 159, 170, 194
Esterly, Glenn 187, 212
Evergreen Review 160, 161, 182

Factotum 66, 79, 83, 88, 91, 95, 110, 208–9, 236
Fairmount Motors 72
'Fante' 239
Fante, John 46–7, 53, 55, 104, 235, 236–9, 245
Farewell My Lovely (Chandler) 9
Farmer, Philip Jose 159
'Father, Who Art in Heaven' 114
'Fear and Madness' 130
Federman, Raymond 125
Ferlinghetti, Lawrence 2, 124, 193, 197, 236
Fett, Heinrich (uncle) 7, 227, 229–30
Fett, Katherine *see* Bukowski, Katherine (mother)
'Fiend, The' 206–7
finance 56, 67, 68–9, 70, 77, 88, 100, 115, 155, 159, 163–4, 175–6, 209, 234–5, 236, 245
'Fire Station' 87
Fitzgerald, F Scott 104, 179
Flower, Fist and Bestial Wail 113, 122, 151
Flying Aces 20
Fogel, Al 247
Fox, Hugh 165
Free Press 156, 178, 184, 190, 194, 200, 206, 207, 222
'Freedom' 92
'Freeway Life, The' 254
Freyermuth, Guindolf 249
Frye, Barbara *see* Bukowski, Barbara (wife)
'Fun Times: 1930' 21

'Garbage' 75
Genet, Jean 124, 133
Genius of the Crowd, The 153
Ginsberg, Allen 2, 103, 124, 127, 130, 131, 137, 145, 152, 195, 197, 198
'Girls, The' 150, 217
Goebbels, Josef 60

Graphic Arts Center 110
Great Depression 25, 31–32, 49
Greene, Graham 179
Griffith, EV 113
'Guts' 168
Gysin, Brion 170

Hackford, Taylor 191, 203
Haddox, Jim 34, 36, 44
Hall, Iris 216
Ham on Rye 5, 10–12, 13, 14, 18, 22, 24, 28, 33, 36, 44–5, 48, 49, 54, 236, 244, 246–7
Hammett, Dashiell 47, 260
Hamsun, Knut 60, 127, 179
'Hard Without Music' 68
Harlequin 106, 110
Harper's 53, 69
Hatcher, Jimmy 54
health 97–100, 138, 144–5, 146, 199, 241, 263–4
  acne vulgaris 30, 33–4, 35
  constipation 15–16
  haemorrhoids 151–2
  leukaemia 264–5
  starvation 77–9
  TB 255–7
Hearse 113
Hearst, William Randolph 37, 156
'Hello, Hamsun' 263
Hemingway, Ernest 39–40, 51, 57, 101, 104, 179
Hervey Jr., Captain Harcourt 35
Hirshman, Jack 137
Hitler, Adolf 36–7, 47, 49, 60
Hollywood 254–5
Holmes, John Clellon 137, 180
Hoover, President 29
Hopper, Dennis 249, 250
'Horse on Fire' 126
horse racing 101–2, 112, 114, 115–16, 125, 135, 240, 241, 257–8, 261
'Horsemeat' 126
'How to Get Published' 144
Howard, Douglas 207
Hunchback of East Hollywood, The 44
'Hunk of Rock' 216
Hustler 248
Huxley, Aldous 38, 179

'I Made a Mistake' 215
'I Meet the Famous Poet' 172
'I Shot a Man in Reno' 130
'I Was Born to Hustle Roses Down the Avenues of the Dead' 26–7
'Ice for the Eagles' 13
Igriega, Robert 161
It Catches My Heart in Its Hands 132, 133–4, 135, 143, 144

James, Danny 200
Jeffers, Robinson 126, 127
'John Dillinger and Le Chasseur Maudit' 128
Johnson, Kay (Kaja) 134–5
Jones, LeRoi 124
Journey to the End of the Night (Céline) 145

Kamstra, Jerry 197
Kaufman, Bob 137
Kaye, Arnold 128, 180
Kazin, Alfred 126
Kelly, Robert 155
Kennedy, President 180
Kerouac, Jack 124, 137, 145, 180, 198, 206, 254
Kiepenheuer & Witsch, Köln 181
King, Linda 87, 185–90, 191–7, 209–12, 226
KissKill Press 194
Klein, Allen 3
Knox, Robert 51
Krause, Emilie see Bukowski, Emilie (grandmother)
Kunkin, Art 156, 206
Kurnik, Stanley 136, 137

La Cienga Public Library 38, 46
'Ladies Man' 217
Lamantia, Philip 124, 170, 172
Last Night of the Earth Poems, The 262–3
Laugh Literary and Man the Humping Guns 173, 187
Lawrence, DH 38, 176
Le Monde 232
Lennon, John 1, 103

Levertov, Denise 155
Lewis, Sinclair 38
Li Po 261
'Life In a Texas Whorehouse' 58
Locked in the Arms of a Crazy Life (Sounes) 84
Locklin, Gerald 226, 248, 265
Long, Philomene 265
Longshot Poems for Broke Players 151
'Looking Back' 75
Los Angeles City College 44–6, 48–9, 50–52, 53
Los Angeles Examiner 37, 49
Los Angeles High School 4, 34–5, 40–41, 44
Loujon Press 151
'Love, Love, Love' 68
Love Is a Dog From Hell 163–4, 221, 224–5, 237
'Lover, The' 217

Madonna 250, 256
Mailer, Norman 251–2
'Maja Thurup' 207
Malone, Hank 240
'Man, The' 206
Martin, John 122, 149–51, 155, 175–6, 178–9, 182, 186, 194, 205, 206, 211–12, 213, 214, 222, 225–6, 234, 236–7, 244, 245, 248, 256, 260, 265
Martinelli, Sheri 147, 164
'Master Plan' 71
Matrix 68, 81
McCartney, Paul 1, 103
McClure, Michael 2, 124, 133, 137
McGillan, Tommy 74
McRae, Donald 253
'Me Against the World' 22
Me and Your Sometimes Love Poems 194
Memoirs of a Bastard Angel (Norse) 171
'Mermaid' 227
Merry Company 80
Micheline, Jack 124, 137, 160, 193
Midwest Poetry Chapbooks 151
Miller, Brown 130
Miller, Henry 104, 123, 124, 133, 144, 179, 180, 181, 195

Milliron's Dept Store 93
Mockingbird Wish Me Luck 194
'Monkey, The' 18
Montfort, Michael 227, 229, 230, 248
Morona *see* King, Linda
Mortenson, Abe 36
Most Beautiful Woman in Town, The 194
Mount Vernon Junior High, Los Angeles 29–30
Moyamensing Prison 63
Mullinax, William 'Baldy' 29, 32–3, 34, 36, 41, 48, 51
'Murder of Ramon Vasquez, The' 125, 206
Musso Frank's Grill 47
'My First Affair With That Older Woman' 86, 120
'My Secret Life' 32

Naked Ear, The 106
Nazism 36–7, 47–51, 63
New Vanguard Party 48
New York Review of Sex and Politics 181
New York Times 255
New Yorker 53, 63, 141
'No Neck and Bad As Hell' 191
'No Way to Paradise' 92, 207
Norse, Harold 75–6, 130, 133, 134–5, 152, 170–2, 190, 247, 255
Notes from Underground (Dostoevsky) 80
Notes of a Dirty Old Man 2, 54, 65, 109, 112, 159, 170, 173, 181, 184, 194
Nutall, Jeff 152

'Object Lesson' 68
O'Brien, Pamela *see* Brandes, Pamela
O'Hara, Frank 128
Olson, Charles 124, 128
'On and Off' 29
'On Going Out to Get the Mail' 150
'One For Old Snaggle–tooth' 137
Open City 107, 122, 156–61, 166, 170, 178, 181, 194, 200, 206
Orlovsky, Peter 198
Ortner, Hal 34

Orwell, George 179, 208
'Out of Season' 102
Outsider magazine 122, 123–4, 133, 149
'Overhead Mirrors' 218

Packard, William 249
'Panties' 18
'Passing of a Great One, The' 239
Passos, John Dos 38
Patchen, Kenneth 2, 124, 133
Pelieu, Claude 152, 173
Penguin Modern Poets 13 170
Penn, Sean 145, 209, 249, 250, 252, 256–7, 265
Pepper, Art 10
Perkins, Michael 125, 159
'Piss' 86
Pivano, Fernanda 15, 38, 39, 89, 209, 235
Pivot, Bernard 231
Place to Sleep the Night, A 110
Pleasants, Ben 41, 50, 236
Poems Written Before Jumping Out of an 8 Story Window 195, 227
poetry readings 182–3, 192–3, 197–8, 215–16, 222, 229, 241
'Poop' 15–16
Portfolio: An International Review 68, 73, 111
Post Office 95, 109, 118, 119, 135, 137, 178–81, 184, 194, 226
Pound, Ezra 126
'Practice' 27
'Pretty Boy' 193
Prima, Diane di 124, 152, 160
Prohibition 9, 15
Proust, Marcel 77, 104, 179
Pulp 259–60
Purdy, Al 130, 143, 164, 194, 201

Quixote 106

'Rags, Bottles, Sacks!' 24
Reage, Pauline 195
'Reason Behind Reason, The' 68
Rechy, John 9, 180
relationships
  Barbara Frye 106, 107–13

Frances Elizabeth Dean 135–42, 147–8, 165
Jane Cooney Baker 83–93, 94–6, 97–104, 115, 117–22
Linda King 185–90, 191–7, 209–12, 226
Linda Lee Beighle 219–21, 226–39, 240–9, 254, 255–6, 258, 259, 264, 265
Liza Williams 190–2, 193, 197
Pamela Brandes (Cupcakes) 211, 214–15
Renaissance 124, 155–6, 159–60
'Result' 239
'Reunion' 100
Richardson, Mr 45
Richmond, Steve 14, 130, 145, 152–3, 160, 173, 194, 195, 248
Robson, William J 182
Rockmore, Noel 144
Rodrigues, Spain 191
Rolling Stone 212
Roman, Jim 81, 145, 164
Roominghouse Madrigals, The: Early Selected Poems 1946–1966 253, 256
Rourke, Mickey 250–1
Run with the Hunted 151

Sade, Marquis de 195
Salinger, JD 236
San Francisco Chronicle 193
Sanderson, Mr 40–41
Saroyan, William 46, 47, 64
Sartre, Jean Paul 256
Scarlet 214, 215
Schwarzenegger, Arnold 247
Schwinn, Hermann Max 48
Sedgate, Minnie 142, 143
Selby Jr., Hubert 195
'Seminar, The' 170
Septuagenarian Stew: Stories and Poems 253, 256–7
7 Poets Press 151
sexuality 64, 69, 85, 87, 88, 94, 107, 168, 187–8, 214, 216–17
Shakespeare Never Did This 228, 230, 236
Sherman, Jory 116, 123, 126

'Shipping Clerk with a Red Nose, The' 203
Shuwarge, Ray 34
Sims, Mrs 16
Sinclair, Upton 38
'Sloppy Love' 86
'Snails' 30
Snyder, Gary 124, 133, 137, 197
Solomon, Carl 133
Sounes, Howard 84, 107, 216, 223
South of No North 101, 151–2, 167, 170, 206, 207
Southern Pacific Railroad 56–7
'Sparks' 105
Spender, Steven 127
Spillane, Mickey 91, 260
Stangos, Nikos 171
Stieglitz, Alfred 203
Stoner, Bob 34
Stonybrook 182
'Stop Staring at My Tits Mister' 207
Stories and Novels 227
Story 64, 67, 69
Strachan, Don 189–90
Straight Life (Pepper) 10
'Streetcars' 28
'Stride, The' 38
'Suggestion for an Arrangement' 239
suicide attempts 30, 96
Sullivan, Frank 20, 32–3
Sult (The Hunger) (Hamsun) 60
Sunbeam Lighting Co. 93
Supreme Lighting Co. 105–6

Tales of Ordinary Madness 54, 194, 236, 246
Taylor, Courtney 63
Tester, Keith 116
'The Fire Station' 3
'These Mad Windows That Taste Life and Cut Me If I Go Through Them' 165
Thomas, John 154–5, 265
Thompson, Jim 260
'Those Girls We Followed Home' 29
'Those Marvellous Lunches' 22
'340 Dollar Horse and a Hundred Dollar Whore, A' 135
Times Literary Supplement 247

'To Kiss the Worms Goodnight' 150
Townshend, Pete 242
Trace 106
'Training For Kid Aztec' 56
Tribute to Jim Lowell, A 153
Trocchi, Alexander 180
Trotsky, Leon 103
'Trouble with Spain' 191
'True Story' 92, 150
'Twelve Monkeys Who Won't
    Copulate Properly' 172
'20 Tanks From Kasseldown' 68
'Twins, The' 114

'Unaccommodating Universe, The' 263
University of California, Santa Barbara
    164, 176
Untermeyer, Louis 126

Vinkenoog, Simon 152
'Violin Player, The' 240
Virginia Road Grammar School, Los
    Angeles 15–17
Vogue 195
'Voice In a New York Subway' 68

Wakoski, Diane 133, 155
Wantling, Ruth 180, 222, 223
Wantling, William 104, 164, 194, 222
War All the Time, Poems 1981–1984
    126–7, 217, 253
Watts riots 145
Way the Dead Love, The 166, 169
'Way to Review a Play and Keep
    Everybody Happy But Me, The'
    155

Webb, Jon 100, 116, 122, 123, 132,
    133, 142, 143, 144, 145, 155,
    157–8, 203
Weissmuller, Johnny 238
Weissner, Carl 152, 155, 161, 164,
    170, 174, 177, 178, 179, 181, 188,
    191, 192, 195, 197, 214, 215, 222,
    227–8, 229, 232, 264
Welch, Denton 179
Wennersten, Robert 64, 71, 127
West, Nathanael 9, 47, 179
Williams, Liza 186, 190–2, 193, 197
Williams, Miller 144
Williams, William Carlos 103, 128,
    224
Winans, AD 75, 121, 223, 227
'Wine of Forever, The' 239
'With Vengeance Like a Tiger Crawls'
    115
Wolfe, Thomas 40, 53
Women 190, 192, 195, 197, 203, 215,
    216, 220, 221–2, 223, 224, 225,
    237, 244
Wormwood Review, The 124

'Yankee Doodle' 105
'Yes' 194
'You Don't Know' 69–70
*You Get So Alone at Times That It Just
    Makes Sense* 253

Zapple 1, 3